STAINED
GLASS

STAINED GLASS

Lawrence Lee, George Seddon, Francis Stephens

With photographs by Sonia Halliday and Laura Lushington

LONGMEADOW

First Published in Great Britain in 1976
by Mitchell Beazley Publishers Limited

This edition published in 1992 by Longmeadow Press
201 High Ridge Road, Stamford CT 06904 U.S.A.

© Mitchell Beazley Publishers Limited 1976
All rights reserved
ISBN 0-681-41639-4

Editor Daphne Wood
Art Editor Sue Casebourne
Assistant Editor Susie Courtauld
Editorial Sue Farr, Jinny Johnson, Yvonne McFarlane, Sarina Turner, Lira Winston
Design Michael Rose, Kevin Maddison
Picture Research Jan Jones, Susan Pinkus
Editorial Assistant Margaret Little
Production Hugh Stancliffe

Publisher Bruce Marshall
Art Director John Bigg
Executive Editor Glorya Hale

Consultants
Michael Archer, Victoria and Albert Museum, London
Dr Rüdiger Becksmann, Deutscher Verein für Kunstwissenschaft, Stuttgart
Yvette vanden Bemden, Corpus Vitrearum Medii Aevi, Brussels
Stephen Bridges, Stained Glass Association of America, New York
Alfred Fisher, Chapel Studio, England
Dr Ulf-Dietrich Korn, Landeskonservator, Westphalia-Lippe
Dr Dietmar Lüdke, Augustiner-Museum, Freiburg
Professor Roy Newton
Françoise Perrot, Corpus Vitrearum Medii Aevi, Paris
Dr Elisabeth Schürer-von Witzleben
Richard Sharpe, Trinity College, Cambridge
The late Professor Hans Wentzel

Produced by Mandarin Offset
Printed and bound in Hong Kong

Foreword 6

The World of Stained Glass
Lawrence Lee
The Medium of Glass 8
Glass in the Ancient World 10
Beginnings of an Art Form 12
The Church and its Planning 14
The Architectural Challenge 16
Painting with Light 18
Webs of Stone 20
The Circle and the Rose 22
Sources of Inspiration
　The Bible 24
　Sacred and Profane 28
Spirits of Good and Evil 30
The Language of Symbols 32
Saints and their Emblems 34
The Family Tree of Christ 36
Faces of Christ 38
Donors—Self-perpetuation and Piety 40
A Framework of Glass 42
The Natural World 44
The Ancient Tradition of Heraldry 46
The Art of Blazoning in Glass 48
Reflections of the Times
　Architecture 50
　Details of Daily Life 52
　Fashions 54
The Changing Art of Portraiture 56
Tributes in Stained Glass 58
The Art and the Artist 60

The History of Stained Glass
George Seddon
ELEVENTH AND TWELFTH CENTURIES
The Cathedral Age 64
THIRTEENTH CENTURY
The Age of Gothic Art 72
FOURTEENTH CENTURY
The Age of Turmoil and Innovation 84
FIFTEENTH CENTURY
The Age of Transition 100
SIXTEENTH CENTURY
The Age of Decline 124
SEVENTEENTH AND EIGHTEENTH CENTURIES
The Impoverished Years 142
NINETEENTH CENTURY
The Age of Revival 146
TWENTIETH CENTURY
The Age of Expanding Horizons 158

How a Stained-Glass Window is Made and Restored 176
Francis Stephens

Gazetteer 195
Glossary 199
Index 200
Acknowledgements 206
Bibliography 207

Stained glass is unique among the arts of the world because of the relationship that exists between glass and light. We see colour on a painted surface through the reflection of light; the colour we see in a stained-glass window is from the light refracted through it. The colours of the glass are deadened by reflected light, and when darkness falls a stained-glass window cannot be brought to life.

Essentially a dynamic, daylight art, stained glass is energized through its relationship with light and changes according to the time of day, the seasons and the weather. All affect—sometimes subtly, sometimes dramatically—the image that is perceived, for stained glass is the most ancient and cunning form of kinetic art.

Light, the intangible phenomenon by which the world is made visible, has, since time immemorial, been symbolically equated with goodness, revelation and beauty and has, therefore, been a focal point of the philosophies and religions of mankind. The Old Testament account of the first day of Creation, for example, begins, "And God said, Let there be light: and there was light. And God saw the light, that it was good: and God divided the light from the darkness." And in the New Testament, John the Evangelist describes Christ as the true light and the light of the world.

The flowering of the art of stained glass in the Middle Ages can be traced back to the influence of Plato and the Neoplatonists. The Neoplatonic philosophy of light was expounded in the fifth century by the Syrian mystic Dionysius the Areopagite and it was his writings that inspired, seven centuries later, Abbé Suger, the father of Gothic architecture, to fill his Abbey Church of St Denis, near Paris, with "the most radiant windows" to "illumine men's minds so that they may travel through it [light] to an apprehension of God's light". Thus began the golden age of Gothic architecture and stained glass.

The concept of the spirituality of light is also deeply rooted in the Jewish religion, but until comparatively recently the windows of synagogues were glazed with clear glass so that worshippers would be filled with reverence by the sight of the sky. The medieval Christian Church, however, employed coloured glass deliberately, aware that

colour has a spiritual quality as well as a sensual appeal. Even for modern man the rainbow, the light of the sun broken into its component colours, is a thing of wonder. And the rainbow, according to Genesis, was God's covenant with man after the Flood.

At the end of the Dark Ages, when the boom in church building began, churches and cathedrals came ablaze with the colour of stained glass. The effect must have been staggering. Going to church meant not only spiritual instruction and comfort, but entry into a magical self-contained world. At one level stained glass was the medieval equivalent of the cinema, at another it was the agent of a mystical experience that made man more receptive to God. It was, and indeed still is, essentially an atmospheric art. As the French novelist René Bazin wrote, a stained-glass window is "une atmosphère avant d'être une image".

Since the Middle Ages the art of stained glass and stained-glass windows themselves have undergone many vicissitudes. Windows have been destroyed by wars, iconoclasm, vandalism and neglect and they have been ruined by "restoration". In the seventeenth and eighteenth centuries the art itself was devalued by its practitioners, for their techniques of painting with enamels on glass sacrificed the luminous colour which was its essence.

From the middle of the twentieth century, however, there has been a splendid revival. Beginning in France and Germany, it spread to the United States and the influence of the new movement is being felt in many other parts of the world, including Ethiopia, Australia and Japan, which have no tradition of stained glass. It has long ceased to be an exclusively religious art, and its future may well be increasingly secular.

Stained Glass is not an In Memoriam volume, for, although at times it dwells lovingly on the past, those who have contributed the illustrations and the text are enthusiastic about contemporary work and confident for the future. The book is, rather, a guide to the rich artistic heritage preserved in the churches and cathedrals of Europe and to the highlights of contemporary work. It charts the origins and the flowering, the decline and the eventual revival of this intriguing art.

In assembling their magnificent collection of photographs to illustrate the book, Sonia Halliday and Laura Lushington travelled widely in Europe for more than four years photographing unfamiliar as well as famous stained glass. Spanning a period of nine centuries their photographs reveal the exquisitely impressionistic quality of the art form and the extraordinary images which it depicts.

The religious and secular images in the glass, their intellectual, social and aesthetic context and the decorative, symbolic or sacred designs into which they are woven are the theme of Lawrence Lee's *The World of Stained Glass*. From an analysis of glass itself and a description of its role in ancient civilization he suggests the origins for this Christian art form. He describes its contribution to the architectural symbolism of a church, its relationship to architecture and to light and the details of everyday life which are as much a part of its imagery as is its prolific symbolism.

The History of Stained Glass, written by George Seddon, is a fascinating exploration of the history of art and of history itself from the eleventh century to the present day. The styles and themes of stained glass at different times and in different countries are shown to be interdependent upon the current philosophies, events and technical and aesthetic innovations. Stained glass is viewed not in artistic isolation but in relation to the paintings, manuscripts, tapestries and engravings which paralleled and influenced its development and which in their turn were influenced by it.

To a greater extent than most art forms, stained glass depends upon skilled craftsmanship and it is with this aspect of the art that the third section of the book is concerned. Here Francis Stephens describes the creation of a window from the first sketch to its installation in a building. The account of restoration relates to the work and modern techniques perfected at Canterbury Cathedral. It explains the reasons for the deterioration of stained glass and the ways in which it can be most sensitively repaired.

Stained Glass is, above all, a guide to the essential experience of seeing stained glass in its own environment as a distinctively dynamic medium. No art form took its spiritual role so literally as did this one, whose images were not merely illustrated but were activated through light—a phenomenon which was considered to be divine. Seen within the buildings for which it was designed, stained glass, with its moody changes of tone and colour, controlled by no human agency, continues to create the illusion of a supernatural drama.

The Medium of Glass

Bombarded by meteorites, the Moon's basaltic rocks have formed spheres of glass, covering the planet with glassy dust. The micrograph of a fragment of lunar rock, above, shows the calcium and aluminium silicates which in great heat fuse to form glass.

A tektite, above, is a natural glass found in a few areas on Earth. Vitrified from silica and such subsidiary elements as soda, lime and iron, tektites range from the minute to more than four inches. They probably originate in outer space.

Obsidian, above, a black or dark red glass formed in volcanic eruptions, is found in several parts of the world. Harder than window-glass, it always has, when chipped, smooth, curved surfaces and sharp edges. Early man used it for arrow-heads.

Quartz, a crystalline form of silicon dioxide, is the common mineral which is used as the basis for most man-made glass. The piece, above, magnified three times, is one of many varieties. Its prismatic white crystals are set in chalcopyrite.

What is this material, fused from the sands which have gathered during millions of years' erosion of the Earth's mantle? What is the material that lay in profusion as tiny marbles on the Moon, untouched until the feet of the first astronauts trod them into the yielding dust? As they explored, the astronauts found, to their amazement, that these marbles were glass.

Glass is a natural substance, a supercooled silicious liquid, that is, a liquid that becomes solid without having the usual freezing point. Natural glass is likely to be found almost anywhere in the universe. Indeed it comes to Earth occasionally from outer space as globules of silica, of meteoric origin, which have fused to form glass in the heat which is engendered by their entry into the Earth's atmosphere. These globules are called tektites. Natural glass is formed on the Moon by volcanic action and the bombardment of its surface by meteorites. On our own planet, natural glass is sometimes formed by the rapid cooling of highly silicious volcanic lava. Lightning, too, may produce a kind of glass, known as fulgurite, by striking a metallic ore through sand and fusing the sand in the process.

Although man-made glass had a long history—more than four thousand years—even today scientists do not know the precise nature of this enigmatic substance. All they can say is that it is formed by melting certain minerals and cooling them in a way which prevents crystallization, giving a supercooled liquid that is so stiff, or of such high viscosity, that it has most of the properties of a solid.

The main ingredient of almost all glass is silica, which may be sand, quartz crystals or flint. However, because pure silica vitrifies, or turns to molten glass, only at about 3100 degrees Fahrenheit, it is used exclusively to make special heat-resistant glass. For most glass in common use, including that used for stained glass, a flux, usually soda ash, and a stabilizer, such as limestone, are added to the silica and the mixture is then melted at a lower temperature of about 2700 degrees Fahrenheit. Cullet, or scrap glass, is sometimes added to assist melting.

As the raw ingredients are heated, they gradually decompose, giving off gases and forming a bubbling liquid in which every particle of silica is finally dissolved. There are many ways of shaping this liquid—pressing, blowing, drawing, floating, casting and rolling—and the possible final shapes are multitudinous. Most stained glass is made into sheets from a blown bubble of molten glass. The bubble is either moulded and split, formed into a cylinder or spun, providing the characteristic seams, bubbles and variations of thickness of stained glass.

The final cooling, or annealing, is a crucial part of the manufacture of glass. As a liquid, glass tends to cool rapidly on the outside, and this creates tensions which can easily cause the glass to shatter. Like all treatment of this brittle substance, the cooling has, therefore, to be controlled and gradual.

Glass which has been made from a pure mix of silica, soda and limestone is transparent and colourless. Unlike such solids as wood and painted canvas, which reflect light, the molecular structure of glass allows the energy of the light to pass through directly so that in a perfect sheet of glass the light rays enter and emerge at the same angle with their original brilliance unaltered. Variations in thickness, however, and small flaws in the glass can deflect the rays of light and these changes, which concentrate or diffuse the light, can create a fascinating and ever-changing shimmer and iridescence. It is for this reason that stained glass is manufactured by a process which encourages imperfections.

To colour glass, extra substances have to be added which will stop certain of the wavelengths of light from passing through the glass. These unabsorbed wavelengths give the glass its colour. Probably the first colouring of glass was

Commercial sheet glass is made mechanically by passing molten glass through rollers. The rollers can be patterned. For reeded glass, for example, one of the rollers is ridged.

Clear commercial reeded glass

Flashed green on white muff glass

Flashed ruby on yellow muff glass

Flashed glass has two or more layers of colour. Usually a thin "flash" of deep colour overlays light-coloured or white glass. A tiny blob of molten dark glass is gathered up, cooled, and then dipped in a pot of light-coloured glass. The blob is then blown into a bubble, which expands with distinct layers.

Pale streaky gold-pink muff glass

Muff glass is the antique stained glass which is still hand-made in the same way as it was in medieval times. It is sometimes known as cylinder glass. A blob of molten glass is collected on a blowpipe and blown into a long bubble. The ends of the bubble are cut off, leaving a cylinder which, when cut down one side and heated, opens to a flat sheet. The sheets have an infinite variability of texture, thickness and colour.

accidental. By Roman times, however, such colourants as copper and cobalt were consistently used to give greens and blues. Even today, the chemistry of glass colouring is complex. Much depends on the preparation of the mix and how and when the colour strikes or develops its true hue in the course of the melting.

There are two basic methods of colouring glass. Certain metal oxides can be dissolved in the glass, and the molecular structure of the solution is such that it absorbs wavelengths of certain colours. Glass to which iron oxide has been added, for example, is green. In the other basic method, chemical particles may be dispersed, or suspended, in the liquid. If they are approximately the same size as the wavelength of light, certain colours will pass through the glass while others are stopped. Particles of gold, for example, are dispersed through the glass to give the characteristic ruby colour of stained glass.

It is almost miraculous that very early in the history of civilization, man, as a result of his ingenuity, almost fully developed glass—this amazing substance which sparkles with diamantine brilliance, which has as fascinating an iridescence as an opal and which can be as deeply infused with colour as a ruby. Quite apart from the story or image which a stained-glass window may convey, it is the jewel-like qualities of glass which make it a unique work of art.

Dalle de verre is thick, modern cast glass, which is used, for example, in concrete-set windows. It is made by pouring molten glass into moulds. The pieces are usually rectangular, like this slab of selenium yellow, about one foot long and one inch deep. The French name means glass flagstone.

Streaky blue muff glass

Pot purple muff glass

An unusual piece of *dalle* which has been cast in a circular mould and coloured irregularly by unevenly dissolved iron oxide.

Pot glass is antique glass which is one deep colour throughout its thickness.

The piece of amber *dalle*, left, has been faceted, or chipped, for highlight effects.

Pot blue Norman slab

Tinted amber muff glass

Crown, or spun, glass was probably the earliest stained glass. It was made by twirling a bubble of glass on a rod, and cutting one end open so that under centrifugal force the bubble opened to a large circular sheet. The central knob, where the rod was attached, is also found in modern bullion glass.

Norman slab, a very uneven glass, was made by blowing and moulding a bubble of glass into a box shape and dividing the box down the sides. The pieces are thickest in the centre. This type of glass, which was invented during the nineteenth-century Gothic Revival, is no longer made today.

THE COMPOSITION OF GLASS

Glass in its purest form is silicon dioxide, or silica. Chemically, this means that each molecule of glass is composed of one atom of silicon and two atoms of oxygen. In silica, which is a solid, the atoms have a rigid order. In glass, right, which is a supercooled liquid, the atoms are arranged irregularly.

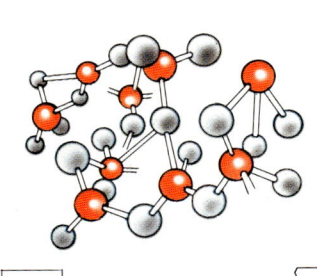

When heated to above 3000°F, atoms of pure silica are reordered to form perfect glass (1). But as the Romans discovered, with lime and soda additives (2) glass can be made at lower temperatures. Fifty per cent lime and potash (3), medieval glass vitrified easily, but corrodes readily.

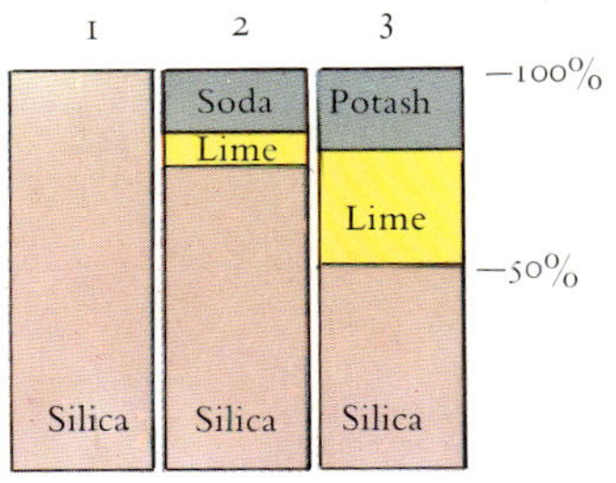

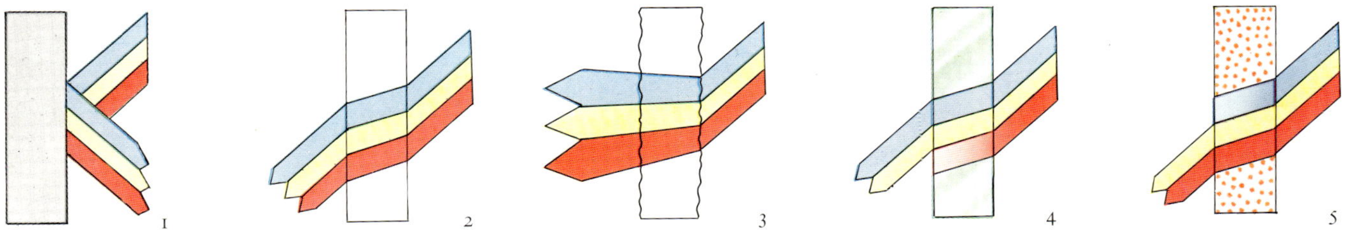

On striking a white solid, light is reflected (1). When light strikes clear glass with parallel, flat surfaces, it emerges at the same angle as it enters, passing through virtually unchanged (2). If the glass is flawed, the light tends to emerge at an altered angle and concentrates into sparkles or diffuses (3). When metallic oxides are dissolved in the glass, some wavelengths are absorbed, giving the effect of colour; iron oxide absorbs red light to give green glass (4). Glass can also be coloured by molecular particles dispersed within it and which absorb light. Cadmium selenium, for example, makes orange (5).

Reamy glass, which has an irregular rippled effect, is made from a mixture of glass of different hardnesses. It is usually white mixed with a colour. This cylinder of reamy blue will be incised down the side and placed in a hot kiln, where it will open to form a flat sheet of muff glass.

Glass in the Ancient World

Of unknown provenance, this glass fragment portraying a royal Egyptian dates from c. 1400 to 1200 BC. Now in the British Museum, London, it was probably part of a temple inlay.

The biological characteristic that distinguished man in the course of the development of species was his use of tools. Man is a tool-maker, able to extend the use of hand and arm with implements from his environment, rather than evolving a specialized anatomy to serve his needs. His highly developed brain, giving him powers of prediction, or imagination, could be said to be the most sophisticated tool of all. And when he learned how to make appropriate tools to mould materials to his will, man became an artist as well as a hunter, for the mastery of forming weapons in heat extended to the making of artifacts that were the beginning of art.

This power of extension accorded to man by tools was demonstrated particularly in glass, for, while it is possible to model clay to the shape required and fire it afterwards, molten glass cannot be shaped directly by hand. The whole history of this singularly beautiful material—from the little globules of roughly fashioned beads to moulded vessels, to a blown bubble of glass and the fully automatic glass bottle industry of today—has been rendered possible only by tools.

Glass is generally thought to have been invented about 3000 BC, and its discovery may well have been accidental. Pliny's account in *Historia Naturalis* (Natural History) of Phoenician sailors finding vitreous material among the embers of a beach fire may be apocryphal, but it is definitely known that in the third millennium the Egyptians, the Sumerians and the people of the Indus Valley civilization were able to make faience—an opaque paste of sand coated with glaze. They had made the chemical discovery that alkaline silicates fuse like metals, and that such silicates can be made by heating silica—sand, flint or quartz crystals—with potash, a product of burning wood, or with natron, a mineral found in the western desert of Egypt. Between 1554 and 1075 BC craftsmen in Egypt discovered a process for making clear glass which could be fused and cast like metal. It was cast into rods that while hot could be moulded on a sand core into vessels. These vessels were considered by the wealthy to be superior to pottery. This same process was used to make imitations of precious stones.

The terminology of glass has been found on cuneiform tablets dating from the second millennium BC. A recipe for glaze and references to glass-making are recorded on tablets found at Nineveh which date from the seventh century BC. Three different furnaces are mentioned—"furnaces for metal", "furnaces with floor and eyes"—presumably holes from which the metal was gathered from an underground tank—and "furnaces of the arch", a heated chamber for annealing. Shallow fire-resistant crucibles seem to have been the earliest form of receptacle for melting the raw materials and these are believed to have been used at Tel-el-Amarna, in Egypt, in the reign of Amenhotep IV (1379–1362 BC).

From the Near East, glass-makers gradually extended their workshops to all parts of the Mediterranean, spreading through the Aegean to Cyprus, Crete, Greece and Italy. The conquests of Alexander the Great opened up Egypt and Asia to the culture and economic system of Hellas. The colonies that were founded, notably Alexandria, became settled with Greek or Hellenized officials, bankers, merchants and craftsmen. From this there emerged a cultural cross-fertilization of the Classical with the Oriental world which was clearly reflected in the artifacts of this period.

With the invention of the blowing iron, probably in Syria during the second century BC, an entirely new field

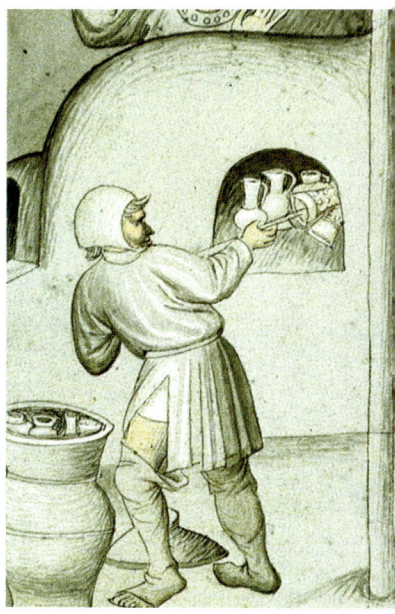

Medieval glass-makers at work are depicted, right, in a Flemish fifteenth-century version of the apocryphal Sir John Mandeville's *Travels*. The wall of the oven has several apertures through which the fire is controlled, crucibles are adjusted and the molten glass is withdrawn using metal rods. The twelfth-century German monk Theophilus advised the glass-blower, in his treatise *Upon Various Arts*, to "bring the tube to your mouth and blow slightly, and instantly removing it from your mouth, hold it near your cheek, unless in drawing breath, you may by chance attract the flame into your mouth".

Dark green beads of faience—an early composite glass of quartz paste—form part of a falcon collar from the tomb of an Egyptian queen. They date from the twentieth century BC.

Unguent vessels from Egypt's eighteenth dynasty (1570–1320 BC) were made of glass poured on a sand core. Contrasting coloured glass threads were "combed" into zigzag patterns.

The relaxed pose of two princesses in moulded red glass indicates their origin in Egypt's Amarna period (c. 1379–1362 BC), an era typified by a naturalistic style of art.

Worn to ward off the evil eye, scarabs represent the sacred beetle of the Ancient Egyptians. This glass-paste scarab, buried with a mummy, dates from about 600 BC.

Of Egyptian origin, this seventh-century BC blown-glass drinking cup has an applied annular handle. The pinched decorative effect was achieved by squeezing the molten glass with tongs.

was opened up. The ability to "gather" metal and blow it into a hollow bulb, to reheat it in the open door of the furnace and to repeat these processes as often as necessary for the proposed shape, led to the manufacture of a far greater variety of articles, including bottles and dishes with a wide range of decorative motifs and handles.

By the first century AD, glasses which had originally been opaque or inadvertently coloured by impurities in the raw batch could be made transparent and colourless or could be coloured by design rather than by accident. About this time, glazed windows became a feature of the houses of the rich, especially in northern Europe. In the letters of the younger Pliny there are references to windows in his detailed description of his house at Lausentium. By inference it can be assumed that the windows were glazed, probably with a lattice of panes of glass set in wood or bronze frames: ". . . It has windows on both sides, but more facing the sea, as there is one in each alternate bay on the garden side. These all stand open on a fine and windless day and in stormy weather can safely be opened on the side away from the wind. . . ."

The Italians developed an openwork glass technique, a splendid example of which can be seen in the British Museum —the so-called Lycurgus Cup, which dates from about the early fifth century AD. On the basic thick, greenish-coloured vessel, a figure among vine branches has been most cunningly carved so that in transmitted light both the background and the carved image are reddish and translucent. In reflected light the whole cup is green and opaque. The skill of the undercutting of the vine tendrils is remarkable.

Throughout the disintegration of the Roman Empire during the fourth and fifth centuries AD, local glass-makers continued to practise and develop their trade so that, by the seventh century, when the Christian Church was established on a European basis, there had been in southern Europe a considerable cross-fertilization of traditions. Archaeological evidence traces the spread of glass manufacture from the Near East through the valleys of the Rhine and the Rhône to northern France—and eventually to England. A tombstone discovered at Lyons, which bears the inscription "an artist in glass of African Nationality and a citizen of Carthage", is a testament to the amazing spread of glass-making.

The unusual visual effect of fifth-century AD Roman cage-cups, or *diatreta*, is due to the presence of manganese and colloidal gold in the glass. In almost magical transformation, the vessel, an opaque green when seen in reflected light, above right, turns a deep ruby red in transmitted light, above left. The reticulated decoration was produced by cutting and grinding the cast glass. In a scene from Greek mythology on the bowl of the cup, King Lycurgus meets his death at the hand of Dionysus, god of wine.

The flowery design of Ancient Roman *millefiori* glass evolved out of the mosaic technique perfected in Alexandria in the first century BC. Twisted glass threads finish the rim.

The eroded glass of this first-century AD Roman vase, found at Reims, produces an iridescent effect. All but the neck and handle, which are shaped by hand, has been mould-blown.

Glassware from first-century AD Syria was often decorated with "snake trails", as seen around the centre of this small opaque vessel. Mould-blown to the neck, it was finished by hand.

The famous Portland vase dates from first-century AD Rome. A fine example of cameo glass, the carved outer layer of white glass stands in relief against a dark background of blown glass.

Blue threads delineate the "face" of a third-century AD Rhenish–Roman glass helmet-flask. The vessel is embellished further by a transparent coiled glass bird on a red-berried twig.

Beginnings of an Art Form

ARTISTIC FORERUNNERS

The art of setting jewels in gold is thought to be one of the earliest forerunners of the art of stained glass. This crown is said to have been made in the tenth century for the Holy Roman Emperor by the workshop of the Benedictine Abbey on the Island of Reichenau in Lake Constance, Germany. It is composed of eight hinged panels, upon four of which justice, wisdom, longevity and humility are personified by biblical figures in enamel on gold. The crown is encrusted with precious stones, which are held in place by gold claws, or cloisons, on raised filigree settings.

The inscription on this jewel, "Alfred ordered me to be made", suggests that it was created in the ninth century for Alfred the Great. The figure, depicted in cloisonné enamel, is as unidentifiable as the purpose of the object itself. Cloisonné enamel, in which the colours are separated by thin metal strips, is believed to have inspired stained glass.

Stained glass as an art form was anticipated by the glittering mosaics whose patterns, composed of many pieces of coloured glass, lined the walls and domes of early Christian churches. The magnificence of those at Ravenna established the city as the artistic capital of the Byzantine world during the fifth and sixth centuries. The Arian Baptistery, built by Emperor Theodoric, who had conquered Ravenna in 476, has in the centre of its vault a golden mosaic showing the Baptism of Christ surrounded by the radiating figures of apostles.

An excellent example of traditional Islamic fretwork, this pierced marble window in the Topkapi Palace, Istanbul, is filled with coloured glass forming the pattern of a flowering plant through which the light filters. Muslim law against depicting living creatures led to the development of exquisite floral or geometric designs on tiles and carpets as well as in mosaics and stained glass.

Stained glass is, basically, a Christian art, for it had no existence until the Christian era. It is the art form which could be said to have profoundly distinguished Christian churches from the temples of the Pharaohs or the Athenians, by making their windows vehicles of spiritual expression rather than voids between massive columns. One has only to gaze at the fenestrated harmony of the east end of Bourges to realize that it is not a monument, not a beautiful exercise in proportion to celebrate a Classical ideal, but a casket, a celestial musical box, its visual music speaking only because it has transformed daylight to announce a god of light.

It is virtually impossible to pin down the origins of stained glass to one place or one time for it is an art form that defies the school-book approach to history, in which events are measured marks on a chronological ruler. When all the historical evidence is sifted, a gap still remains at the beginning which, until a convincing discovery is made, can be filled only by the imagination, by envisaging history as a fluid, multidimensional whole. Viewed in this way, history resembles the starlit night sky, a planetarium where it is possible to see ends before beginnings: to see the star of Dante shining as brightly now as it did at the birth of the *Divine Comedy*; to see the ever-twinkling star of Jane Austen in the same glance as the great Romanesque galaxy. And in this galaxy, seemingly from nowhere, a new star is suddenly born—the star of stained glass.

Whenever and wherever stained glass first evolved, it did not spring up in an artistic vacuum. Similarities in materials and techniques can be discerned between stained glass and other medieval art forms, including mosaics and enamel-work. At first, in Classical times, a means of embellishing floors, mosaics were later adopted by the Christian Church for wall decoration and domes. Instead of the hard-wearing stones or ceramic pieces of the Classical pavements, wall mosaics were composed of small pieces of coloured glass fitted together to create bold, coherent designs—a similar technique to that used by the medieval stained-glass artist.

The idea of using a framework of lead to hold together the pieces of glass may well have been inspired by the art of the goldsmith and the cloisonné enameller. Imagine, for example, a man watching a goldsmith at work. With the alert, empirical mind of the experimental scientist, he sees how easily the goldsmith bends strips, or cloisons, of gold around pieces of coloured glass to hold them together in a patterned cluster. Knowing that coloured glass could, by the Middle Ages, be made in reasonably large pieces, he suddenly thinks of lead instead of gold—a cheap and malleable metal, which could hold a pattern of glass panes as a jewelled window rather than as a jewelled brooch.

The strips of metal used by the cloisonné enameller to enframe areas of coloured enamel are, with their raised outlines, even more suggestive of lead-lines in a stained-glass window. Indeed, it was but a step, artistically, from the enamelled reliquary adorned with saints looking out from their casket to saints looking in from their transparent setting in architecture.

Another important discovery was linked with the invention of casting, or milling, a strip of lead with a section that could be shaped and jointed to hold glass in a transportable panel. The artist discovered that iron filings, ground to a paste with a flux of powdered glass, could be painted on the glass for such details as facial features, hands and drapery, and then fired at a temperature just short of melting point.

Traces of the gestation of stained glass are scanty. Even before Charlemagne's image had blurred on the coinage of Europe, some of the more progressive ecclesiastics had had their churches glazed. Already in the sixth century, for example, St Gregory had the windows of St Martin of Tours in France glazed with coloured glass. In the following century, c. 675, Benedict Biscop, the abbot of Monkwearmouth, in what is now Sunderland, employed Gallic

Excavations in 1932 at Lorsch Abbey in Germany unearthed fragments of stained glass which are thought to date from the ninth or tenth century. In spite of the dark gaps of missing glass, a head of Christ is suggested by this reconstruction of the ancient pieces, believed to be the earliest existing pictorial stained glass.

glaziers in his monastery church. Such early windows varied considerably in form. The apertures were not necessarily filled entirely with coloured glass. Sometimes they were filled with alabaster, marble or even wooden boards, which were pierced with holes into which coloured glass was inserted. This technique may well have been adapted by the first Christian builders from the fretted windows of the Levant, their ornamental network of stone or wood often punctuated with glass.

The Tours windows have not survived, however, and the glass excavated at Monkwearmouth shows no trace of painted design. The first and, so far, only glimpse of daylight in this tunnel of uncertainty, the real prototypes of stained glass, are the fragments from Kloster Lorsch in Germany, the head of Christ from Wissembourg in Alsace, and the famous five prophet windows in Augsburg Cathedral. Whatever technical developments preceded them, the Augsburg windows show an assured technique and style—enough to indicate that the art had been practised for some considerable time before the windows were created.

Inevitably, therefore, stained glass must appear in history as a fully fledged art form whose antecedents are lost.

There is, in fact, a sudden arrogance about the use in churches not of white glass but of expensive coloured glass on a monumental scale, when up to that time glass had been used only for jewellery, utensils and small-scale domestic glazing in the houses of the rich Romans or Byzantines.

Those who guided the beginnings of stained glass would have been aware of a movement of creativity in other artistic spheres that had metamorphosized the Classical and Oriental conventions of divine imagery. By a gradual process, which must have incorporated one artist's insight and another's technical invention, the grim hieratic Pantocrators of the Byzantines softened to the gentle smile of the Gothic angel, the expressionless goddesses of the Classical world gave way to the tender Mother of God—Notre Dame de la Belle Verrière in the cathedral of Chartres.

And behind this creativity there must have been a driving force, which exerted an unconscious, all-embracing influence. It was a force that was continuous, from the catacombs of Ancient Rome to the medieval glass of Canterbury Cathedral, moving from sign to symbol, from symbol to subject, until the whole story of God and man was made incarnate in light.

The Church and its Planning

Imagine flying low over a cathedral city. Immediately striking are the shape of the cathedral and its dominance over the buildings which surround it. Not until the Industrial Revolution was there any building, apart from palaces, to compete with the cathedral in a city or the church in a village. From the air, too, the cathedral's lovely symmetry of form, its plan, is apparent.

The word plan is used by architects to describe the simple form of a building as outlined by its walls, but behind the word, when applied to a house of worship, lies a deeper meaning, which, to the medieval mind, embraced preconceived concepts of a divine order. It was this order that dictated the dimensions and proportions which the builders translated into materials of stone, wood, metal and glass. From the air, even without an architect's training, it can be seen that the planning was not haphazard. It was creative engineering—the achievement of a stable structure of great height and complexity yet with the appearance of both lightness and grace.

The cathedral was created by men of divine effrontery as a house for God—not for a god of darkness and forest magic, not for a god of random arbitrary power, but for a god of perfect geometry. In the ancient world, the study of number, expressed through geometry, was considered a means of understanding the ideal order that had fashioned the universe, and the geometry of Greek mathematics was inherited by the Christian Church and widely used in church planning. When it became necessary to design large buildings for the increasing congregations, it was the churchman who laid down the principles from which the master mason would extrapolate the dimensions and proportions of the building, based on circles, triangles and squares. In addition to this geometrical tradition, the practical churchman and his master mason brought great empirical judgement to the solutions of the physical problems of site and availability of materials. But, more important, in the process they often made adventurous leaps of imagination, which resulted in new and unpredicted forms.

The form on which the plans of most medieval churches and cathedrals in England, France, Belgium, Germany and Italy are based is that of the Latin cross, a two-armed structure, the short arm of which forms the north and south transepts. This cruciform plan may have developed from that of the Early Christian basilica or it may have been suggested by the cruciform tombs built during the reign of the Emperor Constantine. Whatever its origin, the plan was modified during the Middle Ages because of the need to accommodate an ever-growing clergy and congregation. Aisles, transepts, ambulatory—the aisle or walk around the east end of a church behind the altar—and subsidiary chapels all provided additional space. In France, the chapels were often built to form a semicircular ring known as a *chevet*. Double transepts, which extended the eastern end of the church, originated in Cluniac monasteries and were introduced to England by William of Sens, one of the architects who rebuilt the choir of Canterbury Cathedral. They were subsequently incorporated into many English cathedrals, including Salisbury and Lincoln. This innovation was of particular importance in England because many of the cathedrals were monastic churches and provision had to be made for large numbers of clergy. It is possible that the preaching friars, the Franciscans and Dominicans, called for the increase in the size of the nave in some churches, in order to accommodate a larger congregation, but this certainly occurred more and more as a result of the Reformation, with its stress on the participation of the laity.

At the dark intersection, or crossing, of the transepts and the nave, there arose a central tower with a clerestory. This was often known as a lantern because of its light-admitting function. In France, however, the transepts were relatively high and the crossing was lit by the windows in

Many Christian churches in the early Middle Ages were built on pagan sites, after the idols had been destroyed, so that people could worship in familiar places. However, sacred significance continued to be ascribed to the stones with which holy areas were enclosed and to spring water, which was believed to imbue these chosen spots with supernatural powers. Attitudes about good and evil were incorporated into the church building itself. The north side of the church, for example, was associated with darkness and evil, and only the profane were buried on the north side of the churchyard. The south, in contrast, was considered the side of enlightenment and goodness. These beliefs were later reflected in the decoration of the church, where appropriate subjects were represented on each side. Frescoes, carvings, sculpture and stained glass were all designed to show the penitent the path to redemption. To enter the church was to embark on a spiritual journey akin to pilgrimage, a journey dictated by the symbolic structure of the building. The ascent of the western steps, which graced the entrance of many cathedrals, implied a religious elevation; the progression along the nave signified a voyage; and the entry into the chancel represented an admittance to the heavenly regions.

Romanesque carvings on capitals were invested with symbolic power. An Annunciation is combined with the Classical acanthus leaf on this capital in Monreale Cathedral, Sicily.

the end walls. Western towers are a feature of French, German and some English cathedrals, a containment for the double thrust of the side and end walls. They also mark the importance of the west end as a ceremonial entrance, for it is here that the new archbishop ritually enters his cathedral for the first time. Through this entrance, too, thousands of pilgrims pass to gaze at the superb vista of the nave and to catch a glimpse of the choir beyond the great chancel screen. In German cathedrals the western towers were a traditional symbol of secular power balancing the concentration of ecclesiastical power at the eastern end.

From the outset, the building was orientated on an axis that marked the rising sun, the head of the church always directed towards the east. The north side, associated with evil and regarded as a region of darkness and cold, became the place of the Old Testament, while the south side, with its relative light and warmth, was consecrated to the New Testament. The west end became the region of history, and, in most cathedrals, there are representations of the Last Judgement, or Doom, either in sculpture above the porch or in the west window.

In the twentieth century, the traditional, basically rectangular plan has been increasingly criticized as inadequate for the setting of new forms of worship, and the design of new churches, since the Second World War, reflects a tendency towards radical and, at times, eccentric planning. In many modern churches, the old rectangular plan of nave, narrow chancel and fixed eastern altar has been largely abandoned in favour of circular, square or asymmetric plans with a free-standing altar at or near the middle of the building.

The planning of the church has been an organic growth, a plant eventually bearing flowers of infinite variety, but always from an order laid down in its seed from the early days of the primitive Church.

Although most English cathedrals have a square east end, many French and German churches and cathedrals, such as Altenberg, above, terminate in a *chevet*, or semicircular ring of chapels radiating from the ambulatory.

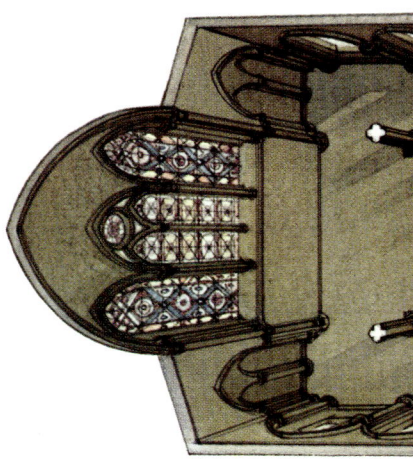

The north was associated with darkness, and sometimes with the Church's enemies, such as this figure with a bishop's head impaled on his sword, from a north clerestory window in St Mary's Church, Fairford, Gloucestershire.

Church ceilings, especially in the chancel, were associated with heaven. In Gothic churches, celestial symbols, like this angel trumpeter in the cloisters of Norwich Cathedral, were carved on the roof bosses.

Saints feature prominently in windows on the south side, the side of goodness, light and the New Testament. This detail from Fairford Church shows St Bartholomew holding the knife with which he was flayed and reciting the part of the Creed attributed to him—"I believe in the Holy Ghost."

The need for repentance is emphasized by sculptures of the Last Judgement, which, like this example from Notre Dame, Paris, are carved above western doors. The medieval theologian Durandus compared the western entrance, through which the laity approached redemption, to Christ's words, "I am the Way."

THE CHANGING PLAN

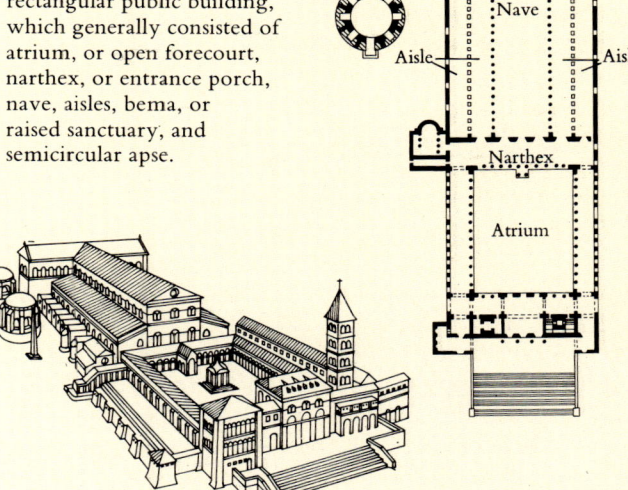

Early Christian churches were based on the plan of the Roman basilica, right, a rectangular public building, which generally consisted of atrium, or open forecourt, narthex, or entrance porch, nave, aisles, bema, or raised sanctuary, and semicircular apse.

Old St Peter's, Rome, was built in 330 by the Emperor Constantine, who in 312 had accepted Christianity. Its architecture is based on the design of the basilica. The cruciform plan of medieval churches is thought to have evolved from the rudimentary transepts.

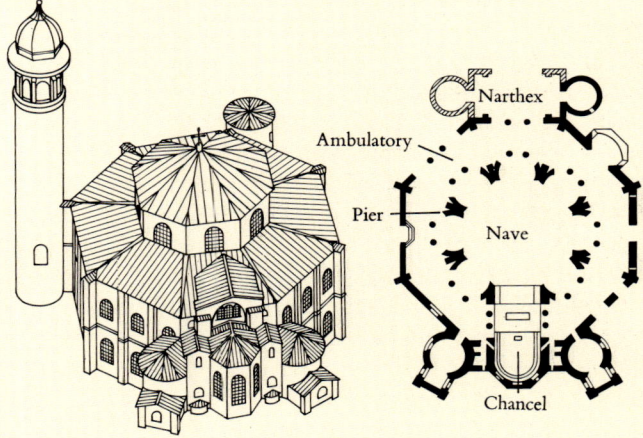

An alternative to the basilican plan was the domed, centralized design based on the architecture of Byzantium. One of the finest examples of this is the octagonal Church of San Vitale at Ravenna, which was built in the sixth century by the Emperor Justinian.

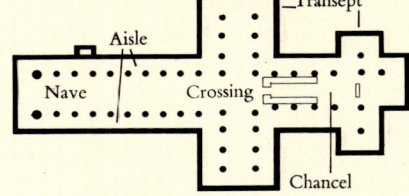

Double transepts, originally a feature of Cluniac churches, were characteristic of many medieval English cathedrals and churches, including the thirteenth-century Beverley Minster, near York, above. The transepts provided space for a large choir of monks or canons or for subsidiary altars.

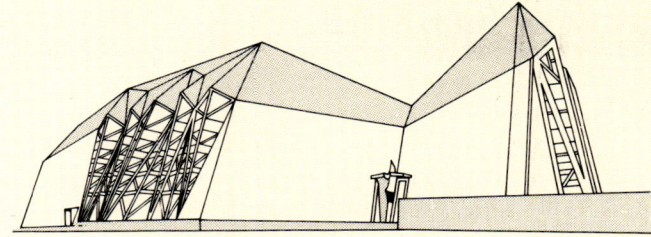

A traditional symbol underlies the plan of the modern First Presbyterian Church in Stamford, Connecticut. The church is in the shape of a fish, which, since the second century, has been a symbol for Christ, the Greek initials for Jesus Christ Son of God Saviour spelling *Ichthus*, the word for fish.

15

The Architectural Challenge

Architecture is often called "the mother of the arts" and this rather generalized term is particularly true of its relationship to stained glass, for without the framework of a building windows could not exist. Before the advent of this uniquely Christian art, windows were more or less utilitarian. They provided light and air for the poor, but only the rich could afford to have them glazed. The exploitation of light did not extend beyond simple lattice-work or, in the East, elaborate fretting of stone or wood, which was sometimes set with small fragments of glass. Rather than exploiting light, however, this was actually a modifying or subduing of light in countries where small windows were favoured to reduce heat and glare.

The full exploitation of the window as an art form was, perhaps, possible only in northern Europe, with its preponderance of dull days. The introduction of the optimum amount of light became the natural goal of architects of churches and cathedrals. Although the first stained glass was made for the single semicircular-headed windows of the Romanesque style, and these windows grew to be quite large, it was Gothic architecture, and the great expanses of glass which were its hallmark, that finally made the glazier as important as the mason.

From the disposition of the parts of the church or the cathedral on the horizontal plane, there evolved the superb vertical planes made possible by the evolution of the pointed Gothic arch. There was the great western entrance surmounted by a rose window; the nave, with its splendidly glazed aisles, divided into bays rising above the arcades through triforium to clerestory; the transepts branching from the transition of the nave and choir, each with its range of windows and its end wall often adorned with another rose; the screened choir through which the light from the high windows of the eastern apse was ever present, in contrast to the dark, mysterious apse of Byzantine churches.

All this came into being because inspired master masons and master glaziers worked with the common goal of attaining height and light. These innovations did not occur suddenly, but evolved organically out of a step-by-step tradition stimulated by intuitive invention. Sometimes the inventiveness was reckless, as at Beauvais, where the height of the cathedral grew too great for the foundations and the whole structure collapsed. However, as more and more complex buttressing counteracted the thrust of the vaults, walls became screens of multi-light windows filled with stained glass that has never been surpassed.

From this high peak of co-operation between mason and glazier in the Middle Ages there was a gradual decline. The growing importance of secular buildings, from the fifteenth century onwards, weakened the partnership that had lasted for more than four centuries. As a result of the revival of Classical ideas brought about by the Renaissance, windows were again planned as plain glazed areas, the function of which was to light up the modelling of columns, pilasters and rich coffered ceilings. In the eighteenth century, anything Gothic was considered barbarous and this attitude persisted until the Romantic revival of medieval art and craftsmanship in the nineteenth century, which produced many large churches and one or two cathedrals. But, being imitative of a past age and created by stained-glass firms who tended to copy medieval styles blindly in inferior glass, the windows were stereotyped and sometimes very bad.

The modern revolution in architecture, and the use of new constructive methods and materials—notably reinforced concrete—has vastly increased the scale on which the glazier can work. Larger areas than ever before can now be spanned to give whole shimmering walls of glass, supported only by slender concrete or metal frames. Once again the glazier has had to meet a new challenge posed by the architect—to transform a building into a vibrant harmony of masonry and glass, of form and light.

The first Christian churches were built according to prevailing Roman traditions and seem to have been based on the basilica, the Roman Hall of Justice. Windows in these early churches were small and some were filled with pierced marble or alabaster slabs, which gave a muted light, revealing the chief glory of the interior—the mosaics. When Christianity became the official religion of the Roman Empire, the imperial centre shifted from Rome to Constantinople, and here the style known as Byzantine reached its apogee in the great Church of Hagia Sophia. Here the Classical style, with columns supporting an entablature, or framework, and a roof, was fused with the Oriental tradition of a square plan surmounted by a dome. The series of compartments growing out from the central area of the dome made possible a variety of semi-domes, their surfaces vehicles for yet more mosaics.

Windows were relatively small, with stone lattice-work which was sometimes glazed with clear glass. Romanesque, as its name implies, was a style devised from surviving Roman buildings in Europe and was developed by Christian builders influenced by the Oriental ideas that had spread from the Near East. As mosaics were the glory of the Byzantine church, exquisite sculpture embellished the porches and external arcading of Romanesque churches.

The solid, earth-bound appearance of the Romanesque church was created by walls often eight feet thick. After 1000, the first stone barrel, or tunnel, vaults began to replace flat timber roofs and the walls were designed to resist the thrust of these vaults over the nave. Later, vaults intersected at right angles to form cross vaults, and the underside, or groin, of this intersection formed ribs, the prototypes of the highly moulded Gothic vaults. Extra support was provided by a gallery over the side aisles. Windows, which weakened the structure, were kept to a minimum. In southern European churches, for example San Michele, Pavia, in section, right, the windows were small with rounded arches. In northern Europe the need for greater illumination resulted in larger windows, and the first appearance of stained glass.

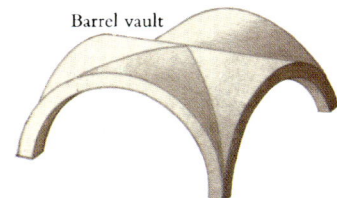

Barrel vault

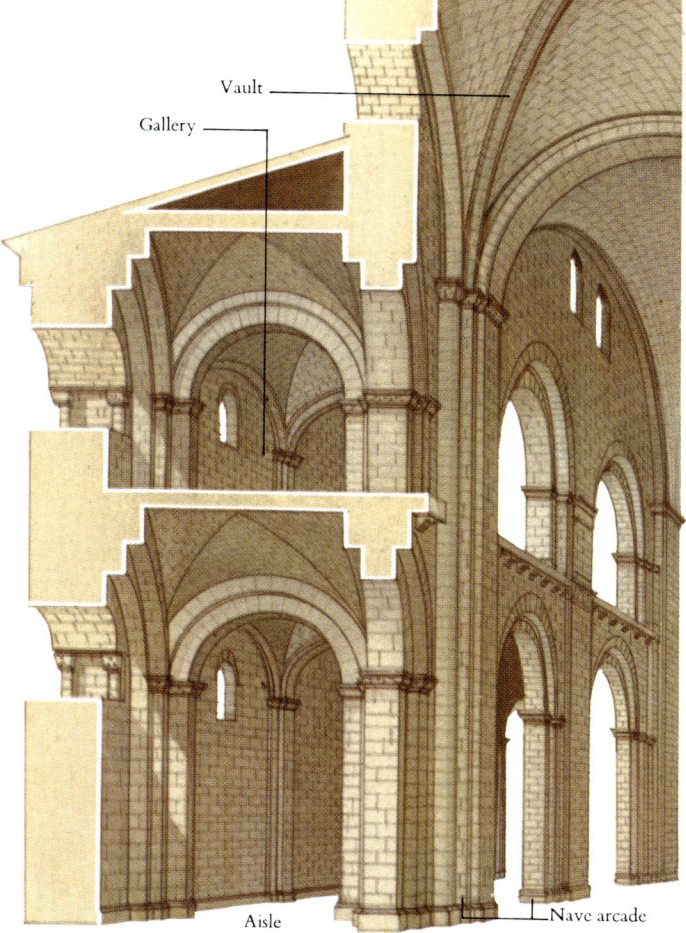

Vault
Gallery
Aisle
Nave arcade

Speyer, one of Germany's few well-preserved Romanesque cathedrals, was founded in 1030 and remodelled at the end of the eleventh century. It is distinguished by its four towers and two domes, by its sturdy simplicity and monumental scale. From east to west it measures 435 feet—almost the length of Chartres. The spacious nave, left, spanned by bays of groin vaulting, stretches towards the apsidal east end.

The term Gothic, meaning barbarous, was applied, in the seventeenth century, to the architecture of the Middle Ages, which had rejected the Classical architectural forms. The delicacy and soaring height of Gothic cathedrals were achieved through a combination of structural innovations—the pointed arch, ribbed vault and flying buttress. The pointed arch and ribbed vault had appeared in Durham Cathedral in the eleventh century.

Buttresses were also used by Romanesque builders, but had been hidden under lean-to roofs. The first truly Gothic building in which these three features were incorporated was the Abbey Church of St Denis, rebuilt by Abbé Suger in 1140. Light was controlled through the medium of stained glass to create a dynamic art form, which, like the aspiring verticality of the architecture, perfectly expressed the religious temperament of the age.

In Renaissance architecture, windows had become relatively small, clear glass voids, but they were reinstated as a frame for stained glass with the Gothic Revival in the nineteenth century. The largely romantic reversion to a Christian "Golden Age" stimulated church building and the often unfortunate restoration of many medieval churches. Windows once more became multi-lighted and were filled with stained glass which attempted to emulate that of earlier centuries. In the twentieth century, the radical change in building methods that followed the use of steel frames revolutionized the role of the window in architecture. Walls are virtually unnecessary as support and may be composed almost entirely of glass. Modern churches vary in shape from the eccentric "Fish" church in Stamford, Connecticut, to the chapel at Ronchamp, France, which looks like an African kraal.

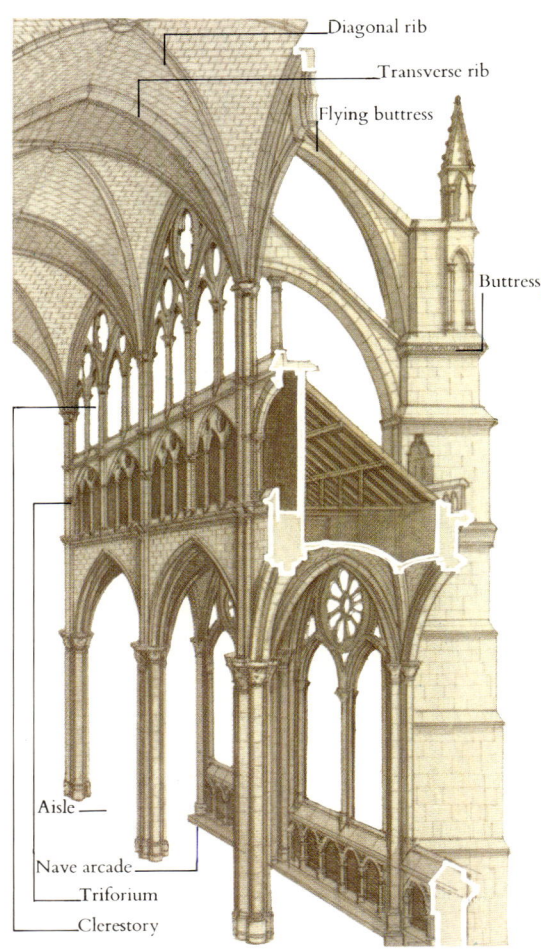

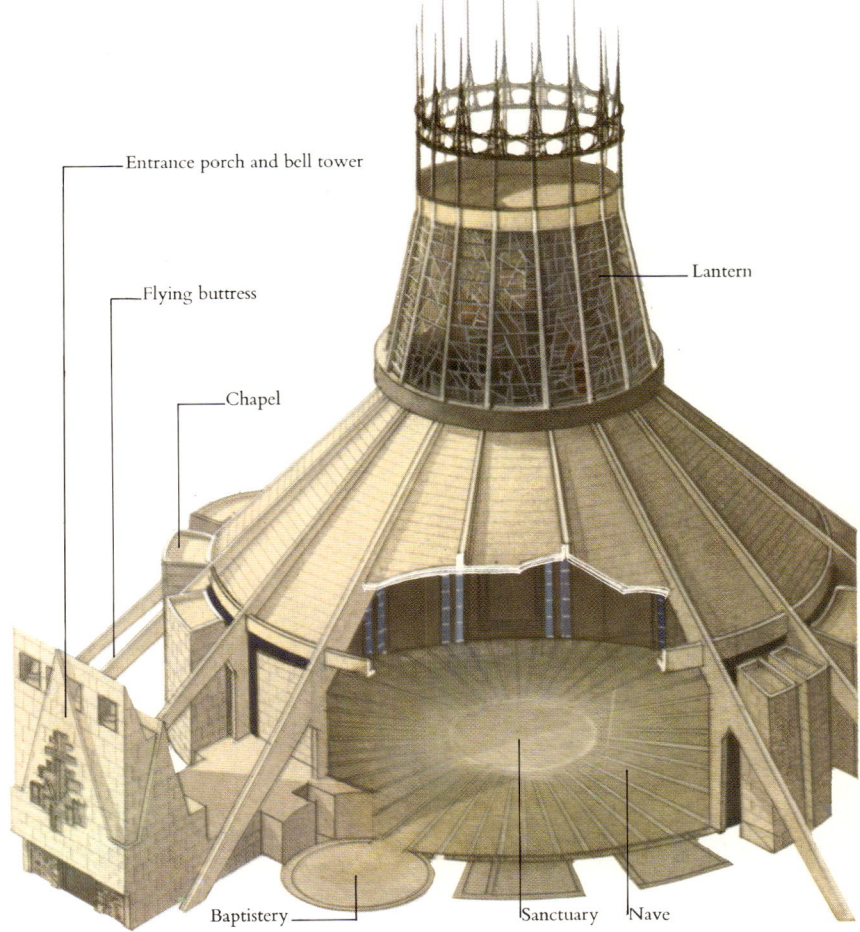

Built between 1220 and 1228, Amiens Cathedral, shown in section, left, was one of the first Gothic cathedrals. Instead of being countered by massive walls, the thrust of the nave vaults was transmitted across the aisles by flying buttresses to stout buttress piers. The structural security afforded by this system led to thinner walls and more and larger windows. The gallery was replaced by a triforium, which was sometimes glazed. The pointed arch, which could span areas of varying dimensions, increased the height of the building, and the vaulting of the arches was strengthened, and decorated, by a network of diagonal and transverse ribs.

Chartres Cathedral is supported by flying buttresses, above, whose double arches are reinforced by spokes.

Light floods through the tall clerestory windows of Amiens, right, the French Gothic cathedral whose three-storeyed nave soars to 138 feet.

Frank Gibberd's circular design for Liverpool's Roman Catholic Cathedral, above and left, opposes the hierarchical structure of medieval church architecture, in which clergy and congregation were segregated. At Liverpool they worship together around a central altar. The framework, built with concrete reinforced by steel, is extended by flying buttresses, which give the cathedral its rising, tent-like appearance. Their function is, however, decorative rather than structural. A crown of spiky pinnacles rests on the domed lantern, in which stained glass by John Piper and Patrick Reyntiens symbolizes the Trinity in three bursts of colour against gradations of the spectrum. Blue windows, also by Piper and Reyntiens, define the bays surrounding the sanctuary.

Painting with Light

The colours of stained glass change continually according to the variations of transmitted light. The glass in the fourteenth-century west window of Altenberg Church in Germany, for example, is illuminated, top, by the brilliance of direct sunlight. The same glass deepens in tone when the sun is obscured by cloud.

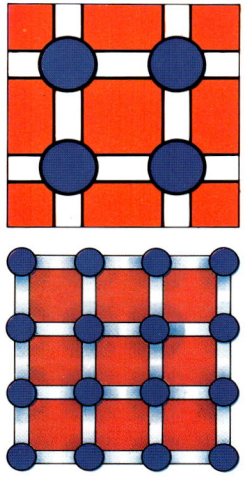

In the nineteenth century Viollet-le-Duc, the French art historian, devised diagrams in an attempt to demonstrate the unequal irradiation of translucent colours. Red, blue and white were said to irradiate equally, top diagram, when seen from a short distance. At a distance of approximately sixty-five feet, lower diagram, the glass seemed to be dominated by blue, the colour with the strongest powers of irradiation. Consequently, the adjacent reds appeared violet while the leads and strips of white were tinted with blue. Viollet-le-Duc's conclusions are controversial. James Rosser Johnson, for example, a modern academic, meticulously repeated the experiment and did not observe any distortion of colour.

Before a stained-glass artist can be judged by the usual criteria of the fine arts, including design, proportion, tonal control and colour, the skill with which he has understood his "canvas" must be appreciated. Stained glass is the only art form that relies entirely on natural daylight for its effect. Every other art form, from painting and sculpture to tapestry and jewellery, is designed to be appreciated by reflected light. In creating such works of art, no great problem arises for the artist. He controls his colours or his shapes knowing that the purely physical reflection in the spectator's eye will be exactly as he plans it.

With a stained-glass window, however, the artist must control a powerful energy which will be transmitted through his medium of expression. He has to paint with light itself. While the painter or sculptor can arrange for the best possible lighting of his work and knows that in essence it will remain more or less unaltered, this is not so with stained glass.

When a window is fixed in its permanent frame in a building, it becomes subject to radical alterations of intensity from influences outside the artist's control. The medieval glazier, in this respect, had a great advantage over his twentieth-century counterpart. He had a setting for his windows that had grown with his own tradition. The architect, therefore, understood his problems and did not present him with an environment that militated against his work, as so often happens with modern buildings.

The colour of the glass, when the window is installed, may be bleached and the effectiveness of its paintwork diminished by strong sunlight. Sometimes the sun may shine only on part of the window's surface with disruptive consequences. The light may advance some colours and make others recede. It may cause two juxtaposed colours, such as red and blue, to combine in an unintentional hue.

Serious disruption may occur, too, from trees or buildings in the vicinity. They may make the lower half of the window dark and the upper half light in contrast. Blue skies or dark clouds may alter the whole colour pitch of a window. A stained-glass window is also subject to halation, the phenomenon of light flooding around a solid object and producing a blurred effect. As a result of halation, a black line appears to have its edge eroded and thus seems thinner than its actual width, or a patch of white surrounded by solid black can appear larger than it is. In York Minster, for example, there are restored portions of fourteenth-century windows surrounded by clear glass, and here can be seen the baleful effect of competing light values which the restorer, concerned with archaeological exactitude rather than aesthetics, failed to appreciate.

By far the most serious effect of halation is glare—a bright mass of uninhibited light either within a window or coming from a nearby source. In the new Coventry Cathedral, for example, the ten nave windows are angled in such a way that they are seen fully only from or near the altar. From this viewpoint, the great expanse of the clear glass at the west end overpowers the muted light of the stained glass of the nave windows, causing them to appear relatively dull by contrast. The eye resolves the problem by adjusting to the bright light, in much the same way as a photographer stops down the aperture of the lens of a camera. Blotting out the white light by holding the hand between it and the eye proves that the stained glass admits far more light than it might seem to. As soon as the eye has become adjusted to muted light the colours begin to glow and expand to their true value.

This unfortunate condition of glare, resulting from light windows in proximity to richly coloured windows, can be seen in many churches and cathedrals. The only way an architect can have stained glass and still achieve a "light" interior for his church is to fill the windows with grisaille—clear glass enriched by painted patterns. Much of the sublime impact of the windows of Chartres Cathedral, on the other hand, is due to the fact that the extensive stained glass is all within the same tonal range and is undisturbed by any nearby white light source. Such a cathedral is in fact the perfect architectural environment for stained glass—a giant black box with virtually all its apertures filled with coloured glass.

The glazed "canvas" is subject to a mass of conflicting stimuli from the differing behaviour of the wavelengths of colours and their intensities as they reach the eye. The complicated problem of what happens to various colours when they are seen by transmitted light has preoccupied many theorists. The most widely quoted is Eugène Viollet-le-Duc, the nineteenth-century French art historian. In an article, "Vitrail", published in 1868, he attempted to systematize the laws and principles which, he believed, underlay all medieval stained glass.

Viollet-le-Duc was mainly concerned with the phenomenon of irradiation, the optical effects of transmitted light through translucent colours, and the fact that this irradiation is unequal according to the colour—some colours recede and others advance, or spread. The most common example of this is demonstrated by the alleged tendency of reds to recede and that of blues to advance, often gathering a power out of proportion to the area they occupy. Yellow appears to remain neutral, advancing only if its colour is moved along the spectrum from the red to the blue end, that is from deep orange to pale lemonish yellow.

Most artists, as is their unruly way, view theorists with irreverence or scepticism, an attitude which has received unexpected support from a modern academic. James Rosser Johnson, a distinguished American art historian, has made a penetrating and imaginative study of the glass at Chartres in which he tested the "principles" of Viollet-le-Duc scientifically and aesthetically and found they suffer to some extent from the old disease of facts being made to fit theories.

The broad observations of Viollet-le-Duc are, of course, correct in so far as colours present different optical values, but he, and other theorists, tended to explain their differences only in dogmatic scientific terms. As Johnson points out, the deeper the shade of blue, the colour most often used as an example in this connection, the less the colour expands. Even reds, which are normally said to have low brilliance and high saturation, have different optical values. If, for example, a piece of deep copper ruby antique glass is placed next to a piece of glass coloured red by the non-metallic element selenium, the brilliance of the selenium-coloured glass compared to the antique glass is striking. Because of its ability to radiate, selenium ruby glass is used in traffic lights, where its function is to assist the driver's eye in bright surrounding light. This kind of brilliance is the opposite of the depth and tonality of colour which the artist requires to eliminate coloured glare as well as white light glare.

In a stained-glass window the artist creates an area of coloured light, modified by monochrome paint, which offers itself as a kind of music of light, instantaneous in space, energized by the physical properties of light waves in the same way that music is energized by the behaviour of sound waves. Like the great composer, the glazier "musician" knows how the various "sounds" of light will behave as they pass through different colours. He knows how to control the irradiation of some "chords" so that they do not overpower the essential theme of his composition. This knowledge is the subtle combination of workshop rules, inherited from a long and living tradition, and his own intuitive co-ordination of coloured images.

Early in the twentieth century, the Spanish architect Antoni Gaudí restored the interior of the cathedral of Palma in Majorca to regain the original medieval effect. The strong morning sunlight shines through the Star of David east window to mingle with the windows of the side nave and central apse in a harmony of light and colour.

Webs of Stone

Angel musicians, besides their lyrical charm, are frequently used in tracery because they can easily be adapted to fit the irregular spaces. An angelic orchestra, including this figure blowing a horn, appears above the sixteenth-century Jesse Tree in Autun Cathedral, France.

The tracery of the sixteenth-century Noah window in St Neot Church, Cornwall, is composed of three Perpendicular shapes. The nineteenth-century central panel, above, shows God with symbols of his creation. Within the globe is a miniature landscape in which night and day are juxtaposed.

Geometric tracery, right, which survived a fire in 1298, surmounts the fourteenth-century lancets in the south aisle of Strasbourg Cathedral. Concentric bands of stars, circles and rosettes, enriched by deep reds and oranges, surround the central Virgin and Child, as well as the attendant angels below. An unusual motif, in the same window, above, resembles a wheel of fire.

Tracery, the ornamental stone patterns which distinguish Gothic architecture, was probably derived from Byzantine windows and pierced marble screens. Medieval tracery originated as a result of the purely practical need to terminate two or more mullions, the vertical stone shafts dividing window lights, within the frame of a pointed arch. This problem did not exist with the round-headed single lights of Norman, or Romanesque, windows. In Gothic buildings, however, where two or three lancets were grouped together to form a single window, an uncomfortable space occurred above and between the points of the lights. At first this space was filled by small, circular, quatrefoil or trefoil lights, which were given the characteristic petal or clover shape by the use of the cusp, a projecting point at the intersection of two arcs. These simple, static shapes were known collectively as plate tracery because they appeared to have been carved out of a plate of solid stone.

At Reims, in the early thirteenth century, a new form of tracery—bar tracery—appeared. Stonework lost its natural appearance of weight and solidity. Instead of being "punched" with holes, it was pared away and filleted, until slim stone bars, or ribs, formed the skeleton of the geometric shapes used in plate tracery. The foliated circles of this geometric phase were balanced with formal elegance and admitted patterns of light through myriad openings. Tracery became less rigid in the fourteenth century as a result of the gradual development of curved openings which resembled leaves, petals and flames. Visual movement, captured paradoxically by unbending stone, was the essence of succeeding styles of tracery, which were appropriately called flowing, curvilinear and flamboyant. Stonework, skilfully shaped into sinuous patterns that echoed each other yet were never dull or repetitive, appeared to flow and undulate in rhythms which suggested growth and movement in nature.

The tendency to make windows taller culminated in the massive multi-light windows of England's Perpendicular period, which began in the late fourteenth century, and it led also to a less flowing type of tracery. This style of architecture, with its flattened arch, which reduced the area above the springing line, the point at which the mullion curves, precipitated the decline of tracery.

Stained glass, which had to be adapted to the somewhat awkward problems tracery imposed, either reinforced or subtly suppressed the pattern created by the stonework. Sometimes, a group of tracery lights was isolated by the related designs of its stained glass. In other instances, fillets of clear glass, or narrow borders around the individual panels, emphasized the glass by admitting haloes of light whose brilliance eclipsed some of the stonework. Increasingly, after the fifteenth century, the stone was disregarded and the glass often carried its theme from one section of a window to the next, and even extended it into the tracery. The effect created was that of a picture on which a stone pattern had been imposed, rather than an integration of stained glass and stone.

Traceries often contain the only original glass of old windows, and their imagery makes a fascinating study. Before the glaziers chose to ignore the patterns of the tracery lights, symbols were among the most common and most convenient motifs, because they could be designed to fit odd shapes and could also add significant comment to the theme of the main window. If the subject of the main window was the Crucifixion, for example, the tracery lights would carry the emblems of the Passion—which included nails, a crown of thorns and spears. Symbols were often combined with angels, who either carried the emblems or played various

THE DEVELOPMENT OF TRACERY

The circle and its subdivisions, or *mouchettes*, below, provided the basic forms of Gothic tracery. The earliest style, plate tracery, consisted of a circle punched in the stonework above the lancets. The circle gradually developed cusps and became a foliated form, such as a quatrefoil. In the thirteenth century, the stonework above the lancets was filleted into bar tracery, its slender bars forming geometric shapes. Fourteenth-century bar tracery became more dynamic, developing into styles known as reticulated and flowing, both distinguished by the ogee, or S-shaped curve. In fifteenth-century France this tradition culminated in flamboyant tracery, while in England it was succeeded by the Perpendicular style. Curves were replaced by straight lines and tracery was minimized by the flattened arch and extended mullions. In a later, rectilinear, variation upright panels surmount the lancets.

The circle and its subdivisions

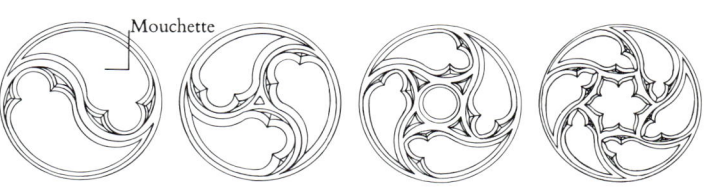

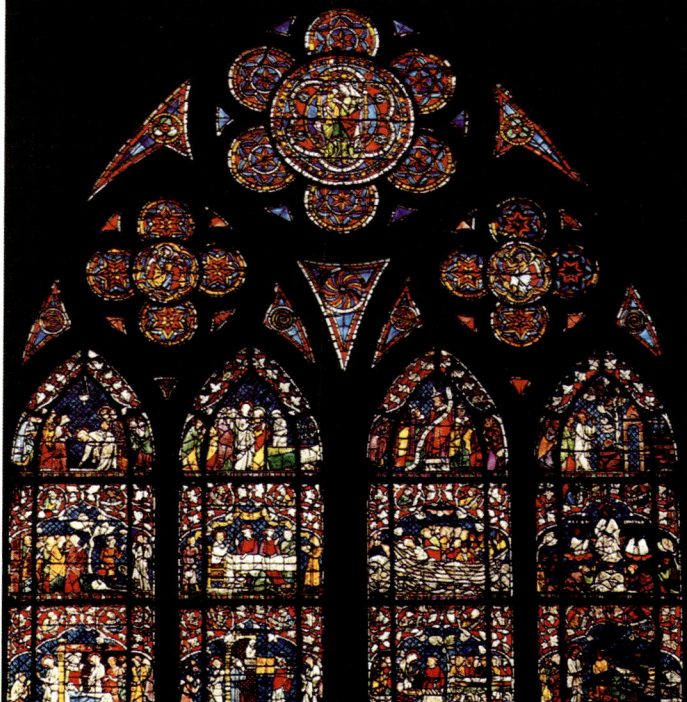

Trefoils of fourteenth-century reticulated tracery, a transitional phase between the balance of geometric and the rippling effect of flowing, satisfyingly depict and echo the triangular forms of bishops' mitred heads in this window in the Lady Chapel at Wells Cathedral, England.

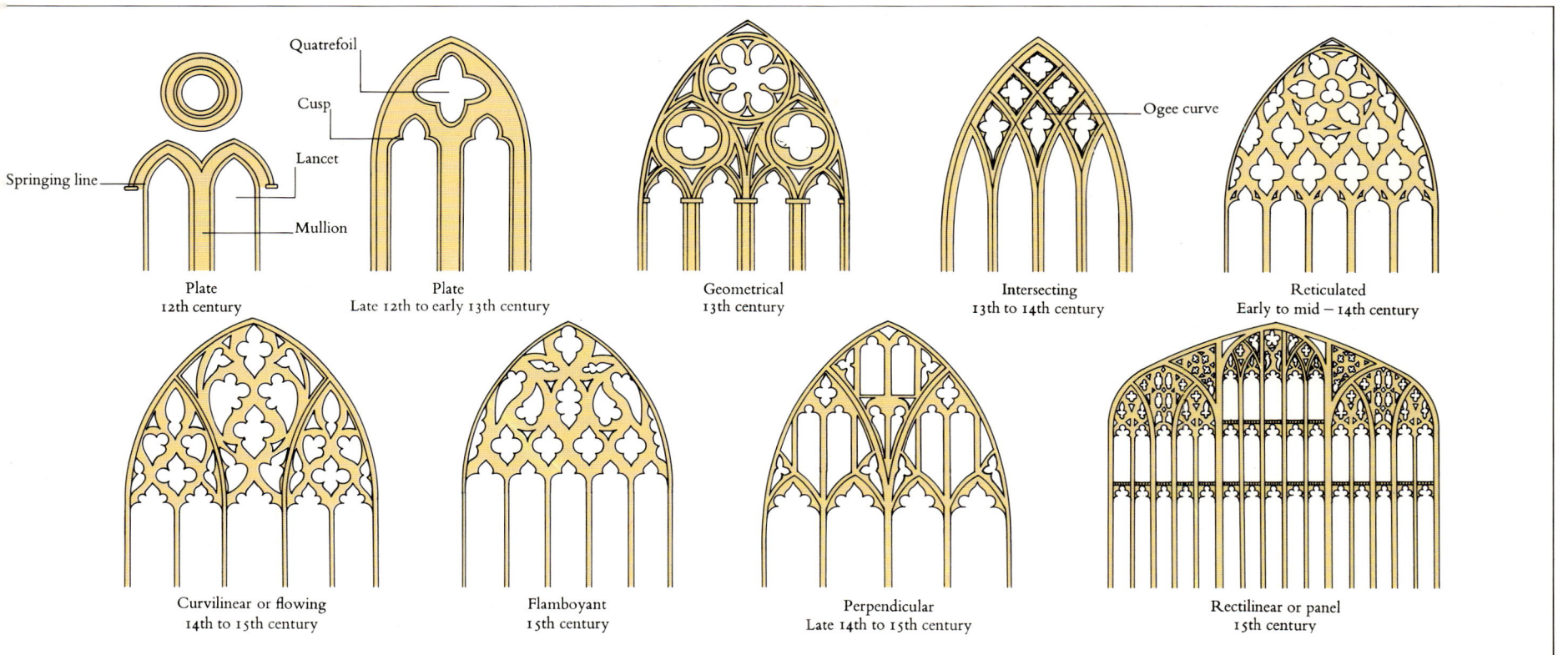

musical instruments. These angels are among the most charming inventions of the glass-painter's art and they fill the appropriate areas of tracery with unconscious ease.

The return to the Classical style in architecture in the sixteenth century—a development that followed the flowering of the Renaissance—spelled death to tracery. It might be said that a vestige was left in the semicircular, arched windows of such well-known Italian buildings as the Palazzo Strozzi in Florence, where the central column, or mullion, divides to make two smaller arches, and the space above is embellished with a circle. But these are only architectural features and in no sense were they conceived as settings for stained glass. Tracery, therefore, virtually died out until the Gothic Revival in the nineteenth century, when, with the abundance of new church building in the "Gothic" manner, almost every style of tracery, from simple to flamboyant, was used.

The beginning of the twentieth century was characterized by many emergent styles in building form and technique, but by far the most influential factor in the appearance of modern buildings is the dominance of reinforced concrete technology. Nevertheless, tradition dies harder than technologies, and, until comparatively recent times, church architects had to design churches "that looked like churches". Attempts to do this and yet to defer to more radical thinking are reflected by a return to the simplest of all tracery schemes in the windows of some churches of this period. In, for example, a three-light window, the mullions simply divide at the springing line, and, using the same arch as that of the main arch, curve to left and right, bisecting each other to form roughly diamond shapes within the head of the window opening.

Apart from such compromises, however, the mainstream of modern architecture is set on a course which once more seems to preclude tracery. Yet history takes no notice of even expert forecasts. Perhaps the famous "Fish" church, in Stamford, Connecticut, will become the prototype of a new form of tracery, which embraces not only the window but the whole roof; and this because stained glass, in its undoubted revival, again demands a new architecture.

Stained glass, designed by Burne-Jones, fills the east window in the Latin Chapel of Christ Church, Oxford. A circular opening at the head of the geometric tracery is complemented by the curves of the design, in which a ship of souls is steered by angels beneath a crescent moon.

The undulating rhythm of flamboyant tracery developed to the fullest in fifteenth-century France. Tracery lights in Evreux Cathedral, above, with typically curving bars of stonework, depict angels against scarlet backgrounds, which emphasize the flame-like, or flamboyant, quality of the tracery.

Rectilinear panels of tracery in the sixteenth-century east window of King's College Chapel, Cambridge, are formed by the vertical continuation of the mullions to the flattened arch of the window. In the centre of the tracery lights the arms of Henry VII are displayed on the banner carried by the red dragon.

The Circle and the Rose

These Early Christian symbols, based on the ancient forms of cross and circle, are carved on the walls of the Basilica of St John at Ephesus, which was built by the Emperor Justinian in the sixth century. They resemble the patterns of early rose windows.

Circular rose, or wheel, windows represent one of man's most profoundly sacred symbols. Since the earliest days of recorded history, the circle in a variety of forms has been used in rites: there are sun wheels in neolithic rock paintings; the circle of the sun was worshipped by many cults; the circle as a symbol of eternity has persisted into Christianity; the circle, or *mandala*, is of importance in Asian mysticism. Carl Gustav Jung, the Swiss psychiatrist, in his book *Man and his Symbols*, describes rose windows as some of the most splendid examples of *mandalas*, which, within a European, Christian tradition, express man's sense of the eternal in the universe—and in himself. The circle is, too, the very basis of geometry, the starting point from which all arcs and bisections evolve.

Simple wheel windows, quite common in the Romanesque period, were the earliest rose windows. They were small, round openings, in which stone tracery radiated out from the centre like spokes, giving a wheel-like effect. They were placed over the west door because this gable offered the mason and the glazier the largest flat plane in the building. One of the earliest examples of a wheel window is in the west façade of the twelfth-century Church of San Zeno Maggiore in Verona.

It was, however, the combined genius of the Gothic masons and glaziers that transformed the gables of many cathedrals into immense circular webs of light and colour. As Gothic tracery developed, so the patterns of stone threading across these circular windows became more and more elaborate, until they evolved to form the image of a many-petalled, flamboyant flower.

The imagery in most rose and wheel windows is inevitably subordinated to the radiating lines of the interlocking tracery. The major exceptions are the Italian *occhio*, or eye window, and its Spanish equivalent, the *ojo de buey*, or bull's-eye, one of several kinds of Spanish rose windows. Devoid of stone tracery, the glass panels in these windows are supported by ironwork that radiates from a central point or is arranged in vertical or horizontal bars. Although the circular form of these windows is emphasized by abstract borders, the central compositions are not adapted to the circular shape and would be equally suited to rectangular openings.

Two of the most popular themes depicted in all rose windows are the glorification of Christ and the Virgin, and Christ as the Apocalyptic Judge. Secular subjects are also used. They include the labours of the months and the signs of the zodiac, excellent examples of which are in the fine fifteenth-century roses of Angers Cathedral. German glaziers often rejected such figurative subject matter in their rose windows in favour of decorative patterns of foliage. And the distinctive roses in the cathedrals of Valencia and Palma in Spain have the tracery arranged to form a Star of David, which is filled with abstract patterned glass rather than figurative detail.

The logic of a wheel motif involves the rotation of the design within it. There comes a point, therefore, when a figure would logically have to stand on its head. Figures—usually only head and shoulders—are, in fact, often depicted upright. The rotation of the design may contribute positively to a moral or symbolic purpose, as, for example, in the western rose of Amiens Cathedral. Around the upper half of the rose is a semicircular stone wheel of fortune in which a chain of prosperous people climb to the apex of the circle only to descend as beggars.

The realism, or lack of it, in the stained glass of rose windows should be unimportant; everything is dominated by the radiation of the spokes and the circular intervals that bisect them to form an exquisite flower-like image. If the abstract qualities of a rose window are fully appreciated, there will be no contradiction in the idea of figures rotating with their feet towards the centre—"like herrings in a barrel", as the stained-glass artist and author Lewis Day once

The Development of the Rose
The twelfth-century round window, divided by crude stone spokes, was succeeded in the thirteenth century by a circular arrangement of holes in the shape of a large rosette. The development of bar tracery, in the mid-thirteenth century, led to the wheel window, whose splendour was achieved by the radiation of many slim spokes. From the fourteenth century onwards the curves of flowing tracery transformed the geometric wheel into the shape of a many-petalled flower.

Romanesque wheel window in the Church of San Pedro, Avila.

Thirteenth-century plate tracery in Chartres' west rose.

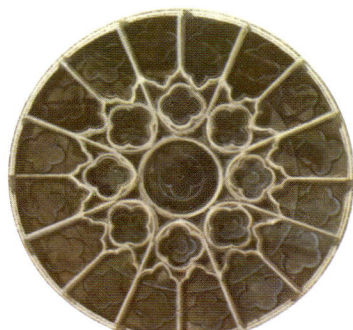

Thirteenth-century bar tracery in the west rose of Reims.

Early sixteenth-century flamboyant south rose of Amiens.

An Italian *occhio*, filled by a single circle of pictorial glass, is distinguished by the absence of tracery. Paolo Uccello designed this Nativity for the dome of Florence Cathedral with the pure colour and perspective characteristic of his paintings.

The Bishop's Eye in Lincoln Cathedral was designed in the fourteenth century with curvilinear tracery. Two large leaf shapes are formed by a network of stone branching from vertical bars instead of radiating from a central point.

Tracery openings on the exterior of Chartres' west rose appear to contract when seen from within the cathedral. The glass, arranged in the form of a huge blossom, achieves a brilliant intensity in contrast with the surrounding darkness.

Through the ingenious use of bar tracery, the large black cross, superimposed diagonally upon a smaller one, appears to revolve around its brightly coloured axis in this spectacular window in the Church of St Lorenz, Nuremberg.

Flamboyant tracery, which flourished in sixteenth-century France, fills the north rose of Sens Cathedral. Petal-like medallions, in which angels play musical instruments, form the shape of a flower around the central figure of Christ.

described them. The fenestration can, in fact, be appreciated as something without top or bottom—as a phenomenon that floats in directionless space. The superb roses of Notre Dame in Paris, for example, seem to turn, yet to remain forever still, an illusion created by the repetition of concentric rings of radiating light in a rhythm of glass and stone.

Medieval glaziers seemed to appreciate the need to adapt the glass in rose windows to the stonework and, especially when the masonry became complex, they outlined the areas of glass with light borders, causing halation, which makes the web of stone seem even more insubstantial. They occasionally reinforced the circular effect by carrying a border round a window, passing it through the lights and ignoring the stonework moulding, or cusping. This type of halation, which causes stonework to be obscured by light, can be observed by studying the width of the mullions from the outside of a rose window and then from inside the building. It can then be seen how light expands the openings, so that a vast expanse of glass appears to be contained within apparently minimal stonework.

It is difficult to choose any particular rose window as outstanding. There are so many fine ones in the cathedrals of northern Europe and England and everyone will find his own favourite. For the nineteenth-century French author Huysmans, for example, the north rose of Chartres Cathedral was obviously a favourite, evoking the memorable description "it was . . . lit by sparkling flowers growing just like fiery saxifrage, in holes in the wall".

It is a great delight to study rose windows both from a distance and, with the help of binoculars, in detail, first working out the basic lines as the mason laid them out and then seeing how, by clever accents of light and colour, by circles at the widest part of tapering lights, circles in the centres of the outer trefoils and continuous concentric bands and gleaming eyelets of pure colour, the glazier accepted the challenge of this unique aspect of his art.

The design of a rose window often involves a compromise between abstraction and realism. At the centre of the west rose of León Cathedral, the Virgin and Child are surrounded by a ring of apostles whose arrangement, dictated by the logic of the circle, is illogical since some are standing on their heads.

A giant rose window, forty feet in diameter, creates a burst of light and colour at the western end of Reims Cathedral's lofty nave. Completed in the middle of the thirteenth century, this rose is one of the first to have been designed with bar tracery, the dramatic system of stone spokes which transformed circles of blossoms into radiating wheels.

Sources of Inspiration – the Bible

Illuminated manuscripts which effectively combined words and paintings were a fruitful source of religious instruction. They were also an important means of spreading artistic ideas, and the development of their design influenced the development of murals, panel-painting and stained glass. A centre for the production of early English illuminated manuscripts, the abbey founded by St Augustine in 597 at Canterbury is thought to be the origin of the eighth-century psalter, above, which is now in the British Museum. The stiff figures of King David and his acolytes, reminiscent of stained-glass images, are enclosed by a massive, Romanesque arch decorated with geometric and curvilinear motifs, which were later used in the wide borders of Romanesque stained-glass windows.

From the beginning of the Christian era, the Bible, together with manuals of instruction and exegesis written by the early Fathers and scholars of the Church, was the fundamental source of thematic material for artists. And the way in which this material was visually presented was largely determined by the Church. As early as 787, the Second Council of Nicaea, the Seventh General Council of the Christian Church, ordained that "the composition of religious imagery is not left to the initiation of artists, but is formed upon the principles laid down by the Catholic Church and by religious tradition". Whatever inspiration there may have been in the work of an individual artist, in the choice of subject and, to some extent, in its treatment, the medieval painter, sculptor or glazier was by no means his own master.

Although medieval craftsmen were often educated, and many were fairly cultured, there is no doubt that they were dependent upon the works of traditional scholars for guidance in the decoration of cathedrals and churches. Even when Michelangelo, with all his unruly individualism, was commissioned by the Pope to paint the Sistine Chapel in Rome, the subject he was to illustrate was, broadly, the same scheme of salvation that had been the theme of the pre-Renaissance painters. And the early Eastern Orthodox Church not only dictated which Old and New Testament subjects were to be depicted, but where they were to be placed on the walls and domes of the churches. This ruling remained virtually frozen until the nineteenth century.

The early Fathers were keenly aware of the effect of beauty on worshippers and they wanted religious art to exploit the intrinsic seduction of stone, wood, gold, silver, enamel, mosaic and glass. But, at the same time, they believed that works of art had to teach and the imagery had to be so designed that it was instantly recognizable, in accordance with iconographic tradition.

A favoured instructive device was that of types and antitypes. Significant events or characters from the Old Testament, known as types, were counterpointed with scenes which they were thought to prefigure in the New Testament, antitypes. The play that clerics and scholars made on these themes, despite their avowed purpose of instruction, was often stretched to the limit of mystical interpretation. Popular subjects which were thus linked included Jonah being swallowed by and miraculously delivered from the whale and Christ's Entombment and Resurrection; and the Queen of Sheba presenting gifts to Solomon was coupled with the Adoration of the Christ Child by the Magi. Medieval glaziers quickly adopted this instructional device. One of the most extensive of all early stained-glass typological schemes was commissioned by Abbé Suger for the twelfth-century Church of St Denis, near Paris. Suger himself decided upon the subject matter, which included such scenes as the veil being taken from Moses' face counterpointed by Christ unveiling the Law.

The most popular Old Testament stained-glass themes, other than those which were used in conjunction with New Testament scenes, were those which were singled out in church services, either in prayers or to make moral points in sermons. In England, for example, the favourite images of the deliverance of Isaac from sacrifice and of Daniel

The medieval belief that biblical events unfolded according to a preordained pattern is expressed in the scheme of type and antitype. Old Testament stories, known as types, and their New Testament counterparts, antitypes, are juxtaposed in the thirteenth-century Poor Man's Bible windows, detail right, in Canterbury Cathedral. The angel's warning to the Magi in the centre panel is prefigured by the admonishment of the heretical King Jereboam, on the right, and, on the left, by the petrification of Lot's disobedient wife.

Moses' spies returning with proof of the Promised Land's fecundity were considered a prefiguration of the Crucifixion. The grapes, signifying Christ, are ignored by the spy in front, symbol of Jews, but regarded by the other spy, symbol of Christians. This event is depicted, above left, in the fifteenth-century Koberg Bible, and, above right, in a contemporary window in St Lorenz, Nuremberg.

from the den of lions gained their initial popularity in the ninth century when prayers were offered during the Viking raids. Such scenes always stressed God's omnipotence and illustrated the dramatic moment of his intervention.

The artist's choice of New Testament subjects was largely confined to those associated with the major church festivals, since one of the purposes of works of art, whether stained glass, sculpture or painting, was to explain the significance of the festivals to the congregation. The events which were depicted provided about fourteen subjects and included the Birth of the Virgin, the Annunciation, the Nativity, Christ's Entry into Jerusalem, the Passion and the Assumption of the Virgin. Apart from this comparatively limited range of Gospel themes, glaziers were also permitted to illustrate the Holy Sacraments and such moral allegories as the Virtues and Vices and the Seven Deadly Sins. Depictions of the Last Judgement, replete with bubbling cauldrons and grotesque demons, were also popular.

Many of the more vivid details in illustrations of New Testament scenes—and some which have come to be regarded as traditional features—were drawn not from the Bible but from the apocryphal gospels and from books which recorded the visions of medieval mystics. For example, two of the best-known animal protagonists, the ox and the ass in Nativity scenes, are not mentioned at all in the Gospels. They are, however, included in the account of the Birth of Christ, in pseudo-Matthew's apocryphal gospel and their significance is reinforced by lines from *Isaiah* I, 3: "The ox knoweth his owner, and the ass his master's crib: but Israel doth not know, my people doth not consider." These

The prophet Jonah, left, is disgorged on to dry land after spending three days and three nights in the belly of the "great fish". In St Matthew's Gospel, Christ refers to Jonah's maritime imprisonment as foreshadowing his own entombment "for three days and three nights in the heart of the earth". Jonah's deliverance was consequently seen as a prefiguration of the Resurrection. The fish, not specifically recorded as a whale, provided an opportunity for artists to invent alarming sea monsters, such as this vicious creature in a fifteenth-century window from the Convent of St Lambrecht, Austria, and now in the Landesmuseum, Graz.

Sources of Inspiration – the Bible

The drawings in the twelfth-century Guthlac Roll, now in the British Museum, may well have been made specifically for use by stained-glass artists. Each of the eighteen drawings of the life of St Guthlac, detail above, are only approximately six inches in diameter. Their unusually small size seems to confirm the theory that the roll was prepared by an illuminator as a set of medallions from which the glazier could draw his full-size cartoons, or working designs, for a window.

words were interpreted as a prophecy of the manger of the Christ Child in Bethlehem, and the Jews' refusal to recognize Christ was contrasted with the adoration of the infant by the humble animals. The animals were included in Nativity scenes so that this point could be made.

For all their subject matter, whether from the Old or the New Testament, whether apocryphal or legendary, medieval artists and craftsmen drew upon common sources of design. In the early Middle Ages, the chief repositories of illustrated source material were the monasteries, and it was in the monasteries that the art of manuscript illumination blossomed. Indeed, the close similarity of style between illuminated manuscripts and their counterparts in wall paintings and in stained glass suggests that the same artists sometimes were involved in all these art forms. Certainly, the frequent use of roundels or other semi-architectural shapes to enclose figures and the recurrence of other similar details in miniatures, carvings, paintings and stained glass points to a general practice of copying designs from a common source.

In the early Middle Ages a certain stylization and repetition was inevitable in the designs for stained glass. Since there was no paper, the glazier had to draw his original sketch on parchment and prepare his cartoon on whitened boards. Although the parchment sketches could be kept, the practical difficulties in keeping a large stock of the boards tended to inhibit experimentation with subjects. A careful study of medieval windows reveals that many figures have been drawn from the same cartoon. The basic figure is varied by the introduction of different symbols, as in the case of apostles or saints, or, sometimes, by simply reversing the figure or by changing its sex.

The medieval glazier was not only influenced by the contemporary visual arts but by the largely unwritten mass of traditions passed on from one master craftsman to another. There was, too, the visual impact of the Passion plays, which were performed by itinerant actors at great festivals of the Church. Some windows seem to reflect the small compass of the stage and the expressive gestures of actors. The tapestried backgrounds of the windows in Great Malvern Priory Church, Worcestershire, are believed to have been inspired by the stage backdrops.

Two major technological developments greatly extended the sources of design available to the stained-glass artist—the inventions of paper and printing. Filtering into southern Italy in the thirteenth century from Moorish Spain, the manufacture of paper gradually spread through northern Italy to Germany, France and England. It revolutionized the preparation of the cartoon. No longer did the glazier have to design the cartoon on whitewashed boards, but could instead work on paper scrolls, which could be preserved far more easily than boards and could be handed down from one generation of glaziers to another.

The development of printing with wooden blocks in the fourteenth century led to the appearance of such devotional books as the *Biblia Pauperum* (*Poor Man's Bible*), an

REFLECTIONS OF THE THEATRE

Theatrical effects and stage designs used in medieval miracle plays are frequently reflected by the imagery in stained-glass windows. On the festival of Corpus Christi, kept in honour of the Holy Eucharist on the Thursday after Trinity Sunday, miracle, or mystery, plays were performed by members of local trade guilds in the streets of such cities as York, Coventry and Chester. Based on biblical themes and supported by apocryphal tales, these sacred dramas were also an opportunity for euphoric irreverence, and scenes whose comic potential was too great were periodically suppressed by the Church. The print, below, of a mystery play being re-enacted in eighteenth-century Coventry shows the mobile theatre with its dressing-room below the stage.

The Massacre of the Innocents, above, in the fifteenth-century east window of St Peter Mancroft Church, Norwich, is presided over by the figure of Herod, who calmly dismembers a child with his sword. The box-like throne on which he sits resembles the architectural structures used in the medieval theatre, and the mantle hanging over the front suggests a curtain used as a screen.

An unusually bloated serpent with a man's head, right, is twined round the tree of knowledge in the sixteenth-century east window in the parish church of St Neot, Cornwall. The distended coils and male rather than traditionally female head suggest that the image was inspired by a theatrical serpent, played by an actor in an elongated green sack.

invaluable source of design material for the glazier and a summary of the prophetic parallels between events from the Old and New Testaments. Most of the illustrations in the *Biblia Pauperum* comprised New Testament scenes surrounded by Old Testament types.

Another widely used source of design material was the *Speculum Humanae Salvationis* (*Mirror of Human Salvation*), which dates, in manuscript form, from at least the thirteenth century. It was one of the first devotional books to be printed with movable type in the fifteenth century, which greatly increased its circulation. On a somewhat more extensive scale than the *Biblia Pauperum* it relates in text and pictures the Bible story from the fall of Lucifer to the Redemption of Man.

Among the surviving stained-glass windows based on designs in these two kinds of book, St Mary's Church at Fairford in Gloucestershire has one of the most complete existing schemes of windows setting forth the plan of salvation based on the *Biblia Pauperum*. And the glaziers of Great Malvern Priory Church are believed to have based their designs on woodcuts in the *Speculum Humanae Salvationis*.

The modern preoccupation with originality as a prerequisite of great art makes it difficult to understand how artists in the Middle Ages were apparently content to adhere to strict and often artistically inhibiting rules, to illustrate what were in fact stock subjects, to copy other artists and, generally, to take any shortcut available. Unlike modern artists, who feel compelled to create their own ideas and are judged by the originality of those ideas, the medieval artist was commissioned by the Church, a power outside himself which had instilled its teaching in him since birth and an all-pervading organization which, although he might at times resent it, he would not question. Another consideration was the sheer volume of the work which had to be done by the workshops which were attached to cathedrals, abbeys and larger churches. To the medieval glazier the excellence of the finished window was sufficient justification for working along the lines he had to. And it is in these early windows that the stature of the individual artist can be seen.

From the representation of Old Testament subjects to scenes from Christ's Passion, stained-glass windows were the visual teaching aids of Christendom, which was complete in its embrace of all the material means by which men could learn immaterial truth, profound in its theology, but expressed through symbols and allegory so that all who saw might understand. Christ was once again incarnate in the Word made flesh—the flesh of stone and glass and lead created by a host of mortal artists and craftsmen who bent their wills to the will of the material they used, making it speak not for themselves but for all—not as trivial or arid diagrams, but as works of art. In many instances the artist transcends the concept to produce works of art that are an ineffable synthesis of material, skill and imagination. These go beyond mere teaching—unless the sudden instinctive recognition of beauty is the greatest lesson of all.

The production of religious texts and pictures was revolutionized by the invention of printing from wooden blocks in the fourteenth century, followed by the invention, in about 1450, of movable type and the printing press. Illustrated for the first time in the *Danse Macabre*, published in 1499, the printing press is visited by embodiments of death. Skeletons, claiming all men equally, grasp the compositor at his typecase, the pressman at the press and the bookseller in his shop.

Two of the major sources of design for the medieval glazier were the *Poor Man's Bible* and *Mirror of Human Salvation*. Its teachings arranged according to the scheme of type and antitype, a fourteenth-century manuscript version of the *Poor Man's Bible*, below, shows Christ pierced by the spear, bordered by the creation of Eve and Moses striking the rock. A page from a fifteenth-century blockbook edition of the *Mirror of Human Salvation*, right, shows Jacob's dream of the ladder to heaven.

Sources of Inspiration – Sacred and Profane

Outside the prescribed teachings of the Church a wealth of subject matter awaited the glazier in secular literature, from pagan myths and legends to fables and, later, to fairy tales. Until the fifteenth century, however, the influence of the Church was paramount and secular subjects, with the exception of heraldry, were virtually taboo.

Of the peripheral religious subjects which were not strictly inspired by the Bible, the lives of the saints and the legends surrounding the Virgin Mary provided the medieval glazier with ample opportunity for exercising not only his creative skills but his imagination. Cathedrals and churches throughout Europe and England abound with windows illustrating these themes in colourful and often, in those depicting the martyrdom of saints, gruesome detail.

A determining influence on the iconography of such windows was the *Legenda Aurea* (*Golden Legend*), a vast hagiographic work compiled in about 1275 by Jacobus de Voragine, a Dominican monk who later became Archbishop of Genoa. It encompassed not only the lives of the saints and Apostles but legends of the Virgin Mary and other narratives relating to the Church's festivals. It earned De Voragine high praise: one of Caxton's assistants, who delighted in the name of Wynkyn de Worde, said of it, "Like as passeth gold in value all other metals, so this legend exceedeth all other books."

To this same conceptual twilight between the Bible and non-biblical but derivative themes belongs the unique Pricke of Conscience window in All Saints' Church, North Street, York. Based on a fourteenth-century poem by Richard Rolle, a Yorkshire recluse, the window illustrates, in a series of vividly detailed panels, the calamities attending the end of the world.

With the revival of interest in Classical literature during the Renaissance and the decline in the power of the Catholic Church in northern Europe during the Reformation there began to be an increase in the depiction of secular subjects in stained-glass windows. This trend was reinforced by the proliferation of mansions for the rich, which replaced their

The fated lovers in a tale in Ovid's *Metamorphoses*, Pyramus and Thisbe are depicted in a Swiss panel of 1551, above, now in the Landesmuseum, Innsbruck. A fly, a common visual conceit of the sixteenth-century glazier, hovers over the dying Pyramus, observing the melodramatic scene.

The legendary Ganymede, a mortal distinguished by his exceptional beauty, is depicted in this sixteenth-century German window, right, being borne away by an eagle to become cupbearer to Zeus on Olympus. Made for a family of wealthy merchants, the Tuchers, the window is still in their Nuremberg house, now a museum.

The fishermen of England donated the Isaak Walton window to Winchester Cathedral in 1914. It shows Walton, author of *The Compleat Angler*, published in 1653, seated in the midst of his fishing tackle in the idyllic setting celebrated in his book.

embattled and often spartan castles. Such homes, with their large halls, staircases and private chapels, offered the glazier wide scope for his creativity.

Among the most popular subjects for domestic buildings—apart from heraldry and portraits—were Greek and Roman myths which could be made to symbolize the achievements of the family or could serve as stained-glass equivalents of the fashionable Italianate oil paintings. The Nuremberg museum which was originally the home of the wealthy Tucher family has, for example, sixteenth-century windows that depict various characters from Classical myths, including Ceres, the Roman goddess of food plants, in her serpent-drawn chariot and Ganymede, the cup-bearer of Zeus in Greek mythology.

Fables, narrative poems, fairy tales, the Arthurian Romances, children's classics and even nursery rhymes have also provided the stained-glass artist with thematic material. Aesop's fables are illustrated in staircase windows, dating from *c.* 1867 in Rendcomb College in Gloucestershire. In the church at Daresbury in Cheshire, the birthplace of Lewis Carroll, there are twentieth-century windows depicting scenes from *Alice in Wonderland*. The beautifully executed figures are based on those in the illustrations by Sir John Tenniel. And in the German Classroom in the University of Pittsburgh there are twentieth-century panels depicting scenes from the Grimm brothers' fairy tales.

Not only has secular literature inspired the stained-glass artist but the work of the glazier has also served as a source of inspiration to writers. The nineteenth-century French novelist Gustave Flaubert based one of his short stories, the *Legend of St Julian Hospitator*, on a fourteenth-century window in Rouen Cathedral that depicts the life of the saint in thirty medallions. And the thirteenth-century Five Sisters window in York Minster inspired Charles Dickens to include in *Nicholas Nickleby* an apocryphal account of how the window acquired its name.

Perhaps one of the most evocative of all literary passages inspired by stained glass is in *Swann's Way* by Marcel Proust. He eloquently describes a window in the parish church of Combray: ". . . the next instant it had taken on all the iridescence of a peacock's tail, then shook and wavered in a flaming and fantastic shower, distilled and dropping from the groin of the dark and rocky vault . . . a moment later the little lozenge windows had put on the deep transparence, the unbreakable hardness of sapphires clustered on some enormous breastplate. . . ."

King René of Anjou married Isabella of Lorraine in 1420. The author of poems and romances, René retired in 1442 to Aix-en-Provence, where his court became a haven for poets and artists. The honeymoon of René and Isabella inspired stained-glass panels by Rossetti, Burne-Jones and Madox Brown. Rossetti's panel, *Music*, above, illustrates one of the imaginary scenes, which centre around architecture, painting and sculpture as well as music. The panels, made in 1861, are now in the Victoria and Albert Museum, London.

Tenniel's drawings for Lewis Carroll's *Alice in Wonderland*, above, were translated into stained glass, right, by Geoffrey Webb for the church at Daresbury, Cheshire. The window marked the centenary of Carroll's birth there in 1832.

The dainty figure of Little Red Riding Hood, above, with the inscription "Rotkäppchen", is the subject of one of twenty-four panels, inspired by the Grimm brothers' fairy tales, in the German Classroom of the University of Pittsburgh. The panels were designed by Mrs Orin E. Skinner of Connick Studios, Boston.

Spirits of Good and Evil

From the earliest times concepts of good and evil spirits, or of good and bad luck, have persisted. The Early Christian Church absorbed many pagan festivals and seasonal rituals into its calendar, transposing them to festivals of saints or to such convenient anniversaries as Christmas and Easter. The Church of the Middle Ages was absolute in its authority over men's minds. All else, including animals and plants, unbaptized infants, disease, natural calamities and unexplained phenomena, was outside the fold and was believed to be under the control of the Devil.

The concentration on the miraculous in religion tended to reinforce superstition, including those superstitions concerned with "the old religion", or paganism, which, although condemned by the Church, nevertheless seemed to infiltrate its sanctuaries. Hence it is that in many medieval churches there are monstrous images at the porches, gargoyles at the eaves and devils in the windows.

Whatever may be thought of the co-existence of Christianity and paganism, there is no doubt that the medieval Church had a far superior concept of angels to that of the modern Church. The angel in one of the clerestory windows at Chartres, for example, is not a comforting figure who happens to have wings, but a vigorous spirit in the form of a man yet belonging to another order of beings. The Lord "maketh his angels spirits; his ministers a flaming fire" (*Psalm 104*) is clearly the metaphor that the Early Church adopted in its conceptualization of heavenly beings. Some of the noblest portrayals of angels are those found in the icons of the Orthodox Church. The famous Old Testament Trinity—the thirteenth-century icon, attributed to Andrei Rublev, showing the visitation of three angels to Abraham—is one of the best examples. At the other end of the scale, in the rustic simplicity of village churches, the most charming little creatures smile down from tracery lights. Guilelessly they hover, playing instruments, bearing the emblems of the Passion or, in the case of the seraphim, they stare with near cross-eyed intensity amid a flurry of many wings.

An artist is, however, always aware of opposites. A positive needs a negative, good presupposes evil and light shines in darkness. The medieval artist was allowed the expression of such contrast by the Church's belief in the "last things"—the apocalyptic end of the world and the judgement of souls. The place for representing these subjects was usually over the main door at the west or on chancel arches. The west window in St Mary's Church at Fairford in Gloucestershire is the best example in England of the Doom theme, and the artist clearly took enormous delight in the dramatic use of reds and blues in the glass as well as in the detail of his painting. In the window, St Michael—the archangel who cast out Lucifer, the prototype of the fallen angel—is shown weighing the souls. The good souls are human figures while the bad ones are transformed into devils. The weighing of the souls was, in its didactic symbolism, a popular subject for the medieval glazier, who often treated it with grotesque humour.

Graceful, robed angels were a favourite vehicle for expressing the Pre-Raphaelite ideal of female beauty. The window, left, an excellent example, was designed by Burne-Jones for Rottingdean Parish Church, England.

A rebec, a medieval stringed instrument, is played by the angel in the fifteenth-century panel, right, in the Victoria and Albert Museum, London. The feathered leggings may be derived from the costumes worn by angels in mystery plays.

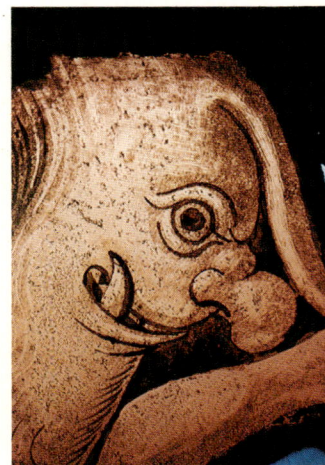

The horrors of hell and the joys of heaven are expressed in the powerful bas-reliefs with which the twelfth-century sculptor Gislebertus decorated the Burgundian cathedral of Autun. Carved Romanesque capitals have been removed to the cathedral museum, where their detail can be easily seen. On one of these capitals, above, winged devils assist in Judas' suicide.

The depths of the infernal regions depicted in the sixteenth-century Last Judgement window, left, in Fairford Church, Gloucestershire, are inhabited by Satan. He is represented as a double-headed monster, illuminated by the red glow of hell. The face with bared teeth in this detail represents Satan's stomach; above it a second head receives a stream of damned souls through its mouth.

Scenes from the Last Judgement in the fifteenth-century north rose in Evreux Cathedral include the capture of souls by red devils. At the bottom of the window, above, is this composite creature with a devilish face and the hindquarters of an animal.

Satan, chained to a pillar in hell, is portrayed with pointed ears and a beak-like nose in this detail from a fourteenth-century Resurrection window in the St Lawrence Chapel, Strasbourg Cathedral. Demoniacal heads, one of which peers over his shoulder, surround him in red medallions.

Religion, cleansed of superstition, had progressed, like civilization, from the ignorant naïveties of the Middle Ages —such was the widely held belief in northern Europe in the nineteenth century. The representations of angels and devils in medieval art were viewed with amused superiority and these other-worldly spirits were generally considered to be crudely executed compared with the contemporary, academically accurate figures.

Imbued with the sentimentality characteristic of this period, church art made much of angels as guardians for children or as doleful attendants at the death of loved ones, as witness the many winged marble maidens in churchyards and their counterparts in stained-glass memorial windows. The influence of the Pre-Raphaelite movement, however, blew a fresh breeze through the morbid atmosphere of much of the stained glass of the nineteenth century. The clear-eyed innocence of the angels of William Morris's windows suggests a folk memory of Arcady, where evil had not yet stalked the world.

Devils seem to have been suppressed in nineteenth-century religious art. Presumably such devils as those in the sixteenth-century Doom window at St Mary's Church were regarded as comic and childish, belonging to the world of fable. Although the orthodox believed implicitly in heaven and hell, their concepts were vague: unending, blissful family reunions in the sky or an unending misery in fire that burned but did not consume in some undefined region "below". Non-Christian peoples were considered heathen, without the light of Christ, destined for exclusion from heaven, but their paganism obviously fascinated the Victorians and may have found an echo in their own imprinted, sub-Christian belief. It is doubtful if such imprinting of early belief has ever been eradicated from man's subconscious. Even today, a "good" Christian may not see any inconsistency in consulting a horoscope or avoiding a gypsy with the "evil eye".

In modern religious art, angels are used as a device to symbolize heavenly spirits, but devils are still missing in a definite form. In the multicoloured window on the south side of the nave of Coventry Cathedral, the image of the beast with seven heads—from the *Book of Revelation*—is depicted and, in the purple windows, evil is represented by large black arrows. Very dark abstract shapes are sometimes used to suggest the negation of light, but to personify Satan or his minions is not acceptable to modern theological thought. Perhaps only in modern painting can expressions of evil be seen in horrific forms. Some of the paintings of Francis Bacon, for example, convey a feeling of decay and disruption, man in some process of damnation, but without the hope of salvation fundamental to Christian doctrine.

The Language of Symbols

Since the unseen realities that man has always believed to lie behind the observable world are sometimes too fearful, too holy or too abstract to be represented, he has from earliest times translated them into a language of symbols. First-century Christianity, having rejected the religions which depicted their gods as half-animal composites, or as very fallible human beings occupying despotically conducted Olympus, expressed its belief through the cross, one of the starkest and oldest of symbols. From this single crossing of two lines there evolved the *crux dissimulata*—the disguised cross of the Roman catacombs—the Celtic cross and many other elaborations. Symbolic abstraction was extended by the sacred monogram, which combines the first three letters of the name of Christ in Greek, or by circles, squares and triangles that embody such complex ideas as eternity, the Trinity and salvation.

But man's need to express religious concepts in sensually evocative images, rather than in abstract symbols, could not be repressed for long. When Christianity became established as the State religion under Emperor Constantine, in the fourth century AD, this creative urge erupted in all the splendour of mosaics. They were mosaics which showed Christ as Creator, as Saviour or as Good Shepherd, surrounded by his four Evangelists, who were often in symbolic guise—St Matthew depicted as a winged person resembling an angel, St Mark as a lion, St Luke as an ox and St John as an eagle. Animals were used to symbolize special characteristics ascribed to the Evangelists. The eagle, for example, represents far-sightedness and the spread of the Gospel. Such symbols were in effect sanctioned by the use of animal metaphors, not only in the Old Testament but also in the New Testament, which culminates in the powerful images of the Apocalypse—the four horsemen, the archangels, the dragon with seven heads, the beasts that surround the throne and the lamb that was slain.

The imagery is at its most extreme in the sculpture of the Romanesque period—on the portals of west doors, on the façades surrounding them and on the capitals of columns. Figures of the Godhead, the Virgin Mary and the Apostles became more sophisticated and, as the Gothic Age approached, increasingly human. This change in style marked the development of Christian consciousness from the remote, almost hostile, hieratic figures of Orthodox icons to the lyricism and humanity of the figures in the finest of Gothic sculpture. In stained glass the severe, almost diagrammatic Christ in Majesty, who overawed the faithful in Byzantium, became the human, suffering Son of Man. This is symbolism in its deepest sense, communicating concepts by creating understandable metaphors.

Visual convention had to be precise and unambiguous for a largely illiterate population. Gestures conveyed benediction or damnation, for example, by the arrangement of the fingers. A bishop had to be recognizable as a bishop and so wore his mitre even when shown in bed. And how better could a damned soul be recognized than by being depicted as a devil?

Colours, numbers, letters, geometry, flowers and trees all played a part in the visual textbook of the Faith. The circle, for example, represents the eternal and sacred, the square conveys earthly order. The Greek Alpha and Omega signify the Beginning and the End. Seven is a mystic number, which divides into three and four, potent numbers representing the Trinity and the four Evangelists. Blue came to symbolize heavenly things, red the blood of the martyrs and white purity.

Unfortunately, few, if any, complete ensembles of medieval windows survive in their original form, so that today it is difficult to follow the visual narrative with the ease of the medieval peasant. It is certain, however, that the figures, animals, birds, fish and other objects were, for the most part, not placed in the windows by the whim or the eccentricity of the artist. Often of symbolic significance, they were depicted according to certain conventions, but the delightfully fresh interpretation of familiar subjects and the sly visual asides show that the artist was not imprisoned in a cast-iron system that gave him no opportunity to express himself. He did, however, have the advantage of a commonly understood symbolic scheme within which he could move with relative freedom.

Although the spread of literacy lessened the need for symbolism, and lettering giving names of saints or appropriate quotations from the Bible on scrolls surrounded figures, emblems were still carried. Indeed, the use of symbols never completely died out. Traditionally designed windows retain the old symbols, and even modern abstract works use conventional iconography as starting points for designs. The Holy Ghost as tongues of fire is difficult to resist when the artist has ruby glass at his disposal. The purity and sparkle of the water of Baptism has never been more imaginatively shown than in the twentieth-century baptistery windows at St Maria Königin, Cologne, and Léger's emblems of the Passion in Audincourt Church are instantly recognizable in their monumental simplicity.

In the art of the seventeenth century there developed a new type of depiction of the Immaculate Conception, the creation of the perfect Mother of Christ, influenced by the pregnant woman in the Apocalypse who is clothed with the sun, stands on the moon and is crowned by the stars. It is exemplified by this seventeenth-century window in Troyes Cathedral. Most of the surrounding symbols are derived from the *Song of Solomon* in which a bride, interpreted as the Virgin, is likened to a lily, a sealed fountain, an enclosed garden and a rose. The "flawless mirror ... of God", with which she is compared in the *Book of Wisdom*, is also shown.

Since the twelfth century, God the Father has frequently been personified as a bearded patriarch. Fifteenth century; York Minster.

St Francis's vision while receiving the stigmata was conventionally shown as a winged crucifix. Sixteenth century; Brussels Cathedral.

A lily, symbol of purity, blossoms in a vase between Mary and the Angel in this Annunciation scene. Fourteenth century; Chartres Cathedral.

The three Magi are traditionally identified by crowns, which they are shown wearing even when asleep. Early thirteenth century; Canterbury Cathedral.

The Trinity is sometimes depicted as a person with three faces. Sixteenth century; Notre Dame Church, Châlons-sur-Marne.

The six-pointed Star of David is the symbol of Judaism. Twentieth century; by Evie Hone, All Hallows, Wellingborough.

God, frequently represented only by a hand, gives the tablets of the Law to Moses. Twelfth century; by Master Gerlachus, Münster Landesmuseum.

The dove traditionally symbolizes the Holy Ghost. Twelfth century; by Master Gerlachus, Münster Landesmuseum.

A sacrificial lamb, symbol of Christ, carries a banner, the emblem of the Resurrection. Thirteenth century; Darmstadt Museum.

The arms of Christ, curved like branches, symbolize growth. Fourteenth century; from Constance Cathedral, now in Freiburg Cathedral.

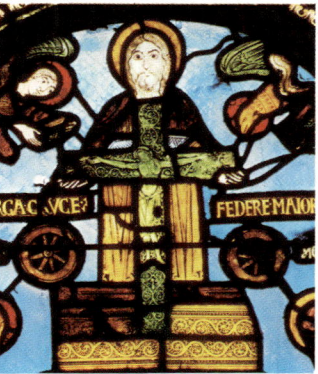
The crucifix, green like a plant, signifies growth and rebirth. Twelfth century; Abbey Church of St Denis, Paris.

Christ, with cruciform halo symbolizing divinity, makes the gesture of blessing with his right hand. Fourteenth century; Freiburg Cathedral.

The mourning Virgin, conventionally pierced by seven swords, and the emblems of the Passion. Sixteenth century; St Mary's, Shrewsbury.

Traditional depiction of demon waiting to snatch wicked soul of impenitent thief. Sixteenth-century; Notre Dame Church, Châlons-sur-Marne.

A lion is conventionally seated upon a step leading up to the throne of King Solomon. Fourteenth century; Münster Landesmuseum.

A female-headed snake, the traditional embodiment of evil, tempts Adam and Eve in the Garden of Eden. Fifteenth century; Ulm Cathedral.

An almond-shaped aureole of light conventionally emanates from the Virgin. Sixteenth century; Great Malvern Priory, Worcestershire.

The soul, often personified as a diminutive, naked child, is weighed by St Michael. Fourteenth century; Eaton Bishop Church, Herefordshire.

The seven-branch candlestick, described in *Exodus*, signifies the Old Testament. Twentieth century; by Evie Hone, All Hallows, Wellingborough.

A small man climbing a tree to see Christ is a conventional feature of Entry into Jerusalem scenes. Fifteenth century; Ulm Cathedral.

Wavy lines are the stylized convention for depicting water, as in this miraculous draught of fishes panel. Thirteenth century; Canterbury Cathedral.

Judas taking the fish, a symbol of Christ, is traditionally a feature of the Last Supper. Thirteenth century; Bourges Cathedral.

The tricoloured rainbow conventionally symbolizes the Trinity and forms Christ's throne. Sixteenth century; Fairford Church.

The guards mentioned by St Matthew are traditionally shown sleeping near Christ's tomb. Fourteenth century; All Saints' Church, North Street, York.

Saints and their Emblems

St Mark the Evangelist, from a sixteenth-century window in the parish church of St Neot, Cornwall. His symbol, the lion, generally winged, is a representation of power and royal dignity.

The Evangelists and their symbols, combined in animal and human form in a fifteenth-century window in St Lorenz Church, Nuremberg. In this representation of the doctrine of Transubstantiation, the Four put the wafers of the Host through a process from which the bread emerges as the mystical Body of Christ.

St Matthew the Apostle and Evangelist, from a sixteenth-century window in the parish church of St Neot, Cornwall. His symbol, a winged figure of a man, emphasizes the human aspect of Christ, whose genealogy opens the Gospel of St Matthew.

From its narrow connotations in the early days of the Christian Church, the title of saint has evolved in meaning over the centuries. Although no mention is made of saints either by Christ or by his disciples, by the second century the Virgin Mary, the Evangelists and Apostles were recognized as such. The title of saint, however, was first bestowed as an honour upon those men and women who laid down their lives for their faith—the martyrs of the Early Christian Church. During the era of toleration, which began with Constantine the Great's Edict of Milan in 313, the persecution of Christians by the Romans was ended and the title of saint was extended to "confessors"—those who declared their faith to a Roman tribunal but did not die for it. Bishops who defended Christianity against heresy were among the first confessor saints. The formal process of canonization was not adopted until about the tenth century, by which time the veneration of the relics of saints and pilgrimages had become popular practice.

The medieval man had an advantage over his modern counterpart when he looked at a stained-glass window. Born and bred in the fold of the Church he was familiar with the iconography of the times and, looking at a window, would have recognized many of the saints and the scenes which were depicted in it. If he saw a representation of a mature woman clasping a young girl, he would not have to be told that this was St Anne, the mother of the Virgin Mary, and if he saw a king (a king because he wore a crown) playing a harp, he knew him to be King David.

The art of identifying seemingly anonymous saints in stained-glass windows, or in other art forms, lies in the recognition of their distinctive emblems. Although all saints are depicted with haloes and wearing their appropriate dress—bishops with robes, soldiers in armour or kings crowned and robed—the distinguishing feature of each individual saint is his or her personal attribute. A martyr is distinguished from a non-martyr by a crown, which signifies eternal life won by heroism, and a palm, which represents the triumph of the martyr in death, and is often shown with the instrument of his or her martyrdom. A saint who was not a martyr may be depicted with an object emblematical of his or her particular virtue.

Mary, Mother of Christ, has always occupied a prime position in the saintly hierarchy. Although she has no one emblem, the narrative conventions in her depiction make her instantly recognizable—as the Virgin with flowing hair, as the *Mater Dolorosa*, dressed in mourning and lamenting over the dead Christ, or as the Madonna, surrounded by angels and bearing the crown and sceptre, or the orb and cross.

Next in the celestial hierarchy are the four archangels. The first two, Michael and Gabriel, are represented in many windows. Michael, angel of the Last Judgement, is usually depicted with a sword and scales, emblems of justice and the weighing of souls. Gabriel, angel of the Annunciation, holds

EMBLEMS OF THE APOSTLES

Used in art from about the sixth century, symbols or emblems relating to the life or death of each of the twelve Apostles may refer to their former occupations—the fish of Peter, fisherman of Galilee, or the purse of Matthew the tax-gatherer—or to the instruments of their martyrdom—such as the fuller's club of James the Less.

 Key or fish
St Peter

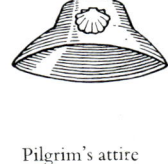 Transverse cross
St Andrew

 Pilgrim's attire
St James the Greater

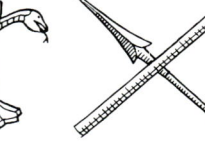 Chalice with serpent
St John

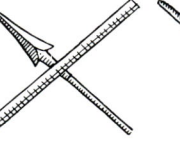 Builder's rule or spear
St Thomas

 Club
St James the Less

 Crozier or small cross
St Philip

 Flaying knife
St Bartholomew

 Purse
St Matthew

 Saw
St Simon

 Halberd or lance
St Jude

 Lance
St Matthias

a lily and is almost always the messenger of salvation. Raphael, who protects humanity, bears the pilgrim's staff and is often represented accompanying Tobias—a reference to his role as guardian of the youth in the *Book of Tobit*, in the Apocrypha. Uriel, known as the interpreter of judgements and prophecies, bears a scroll and a book.

The four mysterious creatures recorded in the vision in the fourth chapter of *Revelation* were adopted as emblems of the Evangelists, the writers of the Gospels. St Matthew has a human, though winged, form, St Mark is depicted as a winged lion, St Luke as a winged ox and St John as the eagle which adorns thousands of church lecterns. The twelve Apostles, also prominent in stained glass of all periods, are often found in tracery in which there is a convenient subdivision of twelve lights. Each apostle has an appropriate emblem which may relate to his occupation in life or may be the instrument of his martyrdom.

The group of saints associated with a particular activity or country are known as the patron saints of Christendom. George, the soldier saint and legendary slayer of the dragon, is the protector of England. St Christopher, with his palm staff, has long been the patron saint of wayfarers and, more recently, of motorists. Sentenced by Diocletian to be shot to death by arrows, Sebastian, patron saint of archers and pin-makers, is widely depicted with the arrow as his emblem. This was not, however, the instrument of his martyrdom, for he recovered from his arrow wounds only to be beaten to death and thrown into Rome's main sewer.

The most popular female saint, after the Virgin, is Mary Magdalene, immediately recognizable by her box of ointment and her long, flowing hair. Since the Middle Ages, she has been the patroness of repentant sinners and her penance has come to symbolize Catholic penance. Another popular female saint is Catherine of Alexandria, patroness of students, scientists, theologians and wheelwrights. She is usually depicted holding a spoked wheel, emblem of her torture and martyrdom.

The number of saints recognized by the Catholic Church runs, dauntingly, into many hundreds. No one hagiographic source, from the medieval *Golden Legend* of De Voragine to the redoubtable *Sacred and Legendary Art* by the scholarly Anna B. Jameson, published in 1890, can claim an exhaustive list. Confusion has inevitably arisen over different names for the same saint and, indeed, legends surround saints who never existed. Although in 1969 some names were purged from the liturgical calendar, some questionable figures still remain among the innumerable saints recognized by the Catholic Church. Perhaps the oddest of non-existent saints was St Decimil, who was never officially canonized. A tombstone was found in Provence bearing the name DECIMIL and prayers were written in his honour. It was subsequently discovered that the stone was not a tombstone at all, but a much-weathered Roman milestone for the guidance of legions marching on Gaul.

St Luke the Evangelist, from a sixteenth-century window in the parish church of St Neot, Cornwall. His symbol, a sacrificial ox, echoes the sacrifice of Zacharias at the opening of St Luke's Gospel.

THE PILGRIMAGE CULT

The dreadful mutilation and martyrdom of St Leodegar, from the thirteenth-century martyrs window in Freiburg Minster. Bishop Leodegar was put to death in the seventh century by Ebroin, a powerful Frankish mayor.

The boy and the gold cup fall from the ship in a scene from one of many miracles of St Nicholas, below, in a sixteenth-century window in Hillesden Church, Buckinghamshire.

Journeying to the shrines of saints or other holy places was common practice in medieval Christendom, where the chief centres of pilgrimage included Canterbury, Rome, the Holy Land and Santiago de Compostela. A pilgrimage was undertaken in the hope of divine intervention or as an act of penance, devotion or thanksgiving.

With the blessing of the priest, the medieval pilgrim set out, in recognizable garb, exemplified by that of St James the Pilgrim, above, from a fourteenth-century French manuscript, and returned wearing the badge of the shrine on his hat and sometimes bearing holy relics. The wide-scale veneration of "sacred" relics led to the dismembered remains of saints being obtained by trickery and violence.

Spain's Romanesque cathedral, Santiago de Compostela, has been a centre of pilgrimage since the Middle Ages. The façade, left, dates from the seventeenth century.

The thirteenth-century gilt copper reliquary from Limoges, below, is decorated with champlevé enamelwork. It is now in the Victoria and Albert Museum, London.

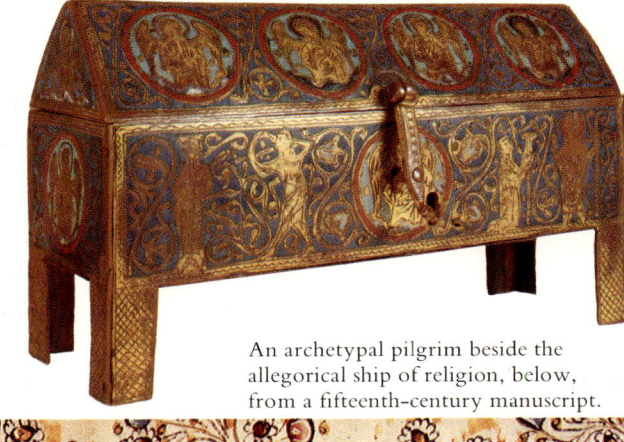

An archetypal pilgrim beside the allegorical ship of religion, below, from a fifteenth-century manuscript.

St John the Apostle and Evangelist, from a sixteenth-century window in the parish church of St Neot, Cornwall. His symbol is the eagle, which exemplifies power and victory and soars to heaven in representation of divine inspiration.

The Family Tree of Christ

One of the first examples of a Jesse Tree is this early twelfth-century manuscript illumination from the St Bénigne Bible at Dijon. Resting in the curve of the initial V, a sleeping Jesse supports the tree. Upon each of its seven branches perches a nimbed dove, representing the gifts of the Holy Spirit.

An ornate mid-twelfth-century Jesse Tree in bronze relief decorates the door of the west entrance at the Church of San Zeno Maggiore, Verona. The branches resemble contemporary liturgical candlesticks.

The overall effect of the stained glass in the monumental Jesse Tree window in Notre Dame Cathedral, Chartres, right, is one of vibrance. Blues merge into violets to create what has been called "a symphony of colour". Glazed between 1140 and 1150, this lancet window in the west end of the nave closely resembles the first Jesse window at St Denis, near Paris. Of the three vertical panels, the central one contains the figures most important to the design. Interposed between a recumbent Jesse supporting the tree and Christ with the seven doves at the top are, in ascending order, four kings and the Virgin. The prophets, representing Christ's spiritual forefathers, echo the central theme of his genealogy in flanking half-medallions.

The Jesse Tree, one of the most popular subjects of medieval art, derives from Isaiah's prophecy of the coming of the Messiah from the royal line of David—"And there shall come forth a rod out of the stem of Jesse, and a Branch shall grow out of his roots" (*Isaiah* XI, 1). The artistic interpretation of the prophecy of Isaiah made Jesse the stem, or root, Mary the rod, or shoot, and Christ the fruit, or flower. The tree is in fact genealogical, tracing Christ's ancestry back to Jesse, the father of David.

The symbol of a tree, first encountered in the Bible as "the tree of knowledge of good and evil", was probably connected with primitive mythologies in which the tree symbolized natural and supernatural life. The rod of Aaron also suggests a miraculous branch, as does the stick thrown down by Moses which turned into a serpent. Christ's death "on a tree" falls appropriately into the interpretation of the tree of life—or of salvation. The medieval mind, always looking for analogies, parallels and fulfilment of prophecies, not surprisingly adapted the tree concept to express Christ's authenticity as Saviour.

God's appearance in the burning bush of the Old Testament, one of the prefigurations of the Birth of Christ, is also believed to have inspired the tree image, and the recumbent Jacob in the story of Jacob's dream may have been transformed into the figure of Jesse, prone at the foot of his family tree. Christ's words "I am the Vine, ye are the branches" underline the basic, all-embracing metaphor of the root and branch of salvation; this may be the reason that so many Jesse Trees are represented with main stems like the "rods" of a vine and with palmate-leaved foliage.

Suger, abbot of St Denis in the first half of the twelfth century, is usually attributed with the idea of representing the Jesse Tree in stained glass. It was on the St Denis window that the twelfth-century Chartres Jesse Tree was modelled. In the thirteenth century there were stained-glass Jesse Trees in the cathedrals of Strasbourg, Le Mans, Beauvais, Angers, Troyes and Soissons, as well as in the Ste Chapelle, Paris.

Early windows depicting this theme show Jesse asleep at the base with figures of kings within the highly stylized branches which culminate in the crowned Virgin. Christ sits in the arch surrounded by the seven doves, which symbolize the gifts of the Holy Spirit. There are figures of prophets in the half-medallions at the sides. By the thirteenth century the tree developed a variety of forms, some angular and some circular. In many windows the background colours alternate—one colour in the side medallions and another in the central ones. The figures themselves changed according to the particular aspect of Christ's genealogy the artist wished to illustrate. In Jesse Trees of the fourteenth century, the branches are less formal, and sometimes spread across the mullions. The figures are treated with less rigidity. From this developed the naturalistic designs of the fifteenth century, which appear three-dimensional.

From the twelfth to the fifteenth century, the extension of the use of white glass and silver stain gradually changed the appearance of Jesse Trees from the original deep-coloured mosaic-like windows to silvery pictures in which rich patches of figure or background colour contrast with leaves, branches and ornamental detail which are delicately executed in paint and stain.

Sometimes the tree form has been used as a device to bring in subject matter other than the ancestors of Christ. At Wissembourg in France and Mönchen-Gladbach in Germany, for example, scenes from the Old and the New Testaments confront each other in several rows of panels. In some windows animals appear as symbols or in place of the usual ancestors. Bible windows from Colmar, fragments of which are now in the Burg Kreuzenstein collection near Vienna, are based on thirteenth-century animal fables. Of the fabled creatures, the "pelican in her piety" feeding her young with her own blood was used to signify the redemption through self-sacrifice of the Crucifixion. The resurrection of the dead, through Christ, symbolized by the lion who revived still-born cubs with its breath, is also found in the cathedrals of Lyons, Bourges and Le Mans.

The Chartres Jesse Tree is the paramount example of the synthesis of architectural setting, design and orchestration of colour, through which stained glass is elevated to an art of outstanding spiritual force. It is one of the few windows to which the term "visual music" can legitimately be applied. At the top of the window, the figure of Christ breaks the rhythm of the glazing bars. The theme or "melody" of the branches of the tree ascends in beautiful arabesques to explode in the seven gifts of the Holy Spirit, while the whole movement is sustained by brilliant arpeggios in the wide, patterned borders. The window could be called a sonata in the key of blue.

The visual possibilities inherent in the form of a tree, whose branches rise dynamically, are used by great artists to create an archetypal image that recalls the tree of knowledge or the tree of life, both common to many ancient religions. In such a work of art as the Chartres Jesse window the tree is transformed into a powerful symbol.

Extravagant canopies dominate the Jesse window in St Lorenz, Nuremberg, left, created by one of fifteenth-century-Germany's leading glaziers, Peter Hemmel von Andlau. The richness of the design can be seen in the detail, above, of prophets and a Moorish king.

Stained glass and stone relief are combined to great effect in this unique fifteenth-century Jesse Tree window in Dorchester Abbey, Oxfordshire. Old Testament stonework prophets counterbalance the delicate representations of Christ's ancestors in glass.

Sens, in northern France, was notorious in medieval times for the *Fête des Fous*. The ass, central object of the festival at which Christian ritual was parodied, is depicted in this detail, above, from the sixteenth-century Jesse Tree window in Sens Cathedral.

Faces of Christ

Austere yet hypnotic, the expression of this eleventh-century face of Christ is created by a design of ornamental simplicity. Originally in the Abbey Church of Wissembourg, Alsace, it is now in the Musée de l'Oeuvre Notre-Dame, Strasbourg, and is the earliest stained-glass image of Christ to have survived intact.

The face of Jesus Christ is quite unknown to us. Putting aside momentarily the Christian claim—that Christ was the Son of God—and thinking of him in terms of great men who have radically changed the course of history, it is remarkable that no account of his appearance by his contemporaries exists. Nor was any authentic description carried by oral traditions to become embodied in the Epistles or Gospels, written in the decades after his death. The many apocryphal descriptions must be discounted. They came later, when his divinity was generally accepted and it was necessary to establish that he was also truly human, in order to combat certain heresies, some of which claimed that he was little more than a spirit with a human body.

The familiar, accepted face of Christ is derived from nothing more than an imagined portrait based on simple deductions. He was a Palestinian Jew, therefore he would be likely to have a beard, darkish complexion and longish hair. With only these suppositions to go on, his face could be the face of any of a thousand young Jewish men—such as might be seen today in the streets of Jerusalem. The rest is pure conjecture based on what he said and how he acted: he was a good man, therefore he must have a good face; he was capable of attracting many and diverse people to his teaching, therefore he must have a dynamic expression; he was one who overcame spiritual and physical temptation and must, therefore, have a face which expresses moral strength and integrity. But this gives no indication of the anatomical disposition of his features. What was the length of his nose? How were the eyelids drawn over the eyes? What shape was his mouth? These questions must remain unanswered. It is in fact to a symbol of a man that artists have put a face of their own making.

These conjectural faces of Christ have always reflected the times in which the artist lived. In the first few centuries AD, when Christianity was establishing itself in a pagan world, Christ was often shown as a Greco-Roman god, clean-shaven, young and virile, suggesting that the second Adam could also be thought of as a second Apollo. Sometimes he was pictured very like the Arcadian shepherd-god Hermes, with a lamb over his shoulder, indicating that here indeed was the true protector of sheep—the Good Shepherd. By the fourth century a new image had taken over almost completely—the fierce ascetic of the Byzantine-influenced Conqueror Christ, reflecting the concept of the Supreme Ruler with bearded face, severe expression and magisterial authority. Thus the mould was made from which the mainstream of artists' images was cast for several centuries.

In medieval Europe, during the thirteenth and fourteenth centuries, the representations of the face of Christ began to show subtle changes. The humanizing influence of the Franciscans, combined with other and more esoteric movements which were beginning to erode the power of Church and State, must have encouraged artists such as Giotto to depict a more human Christ. The expressive faces of Christ in Giotto's frescoes in the Upper Church of San Francesco at Assisi clearly demonstrate a break with the hieratic Christ of Byzantine art.

By the fifteenth century, when Fra Angelico was decorating the Convent of San Marco in Florence, Christ had become Jesus, the gentle Son of Man. This development led naturally to the image of the suffering Christ, the symbol of mankind subjected to torture and death. There was less obvious scope for "the human Christ" in stained glass, because of the severe restrictions imposed not only by the material itself, but by the monumentality of the art, the often boldly stylized designs which were to be "read" from a distance. Nevertheless, the Christ of the Passion was a popular subject from as early as the fourteenth century: by this time he was definitely man and no longer a symbol.

Coincident with, and indeed reflecting, man's growing consciousness of himself as an individual, heir not only to the world of European Christendom, but also to the ancient and highly developed Greco-Roman civilizations before the birth of Christ, the image of Christ underwent another change, echoing the returning passion for the human beauty of the Classical world. The Christ of the Renaissance speaks less of his suffering and more of his perfect manhood. The artist was less concerned with Christ's teaching or his Passion than with aesthetic effect, which was achieved by a combination of the disciplines of accurate anatomy, architecture and perspective.

The pendulum effect of history was demonstrated by the Counter-Reformation when, under the strictures of the Jesuits, Catholic artists were, for example, forbidden to portray nudity for its own sake—thus stifling the purely aesthetic ideal—and were urged to propagate the dogmas of the Church to counteract the spread of the Reformation. Chiaroscuro, or the treatment of light and shade, which was so brilliantly mastered by such painters as Caravaggio,

Severity, suffering, gentleness and triumph have all been expressed in faces of Christ. Paintings by the persecuted Christians on the walls of the Roman catacombs show him as solemn teacher and god-like youth. Byzantine mosaics depict him as a universal king who stares fixedly ahead against a halo in which a cross signifies his divinity. The image of the majestic judge persisted throughout the Romanesque period until the Gothic age, when Christ was increasingly portrayed as an emaciated victim. Transformed into a Classical hero by the Renaissance, and sentimentalized during the nineteenth century, Christ in the twentieth century is again starkly portrayed as a man of sorrows, some depictions being almost Byzantine in their expressiveness.

Second-century fresco, tomb of SS Nereus and Achilleus, catacombs, Rome.

Eleventh-century mosaic, monastery church of Daphni, Greece.

Thirteenth-century stained glass, Bourges Cathedral.

Fourteenth-century stained glass, Königsfelden Church, Switzerland.

Detail, Fra Angelico's fifteenth-century painting *Noli me Tangere*, Florence.

Fifteenth-century stained glass by Hans Acker, Ulm Cathedral.

Sixteenth-century stained glass, St John's Church, Gouda.

Seventeenth-century Dutch enamel, Addington Church, England.

Detail, Holman Hunt's nineteenth-century painting *Light of the World*, Oxford.

Detail, Gauguin's nineteenth-century *Christ in the Garden of Olives*, California.

Twentieth-century stained glass by Evie Hone, Eton College Chapel, England.

greatly increased the range of artistic possibilities in the expression of passionate zeal and devotion. The Spanish painters carried the device of sharp lighting of features in a dark background to the point of morbidity. Of this period El Greco stands out, his Christ of the *Agony in the Garden* seeming, as a result of the picture's total formal involvement of figures, clouds, rocks and ministering angels, to speak of the crisis between the wills of God and man. Yet the face of El Greco's Christ is human.

In theory, at least, Protestantism relied mainly on the written word and rejected art as a means of grace or as a didactic vehicle. When its violent antipathy to the "idolatry" of the Papists subsided, Protestantism turned to the Old Testament for its subject matter. For did not the Mosaic Law prohibit graven images? The result was that portrayals of Christ were rare; when he was depicted, notably in the paintings of Rembrandt, it was generally in domestic settings, which emphasized the ordinariness of the Gospel narratives.

Not until the Gothic Revival of the nineteenth century did Christ again appear as the formal King of Heaven, and then only in imitation of medieval models. In Catholic Europe the propagation of mystical and devotional cults led religious artists to paint pictures which revel in sentiment to the point of bathos, as, for example, Guido Reni's *Ecce Homo*. The Christ of the nineteenth century had become Gentle Jesus, with softened features and a sad expression.

The challenge of the person of Christ to artists of the twentieth century has been mixed. At times he is depicted as a passionate revolutionary facing inevitable martyrdom, at other times his depiction is no more than an excuse for a demonstration of an unorthodoxy intended to shock the susceptibilities of the established religion. Today a depiction of Christ tends to be the projection of a painter's or sculptor's personal image of him.

Only in stained glass, still partly dependent on the Church for commissions, does something of the accepted concept of Christ survive, with the emphasis perhaps on the hieratic rather than the human Saviour. Once more the pendulum of history has swung, but the traverse of its arc comments only on men's changing ideas about Christ. His physical appearance remains an enigma.

Donors – Self-perpetuation and Piety

Theocratic control reigned supreme in the early Middle Ages. The glory of God and the teaching of the truth were all-important and the inclusion of a living human being in a stained-glass window would have been considered inappropriate, if not slightly presumptuous. Yet, by the end of the twelfth century, donors of windows—both ecclesiastical and secular—began to be represented, either at the base of the window or in one of the tracery lights. They were always small in scale compared to the main subject or figure.

The depiction of members of the laity was, however, evidence that there were individuals of sufficient power and wealth to be able to donate windows for churches independently from the ecclesiastical authorities—although presumably with their active co-operation. In the thirteenth and early fourteenth centuries these donors were still content to be subservient to the religious function of the window; they were nearly always kneeling as in prayer, sometimes accompanied by wife and children. From the thirteenth century onwards, craft guilds, too, often made gifts of windows. Although they influenced the choice of subject in parts of the window—the guild windows at Chartres, for example, show, in the lower panels, the work of the various trades—it is rare to find the individual donors themselves represented.

One of the simplest technical forms of showing donors was to paint the whole figure on to white glass, a technique exemplified by a fifteenth-century window in the parish church at Winscombe in Somerset. This rather rustic treatment is common in English windows, possibly because of the economy required in the use of coloured glass, which in the Middle Ages had to be imported. The larger pieces were saved for the main figure while, in some cases, small offcuts of colours were used for the peripheral figures of donors.

In much the same style is an interesting window in the Church of St Leonard at Middleton in Lancashire, which was given by Sir Richard Assheton c. 1520 as a thank-offering for the outcome of the Battle of Flodden. He, his wife and their chaplain are depicted, as well as seventeen of his archers, each holding a longbow on which his name is inscribed—appropriately since Sir Richard, a wealthy landowner, had led the archers at Flodden Field.

English windows of the fourteenth and fifteenth centuries abound with donors of all stations of life and many exhibit fairly sophisticated design and workmanship. Outstanding are the fifteenth-century east window in East Harling Church, Norfolk, and the remains of contemporary windows in Long Melford Church, Suffolk. At the base of the outer lights of the East Harling window are kneeling figures in armour—on the left Sir Robert Wingfield, Knight of the Garter, and on the right Sir William Chamberlain, Comptroller of the Household of Edward IV. Sir Robert was the first husband of Anne Harling, a member of the ancient family which received its name from the parish, and Sir William her second husband. Not far away, at Long Melford Church, there is a whole series of equally splendid ladies, kneeling with hands in prayer and robed in heraldic mantles bearing family arms. Both these windows show how the donor had already, by the fifteenth century, taken a much more prominent place in the design, having, in fact, become equal in size to the figures of the main subject.

The churches of Europe, too, are rich with windows ranging from the fourteenth to the seventeenth century which show the evolution from the small-scale donor to the large groups of benefactors—frequently portraits of kings and queens accompanied by all the panoply of State, including coats of arms. While a rather simple, economical treatment persisted in the work of many of the English stained-glass schools, work in France and Germany developed far more rapidly towards the ideal of greater naturalism. This was accompanied by more obvious skills in highly modelled glass painting, which was less calligraphic than the English and was moving towards the dangerous waters of representation for its own sake. As time went on, a greater degree of realism was evident in the depiction of donors in stained glass. They were no longer stereotypes but real portraits with individualized features and dressed in the fashions of the time. In the Church of St Martin, Montmorency, for example, there is an excellent example of portraiture in the head of the donor, Guillaume de Montmorency, Chamberlain and Councillor to Charles VIII and Louis XII of France. The portrait may well be based on a contemporary painting in the Louvre in Paris, so similar is the likeness.

By the Renaissance, with its emphasis on the works and achievements of man, the importance and size of the donors are magnified until they virtually occupy the entire window. In a sixteenth-century transept window of St Gudule, Brussels, for example, large figures of exalted personages

A donor of stained glass is frequently depicted with a miniature of his gift window within the window itself. Within the grisaille window that he gave to Evreux Cathedral in the fourteenth century, Canon Raoul de Ferrières offers his gift to the Virgin, who is suckling the infant Jesus.

The presumption of sixteenth-century donors is exemplified by the window, right, from the Church of St Martin in Montmorency, France. The donor, Guy de Laval, kneels in the centre light, thus displacing the Crucifixion, shown diminutively on the right. Laval's splendid costume contrasts with the ragged appearance of St Jerome, who stands behind him gazing fervently at the cross and beating his breast with the customary stone.

The minute donor and his wife are dwarfed by the Virgin, the angel and even by the lily in this sixteenth-century Netherlandish Annunciation scene, below, now in the Victoria and Albert Museum, London. Instead of expressing pious humility, the two Lilliputian figures appear slightly comic. Their reduced scale is stylistically unusual for sixteenth-century work, in which donors, particularly in Flemish glass, are generally obtrusively large. The dramatic confrontation between Mary and the Angel is presided over by a symbolic dove beneath ornate Renaissance architecture.

kneel at prayer in a kind of open chapel whose elaborate architecture, executed with enormous virtuosity, spreads across all the lights, creating an impression of worldly pomp rather than devotion. The religious subject, St Francis, is notably inconspicuous.

A comprehensive study of donors could be said to illustrate, in an easily assimilated form, the range and development of the design and painting of windows. It embraces figure drawing and portraiture, changing social and religious attitudes, heraldry, architecture, or the framing of the figures, costume and, perhaps more than any other element in a window, the decline of the art of stained glass into monumental picture-making.

MEDIEVAL ADVERTISING

Medieval craftsmen, threatened by competition, formed exclusive commercial societies, or guilds. They thus monopolized the practice of particular trades, prospered under the shelter of their corporate identities and protected themselves while restricting the customer's choice. They expressed their allegiance to God by donating stained-glass windows to their church or cathedral and advertised their craft by illustrating either symbols or narrative scenes of their work within the windows. These "signatures" gradually encroached upon the sacred subject, sometimes even replacing it.

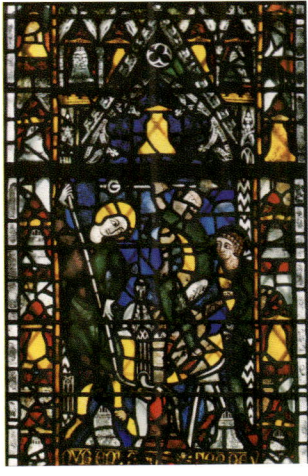

Black puddings, a pig's trotter and a ham are spread out in front of this pork butcher, one of the donors of a fifteenth-century window in the church of Semur-en-Auxois, France.

A fourteenth-century York bell-founder, Richard Tunnoc, promoted his craft by means of a window which he donated to York Minster. Bordered by gold and white bells, he is shown, above, presenting his gift in a central panel. The craft of bell-founding is further publicized by three lower panels in which a bell is cast, tuned and received by St William, the patron saint of York.

The tailors are represented by scissors, above, and the blacksmiths by hammer, pliers and a green creature believed to be a symbol of fire, left, in windows which they and other guilds donated to Freiburg Cathedral in the fourteenth century.

41

A Framework of Glass

Borders in stained-glass windows have both an aesthetic and a practical function. Aesthetically, because a border acts as a glassy frame, repeating the shape of the supporting stonework, it emphasizes the essentially architectural nature of window decoration. A border was sometimes added to a window to make it the correct size for the aperture, thus facilitating the installation in the stone groove. Another practical advantage of a narrow border, or fillet, is that when a window has to be removed for re-leading, the fillet can be broken with impunity, leaving the window intact.

The use of borders in stained-glass windows was, of course, a heritage from other media. Border decoration is, for example, one of the most delightful accomplishments of illuminated manuscripts. Borders were common, too, in mosaics of the Byzantine period. Indeed, the predominating mosaic effect of the border patterns of twelfth- and thirteenth-century windows may have been derived from one of the origins of the art of stained glass, such as mosaic or jewellery.

There was, however, also a more practical reason for the mosaic-like appearance of early stained-glass borders; the inevitable off-cuts and breakages left the glazier with a mass of small pieces of glass which he could readily use to create borders. Although the general effect of the early borders was regular and symmetrical, the various elements, such as foliage and background, were actually made up of glass which differs in shape from one leaf to another or from one apparently similar bit of background to another.

Some of the borders of the early monumental figure windows were very wide—so wide that they sometimes occupied more than half the area of the light. They, and the borders surrounding medallions, helped to create the essentially abstract ornamental style of these early windows.

At first glance, the earliest windows, the so-called five prophets in Augsburg Cathedral, do not appear to have borders. However, the labels bearing the figures' names actually curve to fit the shape of the arch and then continue down each side of the figure, running parallel to the edge, until they reach the foot of the window. Within this there is an additional narrower border, which forms the shafting and the arch of a kind of niche behind the figure. In practical terms, this is an admirable way of breaking up the background while retaining the visual link with the architecture.

The beaded fillet, a thin strip of clear glass with painted bead motifs, occurs frequently within the design of twelfth- and thirteenth-century windows and was a device for utilizing the mass of otherwise unusable fragments left on the glazier's bench. Having cut a number of thin strips of clear glass, the glazier could then paint in the characteristic bead-work—thus turning a dull whitish strip into a border of sparkling diamonds. Furthermore, since the many lead joins were masked by the black intervals between the beads, the effect is of a continuous line or, when surrounding a medallion, a circlet of vibrating points of light.

By the middle Gothic period of the fourteenth and fifteenth centuries, as a result of technical developments in glass-blowing and cutting, glass could be used in larger pieces. The border developed as an outer space between the frame of the window and the newly introduced canopy-work, the depiction of an architectural structure surrounding the figure. One of the simplest forms of the combination of border and canopy is in the St Catherine window in St Catherine's Church, Deerhurst in Gloucestershire. The figure on a red background is enclosed by the shafts of the canopy and the canopy gable, beyond which is a border of alternate red and green separated by squares of white and finally linked to the edge with the yellow beaded fillet. This was an obviously economical method of glazing a large area of background.

Once a basic design structure had been established, the fusion of function and aesthetics in borders offered a multitude of possibilities. Borders evolved quickly from

1 Ornamental foliage and strap-work, twelfth-century Life of the Virgin window, Angers Cathedral.
2 Circles linked by stylized foliage, early thirteenth-century Judgement of Solomon window in north transept of Strasbourg Cathedral.
3 Maple leaf motif, thirteenth-century window in sacristy of Cologne Cathedral.
4 Alternating golden fleurs-de-lys of France and golden leopards of England, fourteenth-century St Frideswide window, Christ Church, Oxford.
5 Chain of ornamental flowers, fourteenth-century St Matthew window, Regensburg Cathedral.
6 Vine leaves and bunches of grapes, fourteenth-century St Catherine window, Christ Church, Oxford.
7 Prophets carrying scrolls beneath arches, fourteenth-century Passion and Entry into Jerusalem window, south aisle of Strasbourg Cathedral.
8 Stylized fleur-de-lys within ornamental foliage, fourteenth-century triforium window at the east end of Evreux Cathedral.

patterns consisting entirely of formalized foliage, to subtle variations on a theme punctuated with rosettes, crowns, animals, heraldic emblems and figures. The same development is reflected by the subsidiary border effects created by the canopy shafting as these shafts became more elaborate. In the Rieter window, for example, in the ambulatory of St Lorenz, Nuremberg, the borders are translated into a tree form which breaks into branches and foliage containing figures and forming the canopy over them.

The transition from the purely decorative and functional border to canopy shafting and the increasingly elaborate "glass architecture" of the sixteenth and seventeenth centuries is further evidence of the decline of glaziers' standards as they began to imitate grandiose pictures of the late Renaissance. Figures appeared in niches as part of a highly modelled Classical façade which spread across the individual lights. The borders, when they existed, were mere decorative frills.

Borders returned with the Gothic revival of the nineteenth century as somewhat slavish copies of medieval work. Most are stereotype patterns and lack the subtle inequalities of the originals. The typical church-furnishers' window of the late nineteenth century had several borders, each with such mechanically repeating elements as foliage, flowers, crowns and monograms, but, because of the precision of shape and exact repetition, the impression they give is generally one of lifelessness.

The abstract designs and massive scale of many contemporary windows preclude the use of borders. Borders still feature in some figurative windows, however, such as the Peace window in Canterbury Cathedral, by the late Hungarian stained-glass artist Ervin Bossanyi. Ears of wheat, heavy with grain, echo the contentment and serenity conveyed by the figures in the main part of the window, as well as providing a framework to the design in the traditional sense.

9 Geometric border, fourteenth-century St Francis window, Königsfelden Church, Switzerland.
10 Fleur-de-lys and crowns surrounding the Trinity in fifteenth-century window in York Minster.
11 An angel within a niche above an architectural motif, fourteenth-century blacksmiths' window in north aisle of Freiburg Cathedral.
12 Fourteenth-century strapwork and fleurs-de-lys, St Joseph's Chapel, Evreux Cathedral.
13 Coursing hounds, sixteenth-century Flemish panel, Victoria and Albert Museum, London.
14 Twining foliage, sixteenth-century window in the Mosque of Murad, Manisa, Turkey.
15 Stylized acorn motif, nineteenth-century St Matthew window, Chetwode Church, Buckinghamshire.
16 Foliaged fleurs-de-lys, nineteenth-century Moses window, Lincoln Cathedral.
17 Twentieth-century abstract border by Jan Thorn Prikker, St James the Great window, Church of St Georg, Cologne.

The shape of a fleur-de-lys at the top of this thirteenth-century window in Merton College Chapel, Oxford, is followed by the border in which fleurs-de-lys alternate with castles of Castile.

The Natural World

Captivated by his words, animals and birds were reputed to have become tame in the presence of St Francis of Assisi. In his sermon to the birds, St Francis is said to have summoned them to praise God for his blessings, whereupon they flew up into the sky in the formation of a cross. His legendary affinity with wild creatures, which he called his brothers and sisters, is exemplified in this fourteenth-century fragment, above, from the abbey church at Königsfelden in Switzerland.

From the tree of knowledge and its tempter, the snake, in the Garden of Eden to Moses' burning bush and brazen snake, Ezekiel's visions of the bird-like seraphim and Isaiah's vision of the slain lamb, the Old Testament is full of imagery involving animals and plants. In the New Testament, Christ used parable and metaphor in such graphic images as the vine, the corn harvest, the lilies of the field and the sheep which were his flock. And the last book of the New Testament gathers together much of its animal imagery in an apocalyptic prophecy of the end of the world.

It was upon the Bible that most of the iconography of the art of the Early Church was based and it was the Bible which inspired those representations of plants and animals whose detail—often as humorous "asides"—is so fascinating in the borders of manuscripts, in sculptured capitals and bosses or in odd corners of stained-glass windows.

As early as the fifth century, bestiaries, books of allegorized natural history depicting animals, some real, some imaginary, were in use as sources of information for artists. For known animals, the bestiaries gave reasonably accurate descriptions culled from various sources, some originating from the writings of Pliny and even Aristotle. But those exotic beasts recorded only in travellers' tales, and often imaginary, were frequently imbued with amazing attributes and provided an excuse for extremely esoteric symbolism.

Among the mythical creatures was the amphisbaena, a winged serpent with a second head at its tail which to the Greeks came to symbolize deceit. In medieval art a second head was often added to any horrific monster. The caladrius was a white bird which foretold the future. Many of the legendary animals have passed into heraldry, including the griffin, the wyvern and the dragon. The phoenix became a well-known Christian symbol of the Resurrection, because it was said to have the ability to be renewed from the ashes of the fire which destroyed it.

Animal imagery was used prolifically on the misericords of churches and cathedrals, particularly in England. The intricate carving testifies to the skill of the medieval carver in representing a story in these carved seat ledges, which offered some support to elderly or infirm clergy during long services.

Glaziers followed the established traditions of carvers in the use of biblical animal symbols. The winged creatures representing the four Evangelists were popular, as were the doves, symbolizing the sevenfold gifts of the Holy Spirit, and the Paschal lamb, the symbol of Christ's sacrifice. Animals were often a feature in scenes illustrating the lives of the saints. St Jerome, for example, is often shown with a lion at his feet, since, according to popular fable, he pulled a thorn out of the paw of a lion which subsequently became his devoted friend. St Francis of Assisi is sometimes depicted with the wolf which terrorized the Italian town of Gubbio in the Middle Ages and which he later tamed.

It was the preaching of St Francis in the early thirteenth century which moved men to think of the animal world as worthy of respect for its own sake and as part of God's creation. Gradually, knowledge of the animal kingdom increased, as trade expanded and Europeans ventured farther into the heart of Asia and Africa and to the Americas. As early as the thirteenth century, Louis IX had brought back an elephant from the Crusades and in the fifteenth and sixteenth centuries many Renaissance princes and noblemen kept private menageries. Maps of the newly discovered territories with their illustrations of exotic beasts also provided information—if not always accurate. The corresponding development of the glass-painters' skills led to a more confident use of animals, less in a symbolic role and more as inhabitants of the natural world, depicted in a fairly realistic landscape. The Nativity, for example, often included realistic sheep, cows and other creatures of the farmyard.

Mythical beasts gradually disappeared, leaving only a few to be used as heraldic charges or supporters in coats of arms.

Plants were not as profusely depicted in stained glass as animals. They were, however, readily adaptable to ornament and were commonly used as such, particularly in window borders, without any specific symbolism. Even the Tree of Jesse had an artistic purpose for the glazier which was almost as important as its dramatic symbolism: the tree form, with its branches and leaves, offered a perfect structure for the disposition of the main groups of interest and rounded off the design with pattern-work.

Some plants are inextricably connected with the doctrines of the Church, the graphic images that the theologians used to teach the illiterate. The vine, for example, was quickly absorbed into the concept of the Jesse Tree, joining the stem of Jesse with the true vine of Christ. The lily has been universally associated with the Annunciation as typifying the Virgin's purity. An imaginative development of the lily theme can be seen in a small panel in Long Melford Church, Suffolk. The lily symbolizes a crucifix, its blooms clustered around the figure of Christ. The cross itself was the tree of life and was linked with the tree of paradise in the fertile minds of sermonizers.

Drawings of plants in the herbals of Gerard and Parkinson, in the sixteenth and seventeenth centuries, provided designers with models for accurate representations in the predominantly illustrative windows of the Renaissance and succeeding periods. By the Victorian era, the artists who illustrated such subjects as the Gospel stories, many of which gave excuse for landscape, made much of their skills in their almost photographic representations of plant and animal life. This sentimental view of nature was also reflected in elaborate backgrounds of flowers and birds. The subsequent attempt of the Pre-Raphaelites to give such subjects some degree of stylization was one more example of their concern to put stained glass once more on what was to them its true course—that of an essentially decorative art.

Birds were a common feature in quarries—square- or diamond-shaped panes of glass. The fifteenth-century quarry, above, now in St Bartholomew's, Yarnton, bears an inscription indicating its original location in an inn.

In medieval art, representations of animals were often exaggerated and comical, as can be seen in the illustrations of a camel from a fourteenth-century English bestiary, below, and animals in Noah's Ark, right, from the fifteenth-century window in Great Malvern Priory Church.

A sleeping or recumbent dog at the feet of a donor is a common motif in the sixteenth-century windows of St John's Church at Gouda. The animal's lifelike pose in the detail from one of the windows, above, is typical of the realism in art which was prevalent at that time. Yellow stain applied to the outer surface of the glass gives the dog its brownish colour.

THE FLORAL TRADITION IN ART

Repeating foliated patterns were a recurring decorative feature of medieval art, as in the thirteenth-century German glass panel, below, originally in Erfurt Cathedral and now in Darmstadt Museum. The developing naturalism of the Gothic Age arose from direct observation of the natural world, whose intrinsic beauty was one of the great discoveries of the time.

The thirteenth-century Chapter House in Southwell Minster is renowned for the lavish yet lifelike foliage which decorates its capitals. The ornate Gothic stonework leaves, right, show a highly disciplined carving technique.

Illustrated herbals were once a common source of reference for stained-glass artists. Clarity of colour and simplicity of design characterize the depiction of madder, belladonna and sweet pea, in a detail, above, from a sixteenth-century Flemish herbal for children.

A more realistic approach to flora, in the famous watercolour of 1503 by Albrecht Dürer, above, and in a contemporary detail from the Passion window in Cologne Cathedral, left, broke away from the traditional mannered technique which prevailed until the beginning of the sixteenth century.

The Ancient Tradition of Heraldry

Military rolls, frequently illustrated in great detail, recorded the arms worn into battle or at tournaments. The detail, above, from a fifteenth-century roll of arms, shows the complementary insignia worn by a combatant horseman and his charger at a tournament.

Heraldry, the systematic use of hereditary symbols centred on a shield, has a long history. Although the rules of blazoning, the formal description of heraldry, did not evolve until after the Norman Conquest, the use of emblems on shields dates back to Ancient Greece and Rome.

As a formal system of identification, heraldry originated in the feudal society of medieval western Europe, and it was from Old French, the language of the ruling classes of this society, that the nomenclature of heraldry evolved, although certain words have their roots in Persian—a direct influence of the Crusades. Over the centuries heraldry spread throughout Europe and, with the help of colonization and the influences of imperialism, to America, Africa and Australasia. During the twelfth century, noblemen and knights began to identify themselves and their equipment, notably their shields, by the use of simple symbols which had clearly defined shapes and contrasting colours. Although the eleventh-century Bayeux tapestry shows warriors with shields bearing such motifs, there was little order to their use at this time. Indeed, heredity was mainly responsible for the systemization of heraldry. At first this simply meant a continuity of insignia within one family to distinguish it from another.

With the advent in the thirteenth century of the great helm, a closed helmet which totally obscured the face, heraldic symbols assumed a practical function, for they facilitated the identification of warriors on the battlefield. The choice of emblem by which a knight wished to be recognized was influenced by the evocation of such animal attributes as ferocity, nobility, cunning and swiftness. Thus the shield, which later evolved as the principal component of a coat of arms, came to be charged, or decorated, with heraldic objects of almost infinite variety and complexity ranging from beasts and birds, both mythical and real, to weapons of war. From the simplest early coats of arms with single emblems, the development of marshalling, or grouping, several devices on a single shield necessitated the division of the shield by one or more lines. These divisions each have a name, such as the bar, the chief, the pale, the bend and the chevron. In 1340, shields began to be quartered in order to show two or more sets of arms to which the bearer laid claim.

Soon the helmet, too, became a means of immediate recognition, when for tournaments the knight mounted on it first a leather and later a wooden device known as the crest. To protect the neck from injury and the sun, a piece of material, known as the mantling, or lambrequin, was attached to the helmet. In battle, the mantling often became torn and hung in ribbons—a trophy of pride attesting the knight's bravery. Between the crest and the mantling was a torse, or wreath, of two colours.

The knight's emblazoned shield and his helmet with crest, mantling and wreath became integral parts of the personal insignia which came to be known as a coat of arms—a term deriving from the decorated surcoat worn by medieval soldiers on top of their chain mail. The coat of

THE ARMS OF THE WORSHIPFUL COMPANY OF GLAZIERS AND PAINTERS OF GLASS

The English guild of glaziers, as it was then called, was granted full arms in 1634. Their shield, upon which stand helmet and crest, is charged with early tools of the trade—grozing irons and closing nails; the lion, which may also be depicted as a demi-lion, recalls the days of royal patronage. The torches carried by the boy supporters allude to the firing of glass.

The shield, or escutcheon, is the most important part of the coat of arms, a reminder that originally the shield bore the knight's identifying motif.

Supporters, as their name suggests, appear to hold up or carry the coat of arms. There are usually two supporters—animals, fabulous beasts or human beings.

The crest, originally a distinguishing feature of medieval knights' tournament apparel, is now a standard part of most coats of arms in northern and central Europe.

The wreath of colours, made up of two twisted bands of silk, was introduced in the fourteenth century to keep the mantling attached to the helmet and to support the crest. In heraldry its function is decorative.

The tournament helmet was widely used in the early fifteenth century, particularly in non-aristocratic coats of arms.

Mantling, a piece of material hanging from the top of a warrior's helmet, protected the head and shoulders. Incorporated into coats of arms, it developed pleats and creases, according to the fashions of the times, and, in the sixteenth century, foliage forms.

The charge, or heraldic motif, in the Middle Ages was usually a simplified stylized animal or bird. Over the centuries the nature of charges has diversified to include railway engines and, as here, the glaziers' nails and grozing iron.

Mottoes range from the war-cry of some ancient houses to less bellicose phrases in Latin or in the language of the country. The glaziers' motto *Lucem tuam da nobis Deus* means God give us your light.

A compartment, or grass ground, serves as a base for the supporters.

arms was, therefore, at one time, literally a protective coat.

The supporters are usually animals or human figures which flank the shield. Their use in England is normally restricted to such people as Peers of the Realm, Knights Grand Cross and certain institutions, although in Scotland and in some European countries they are used more indiscriminately.

The background of the shield on a coat of arms is known as the field, or ground, and it is either a colour, a metal or a fur. Known collectively as tinctures, these colours, metals and furs are used according to specific rules. Because heraldry was originally used to make recognition easy on the battlefield, only the clearest, strongest colours are used, such as red, known in heraldry as gules, blue (azure), green (vert), black (sable) and white (argent or silver). Gold (or) and silver (argent), known in the context of heraldry as metals, are also used. Among the conventionalized furs, ermine is recognizable by the black tails which dot a white background, while the less familiar vair (originally composed of pieces of squirrel fur sewn together) forms a pattern of alternate white and blue shield-shaped pieces. The use of furs probably goes back to the days when shields were covered with real fur.

From the simple functional coats of arms of medieval times to the elaborate and often absurd concoctions of the eighteenth and nineteenth centuries, a vast range of heraldry is reflected in stained glass, a medium to which, with its clarity of colour and design, heraldry is eminently suited.

Shield Shapes

The shield, or escutcheon, the principal component of a coat of arms, varies from simple thirteenth-century forms (1, 2, 3) to more irregular shapes of fourteenth-century Italy and Germany (4, 5). Plain shields of the fifteenth and sixteenth centuries (6, 7, 8) were succeeded by the *cartouche* (9) of the seventeenth century and a graceful nineteenth-century line (10).

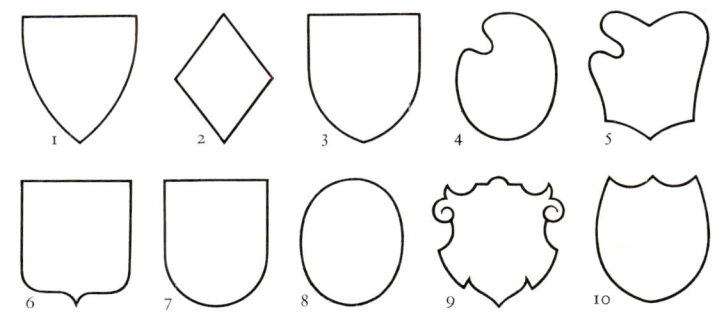

Charges

Shields are decorated, or charged, with animate and inanimate objects. The lion, a common motif, is often depicted passant (1) or rampant (2). An eagle may be displayed (3). The martlet (4), fleur-de-lys (6), mullet (9) and rose (10) may be used as signs of cadency, indicating filial rank. An escallop (5) was a badge of pilgrimage, and the cinquefoil (7) and castle (8) were often part of municipal arms.

Colours

The background of a heraldic shield comprises one of three tinctures: a metal, a colour or a fur whose names derive from Old French and Persian. The metals or (1) and argent (2) are depicted as yellow and white. The five principal colours are azure (3), gules (4), vert (5), purpure (6) and sable (7). The conventionalized furs include ermine (8), white with black dots, and vair (9).

Helmets

The barrel helm (1) and that of a Scottish esquire (2) date from the thirteenth century. In the fifteenth century, the tournament helmet (3) was replaced by the barred helmet (4). An armet (5) was worn by knights and peers and the helmet with closed visor (6) by esquires. In the seventeenth century, the robe of estate (7) was prominent. The arms of a British peer includes several helmets (8).

Divisions

A shield may be divided into grounds of different tinctures. Divisions and colour combinations may include per pale, gules and argent (1), per fess, or and sable (2), per bend, or and gules (3), per saltire, or and sable (4), quarterly, vert and or (5) and per pall, gules, argent and azure (6).

Insignia of Office

Insignia of office may be used in heraldry, as, for example, the batons of the Marshals of France (1). Religious insignia range from the simple pattern of an abbess (2), the stole and mitre of an Anglican bishop (3), the hat and cords of his Catholic counterpart (4) to the ornate papal tiara (5). A coronet is part of royal arms—like those of France's Louis XVIII (6) and Holland's Queen Juliana (7). Civic arms may include a mural crown (8).

Ordinaries

Ordinaries are commonly used charges of geometric shape, encroaching on the background of a shield. The heraldic description of the shields gives first the background tincture, then the name of the ordinary and its tincture. The shields, right, are azure a chief argent (1), or a fess gules (2), argent a pale sable (3), azure a bend or (4), vert a chevron or (5), azure a pall argent (6), gules a saltire argent (7), or a cross gules (8) and or a pile purpure (9).

Supporters

Supporters, animals or humans, often stand on each side of a shield. The lion and the unicorn of English royal arms, right, are among the most familiar of animal supporters. Rarely, a shield is borne by a lone supporter, such as the swan, far right. Widely used elsewhere, in England supporters are the right of peers and certain institutions.

The Art of Blazoning in Glass

The powerful Johann I von Nassau and his simply charged arms in a fourteenth-century glass panel now in Münster Landesmuseum.

Arms of John of Gaunt, in St Albans Cathedral.

Flanked by the coats of arms of his ancestors, Philipp von Daun, Archbishop of Cologne, kneels at the feet of St Peter in the sixteenth-century St Peter and Jesse Tree window which he donated to Cologne Cathedral. Opposite the sumptuously clad figures stands St Sebastian, also dressed in contemporary costume. Among the coats of arms of Von Daun's maternal line is, in the lower right-hand panel, the canting, or punning, arms of the Von Salm family. The charge is derived from the literal meaning of the name—salmon.

There is no better medium than heraldry through which to gain a deeper understanding of the technical and artistic developments of stained glass. Heraldic devices appeared quite early in the stained glass of Europe. At Chartres, in the thirteenth-century window donated by the guild of furriers, a figure holds a cloak whose lining is unmistakably of vair, the heraldic fur, while knights with decorated shields and heraldically caparisoned chargers appear in the aisle windows. In England, the use of heraldic symbols in stained-glass windows was slow to be adopted, but when it became fashionable in the fourteenth century, coats of arms were widely used to identify donors.

A popular alternative to the straightforward coat of arms was the canting, or punning, arms, in which the charge or charges were derived from the literal meaning of the bearer's name. Thus the shield of the English Shelley family bears shells and that of the Wellwoods an oak tree growing out of a well. Canting arms have been popular on an international scale almost from the beginnings of heraldry.

From early use by warriors, great lords and sovereigns, by the fifteenth century heraldic devices had spread to the Church, to landed gentry, municipal government, craft guilds and learned and other institutions and associations. The spread of domestic glass, arising from the increased building of palaces and country mansions with large windows, stimulated the use of family arms as a mark of lineal dignity—a possession much prized by the nobility of the times, as the words of Bolingbroke in Shakespeare's *Richard II* (Act III, scene i) so eloquently indicate:

"Whilst you have fed upon my signories,
Dispark'd my parks, and felled my forest woods,
From mine own windows torn my household coat,
. . . leaving me no sign . . .
To show the world I am a gentleman."

In the sixteenth century, with the advent of the Reformation in Europe, the violent reaction to Catholic doctrine brought about the wide-scale destruction of sacred art and, as a result, glaziers turned their attentions to glass divested of all religious imagery. Heraldic windows in their own right then began to be produced for churches, private houses and municipal buildings.

For two hundred years, Swiss craftsmen were pre-eminent in the production of secular glass. From the end of the fifteenth century, they produced coats of arms of families, cantons and guilds, often taking the engravings of such masters as Hans Holbein and Albrecht Dürer as their source of design—indeed Holbein himself is known to have designed heraldic window panes.

As with the depiction of donors, worldly ostentation superseded the humility proper to a Christian gentleman and religious subjects dwindled or were lost altogether in a mass of armorial bearings. However vainglorious, these heraldic windows of the sixteenth, seventeenth and eighteenth centuries had a great richness and splendour of colour in contrast to the dull opacity of many contemporary "picture windows". This was in large part the result of the observance of demands made on stained-glass craftsmen by heraldry's strict rules of tincture, which dictated the use of armorial colours. The increased complications of the divisions and charges of shields exemplify the ingenuity and artistic skill of glaziers over the centuries. So, too, the aesthetic qualities of stained glass are clearly shown in the treatment of heraldry, which requires sharp colours and a simple bold design.

It seems likely that the first use of abrasion, the removal of coloured areas of flashed glass, was necessitated by the exigencies of small charges on quartered shields, as, for example, in the Tudor arms of England. Here the pattern

The Tudor arms from a sixteenth-century window at Cowick Priory, Devon, and now in the Victoria and Albert Museum, London.

The arms of Countess von Salm from the St Peter and Jesse Tree window in Cologne Cathedral.

The arms of Cardinal Fonseca, chaplain to Ferdinand and Isabella, in Toledo Cathedral.

Sixteenth-century coat of arms in St John's, Gouda, with silver-stained yellow stars.

on two quarters of the shield, of the three gold lions on a red field, was so complicated that leading in separate colours would have been extremely difficult. By abrading—literally grinding down the coloured flash until the basic white glass was reached—the rough shape of the charges was first revealed as white. The charge was then painted and the yellow, which was used to indicate gold, was applied by the use of stain to the back of the glass, giving the effect of two colours on one piece of glass. Where the edges of a motif were irregular, a delineating line of black paint could be applied to the glass surface.

In the sixteenth century the invention of enamels, or ground glass, which was washed on the glass and fired in the same way as black glass paint, enabled artists to colour in not only the basic hues of the field, but also to represent realistically the natural colouring of figures, vegetation and animals. Unfortunately, much of this enamel colouring has proved impermanent and it is common to find eighteenth-century coats of arms with their fields or charges scaled off and returned to their original white glass. In the nineteenth century the more efficient technique of acid-etching was adopted. This involved masking out the background colour with a bituminous paint and then applying hydrofluoric acid to the exposed portion. The masking was removed as soon as the acid had bitten through the flash. Today, separate leaded colours are used as far as possible. Acid-etching and enamelling are used only as a last resort.

In the best heraldic glass, the sharp colours and distinctive devices of the coat of arms are enhanced by the glass-painter. In adapting them to his medium, with its capacity for rich areas of colour clearly delineated by the use of leading, the glazier effectively created a new art form from the science of heraldry.

Seventeenth-century panel from "The Mooress" guild chamber, Strasbourg.

HERALDRY MANIA

In the late fifteenth century it became customary for neighbouring Swiss towns and cantons to exchange small panels of heraldic stained glass. This practice marked a departure from the traditional use of glass in a religious setting to its appearance in council chambers and inns and in town and guild halls. For the next two hundred years, Swiss craftsmen specialized in armorial glass for secular use.

Ensigned with the insignia of the Holy Roman Empire, the arms of the canton of Zurich, above, is surrounded by the arms of the wards of the city. This roundel was created in 1585 by the Swiss glazier Hans Rütter.

The arms of Kyburg, left, from a series of panels of the arms of the cantons, was made by the Swiss master glazier Lukas Zeiner, early in the sixteenth century.

Reflections of the Times – Architecture

A work of art reflects its own times in two distinct ways. First, as the result of influences unconsciously absorbed by the artist, the style of the composition or design reveals an authenticity of period which is more easily recognized than analysed. This intuitive awareness that something belongs to one period rather than to another is often dependent upon no more than a subtle mystery of form. A successful work of art will, for this reason, belong physically to its own time, but it will, spiritually, transcend time. More superficially, a work of art can also reflect its times by depicting contemporary architecture, fashions and objects.

Throughout its history, stained glass developed on a parallel with contemporary painting, from early glass in the style of Byzantine frescoes and the detailed realism of fifteenth- and sixteenth-century windows, which echoed that of contemporary Flemish paintings, to the return to Classicism, which was inherent in Renaissance art. Perspective, which distinguished Renaissance from medieval art, is reflected above all in the representation of architecture.

Dependent upon actual architecture for its framework, stained glass also reflects images of architecture within its design. Architecture was first represented in stained-glass windows in the thirteenth century in the form of stylized ornamental canopies, or niches, which enframed the figures. Similar to the props used in mystery plays, these niches were two-dimensional and lacked any perspective. In England and France they were usually delineated on clear glass and served as light-admitting devices as well as ornamental frames.

In the fourteenth century, canopies gradually became more realistic, mirroring contemporary architecture more accurately. The fourteenth-century east window in Gloucester Cathedral is an excellent example of the depiction within a window of architectural structure and detail. Composed of fourteen lights, horizontally divided into five rows of figures within niches, the entire expanse is virtually a reredos of glass, the structure of the canopies echoing the architectural style of the cathedral itself. Although the development of such canopies was facilitated by the technical innovation of silver stain and the ability to manufacture glass in larger pieces than had ever before been possible, it also testifies to the glazier's understanding of the principles of architectural proportions.

From a simple frame surrounding one figure, the canopy in stained-glass windows gradually expanded with double side columns, which sometimes contained additional niches in which there were smaller figures. The original single-pointed arch proliferated into pinnacles and crocketed canopies which, soaring in the true Gothic tradition, sometimes occupied much of the upper half of a window. Influenced by Renaissance art, these Gothic canopies were replaced by the shell-shaped niches of Classical architecture and they, rather than enshrining one figure, often formed a background to the whole window.

In sixteenth-century stained-glass windows architecture was increasingly illustrated in the form of contemporary buildings and, finally, lost all pretence of assisting the style and structure of the design. It was included for its own sake

THE DEVELOPMENT OF THE CANOPY

Originally the embellishment of a venerated figure and, increasingly, an excuse for letting in light, stained-glass canopies, top right, mirrored contemporary architecture, below right. Crude shapes, suspended above thirteenth-century stained-glass figures, developed in the fourteenth century into elaborate shrines resembling the arcading of Decorated architecture. Tinted with innovatory silver stain, these spiry designs admitted light but often dwarfed the figures. The horizontal bands of canopies, however, unified a group of lancets and framed figures which would otherwise have appeared to float in space. Perpendicular architecture encouraged the height of stained-glass canopies and the impression of verticality was increased by narrow side niches, often filled with small figures. Brassy yellow was partially replaced by light grey or clear glass and the structure of the canopy appeared like a pale silhouette. Mastery of perspective and a return to Classical architecture distinguished the Renaissance canopies. Realistically representing marble edifices with shell-shaped alcoves, their solidity negated the spindly quality of the Gothic style.

Chartres Cathedral. Thirteenth century.

Tewkesbury Abbey. Fourteenth century.

Evreux Cathedral. Fifteenth century.

Auch Cathedral. Sixteenth century.

Lincoln Cathedral, east façade. Thirteenth century.

Freiburg Cathedral, west porch. Fourteenth century.

Chester Cathedral, choir stall, c. 1390.

Palazzo Cornaro, Venice, niche. Sixteenth century.

as an integral element in the pictorial composition. The growing dominance of Flemish glass-painters throughout sixteenth-century Europe accelerated the transition to pictorial architecture until, for example, in the Martha and Mary windows, glazed by Abraham van Linge, in University College Chapel, Oxford, it became complete, even to the inclusion of marble veining on the walls.

It was but a step from showing figures standing inside a realistic building with receding arcades and windows to depicting them surrounded by buildings set in a landscape—a background once again reminiscent of Flemish painting. Many of the charming scenes in sixteenth- and seventeenth-century windows give some idea of urban and rural architecture and an impression of the countryside of the period.

In the nineteenth century, Gothic architecture was once again depicted in stained glass, but it was all too often a stereotyped imitation of the canopies of early windows. It was, characteristically, the Pre-Raphaelites who returned to the creative exploitation of architectural forms in glass, assimilating them into the composition as a whole and producing a harmony between the architectural setting of the window and its intrinsic design.

Modern twentieth-century stained glass has come almost full circle. Rather than reflecting the architecture of today it has become an integral part of the building itself. This is exemplified by the baptistery window of Coventry Cathedral, the lantern of Liverpool Cathedral and Gabriel Loire's *dalle de verre* walls in the Kaiser Wilhelm Memorial Church in West Berlin.

The spires and roofs of Delft and the flat-bottomed boats on the flooded plain beyond are minutely depicted in the Relief of Leyden window, detail above, in St John's Church, Gouda. Commemorating the victory in 1574 over Spanish occupying forces, the window, glazed in 1603, exemplifies the pictorial approach of Dutch glass-painters.

Painted in unusually cool colours by Abraham van Linge, a seventeenth-century window in Christ Church Cathedral, Oxford, shows Jonah sitting resentfully before the repentant city of Nineveh, detail right. Strangely depopulated, the city is depicted in great detail, but without reference to a particular architectural style.

Reflections of the Times – Details of Daily Life

January. Feasting and music-making. French, late sixteenth century, now in Musée Départemental, Rouen.

February. Getting warm at the fireside. English, fifteenth century, now in Burrell Collection, Glasgow.

March. Pruning the trees. English, fifteenth century, Brandiston Hall, Norfolk.

Although the medieval glazier was recording the symbolic or pictorial details of sacred events, he inevitably transposed them from their setting in the eastern Mediterranean during the first century to contemporary Europe. In so doing, he revealed the secular world of his own times.

In early stained glass, reflections of ordinary daily life were merely passing allusions included to make the religious subject more immediate. Thus a Nativity scene would incidentally provide details of contemporary buildings and farming implements. Because of the limitations of glass size and colour, these details were stark and highly stylized, and were frequently out of scale in order to emphasize any underlying symbolic significance.

The fourteenth-century Nativity panel in a window in East Hagbourne Church, Berkshire, exemplifies the early glaziers' minimal use of detail to illustrate a story. Within the simple canopy framework the Virgin and Child are depicted on a crudely drawn bed, in front of which stands a cupboard-like object—the manger. The whole scene is two-dimensional, against a blue diapered background.

Influenced by the increasing realism of contemporary painting, fifteenth-century glaziers attempted more realistic designs, a development heightened in the following century by the availability of coloured enamel paints. This highly pictorial representation of the artist's world is epitomized by a small sixteenth-century Flemish roundel, now in the Victoria and Albert Museum, London, which shows Christ in the House of Simon. This roundel, which represents a peak of technical perfection in the handling of enamel paint, shows exactly how a wealthy man's dining-room would have been furnished in the early sixteenth century, from the table, in perfect perspective, to the beautifully modelled linen-fold panelling and carved cornice in the background.

Fascinating insights into the daily life and customs of the Middle Ages can also be gained from windows which were donated by craft guilds and, more unexpectedly, from those which illustrate the barbarous ways in which the saints of the Early Church were reputedly put to death. In the guild windows, small panels often show the craft of the donors. In the saints windows, implements of various trades, such as flaying knives, axes and grid-irons, are illustrated as instruments of torture or calmly carried by the saints as emblems of martyrdom.

But the secular world really came into its own in both church and domestic stained glass in northern Europe with the panels illustrating the labours of the months—tasks assigned to each month of the year, which varied according to the customs of the country. Comprising a unique social document, the labours recorded in vivid and often charming detail the activities of peasant and noble alike. They were a popular subject in manuscripts known as books of hours, and those lavishly illustrated books commissioned by wealthy patrons were almost certainly used by glaziers as a source of design for their windows.

Labours of the months were usually glazed as roundels or small panels for private houses, colleges or guild halls, although some were made for churches. They gradually became more sophisticated in style and by the sixteenth

July. Reaping. English, fifteenth century, Brandiston Hall, Norfolk.

August. Harvesting. French, late sixteenth century, now in Musée Départemental, Rouen.

September. Picking grapes. English, fifteenth century, Brandiston Hall, Norfolk.

April. Hunting. French, late sixteenth century, now in Musée Départemental, Rouen.

May. Mowing. French, late sixteenth century, now in Musée Départemental, Rouen.

June. Bathing in the courtyard. English, fifteenth century, Brandiston Hall, Norfolk.

century showed a great degree of accuracy and elaborate detail in the representation of contemporary farming and domestic equipment.

Impressions of medieval daily life are conveyed by a few simply drawn details, such as a cauldron bubbling on the winter fire or a sower's wicker basket. Sixteenth-century scenes of courtly and pastoral life are illustrated, contrastingly, in great detail and, stylistically, with the greater freedom and fluidity afforded by the use of enamel paints. The numerous figures are smaller and leave more room for landscape and buildings as well as for different activities to take place simultaneously: while the wheat is being cut in August a labourer eats and drinks, nude bathers wade through a river in the background of a May mowing scene and, within their banqueting hall, the nobility relax after a January feast and are entertained by musicians and a monkey on a ball and chain.

Since modern windows are predominantly abstract, such figurative secular detail is comparatively rare in twentieth-century glass. Much of the stained glass of the American artist Paul Marioni, however, contains unmistakably twentieth-century imagery—including aeroplanes, cars and wash-basins. Perhaps the ultimate examples of reflections of twentieth-century life are the windows done by the Winterich Studio for a restaurant in Ohio; each window depicts a popular sport. In one window there are giant American football players with enormous padded shoulders —as appropriate and evocative of their era of creation as the medieval and Renaissance labours of the months.

FROM SYMBOLS TO OBJECTS

Everyday objects, whose role in early stained glass was symbolic or narrative, were gradually considered interesting as subject matter in their own right. In the medallion of the Marriage Feast at Cana in Canterbury Cathedral, detail below, jars are depicted with the starkness characteristic of thirteenth-century glass. Contrastingly, in the sixteenth-century Birth of the Virgin, right, in the Church of Notre-Dame-en-Vaux, Châlons-sur-Marne, an important part of the composition is St Anne's luxurious bed.

October. Sowing. English, fifteenth century, now in Victoria and Albert Museum, London.

November. Sheltering from a hailstorm. English, fifteenth century, Brandiston Hall, Norfolk.

December. Feasting. English, early fifteenth century, now in Victoria and Albert Museum, London.

Reflections of the Times—Fashions

From the thirteenth to the seventeenth centuries the figures in stained-glass windows were increasingly depicted in contemporary dress. The frieze above traces the development of European costume within this time-span.
Thirteenth century
French (1, 2), English (3, 4).
Fourteenth century
Italian (5, 6), English (7, 8), French (9).
Fifteenth century
Italian (10, 11), Flemish (12), Burgundian (13), German (14), Venetian (15).
Sixteenth century
Italian (16), English (17, 18, 19), Flemish (20), Spanish (21, 22), French (23), English (24).
Seventeenth century
Spanish (25), French (26), English (27, 28), Dutch (29), French (30).

Beginning with the simple stylized windows of the eleventh and twelfth centuries, stained glass has often reflected the fashions of the era in which it was created.

The glaziers of the earliest narrative windows aimed to make the figures easily recognizable and attention to the details of their costume was subordinated to this end. The inclusion of certain elements of dress was considered an adequate indication of the status of the figure—a bishop always wore a mitre, for example, and a king a crown, irrespective of the circumstances in which they appeared. The result, although superbly decorative, was, as with much early glass, thoroughly conventional. The artists sought to portray the type rather than the individual.

By the late twelfth century, a distinctive secular attire had evolved which synthesized elements from western Europe and from the East. This was the era of the Crusades and the general influence of Eastern styles on Western clothes resulted in a covered-up look for people of all social classes, a look reflected in stained glass of the period. Women wore long robes and were usually veiled or wore the chin-enclosing wimple in public. Men were clad in loose-fitting capes with hoods which often finished with a long "tail". This "tail" later developed into the liripipe.

From the late thirteenth century to the end of the fifteenth century, an elongated style prevailed, exemplified most obviously by the steeple head-dress or *hénin*—the fashion counterpart of the soaring heights attained by Gothic architecture. In the late fifteenth century this style was succeeded by an emphasis on breadth in architecture and in dress. The English Tudor hood, worn to great effect, for example, by a lady in the early sixteenth-century east window in St Margaret's Church, Westminster, resembled the gabling of contemporary houses. In the same way, the effect of the padding, or bombast, of Henry VIII's costume reflected the solidity of Tudor architecture. Shoes also changed shape at this time. The long *crackowes*, said to have come from Poland—the length of whose points indicated status, nobles wearing them extended to knee height—were replaced by wider, square-toed shoes which remained popular until late in the sixteenth century.

By the end of the fifteenth century, as a result of increased trade and travel, information about the costumes of people of other lands had filtered through to European glaziers. This information or, sometimes, misinformation

The covered-up look of the clothes of a duchess, left, emphasized by the head-dress, shows the influence of the East on medieval costume. This fourteenth-century panel is from Seligenthal Abbey, Bavaria.

Softly falling robes of "scarlet" —an elastic woollen fabric— are worn by two figures, right, in a fourteenth-century window at Königsfelden, Switzerland.

Much favoured by middle- and upper-class German women, from about 1450 to 1520, was a masculine-style beret in velvet, leather or brocade. The brim could be pinned to the crown, as above, or left to follow the natural curve of the hat. This detail of Mary, a Habsburg queen, is from a mid-sixteenth-century window, now in the Germanisches National-Museum, Nuremberg.

Burgundian countryfolk, left, wearing typical loose-fitting garments of coarse wool or linen, dance around the village linden tree in a late fifteenth-century panel now in Bourges Museum.

altered the representations of such figures as biblical prophets and high priests by giving them the traditional dress of the Palestinians. The glaziers were also influenced by the draughtsmanship of the Italian Renaissance masters. The depiction of robes became more realistic, and folds of drapery were arranged over figures which had now become solid and lifelike.

The German and Swiss styles of slashed sleeves and breeches were fashionable throughout the sixteenth and well into the following century. From the mid-sixteenth century, the formal lines worn by the Spanish court prevailed. This was the age of the lavish, formal ruff, of rigid torsos, of padded hips and of the farthingale.

In the mid-seventeenth century, the essentially French costume of knee-length breeches, wide boots, extravagant, feather-trimmed hats and falling collars was adopted in England by the Cavaliers, the followers of Charles I during the Civil War. Their adversaries, the Puritans, wore less extravagant clothes which were similar to those of their Dutch contemporaries. Later in the seventeenth century a new costume became firmly established in England and France. This consisted of periwig and tricorn hat, tight breeches and stockings worn with a waistcoat and coat.

The tendency to depict costume realistically in stained glass culminated in the late eighteenth century with grandiose compositions showing female figures in fashionable *décolleté* dresses reminiscent of the style of Ancient Rome. Later, the Pre-Raphaelites went back to the Middle Ages, particularly the fifteenth century, as a source of design, in an effort to regain something of the pure pageantry of the past. This medievalist approach is exemplified by the George and Dragon window, executed by William Morris's firm *c.* 1862 from a design by Dante Gabriel Rossetti and now in the Victoria and Albert Museum, London.

In the abstract designs of much twentieth-century glass, there is no place for costumed figures, and in the relatively few figurative representations of biblical scenes, the characters are usually depicted in flowing robes which echo those of medieval narrative windows. Only occasionally are the figures dressed in contemporary costume—as in Hugh Easton's Battle of Britain window in Westminster Abbey. In generations to come it will be almost impossible to envisage twentieth-century dress from the scanty evidence in stained glass.

Wearing the Royal Air Force serge-blue uniforms of the Second World War, pilots are depicted in the Battle of Britain window in Westminster Abbey, detail below. Executed in 1947 by Hugh Easton, the window commemorates the airmen who died during the attack on Britain during the summer of 1940.

The exaggerated slashing of breeches into strips of material stretching from hip to knee was a style particularly popular with European soldiers during the sixteenth and seventeenth centuries. The youth, above, in a detail from a nineteenth-century window in Dover's Maison Dieu, wears a cuirass-shaped doublet over slashed breeches.

Ostentatious feather-trimmed hats, huge falling collars, doublets and breeches of buff leather and wide boots were worn by the Cavaliers during the English Civil War. William of Churton, above, a supporter of Charles I at the siege of Chester in 1645, is depicted in a contemporary Royalist window in St Chad's Church, Farndon, Cheshire.

The Changing Art of Portraiture

Portraiture, in the sense of a realistic likeness, was virtually non-existent in medieval art. In stained glass the simple linear draughtsmanship of early windows, partially determined by the dictates of the medium—that features should be distinguishable often from the towering heights of the clerestory—tended to make all faces boldly stylized. Contemporary religious attitudes also discouraged the realistic portrayal of individuals.

The Renaissance and the Reformation changed artistic attitudes generally and portraiture was no exception. The new doctrine of humanism heightened man's awareness of himself as an individual and this individuality was reflected in portrait painting. Great sixteenth- and seventeenth-century portrait artists, including Holbein the Younger and Rembrandt, achieved the expression of distinctive personalities in their work as well as the penetrating realism which had a far-reaching influence on the subsequent development of the art of portraiture.

In the Middle Ages the only portraits painted on stained glass were of bishops, other members of the clergy, royalty and donors of windows. Few if any were authentic likenesses, the figures depending in large part on costume, inscriptions and setting for identification. Not until the sixteenth century did stained-glass portraits with an obvious claim to likeness appear. Windows became increasingly imitative of oil paintings and while this precipitated the decline of the traditional art of stained glass it did allow greater realism and delicacy of treatment in stained-glass portraiture.

This change in technique, which involved painting with coloured enamels, coincided with the gradual suppression of the exclusively devotional motive of church windows. More in favour was the commemoration, through portraits, of living donors or recently deceased persons of suitable standing—kings, queens and nobles, warriors, clerics and merchants. The tendency towards illustrating secular subjects in stained glass was reinforced by the Reformation with its ban on certain religious images and the consequent circumscription of artists' work in places of worship.

The new realistic approach was heightened by the involvement of portraitists and painters in the preparation of designs for stained glass. The beautifully executed figures of King Charles I and his queen in Magdalen College, Oxford, are the work of the seventeenth-century portraitist, glass-painter and copyist of pictures Richard Greenbury. Similarly, the decidedly realistic figures of Isaac Newton, King George III and Francis Bacon, in an eighteenth-century window in the library of Trinity College, Cambridge, were designed by the Italian artist and engraver Giovanni Battista Cipriani.

The authenticity of portraits in glass of this period can often be corroborated by the existence of a picture of the subject in another medium. The likeness of the stained-glass portrait of Maximilian I, in a sixteenth-century window in St Sebald's, Nuremberg, for example, is supported by two oil paintings of Maximilian by Albrecht Dürer.

With the invention of the camera in the nineteenth century it became easier for the glazier to paint portraits in glass of his patron, of famous contemporary men and women and of dead relatives of the donors of windows. The practice of working from photographs has had some interesting as well as some rather dire consequences. In England, after the First World War, many memorial windows were made using the patriotic subject of St George. In some of these, the heroic face of St George is that of the soldier who is commemorated by the window. Or in a scene depicting, for example, St Anne with the young Virgin Mary, the face of St Anne is that of the departed lady in whose memory the window was commissioned. There is usually a startling difference in the handling of the painting of the head compared to the usual stereotyped style of the rest of the figure. The head would be the work of the "flesh painter"—the highest in the hierarchy of glass-painters in a commercial stained-glass firm—who worked from a photograph of the subject.

As recently as the 1950s this lamentable practice has been perpetrated in no less a place than Canterbury Cathedral. The window by Sir Ninian Comper in the west wall of the north transept shows the British Royal Family surrounded by famous people of the period, including Dr Geoffrey Fisher, Archbishop of Canterbury, and the Duke of Norfolk. The heads, which sit awkwardly on the bodies, are painted from photographs by a portraitist who had little understanding of the design scale or of the conventions proper to the portrayal of a head in the monumental medium of stained glass. This is an example of "photographic" portraiture in glass at its very worst.

Fortunately, since much post-war stained glass is abstract, such gross anomalies are rare. Even windows which honour donors and distinguished people are generally devoid of any attempt at realistic likenesses, and the art of portraiture is all but extinct in modern stained glass.

A fine example of the stylized portraiture of the fourteenth century, the knight, above, from a window in Tewkesbury Abbey, Gloucestershire, is identifiable by his clothes and coat of arms. The figure is one of four in the window which represent members of the De Clare and Le Despenser families, who held the manor of Tewkesbury.

The sixteenth-century stained-glass portrait of Emperor Maximilian in St Sebald's Church, Nuremberg, exemplifies the advance after the Middle Ages in the accurate portrayal of individuals. Designed in the manner of Albrecht Dürer and painted by Veit Hirsvogel, a member of a local family of glass artists, the likeness is supported by a drawing of Maximilian, right, by Dürer himself.

Louis XIII is portrayed in this secular panel in a seventeenth-century building, now the Municipal Library, in the historic French town of Troyes. The portrait, in the Renaissance style, is framed by exquisitely painted details of armour, helmets and weapons.

The heroic visage of the biblical figure Joshua, right, in a window in Hale Church, Hampshire, is in fact a commemorative portrait of an officer struck down in the Boer War. The window is an example of the commemoration of the dead by portraying the individual in a saintly or biblical context.

Twentieth-century photographic-style portraiture at its worst is epitomized by a window in Canterbury Cathedral, designed in 1954 by Sir Ninian Comper and donated by the Freemasons of Kent. It depicts figures of royal personages, officers of state and prelates connected with the coronations of 1937 and 1953. King George VI and Princess Elizabeth appear below.

Ruth and Boaz, ancestors of Christ, are depicted in the detail above from the Jesse window in St Stephen's, St Peter Port, Guernsey. The window was designed by William Morris and Philip Webb in 1864. Morris has successfully incorporated into the window, as the face of Ruth, a drawing of his daughter May, right, which exemplifies the romantic style characteristic of Pre-Raphaelite portraiture.

57

Tributes in Stained Glass

The Swiss hero William Tell, depicted in a sixteenth-century Swiss panel in the National Museum, Zurich, takes aim at the apple on his son's head. Lake Lucerne is in the distance.

Queen Victoria's Golden Jubilee of 1887 is commemorated in this panel from Great Malvern Priory, Worcestershire, showing the Queen and international dignitaries in Westminster Abbey.

Henry of Navarre, in a seventeenth-century panel in Troyes Library, watches with satisfaction as the Spanish troops are driven from Paris during the French Wars of Religion.

Isaac Jogues, a French missionary tortured by Canadian Indians, is shown with missing fingers in the twentieth-century panel by Paul Woodroffe in St Patrick's Cathedral, New York.

Queen Matilda of England sent her daughter a stained-glass window as a wedding present when she married in 1153. Such commemorative glass was, however, an exception during the early Middle Ages for, in addition to their function of letting in light, stained-glass windows were regarded merely as a means of appropriately completing the fabric of a new church or cathedral. The whole building commemorated the Christian Gospel and its stained glass did not specifically memorialize any more than did its sculpture, woodwork or frescoes.

The select few deemed worthy of remembrance in medieval stained glass included saints, particularly those to whom the church was dedicated, and founders or benefactors, who were portrayed as inconspicuously as possible. Occasionally, a window commemorated some outstanding people or events which were not actually depicted. The Great East window in Gloucester Cathedral, for example, is generally believed to be a memorial to the English victory at Crécy in 1346, although no scenes of warfare are illustrated.

With the growing power of the laity from the fifteenth century on, the emphasis in windows changed from celebrating the work of Christ and his saints to commemorating the piety, the good works or the self-importance of contemporary people—to such an extent that, by the sixteenth century, the religious element was often eclipsed. At this time, too, the Protestant abhorrence of religious imagery resulted in a significant increase in secular windows. Historical themes were widely adopted by glaziers, since they were considered relatively inoffensive. One of the most striking of all the historical panorama windows is that of the Relief of Leyden in St John's Church, Gouda. Besieged by the Spaniards in 1574, the citizens of Leyden, under the command of William of Orange, resorted to breaching the dykes and flooding the city so that provisions could be distributed by boat. Everything is depicted in minute detail, including the windmills and the provision-carrying boats.

The practice of donating commemorative windows prevailed throughout the seventeenth, eighteenth and nineteenth centuries and still flourishes today. The numerous examples range from windows in Washington Cathedral in honour of such distinguished figures as George Washington, Robert E. Lee and Florence Nightingale to a window designed by Marc Chagall in memory of a young girl drowned in a sailing accident. In Tudeley Church in Kent this window, a memorial to Sarah d'Avigdor Goldsmid, incorporates several apposite and evocative images, including the image of a girl on a red horse, which reflects Sarah's passion for riding and at the same time expresses a sense of calm and happiness.

Both the historical and the commemorative are embodied in a twentieth-century window in Penshurst Church, also in Kent. The window was glazed in 1970 to mark the village's eight hundred years of parish life. The first priest to be installed there was inducted by Thomas, Archbishop of Canterbury, only a few weeks before his martyrdom and the saint is shown standing by the church at the bottom of the window, while his assassination is depicted above. Groups of figures, coats of arms and many details of significance to the parishioners record the history of the locality.

In contrast, the massive stained-glass windows of Coventry Cathedral are devoid of specific commemorative reference. Their commissioning in the 1950s marked a return to the earliest object of stained glass—the completion of an architectural setting to the greater glory of God.

As a memorial to Dag Hammarskjöld, the former Secretary-General of the United Nations, Marc Chagall designed this window of blue fractured light and images associated with the theme of peace for the UN building in New York.

To commemorate the Battle of Britain and the members of the Royal Air Force who died in it, the window, right, in Westminster Abbey, designed by Hugh Easton and installed in 1947, incorporates the badges of sixty-eight squadrons.

The Art and the Artist

St Luke, the patron saint of artists and physicians, was believed to have been a painter and to have painted a portrait of the Virgin. This idea, dating from the sixth century, inspired paintings and stained glass in which the Evangelist was depicted at work in his studio. The detail above of a fifteenth-century window from the Jakobskirche, Straubing, shows the donation of one of St Luke's paintings to St Pulcheria, a fifth-century Byzantine empress.

The concept of the great artist, which rarely embraced the glazier, evolved during the Renaissance, the age which heralded the degeneration of stained glass. Pre-Renaissance sculptors, glaziers and painters, who were considered, and considered themselves, craftsmen, were on a professional par with clothiers, shoemakers, bakers and other tradesmen. Art, indivisible from craft, was of no special significance and artists, who rarely signed their works, existed within a tradition of artistic self-effacement. They were merely servants of the Church. Civic and royal patronage was not common until the fourteenth century. And then, when a favoured artist was given a position at court, his success often depended more upon his talent to amuse the king than on his creative ability. The humble status of the artist changed, however, as a result of the Renaissance's emphasis upon humanistic ideals. Credited with divine inspiration and lionized by the enlightened élite, artists became the equal of poets, scientists, scholars and philosophers.

The contrast between the Renaissance cult of individuality and the medieval tradition of anonymity resulted in a critical underestimation and depersonalization of medieval art. Because of their literal anonymity, medieval works of art, including stained glass, have been accused of artistic uniformity. However, rather than being uniform expressions of superstitious piety, medieval works of art, from stained-glass windows to frescoes, are distinguished by different degrees of violence, humour, lyricism or devoutness, and in this way reflect the otherwise unknown personalities of their creators. Style can be as distinctive as content and the hand of the same master glazier is detected through such obvious characteristics in his work as the large medallions overlapping the mullions in Augsburg and Ulm cathedrals or the convoluted ribbon frame in windows in Ulm and Regensburg.

Although the title of glass-maker or glazier is affixed to a multitude of names in medieval documents, these mysterious artisans can rarely be credited with specific windows and may even have been the glaziers of clear glass windows. Rare examples of self-disclosure in the earlier Middle Ages are the self-portrait of the twelfth-century German glazier Gerlachus, in a panel which is now in Münster Landesmuseum, and the signature of Clément of Chartres, in a thirteenth-century window in Rouen Cathedral.

By the sixteenth century, however, glaziers had emerged from obscurity. Engrand le Prince in France,

SYMBOLIC SIGNATURES

Rare in early stained glass, glaziers' symbols, the way many signed their work, proliferated in the nineteenth century. The earliest signature in English glass dates from the late fourteenth century, when Thomas of Oxford depicted himself with a scroll inscribed *Thomas maker of this glass* in Latin. In the fifteenth century, John Thornton inserted his monogram and the date in his Great East window in York Minster. Nominal puns of nineteenth-century glaziers and firms include the white friar of Messrs Powell of Whitefriars, Christopher Webb's St Christopher and the sign of Alfred Bell, founder of Clayton and Bell. The Victorian artist Kempe signed himself with a wheatsheaf, an emblem borrowed from his coat of arms.

Thomas of Oxford
Winchester College

John Thornton
York Minster

Charles Eamer Kempe

Messrs Powell of Whitefriars

Goddard and Gibbs

Alfred Bell

Christopher Webb

Sir Ninian Comper

Galyon Hone and Dirck Vellert in England and Valentin Busch in Alsace were among those acclaimed as outstanding stained-glass artists. Unfortunately, this new-found publicity was, in a sense, too late. The Renaissance, which had elevated the position of the artist, gradually threatened and undermined stained glass as an art form. Stained glass became increasingly subservient to painting by trying, unsuccessfully, to imitate its realism and its three-dimensional, illusionistic space. The crucial dependency of stained glass upon transmitted light meant that it was significantly different from painting and the failure of the stained-glass artist to recognize this contributed to its debasement.

The incompatibility of glass with the important artistic changes of the Renaissance was not obvious during the fifteenth and sixteenth centuries and at first the representation of reality in windows seemed a liberation from the constraints of the two-dimensional medieval style. Although there were isolated examples of early stained glass by painters —by Duccio in the late thirteenth century and by Andrea di Firenzi in the fourteenth century—it was not until the fifteenth century that "great artists" combined their talents to decorate one building. Leading painters and sculptors of the early Italian Renaissance were responsible for the outstanding beauty and exhilarating brilliance of the windows of Florence Cathedral. The sculptor Donatello and the painters Andrea del Castagno and Paolo Uccello were perhaps more concerned to honour Brunelleschi's dome than to explore a medieval art form, but Lorenzo Ghiberti, a sculptor who was sympathetic to the Gothic tradition, involved himself completely with the medium.

In about 1500 the painters of northern Europe began to assimilate the current ideas of Italian art and to integrate them with the existing northern style of late Gothic. The German painter and engraver Albrecht Dürer travelled and worked in Italy, where he acquired a scientific attitude to art and a new respect for the status of the artist. Dürer and his famous pupils Hans Baldung Grien and Hans von Kulmbach designed windows and helped to promote the new realism in stained glass. Sixteenth-century glaziers, captivated, too, by the illusionistic abilities of the fifteenth-century Flemish painters Jan van Eyck and Rogier van der Weyden, produced windows with increasingly meticulous landscapes and interiors. As a result of these influences detail became the glazier's overriding obsession—an obsession which detracted from the long-forgotten abstract qualities of stained glass.

The very concept of stained-glass art had radically changed. The medieval master glazier—master not only of his craft but also of his design—had disappeared and with him the principle of using glass as a medium in its own right —as a surface for decorative, two-dimensional picture-making. This tradition had been superseded by realistic pictorial representation, in which lead-work was considered

The glittering *occhio*, above, in Florence Cathedral, demonstrates the adroitness with which the Florentine artist Uccello worked in stained glass. This Nativity window is distinguished by its flat, brilliant colour in contrast to the painting, left, commonly attributed to Uccello, in which the Magi worship Christ against an illusionistic spatial background of sombre brown.

The name of Aldegrever, the sixteenth-century German engraver, is clearly written on the yellow cloak, right, in a sixteenth-century choir window in Ste Foy Church, Conches. But this apparent proof of authorship is misleading. This window, and the others in Ste Foy's choir, were glazed by Romain Buron, a pupil of Engrand le Prince. The reference to Aldegrever is merely Buron's acknowledgement of the engraver's influence.

A unique example of a French thirteenth-century signature, *Clément glazier of Chartres*, is inscribed in Latin, left, in an ambulatory window in Rouen Cathedral. The design of the window itself, and of those surrounding it, however, bears little resemblance to those of Chartres and Clément's work is known to exist only at Rouen.

The Art and the Artist

a necessary evil rather than an integral part of the composition. No longer could glaziers be trusted with the design or the composition of a window—apart from wrestling with the problem of the unwanted black lead-lines. Instead they were commissioned to copy the cartoons of painters.

Influenced by the prevailing style of Neo-Classicism, the art of stained glass reached its nadir in the eighteenth century, as exemplified by the pasty, moralistic figures in the stained glass of Sir Joshua Reynolds. The academic imitation of Classical images became the target for the nineteenth-century Gothic Revivalists, but, despite the Gothicists' good intentions of rescuing stained glass from its academic trough and of overthrowing its lifeless antique images, the art foundered.

One such unsuccessful rescue attempt was the establishment, with strong government support, of a stained-glass studio at the Sèvres porcelain factory in France. Pottery-painters, skilled in the use of enamels, were employed to execute the designs of such artists as Eugène Delacroix and Jean Ingres. A similar experiment in Germany, inspired by Ludwig I of Bavaria, led to the mass-production, in Munich workshops, of equally mawkish windows.

Stained glass was finally saved, in the second half of the century, from the suffocating embrace of sentimentality by the Pre-Raphaelites. Like their predecessors, the Pre-Raphaelite painters were passionate medievalists, but they avoided the depressed derivative style of the Gothic Revivalists. Importance of symbolic content, observation of nature and a concern for good craftsmanship, including a proper regard for the lead-line as an element of design, were Pre-Raphaelite principles which William Morris and Edward Burne-Jones applied to stained glass, thus restoring to it its individuality and translucence.

The characteristics of early glass—simplified, two-dimensional form and flat, pure colour—are closely related to the concerns of twentieth-century abstract painting. In France particularly, artists such as Braque, Léger, Matisse and Chagall have exercised a radical influence on stained glass. Both Braque, a founder of Cubism, and Léger, a painter who extended Braque's Cubism to the world of machines, adapted their artistic preoccupations to the demands of stained-glass windows. Instead of the analytical studies of still life, painted in subdued colours, Braque's windows in the Chapel of St Dominique, Varangeville, depict bold, bright, flat shapes. Léger, in his windows for the Church of the Sacred Heart, Audincourt, abandoned the geometric modern machinery and bovine robot figures of his paintings to produce large organic forms interwoven with basic Christian symbolism. Simplicity of form and unrealistic colour distinguish both the paintings and the stained glass of Henri Matisse. In the Chapel of the Rosary of the Dominican nuns at Vence, his windows of radiant clarity depict floral patterns, in brightly coloured unpainted glass, which, when illuminated by strong sunlight, are repeated on the floor of the chapel.

The visionary imagery of Chagall's paintings is immediately recognizable in his stained-glass windows in Assy, Metz, Jerusalem, Zurich, Tudeley and New York. Unlike Matisse, Chagall applied paint to the surface of the glass, but his windows lose nothing of their brilliance and his leading cleverly emphasizes the rhythms of the figures, the wheels of light and the strange beasts which sweep across his ethereal, predominantly blue expanses of glass.

Conversely, Georges Rouault, a painter who trained as a glazier, designing windows for Assy Church, consciously imitates the appearance of medieval windows as an expressionistic device in his paintings. Fired by moral and religious beliefs, he depicts depraved or tortured figures,

The eclectic eighteenth-century painter Sir Joshua Reynolds was an undistinguished stained-glass designer. The vivacity and the accuracy of detail, for example, in his portrait of the actress Mrs Abington, right, are missing from Justice and Prudence, left, two of the Virtues which he designed for New College Chapel, Oxford. Poised beneath perfunctory canopies, these opaque women obscure the qualities they were intended to embody. The windows were painted in enamel by Thomas Jervais, who did not understand that stained glass must be translucent.

painted in deep, violent colour and outlined with heavy black lines. Although Rouault might seem to be uniting two traditionally incompatible art forms, he merely feeds off the seductive archaism of stained glass.

Whereas in previous centuries the intervention of painters and the subsequent attempt of glaziers to imitate painting led to a decline and debasement of the traditional art, in the twentieth century artists have had a radical, invigorating effect on stained glass and have helped to reinstate it as an art form in its own right. Successful twentieth-century stained glass does not depend upon medieval imagery or style, but it has, to a large degree, been revived by the modern painter's affinity with the medieval principles of stained-glass design.

Distinguished by its dream-like clarity and extravagant, artificial colour, the window below, in Prague Cathedral, was designed by the Czech Art Nouveau artist Alphonse Mucha. Merging with a radiant, golden centre which shows the Bohemian prince Wenceslas with his grandmother, the border of greenish blue and violet incorporates decadent *fin de siècle* beauties reminiscent of the curvaceous figure, right, of the actress Sarah Bernhardt dressed as Lorenzo de Medici in one of Mucha's posters.

A twentieth-century Hungarian painter who was aware of the expressive and dynamic qualities of stained glass, Ervin Bossanyi designed the windows for the south choir of Canterbury Cathedral. The primitivism of folk art, apparent in his painting, below, is imbued with symbolism in his Peace window, bottom. The flower offered to Christ by children of many races is made of faceted glass and flashes white rays, symbolizing peace, when caught by the sunlight.

THE ELEVENTH AND TWELFTH CENTURIES
The Cathedral Age

The tenth century was the watershed of the Middle Ages. Behind lay five hundred years of barbaric decadence which followed the fall of the Roman Empire. Ahead lay a new European civilization.

In the darkest hour before this dawn, however, Western Christendom suffered more from invading hordes than it had at any time in the five preceding centuries. Muslims struck at the heart of Europe from the south, Vikings from the north and west, and Hungarians and Slavs from the east. Yet even then the vital foundation was being laid on which a bright future was to be built—a growing population, recovering at last from the vast losses resulting from the appalling plague of 742. With the coming of a more peaceful era, which also coincided with an improving climate, this population explosion brought about a revival in agriculture, which was of great benefit to feudal landowners and to the Church. The accompanying commercial expansion was even more remarkable, and it created a new, wealthy and eventually powerful class in society—the merchants.

Such were the material advances which made possible the eventual flowering of medieval culture. The form it took was decided by the fact that this was Christendom. Through the darkest of centuries the Church, whatever its weaknesses, had not lost its influence and the faithful had not lost their faith. In the eleventh and twelfth centuries, unbelief was totally alien to the medieval mind. Without belief in God, his angels, his saints and his Church what hope would man have, constantly besieged as he was by the Devil and his cohorts of demons? In these two centuries, the Church possessed more authority and was a more integral part of everyone's life than at any time since.

As villages and towns grew larger and more affluent, the boom in church building began; it was to last for three hundred years, until the middle of the fourteenth century. During that period, thousands of parish churches and eighty cathedrals were built in western Europe. Another factor contributing to this building boom was that the year AD 1000 had been confidently predicted as the date for the end of the world. When this proved wrong, the relief was unbounded and the effect striking. Ralph Glaber, a monk of St Bénigne in Dijon, described how "towards the third year after the year one thousand" the great rebuilding of minsters, cathedrals and village churches began. "Christian people vied with one another in erecting the fairest and richest churches. It was as if the whole world with one accord, casting off its ancient rags, was clothing itself anew in a white robe of churches." The cathedral became the status symbol of wealthy towns, gradually eclipsing the abbey as the main centre of religious and artistic activity. Here, too, in the vast naves, merchants congregated and business transactions were carried out. Many cathedrals were also centres of learning, having schools attached to them, as at Chartres. From these schools the first universities were to evolve in the twelfth century.

Genuine religious zeal, as well as a certain amount of pressure from the Church, ensured that there was no lack of money. Kings, princes, barons, knights, squires, merchants and clerics competed with each other in showering money on their churches, even in their wills, in the hope that thereby they would find favour with God in their lifetimes and their souls would find repose in death. Rich and poor gave in the same hope. Thus devotion to God combined with the new affluence to create the Cathedral Age—the inaugural age of stained glass.

Most of the cathedrals built in the eleventh and in much of the twelfth century were Romanesque. This was a powerful style of architecture based on Roman traditions, but influenced by Byzantium, the Near East and Asia. Characteristically, the Romanesque church had rounded arches and massive walls, which, because they were load-bearing, could not be weakened by being broken up with large expanses of window. The style of the Romanesque glazier was, therefore, necessarily different from that of the following generations of artists, who worked within the framework of the large windows of the Gothic cathedrals that were built in the late twelfth and thirteenth centuries.

The most popular types of window from this early period were the medallion window and the figure window. In the medallion windows, scenes from the Old and New Testaments or the lives of the saints were depicted. They were usually placed along the aisles where they could easily be seen, and they eschewed subtlety so that there should be no mistaking their message. Square or circular iron frames enclosed each medallion scene. The borders surrounding the pictures were exceptionally broad, some up to one-sixth of the window's total breadth.

Figure windows usually showed a single monumental figure in an unlikely pose, with heavy features and an emphatic gesture. They often occupied the clerestory and even at that height the figures had great impact because of their size. The so-called five prophets in Augsburg Cathedral are the oldest such windows, and they are among the greatest art treasures of Germany. In England, a few remain of the eighty-four figures in Canterbury Cathedral which depicted the genealogy of Christ. The most striking figure window is, however, the mid-twelfth-century masterpiece in Chartres Cathedral, Notre Dame de la Belle Verrière, Our Lady of the Beautiful Glass.

Nowhere, even when the cult of the Virgin was at its height in the late Middle Ages, was the Virgin Mary more revered than at Chartres. According to legend, the first cathedral was built above a Druid grotto dating from about 100 BC and dedicated to a *virgo paritura*, a virgin giving birth. The Blessed Virgin herself was said to have written, in Hebrew, to the martyrs who evangelized Chartres, agreeing to her coronation as the church's queen. The cult of the Virgin at Chartres was given great impetus in the ninth century, when, in 876, Charles the Bald, Charlemagne's grandson, gave to the cathedral the *palladium*, the tunic reputed to have been worn by the Virgin at the birth of Christ. This most sacred of relics, together with La Belle Verrière, survived the fire of 1194 which destroyed the Romanesque cathedral. The people of Chartres interpreted these miracles as a sign that while the Virgin Mother, by allowing the cathedral to be destroyed, had indicated her wish for a larger and more magnificent cathedral, she had, by saving the relic, shown her love for the faithful.

When the cathedral was rebuilt in magnificent style, the figure of Notre Dame de la Belle Verrière was installed in the choir, where it is now the centrepiece of a large window, surrounded by thirteenth-century angels. It portrays a seven-foot-tall enthroned Virgin with the Christ Child on her lap, his right hand raised in blessing. His left hand holds a book, showing a quotation from *Isaiah*: "Every valley shall be exalted." The ethereal quality of the colours of medieval glass has never been approached since, and it is the unbelievably luminous blue, set off by ruby and rose, that makes La Belle Verrière so overwhelming.

Romanesque cathedrals seemed particularly prone to being burned down. Canterbury, for example, went up in flames in 1174, Chartres in 1194, while Strasbourg in 1176 was burned down for the fourth time in one hundred years. Other cathedrals collapsed or were replaced by larger buildings, and with changing tastes the Gothic style of architecture began to emerge in northern France, with dramatic effect on the art of stained glass.

Appropriately, the venerated stained-glass image of Virgin and Child, known as Notre Dame de la Belle Verrière, is in Chartres Cathedral, which is traditionally associated with the glorification of the Virgin. The two sacred figures, surrounded by thirteenth-century angels, are depicted in four panels in the centre of this window, which miraculously survived the great fire of 1194.

64

ELEVENTH-CENTURY AND TWELFTH-CENTURY GERMANY
The World's Oldest Windows

Stained glass is fragile and man and nature are destructive. Fire, war, revolutions, Puritans, philistines, restorers and vandals have all taken their toll. It is perhaps, therefore, better to be thankful that against all these odds some stained glass has survived from the eleventh and twelfth centuries than to mourn the loss of so much.

German cathedrals, however, have suffered grievously. For example, a Romanesque cathedral was built at Speyer between 1030 and 1061 and it and subsequent rebuildings were destroyed by fire or war in 1137, 1159, 1289, 1689, 1794 and during the Second World War. But Germany has the distinction of having preserved the oldest complete windows in the world—in the cathedral in the ancient town of Augsburg, which was founded by the Romans in the first century AD.

These windows, glazed towards the end of the eleventh century, portray five Old Testament figures—Moses, David, Daniel, Hosea and Jonas—all that remain of a longer series. They are probably in their original position in the clerestory of the nave, but the frames in which they are fitted are later and perhaps smaller, as several of the figures seem to be hemmed in and others seem truncated. They are still being restored and some glass, for example parts of the hats, has been replaced.

Apart from the windows being unique because of their age, the figures, which are Romanesque in style, are monumental in size and impressive in themselves. They are stern Old Testament characters, more than eight feet tall, who gaze piercingly ahead of them in spite of their squints. The impact of their expressions is all the greater because their faces are disproportionately large. Each prophet holds in one hand a scroll with a Latin inscription. On their splayed-out feet they wear the highly stylized, pointed footwear of medieval knights.

The colours in these windows are very different from the colours of twelfth-century stained glass in England and France. Instead of luminous blues and rubies, the Augsburg figures are predominantly brown, gold, yellow, green and wine, and what little blue is used is a murky grey. These were the colours that predominated in many German churches, both in the Romanesque period and beyond.

The Augsburg figures are boldly designed and, despite their early date, are certainly not primitive; they are the work of skilled, experienced and inspired stained-glass artists. This skill can be traced back to the Abbey of Tegernsee, where there was a flourishing stained-glass workshop. The monks who went from Tegernsee to Augsburg in the eleventh century undoubtedly took their techniques with them. The abbey's influence was widespread throughout Bavaria and farther west. Two other windows still exist which have a style similar to that of the Augsburg windows—a madonna from Flums, in northeast Switzerland, which is now in the Swiss Museum in Zurich, and a Timotheus window from Neuweiler in Alsace, which is now in the Cluny Museum in Paris.

It is difficult to overestimate the contribution made by the abbeys and their monks to the arts of the Romanesque period; the style is largely their creation. Their surge of creativity was the result of the reforming zeal of strong abbots, who were determined to rescue the monks from their secular or Sybaritic activities. The energies they had previously dissipated were now turned to the arts. This was notably so at the Benedictine Abbey of Cluny, whose influence became of primary importance throughout Europe. In Germany it was the Benedictine Abbey of Hirsau, in the Black Forest, which, under the reforming Abbot William, became the leading artistic centre of the Cluniac monasteries, and had a decisive influence on the development of Romanesque art in Germany. The Abbey Church of SS Peter and Paul was the prototype of German Romanesque style, and its famous illustrated manuscripts established the Hirsau school of miniatures.

There is a direct relationship of style between the Augsburg figures and those of the Hirsau miniatures. Indeed, all Romanesque architecture and other visual arts are shaped by common Roman and Byzantine strands. In this instance, stained glass influenced painting, but curiously the later Hirsau miniatures are more wooden and awkward than the Augsburg figures.

The Hirsau miniatures also provide an example of how painting influenced stained glass. For the education of virgins in ways of pleasing "the Heavenly Bridegroom", the monk Conrad of Hirsau produced a primer called *Speculum virginum* (Mirror of the virgin). The frontispiece of this twelfth-century manuscript is a picture tracing Christ's descent from the royal line of David. This is the Tree of Jesse theme, the subject of innumerable and beautiful stained-glass windows in later centuries, but first making its appearance in manuscripts inspired by the development of the cult of the Virgin in the twelfth century.

It is perhaps ironic that the artistic skills spread by the monasteries found greatest expression in the cathedrals of the thirteenth century, which soon outdid in splendour the vast abbey churches of the past. For even during their most morally decadent periods the abbeys were powerful and rich, and their churches reflected their status. The cathedrals, by comparison, were often poor and small. But the positions began to be reversed when, during the twelfth century, the major towns—the cathedral towns—grew wealthier and more powerful, and became the real political, commercial and religious centres. The rivalry between cathedral and abbey was often fierce, but to this day the genius of the medieval craftsman monk is enshrined in many a cathedral.

Germany stayed wedded to the Romanesque tradition long after France and England had turned to the Gothic style. But in one respect a notable German must be considered an innovator; his Christian name was Gerlachus; his surname is not known. In the bottom panel of his mid-twelfth-century Moses window (now in the Münster Landesmuseum) he includes the image of himself at work, the first self-advertisement by a stained-glass artist.

Strongly influenced by Byzantine art and also by the Augsburg prophet windows, the illuminated manuscripts done by the monks of Hirsau Abbey in the Black Forest exemplify the new style of painting which evolved in twelfth-century Germany. This Tree of Jesse, the frontispiece of *Speculum virginum* (Mirror of the virgin) is unusual in that it traces Christ's ancestry back to Boaz, the grandfather of Jesse, who is depicted at the bottom of the tree. Other unusual features are the six Oriental-looking maidens, who personify the virtues, and the leaf formation springing from Christ's head which symbolizes the seven gifts of the Holy Ghost. The *Speculum* was written in the form of a dialogue between the presbyter, Peregrinus, and the virgin, Theodora, who are illustrated in the lower roundels.

Staring with wide-eyed, almost threatening intensity and resplendent in their richly coloured apparel, the Old Testament figures, known as the five prophets, in Augsburg Cathedral are the oldest complete stained-glass windows in the world. They were glazed in the late eleventh century. Three of the windows are shown here: from left to right, Hosea, King David and Daniel.

Self-advertisement and religious imagery are combined in this panel by the Rhenish stained-glass artist Gerlachus. The only known artist amidst a plethora of anonymous twelfth-century master glaziers, Gerlachus depicts himself at the bottom of the panel. The inscription, a punning allusion to his work, invokes God, the king of kings, to be gracious with his gift of light to the artist. In the scene above him, God, shown with a cruciform halo, the symbol of divinity, speaks to Moses from the middle of the burning bush. Moses' crook has turned into a serpent, a miraculous sign of God's presence.

TWELFTH-CENTURY FRANCE

The Dawn of the Gothic Era

Spiritual aspiration is conveyed by the upturned faces and elongated forms of the Virgin and six apostles who witness Christ's Ascension in this twelfth-century stained glass in Le Mans Cathedral. The figure of Christ, to whom they look, is missing. These panels, together with those below it, which depict the remaining six apostles, were glazed in about 1145 and are among the earliest examples of French stained glass.

Were any one man to be called "the father of Gothic architecture" it must be the man who was also called "the father of the French monarchy"—Suger, who, from 1122 to 1151, was the abbot of St Denis, near Paris. The date that Gothic architecture was born might be given as June 11, 1144, the day that Suger's beautiful creation, the abbey church of St Denis, was consecrated in the presence of King Louis VII, the Queen, archbishops, bishops and abbots, many of whom returned home determined to imitate Suger's ideas.

Suger was a remarkable man. Lowly born, he walked with kings. At school he met Louis VI (Louis the Fat) and became a lifelong friend and adviser. He also served Louis VII, unhappy husband of Eleanor of Aquitaine, and he governed France while Louis was away on the Second Crusade. He was a small man, who dreamed grand and magnificent dreams. As head of the royal abbey of St Denis, Suger had the power and wealth to put these dreams into effect, for the greater glory of God, of the French monarchy and of himself.

Five years after he was made abbot, Suger set about the reform of the abbey, which had become materialistic and morally slack. But he had no intention of making it a place only for monks. Unlike St Bernard of Clairvaux, the strict Cistercian, Suger wanted to welcome as many of the laity as possible to the abbey, with its relics of St Denis, the patron saint of France. Indeed, one of the reasons he gave for embarking on building a larger abbey, in about 1135, was to accommodate even greater crowds. Again unlike St Bernard, who fulminated against ostentation in churches where "beauty is more admired than sanctity is revered", Suger believed that only the best objects that man could create were worthy of a house of God.

Suger obviously revelled in looking at beautiful things and he was no dilettante. His involvement in the new St Denis was total and practical. In the detailed record he kept of the rebuilding, there is a revealing account of how he handled the problem of finding beams long enough for the new roof—since all the foresters had sworn that they could not find any tall trees in the area. One morning at dawn, he called his carpenters together and—to the great amusement of the foresters—set off with them to fight a way through the undergrowth of the forest "with the courage of faith". By nine o'clock his faith had been rewarded; they had found the twelve tall trees they needed.

It was Suger himself who devised the subjects for the many new stained-glass windows and arranged for them to be glazed "by the exquisite hands of many masters from different regions". The windows were a major element in Suger's plan, for, as he made clear in his voluminous writings, he was deeply concerned with the symbolic and spiritual qualities of light. In building a church which would be "pervaded by the wonderful and uninterrupted light of most radiant windows" his aim was "to illumine men's minds so that they may travel through it to an apprehension of God's light". In trying to achieve this he was helped by the technical innovations of the new style of architecture, later to be known as Gothic, which made it possible for a great proportion of wall space to be taken up with glass. Proud of his creation, it is little wonder that Suger had himself portrayed in one of the windows—in the act of giving a window.

The windows of St Denis were, unfortunately, largely destroyed in 1793 during the French Revolution. Some of these were restored by the French art historian Viollet-le-Duc in 1848. Fragments and entire windows are also to be found in churches and collections throughout Europe.

Suger's abbey rather spectacularly marked the beginning of a new period of architecture and of stained glass. But it did not result in the immediate death of Romanesque, not

GOTHIC SPLENDOUR

St Denis, Abbé Suger's Gothic masterpiece, was one of the most ornate churches of its time. Inspired by the fifth-century writer Dionysius, who held that visible things mirror the light of God, Suger filled his church with jewelled artifacts and stained glass, the contemplation of which he regarded as a source of divine inspiration.

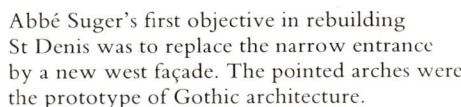

Abbé Suger's first objective in rebuilding St Denis was to replace the narrow entrance by a new west façade. The pointed arches were the prototype of Gothic architecture.

In the Jesse Tree window, one of the "splendid variety of new windows" which Suger commissioned for the abbey church, there is a portrait of Suger presenting the window.

even in France. Only a little Romanesque glass has survived in French cathedrals, but it is of exceptional beauty. One of the earliest windows was that depicting the Ascension in Le Mans Cathedral, of which four panels still exist. A gracefully attenuated Virgin, her blue robes glowing against a red background, looks to the ascending Jesus (now missing from the window). On either side, against a blue background, a trio of apostles gazes upwards; below, on alternate red and blue backgrounds, to which their predominantly yellow and green draperies provide strong contrast, are six more apostles, their faces upturned. The simplicity and elegance of the figures clearly show Byzantine influence, but emotions are depicted in a traditionally Western manner. Compared with the Augsburg prophets, the Le Mans apostles are full of animation.

The outstanding example of French Romanesque glass is the large Crucifixion window, of about 1162, in Poitiers. A blue-haired Christ is portrayed on a red crucifix in a typical Byzantine pose—head to one side, trunk inclined from the hips. Above the central Crucifixion tableau there is a small Ascension scene, in which the groups of disciples and the Virgin are reminiscent of the Le Mans figures.

A later stage in the development of French Romanesque glass is to be seen in the nave of Angers Cathedral. The subjects include the death of the Virgin, the life of St Catherine and the martyrdom of St Vincent. The wide stylized decorative borders are similar to those in Poitiers, but the figures are less elongated, their faces gentler and the folds of their garments more flowing.

The future of French stained glass, however, lay not in Romanesque, but in the new style which in St Denis was Abbé Suger's monument. As the year 1200 passed without the world being overwhelmed by yet another predicted Apocalypse, Europe, and particularly France, was entering the first golden age of stained glass.

The unforgettable beauty of the Poitiers Crucifixion window, right, is created by the graceful elegance of the figures and the sensitivity and often unconventional use of colour—notably the head of Christ with blue hair and the bright red cross. On either side of the cross stand the two soldiers with spear and sponge, whose aggressive postures contrast with the gentle, curved figures of the Virgin and St John. Equally expressive is the upper half of the window, in which the rapt apostles appear to be lifted upwards towards the swirling angels who surround the resurrected Christ. Symbolic figures of the sun and the moon appear as spectators in the foliaged border.

TWELFTH-CENTURY ENGLAND

Marriage of Two Cultures

Martyrdom, fire and war—such were the historic events, and all in the course of a century, that brought about the architectural transformation of Canterbury Cathedral from Saxon to Romanesque and, eventually, to the Gothic building it basically is today. There was a church at Canterbury in Roman times. About AD 600, it was rededicated by St Augustine, who was sent by Pope Gregory I to convert England to Christianity.

Soon after the Norman Conquest all of the old building was pulled down and Lanfranc, the first Norman archbishop, erected a new cathedral in the space of seven years. In style it was nothing more than a Norman cathedral—a Norman cathedral set down in Kent. Twenty years later, Anselm, Lanfranc's successor, replaced it with a building twice as large, and most lavish in its stained glass and wall paintings. That was the cathedral in which Archbishop Thomas Becket was murdered, providing Canterbury with a martyr who made it one of the major places of pilgrimage in Western Christendom. In 1174, four years after Becket's death and a year after his canonization, the choir was gutted by fire.

A Frenchman, William of Sens, was chosen to rebuild the cathedral and he made it much taller, and the choir even longer by adding on the Trinity Chapel in honour of St Thomas. The style he adopted was the new post-St Denis Gothic, already greatly in vogue in the Ile de France, but alien to England (even though there was already some indigenous Gothic architecture, notably at Wells). William of Sens, after being badly hurt by falling off scaffolding, was succeeded by William the Englishman, who was equally French in his outlook. In 1184, only ten years after the fire,

In 1174, the east end of Canterbury Cathedral, above, was damaged by fire and the French architect William of Sens, who was employed to rebuild it, brought the Gothic style to England. In 1178, William was injured and the work, including the Trinity Chapel, repository of Becket's shrine, and the Corona Chapel, built to house the saint's scalp, was completed in the same style by William the Englishman.

The theme of England's only surviving twelfth-century rose window, in the northeast transept of Canterbury, is the Law and the Prophets. The outer quatrefoil is modern, but the central circle, right, dates from *c.* 1178. Beneath arches Moses and a blindfolded figure, representing the Synagogue, hold the symbols of the Law. Around them, personified as women, are the four virtues with their appropriate emblems.

the rebuilding of the cathedral was virtually completed.

The glaziers were undoubtedly as active, energetic and determined as the masons. Who was responsible for the subject matter and style of the stained-glass windows is argued about endlessly and fruitlessly. What is incontrovertible, however, is the striking quality, in subject matter and execution, of the Canterbury glass.

The earliest glass, in the north rose window, seems to have been completed by 1178. Its subject is the Old Dispensation. In the centre square are Moses, with the tablets of stone, and the figure of a blindfolded woman, representing the Synagogue, holding the tablets of the Law. In the surrounding four triangular panels are the cardinal virtues, Justice with scales, Fortitude with a sword, Prudence holding doves and a dragon serpent and Temperance with a torch of fire and a bowl of water. Around them are the four major prophets—Isaiah, Jeremiah, Ezekiel and Daniel. The rest of the glass in the rose was added later. In the south rose window the delicate background of foliage is also the original, early glass, but the figures are Victorian.

It is, however, the great figures of the genealogical windows that are most arresting. They depict the ancestors of Christ and were originally designed to glaze the clerestory. There must once have been eighty-four figures. Of those which survive, only nine figures remain in the clerestory windows. The others are in the west window of the nave and the southwest and northeast transepts. Methuselah is a remarkable portrait in its stylized power, as are the portraits of the Patriarch Jared and of Adam.

The oldest stained glass in England is not in Canterbury,

but in York Minster, whose archbishops were long the rivals of Canterbury's for supremacy among the English sees. A fragment of a Jesse Tree in the minster probably goes back to 1150—and even that early date makes it a hundred years later than the Augsburg prophets. Another panel of twelfth-century glass, now incongruously placed in the vast thirteenth-century grisaille window known as the Five Sisters, shows Daniel in the lions' den.

The story of the minster itself begins in 627, when it was founded by Edwin, King of Northumbria, shortly after his conversion to Christianity. The first building was wooden. It was soon rebuilt in stone, and in the seventh century it was repaired by Archbishop Wilfrid, who put in glass to keep out the birds and the rain. His minster burned down in 1069. It was then rebuilt by Archbishop Thomas of Bayeux, and in the twelfth century it was partly rebuilt by Archbishop Roger of Pont l'Evêque. The minster's architects, unlike those of Canterbury, were late in adopting the Gothic style, but when they did, during the rebuilding from the thirteenth to the fifteenth centuries, all traces of the Romanesque building disappeared. The earliest stained glass fared slightly better, although two small panels, as well as some borders, now in the clerestory windows of the nave, are indeed little enough.

There is a striking resemblance between twelfth-century English and French stained glass. The similarities with Chartres and St Denis are most marked; both had glass workshops which influenced the style of windows in France and England, notably in Canterbury and York. The Tree of Jesse fragment in York Minster, for example, can be matched by Jesse panels in St Denis and in Chartres. There is no irrefutable evidence, but it seems likely that after the Norman Conquest, French glaziers came to England to glaze the windows in the great Norman cathedrals that were being built.

Twelfth-century stained glass was not, however, a national art. It was the art of a religion, and, moreover, it was still the art of one Church. The emergence of pronounced national and regional styles had yet to come.

The earliest surviving glass in England is thought to be this panel in a nave window in York Minster. It shows what is believed to be a king entwined in a branch of a Jesse Tree. Its similarity to contemporary panels at Chartres and St Denis suggests that it was glazed in the mid-twelfth century.

Windows illustrating the ancestry of Christ originally formed a coherent scheme around the choir clerestory of Canterbury Cathedral. In one of the nine windows that remain in the clerestory, Shem, son of Noah, far left, is depicted in the powerful style characteristic of twelfth-century work. Adam after his expulsion from the Garden of Eden, left, belongs to the same series, but the panel has been transferred to the west window.

THE THIRTEENTH CENTURY

The Age of Gothic Art

Gothic architecture, conceived by Abbé Suger at St Denis in the twelfth century, swept through western Europe in the thirteenth century with the speed of the plague. The number of Gothic cathedrals which were begun, completed or were in the process of being built during this period was staggering. France led the way, and her Gothic masterpieces included Chartres, Laon, Amiens, Bourges, Notre Dame de Paris, Reims and Rouen. Salisbury, Wells, Lincoln (which was rebuilt after being destroyed by an earthquake, not by the more customary fire), Winchester and part of York were the main Gothic achievements in England. Germany, which embarked upon Gothic architecture later than France and England, produced Cologne, Freiburg and Regensburg cathedrals, as well as the cathedral in Strasbourg, which was at that time a city of the German Empire. Spain built cathedrals in this architectural style in Burgos, Toledo and León, and one of Italy's finest Gothic buildings is the cathedral of Siena; its façade, striped with bands of marble, shows the influence of northern Gothic modified to Italian taste.

To call the architecture of these cathedrals Gothic would have meant nothing to their builders—the label was not used until the seventeenth century. At the time when the new style came into vogue it was described as *opus modernus*, or *opus Francigenum* to indicate the country of its origin. (Romanesque, used to describe the architecture and art that Gothic superseded, was introduced even later than the term Gothic; it did not make its appearance until the nineteenth century.)

The term Gothic evokes a magnificent cathedral with glorious pointed arches and flying buttresses. But the essential Gothic quality is far more than its outward appearance. Gothic architecture represented an escape from the constraints of the Dark Ages, a new adventurous outlook, an explosion of the human spirit. When, by the fifteenth century, its youthful adventurousness grew into self-satisfied middle age, the life went out of it.

As the Gothic style spread from France throughout Europe it was at first copied and then adapted. The French themselves boldly experimented with techniques that would enable them to build ever more soaring cathedrals—from the modest seventy-eight-foot-high vaulting at Laon, to 120 feet at Chartres, 125 feet at Reims and Bourges, 139 feet at Amiens and 157 feet at Beauvais, where "vaulting ambition" technically overreached itself and the vaulting fell down. While the French Gothic cathedral builders strove for height, the English builders developed a passion for length, and the Spanish for width. Germany made a special contribution to the Gothic style with the *Hallenkirche*, or hall-church, which was characterized by aisles approximately the same height as the nave and choir and by the lack of triforium or clerestory. A typical example, and one of the earliest, is the Church of St Elisabeth in Marburg.

It was climate, however, as much as national preferences which affected the development of stained-glass windows. The ideal of building walls of glass, which was common to architects in France, England and Germany, was not shared by builders in Spain and Italy. In these countries the southern sun was too bright and too hot for vast expanses of glass to be tolerable. Indeed, some of the early large windows were later blocked up.

In northern Europe, as the windows grew larger, the colour of the glass, particularly the blues, grew darker. The aim was not to make the cathedrals dark—although that was often the result—but to give the light a mystical quality. Today, almost eight hundred years later, with so much original glass gone and what remains so affected by age, it is almost impossible to recapture the feeling of religious sensuousness which must have so excited the medieval worshipper. Such an experience might, however, still be possible at Chartres, in France, and at León, in Spain.

A contrary development during the thirteenth century was the increasing popularity of grisaille windows. Made of only slightly tinted glass, their effect depended upon light and design rather than on colour and figures. At first grisaille windows were simple, but later they became more elaborate and medallions were introduced into them. There are several much argued theories to explain the popularity of grisaille glass at a time when the art of figurative stained glass was reaching its apogee. Some of the reasons given are practical: that stained glass was too expensive; that there was not enough coloured glass available to fill all of the new acreage of windows; that the churches had become too dark, especially in sunless northern Europe. But these reasonable explanations are complicated by theological disputes, which centre around the ascetic St Bernard, founder of the Cistercian order.

In 1134 the general chapter of the Order had decreed that the windows in Cistercian abbeys should be of clear glass, without colour or cross (meaning representations of the Crucifixion). This ban must have been frustrating for the Cistercian master glaziers, who responded by creating the most beautiful designs with the leads in which the clear glass was set. There is a fine example, one of the few remaining, in the church of Obazine Abbey in the diocese of Tulle in southern France. But the appeal of such a window is intellectual rather than emotional.

Although Cistercian abbeys were austere, St Bernard reluctantly admitted that bishops, having to provide in their cathedrals for both the learned and the ignorant, "might have to arouse the devotion of fleshly people with material adornments, seeing that they cannot do so with the things of the spirit". But even there, it was emphasized, there was to be no excess.

Grisaille glass was first used more in England (for example, in York, Salisbury and Lincoln cathedrals) than in France, where stained glass was then at its most brilliant. How far the use of grisaille was the result of Cistercian influence it is impossible to say. Their monasteries had spread throughout Europe. When St Bernard died in 1153 there were three hundred and that number grew to more than five hundred by the end of the twelfth century. But by then the Cistercians had relaxed their rules to allow the use of figures in their windows.

In France and England, in the thirteenth century, medallion windows began to oust the figure windows of the previous century. There were also some notable rose windows in this period. The circle is not in the vertical Gothic tradition, but it was too elemental a shape to be ignored. Among the outstanding Gothic rose windows are those at Chartres, Notre Dame de Paris, Laon and Lyons. A rare example of an English rose of this period is in the north transept of Lincoln Cathedral. Although it is much mutilated, a great part of it is thought to be original. Rejoicing in the name the Dean's Eye—because it looks out on the deanery—it depicts the Day of Judgement and the Kingdom of Heaven.

Cathedrals were not the only wonders of the thirteenth century. Small chapels, too, were built at this time and, although they could not match the great cathedrals in grandeur, they often outdid them in splendour. In England there is St Stephen's Chapel, begun by Edward I as part of the Palace of Westminster. Ste Chapelle, built by Louis IX in the courtyard of his palace on the Ile de la Cité, Paris, stands out as one of the minor gems. A cage of coloured glass, it is indeed the epitome of this colourful century.

The north rose in the cathedral of Notre Dame, Paris, epitomizes the dynamic splendour of thirteenth-century French stained glass. Concentric bands of predominantly blue and violet light, divided by dark stone bars, which emphasize their brilliance, radiate in the form of an enormous wheel around the Virgin and Child, who are depicted at its centre.

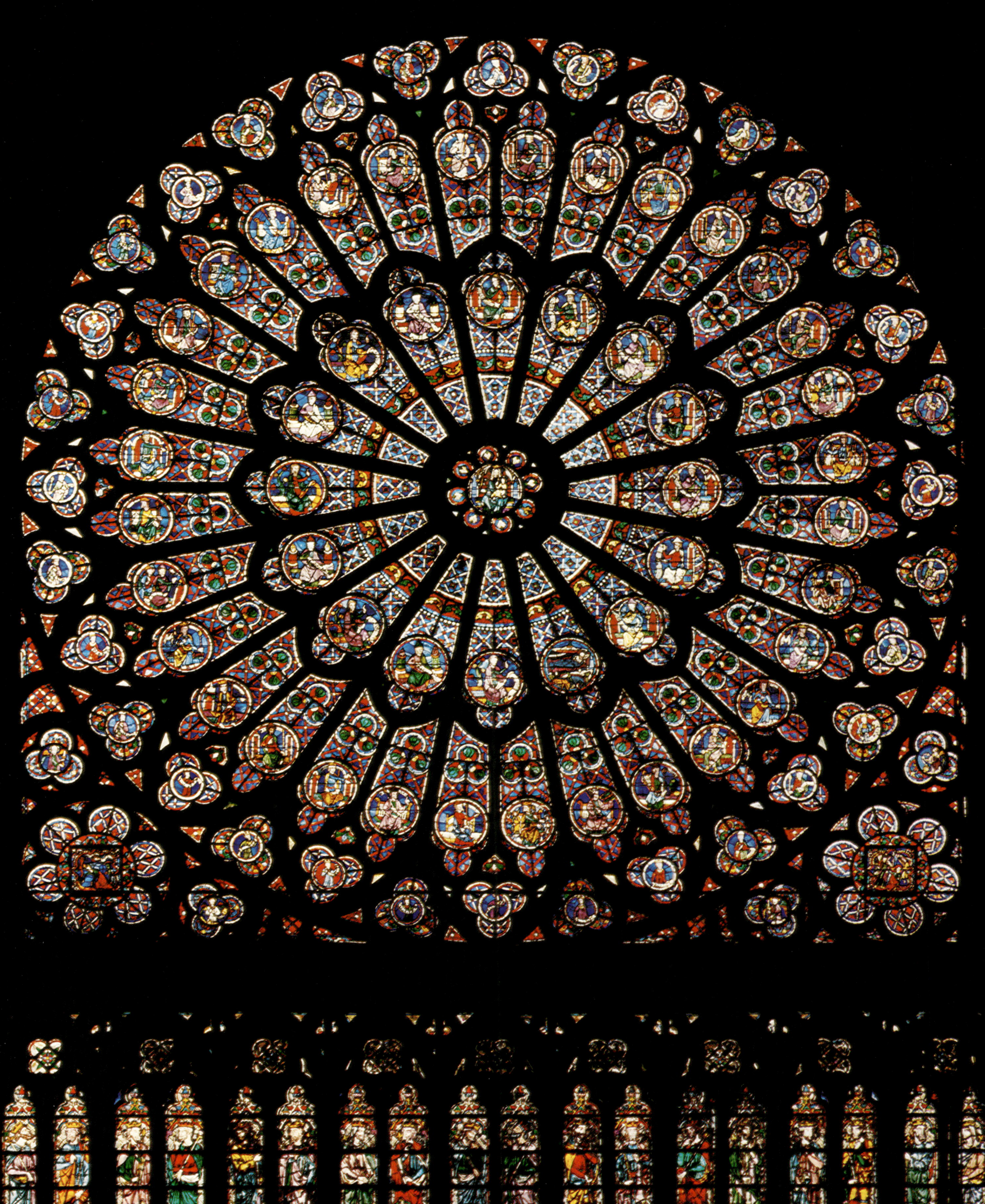

THIRTEENTH-CENTURY FRANCE

Queen of Cathedrals

Multiform medallions depicting angels and doves, kings and prophets, converge upon the image of Virgin and Child in the central rosette of the north rose in Chartres Cathedral. In the lancets below are St Anne and four majestic Old Testament figures who stand triumphantly above scenes of heresy and disaster—the idolatry of Nebuchadnezzar and Jereboam, the drowning of the Pharaoh in the Red Sea and the suicide of Saul.

Almost everything about Chartres Cathedral is beyond normal belief. The barest facts concerning it and the more bizarre of its traditions have an air of unreality. Yet there it is, a manifestation in stone and glass of a city that at times was possessed, not by devils, but by adoration of the Virgin, the patroness of Chartres.

There had been some sort of church on top of the hill at Chartres for centuries. It had been set on fire by the Duke of Aquitania in 743 and by the Danes in 858. Fire also destroyed it in 962, 1020 and 1194. Each time it was rebuilt —six Chartres in all—triumphs of faith and unquenchable energy, culminating in one of the greatest masterpieces of Europe.

Since the ninth century the cathedral's sacred relic, the Virgin's tunic, had made Chartres a city of pilgrimage, adding to its prosperity, its fame and its standing as a centre of scholarship, with its important library and its international band of scholars. Chartres was not only a famous town; it had a strong sense of corporate identity and unity. It lay in the centre of fertile agricultural land, but increasingly its prosperity came to depend on its growth as a trading centre. Many of the factors which made the town so full of vigour were indeed material; the catalyst that turned them into religious fervour was the Virgin.

There was a remarkable instance of this extraordinary fervour when the cathedral was being enlarged in 1145. It became known as the Cult of the Carts. The Abbot of Mont-St-Michel recorded that "men at Chartres began to drag carts, harnessed to their own shoulders, laden with stones and wood, corn and other provisions needed for the new church". Some accounts describe this amazing activity as a great penitential movement that spread through Normandy and the Ile de France; others portray it as a rather jolly outing with the citizens in friendly rivalry in collecting material for the workmen. It did not last long, but it was astonishing in that it so openly brought together all classes of society in the service of the Church.

There was a similar communal outburst of fervour in 1194, after the discovery that although much of the cathedral had been destroyed by fire the Virgin's tunic had been rescued. For this rebuilding, gifts flowed in from all over France and abroad—from kings, the nobility, archbishops, bishops and all other ranks of the Church, and from merchants, guilds, workmen and peasants. Gifts begat other gifts; as St Bernard had written, "Money brings money; for I know not how, but where most riches are seen there offerings flow most liberally."

By 1222 the main part of the new cathedral was complete, and all sculpture and stained glass was in place for the cathedral's dedication in 1260. In fact, most of the windows were glazed between 1215 and 1240—a stupendous achievement, even though many glaziers must have been involved. Their skill was amazingly sure, for they used techniques which did not allow them, while they were creating a window, to see what it would look like when the light was shining through it. Moreover, they could not see—although it was essential to imagine—what effect their windows would have when seen at a distance.

But despite the unpredictable nature of their work, the glaziers of Chartres helped to create a spiritual sanctuary which continues to evoke a sense of awe. The windows glow harmoniously within the subdued light of the vast interior and, framed by the contrasting darkness of the masonry, seem to be suspended in space.

Subtle variations of colour, particularly of blue, are produced by the continually changing quality of light. A radiant sky blue created by direct sunlight deepens to violet and purple as the sun moves away or is obscured. In dull weather the windows have a mysterious dusky glow, yet when pierced by sunshine their diapered borders glitter and their striking patterns of diamonds, trefoils and circles

are delicately emphasized by fine bands of soft yellow light.

A kaleidoscopic effect of light and shadow, through which colours and forms appear and disappear in shifting patterns, is seen most dramatically in the clerestory lancets, where the tall biblical figures appear almost animated by the sudden illumination of their savage expressions and hieratic gestures.

The scale of the gifts to Chartres and the range of the givers is reflected in the windows. Some four thousand donors are shown in figurative medallions—royalty, nobility, churchmen, tradesmen and craftsmen, a panorama of medieval society. In all there are the "signatures" of about seventy guilds, indicating their position and wealth in the town. People are shown at their work. Underneath King David and Ezekiel is a butcher demonstrating how to kill an ox with an axe. Below Moses and the burning bush are two bakers with their newly baked bread. The winemakers' window shows the use of wine at Mass. The furriers gave the Charlemagne window, depicting the Song of Roland; their "signature" is a furrier showing a fur-lined cloak to a client.

Inevitably, many windows were devoted to the Virgin. Among these are the north transept rose and five lancets depicting the glorification of the Virgin. They were the gift of Blanche of Castile, mother of St Louis (King Louis IX of France). In the centre lancet the mother of the Virgin, St Anne, is holding the infant Mary.

St Anne had become another revered saint of Chartres, because her skull, looted by the Crusaders from Constantinople, had recently been bequeathed to the cathedral. Once again Chartres was in the vanguard of a new cult, which did not become widespread in Europe until the fourteenth century, and did not sweep through France until the sixteenth century.

Forty-two windows along the aisles and ambulatory of Chartres Cathedral were donated by the prosperous guilds of the town. The donors "signed" their gifts by illustrating their various trades below the instructive medallions which represent biblical or legendary stories. The Death and Assumption of Mary, right, was presented by the shoemakers, one of whom, seen at work, below, is in the lowest central medallion, as indicated on the key. Above the shoemaker, the central medallions of the window ascend symbolically in alternating circles and quatrefoils. They depict the death, funeral, entombment, assumption and crowning of the Virgin. Her soul, symbolized by a naked child, is received by Christ in one of the lower quatrefoils.

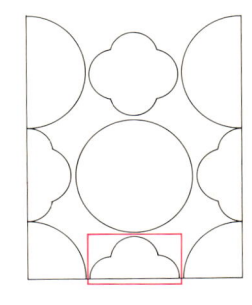

A relationship between commercial activity and religious imagery is established by some of the guild windows, in which the tradesmen's work corresponds to a biblical episode elsewhere in the lancet. The work of the carpenters, coopers and wheelwrights, who donated the Noah window in the north aisle of the nave, is echoed by a scene in one of its medallions in which Noah is building the ark. The wheelwright, left, represents his guild at the bottom of the window.

THIRTEENTH-CENTURY FRANCE

Chartres—Cathedral of Glowing Colour

The stained glass of Chartres covers an area of about twenty-two thousand square feet in 176 windows of unsurpassed beauty. The impact of the jewel-like radiance, the unearthly vari-coloured light suffusing the interior, is overwhelming. The architecture and, indeed, the entire cathedral, seem at first merely a framework for the glass. The oldest glass is in the three windows under the west rose and in the famous Notre Dame de la Belle Verrière, dating from about 1150. Almost all the rest of the glass dates from between 1215 and 1240.

The history of St Nicholas was conveniently vague and was thus the source of many popular legends. In Chartres Cathedral three windows are based upon the fictitious miracles of this saint. One of these windows, in the north aisle of the nave, includes the legend of the Jew and the dishonest Christian, thought to be the origin of one of York Minster's earliest panels, and the legend of the murdered schoolboys, which is also depicted horrifically in Metz Cathedral.

The wide black areas between the medallions of the west rose contrast sharply with the more linear designs of the roses of the north and south. The west rose, less brightly coloured than the older lancets beneath it, shows the Last Judgement. Around the central figure of the wounded Christ are angels and the four beasts of the Revelation. Above is Abraham with the elect, and below the weighing of souls. To the right and left are the twelve apostles. In the outer circle, radiating from the top in pairs of medallions, are instruments of the Passion, four angels blowing the last trumpet, resurrected men, the raising of the dead and hell.

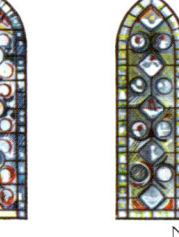

North aisle

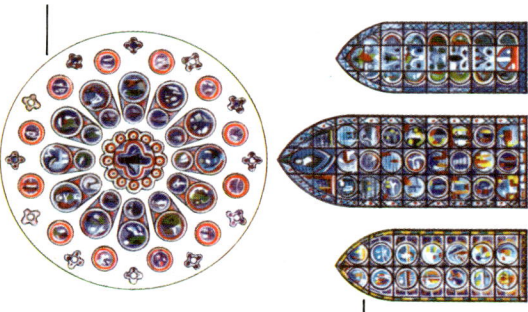

Nave

The three lancets under the west rose, and La Belle Verrière, are the only examples of twelfth-century glass which survived the fire of 1194. The Jesse window, on the right, shows the genealogy of Christ. It is believed to be one of the first windows of its kind and subsequently became the model for many others. The central lancet portrays the life of Jesus from the Annunciation to his Entry into Jerusalem. The story is continued in the Passion window on the left.

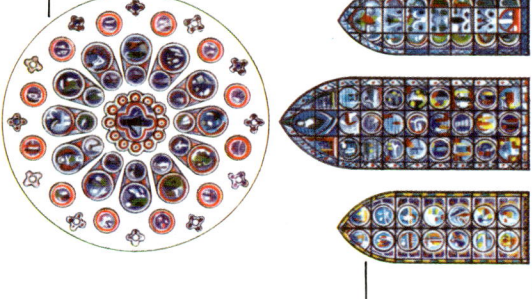

South aisle

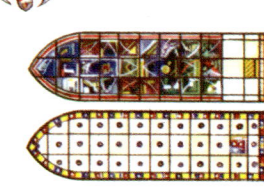
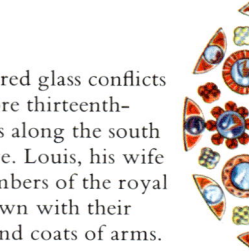

Legends, lives of the saints and stories from the Bible are depicted throughout the sixty-four lancets and *oculi* in the lower storey of the cathedral, along the aisles and ambulatory —so placed that they could be "read". The unity of medieval society under the authority of the Church is exemplified by the large number of windows donated by the tradesmen of Chartres. The windows were status symbols and also a form of advertising. Some guilds, particularly the bakers, who felt professionally inferior, gave several windows. In the clerestory, in paired lancets surmounted by small roses, stand tall figures of saints, prophets and apostles who are drawn with bold simplicity. These huge figures create an impression of austere power which is increased by the intensity of the whites of their eyes, which stare from time-darkened faces.

The Good Samaritan, according to the teachings of the English theologian the Venerable Bede, was a symbol for Christ the Saviour of fallen man. Bede's analogy, with which the scholars of Chartres were familiar, is shown in the Good Samaritan window, where the parable is illustrated, as are the Creation, Fall and Redemption of mankind.

In 1417, Louis of Bourbon, Count of Vendôme, fulfilled his vow to dedicate a chapel to the Virgin on his release from prison in England. Built by the architect Geoffroi de Sevestre, the Vendôme Chapel with its brightly coloured glass conflicts with the sombre thirteenth-century lancets along the south side of the nave. Louis, his wife and other members of the royal family are shown with their patron saints and coats of arms.

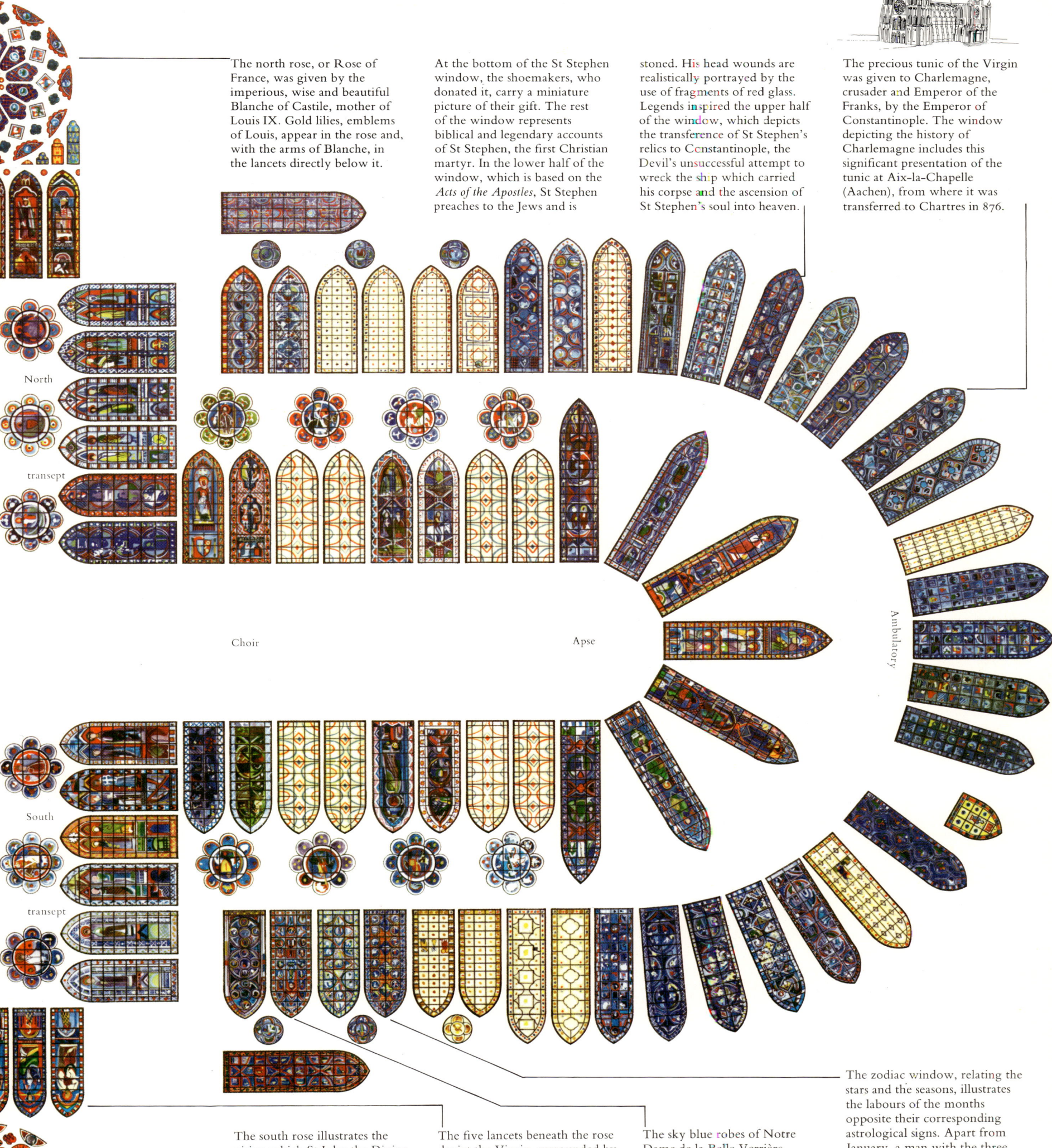

The north rose, or Rose of France, was given by the imperious, wise and beautiful Blanche of Castile, mother of Louis IX. Gold lilies, emblems of Louis, appear in the rose and, with the arms of Blanche, in the lancets directly below it.

At the bottom of the St Stephen window, the shoemakers, who donated it, carry a miniature picture of their gift. The rest of the window represents biblical and legendary accounts of St Stephen, the first Christian martyr. In the lower half of the window, which is based on the *Acts of the Apostles*, St Stephen preaches to the Jews and is stoned. His head wounds are realistically portrayed by the use of fragments of red glass. Legends inspired the upper half of the window, which depicts the transference of St Stephen's relics to Constantinople, the Devil's unsuccessful attempt to wreck the ship which carried his corpse and the ascension of St Stephen's soul into heaven.

The precious tunic of the Virgin was given to Charlemagne, crusader and Emperor of the Franks, by the Emperor of Constantinople. The window depicting the history of Charlemagne includes this significant presentation of the tunic at Aix-la-Chapelle (Aachen), from where it was transferred to Chartres in 876.

The south rose illustrates the vision which St John the Divine experienced on the island of Patmos towards the end of the first century AD and described in the *Book of Revelation*. Christ is in the centre of the window, surrounded by the four symbolic beasts, angels and elders.

The five lancets beneath the rose depict the Virgin, surrounded by the four prophets, Isaiah, Daniel, Ezekiel and Jeremiah. On the shoulders of the prophets are small figures of the four evangelists, whose reduced size symbolizes their dependency upon the teachings of the Old Testament.

The sky blue robes of Notre Dame de la Belle Verrière contrast vividly with the deep blues of the rest of the window. The four twelfth-century panels which form the famous blue Virgin are set in a thirteenth-century window, which depicts angels, the feast in Cana and the Temptation of Christ.

The zodiac window, relating the stars and the seasons, illustrates the labours of the months opposite their corresponding astrological signs. Apart from January, a man with the three heads of past, present and future, the months are represented realistically. August, with Virgo, is a man threshing corn, April, opposite Taurus, is a girl picking flowers and November, with Sagittarius, is a peasant slaughtering his pig.

77

THIRTEENTH-CENTURY FRANCE

The Glory of French Glass

Although Chartres is the cathedral in which Louis IX was christened and which he loved, Ste Chapelle is the small but lavish royal chapel which he built to house and honour the Crown of Thorns and a piece of the Crucifix, precious relics he bought from the Emperor of Constantinople. These two buildings had a dominant influence on the stained glass of France in the thirteenth century, that most glorious period of French glass.

The Chartres influence, paramount in the first half of the century, both in subject matter and in style, can be seen at Bourges Cathedral. The building is impressively spacious and tall, and, after Chartres, has the most extensive cycle of early thirteenth-century stained glass. As at Chartres, there are majestic processions of apostles and prophets, as well as a series depicting the bishops of Bourges, of which eight of the original twenty-six windows remain. In many of the windows the faces of the figures have the same characteristics—prominent, stylized noses, arrogant mouths, similar hair styles and staring eyes—suggesting that one model may have served for all.

The window of the Apocalypse, however, is strikingly different and is reminiscent of the Romanesque traditions of Angers, Poitiers and Le Mans. A cross-fertilization of ideas was, indeed, common in this period, and Bourges itself, along with Chartres, left its mark on the stained glass of Auxerre and Sens.

There were other regional centres of stained glass which were also important. They included Soissons and Laon in the north, Lyons in central France and in the east Troyes and Reims, the royal cathedral. According to legend, when the anointing of Clovis I, King of the Franks, in 496 established Reims as the rightful site for the consecration of French kings, the sacred oil was brought straight from heaven by a dove. In 1200, fire destroyed the cathedral. Although rebuilding was begun promptly, it was long before it was completed; it was barely ready by 1429 for the consecration of Charles VII, on which Joan of Arc insisted. One result of the cathedral's royal connection is an impressive array of kings in both sculpture and stained glass. The great clerestory windows, once filled with figures of the first thirty-six kings of France, paired with the archbishops who consecrated them, have suffered extensive damage, but eight kings and eight archbishops have survived.

The west rose window at Reims is intrinsically beautiful as well as historically important as the earliest example of French bar tracery. In plate tracery, which preceded it, openings were cut out of a solid surface of stone. Bar tracery, built up into intersecting ribwork with slender shafts of stone, was altogether more delicate. As this bar tracery was perfected, rose windows in particular gave the impression of filigree.

Towards the middle of the thirteenth century, a new style of glass-painting began to emerge in the Paris area. This was known as the St Louis style, and it gradually replaced the style established at Chartres as a major influence. While the colours of the St Louis school were still predominantly blue and red, a wide range of hues of purple, yellow and dark green was added. The main change, however, was that instead of glass that displayed meticulous draughtsmanship, as, for example, at Bourges, the impression was created of a rapid sketch with animated figures.

This style was derived from the windows of the Chapel of the Virgin at St Germain des Prés in Paris, but it was at Ste Chapelle, built between 1243 and 1248, that it came to its full glory. The windows at Ste Chapelle belong to one of the grandest of concepts. There are—now much restored—more than one thousand separate medallions and panels,

The ethereal quality of Gothic architecture is epitomized by the Ste Chapelle in Paris. This shrine of thirteenth-century stained glass was built by Louis IX to contain relics which he had acquired from Baldwin II, Emperor of Constantinople.

Christ, the judge and the redeemer, appears with a two-edged sword between his teeth in a medallion from the Apocalypse window in Bourges Cathedral. The window shows the vision of St John in the *Book of Revelation*. Its design is influenced by the windows of Chartres, glazed a few years earlier, in which similar patterns of circles and quatrefoils surround dim forms and deep, glowing colour. Symbols numbering seven, a number which has been held sacred since pre-Christian times, recur throughout the vision and in this detail, left. Christ stands among seven candlesticks, which symbolize the seven churches to which John was told to write. In his left hand he holds seven stars, representing the angels of the churches, and in his right hand a book sealed with seven seals.

depicting episodes from the Old Testament, the books of the Prophets and the lives of Christ, John the Evangelist and John the Baptist. Heraldic emblems—the lily for France and her king, Louis IX, and the castle of Castile for his mother, Blanche of Castile—figure prominently in the borders. On the basis of stylistic and circumstantial evidence, it is believed that at least ten different artists and three distinct stained-glass workshops contributed to the original glass.

The chapel appears to be made of glass, with the windows replacing walls between the piers which hold up the vault. The figures who tell their stories in the medallions are slim and elongated; the leading is vigorous and the colours are glowing. When Henry III of England saw the chapel he was so filled with envy that he is supposed to have said that he wished he could carry it all away on a cart. Even now, with so much glass lost or heavily restored, the effect of Ste Chapelle remains ethereal and hypnotic.

The influence of Ste Chapelle can be detected in the two magnificent transept roses at Notre Dame in Paris. The mid-thirteenth-century north rose window depicts, at the centre of its huge radiating wheel, the Virgin enthroned with her Child. Some eighty priests, judges and kings from the Old Testament encircle the Mother of God. The southern rose, thought to have been completed a decade later, glorifies Christ, who is surrounded by apostles, saints and angels.

John Ruskin, the great nineteenth-century art critic, wrote: "The true perfection of a painted window is to be serene, intense, brilliant, like flaming jewellery; full of easily legible and quaint subjects, and exquisitely subtle, yet simple in its harmonies. . . . This perfection has been consummated in the designs, never to be surpassed, if ever again to be approached by human art, of the French windows of the twelfth and thirteenth centuries."

As the thirteenth century came to an end, France was approaching the economic and social upheavals of the Hundred Years' War. There were also serious repercussions for the arts. The nobility and monarchy had little money to spare, most of it being channelled into the war. Consequently, the next century was to see a diminution of the creative purpose, which, until then, had made France pre-eminent in art and architecture.

Severe but majestic, this monarch, in the royal cathedral of Reims, is one of the survivors of a thirteenth-century series of the first thirty-six kings of France and the archbishops who consecrated them. The figures originally filled the entire clerestory.

THIRTEENTH-CENTURY GERMANY

From Romanesque to Gothic

Relics of the dead were life-blood for the medieval Church. The cult of relics goes back to the fourth and fifth centuries, but at first it was widespread only in the Eastern Church; such great cities as Constantinople and Antioch began to accumulate great stocks of relics through the wholesale exhumation of bodies of the martyrs. The Western Church eventually overcame its distaste at what it regarded as the violation of graves, and by the ninth century a great trade in relics flourished between East and West. In Rome there was even an organization established to unearth, sell and deliver relics to churches throughout Europe. During the Crusades, thousands more relics were brought back as sacred loot, and, by the end of the Middle Ages, few altars were dedicated which did not contain some relic of a martyr.

In 1164, as booty of war, Cologne acquired its most famous relics from Milan. They were reputed to be the bones of the Magi who took gifts to the infant Jesus in Bethlehem. Little is known about the Magi, the wise men from the East who were mentioned in St Matthew's Gospel, and it was popular tradition which put crowns on their heads. While the Western Church gave three as their number, the Eastern Church said there were sixteen of them. And no one could agree about their names or from which country they had travelled to Bethlehem.

Housed in an ornate shrine—the largest of its kind in Europe—the bones of the Magi made Cologne a leading centre of pilgrimage. So when the old cathedral burned down in 1248, work began at once to build a bigger and more magnificent building, which was not, astonishingly, completed until 1880. Thus Cologne Cathedral was raised on the bones of kings for whose existence there is absolutely no historical evidence. Faith not only moves mountains; it also creates wonderful works of art. Among such works of art in Cologne Cathedral, in addition to the shrine, are several windows depicting the Adoration of the Magi.

The oldest, dating from the mid-thirteenth century, is the Bible window in the Chapel of the Three Kings. This window, the oldest in the cathedral, is more than forty-five feet high, with two lancets divided into eleven panels, each panel containing about four hundred pieces of glass. The twenty themes are types from the Old Testament and antitypes from the New Testament: the creation of Eve is set against the birth of Mary; the Queen of Sheba bearing gifts to Solomon is matched by the Magi offering their gifts to the infant Christ; Jonah cast up on the shore has as its antitype the Resurrection. Behind these biblical scenes is a green tree of life, the tendrils of which hold the paired figures of kings and prophets.

Few thirteenth-century typological, or type and antitype, windows have survived in Germany, but as well as the Bible window in the Chapel of the Magi, Cologne possesses another, with livelier figures. Donated jointly by the German philosopher and theologian Albertus Magnus and Siegfried von Westerburg, Archbishop of Cologne, the window was originally in the Dominican Church of the Holy Cross and it was not moved to the cathedral until the end of the nineteenth century.

The cathedral itself was the first to be built in Germany in basically French Gothic style. Much of Germany, especially the eastern parts, which were farther away from French influence, remained firmly attached to Romanesque architecture. Even in Cologne the feverish building of Romanesque churches continued well into the thirteenth century; the last, St Kunibert's, was finally consecrated only a year before the new Gothic cathedral was begun.

St Kunibert's has the best collection of thirteenth-century Romanesque glass in Germany. The windows are wide and roundly arched, the borders are broad and the foliage stylized. The colours are not the overwhelming blues and reds that the French delighted in, but include a fair proportion of yellows and greens. Moreover, the elaborate geometrical frames which surround the scenes in the window depicting the life of St Kunibert, the church's patron saint, are wholly German and nothing like them is ever encountered in French stained glass.

The figures in this window are slim, elegant and courtly, thoroughly in keeping with what was the Age of Chivalry. They have their counterpart in German secular art. From 1200, for two centuries, Germany was in the grip of a craze for courtly lyric poetry that extolled the knightly virtue of *Minne*, devotion or love. At the beginning, the exponents, known as the *Minnesänger*, were generally minor noblemen who sublimated in their poems their devotion to unattainable ladies. Later, however, the pastime spread to all classes of society, and the devotion became less sublimated. Many illustrated collections were made of the poems

With its wide border of highly stylized foliage and its rounded head, the early thirteenth-century St Cecilia window in St Kunibert's, Cologne, is unmistakably Romanesque. Yet in the slender, youthful figure and the gentle expressive features of the saint there is already a trace of French Gothic influence. In her left hand St Cecilia holds the sword with which she was martyred.

and the chivalrous elegance portrayed in these is matched in the St Kunibert figures.

St Kunibert's also has some striking single-figure windows depicting virgins—and virgins are as much a subject of Cologne's religious folklore as are the Magi. One of the saints depicted is the somewhat nebulous St Ursula, who, according to an inscribed stone in the Cologne church which was dedicated to her, was martyred in the fourth century along with other virgins—the number varying implausibly between eleven and eleven thousand. Another version of the story says that they were British virgins slain by Huns a century later. But whoever the virgins were and however many of them there were, they are still commemorated in the eleven flames of Cologne's coat of arms, along with the three crowns of the Magi.

Among the other magnificent German churches and cathedrals influenced by the French Gothic style in the thirteenth century, St Elisabeth's in Marburg and the cathedrals of Freiburg and Strasbourg (then in the German Empire) have outstanding collections of thirteenth-century stained glass. The oldest glass in Marburg is still in the Romanesque tradition and includes windows showing scenes from the Creation surmounted by monumental figures and scenes from the life of St Elisabeth. The style of the glass in Strasbourg and Freiburg ranges from late Romanesque to late Gothic, although in Freiburg the changes in style have been blurred by much restoration.

In the centuries that lay ahead, German conservatism was to be often in evidence. Just as Germany was loath to give up Romanesque architecture, so she also stayed loyal to Gothic traditions longer than the rest of Europe, both in architecture and stained glass.

The crane hovering idly over the unfinished cathedral, as in the fifteenth-century woodcut, above, was a familiar sight in medieval Cologne. By the mid-sixteenth century, only the choir and a temporary wall at the west end were finished. In the 1800s the cathedral became a symbol of a united Christian Germany, which inspired the continuation and, in 1880, the completion of the building.

Its shimmering gold surface enriched with coloured enamel, filigree and precious stones, the Three Kings shrine, containing the relics of the Magi, was one of the greatest pilgrim attractions of the medieval world. Carved figures of prophets and apostles adorn the sides of the shrine. The front and back show scenes from the life of Christ, including, above, the Adoration of the Magi.

Not surprisingly, because of Cologne's prized relics, the Adoration of the Magi was one of the most popular themes of medieval Cologne art. It first appeared in stained glass in the oldest window in the cathedral, the mid-thirteenth-century Bible window, below, in the Chapel of the Magi. The kings are of disparate ages, the traditional way of depicting them in medieval iconography.

Introduced to the Rhineland by French Cistercian monks, grisaille glass was adapted and embellished by German glaziers, notably in the abbey church of Altenberg and in Cologne Cathedral. In the detail, right, from a thirteenth-century grisaille and figure window in Cologne Cathedral, the flower-like patterns with their richly coloured centres are further enriched by bands of red and blue. Delicately drawn foliage fills the geometrical shapes within the flower forms and is repeated in the border. The panels were originally in the Dominican Church, Cologne.

THIRTEENTH-CENTURY ENGLAND

Medieval Miracles

THE PILGRIM CITY

"And especially from every shire's end of England to Canterbury they wend the holy blissful martyr for to seek."

The pilgrimage to Canterbury, which was embarked upon so enthusiastically in the Middle Ages, has been immortalized by Geoffrey Chaucer's *Canterbury Tales*. The poem reflects the variety of people who visited Becket's shrine and who increased the wealth of Canterbury, especially on feast days which commemorated the martyrdom or the transference of the relics from the crypt to the Trinity Chapel. The name of the city has entered the language in many ways. "Canter" comes from the "Canterbury gallop", an easy, moderate gait. Canterbury bells, gain their name from the shape of the bells worn by pilgrims' horses.

Revered as a man of integrity, courage and good works by his followers, dubbed "our traitor" by Henry II and regarded by some as a fanatic in his sudden renunciation of the world, Becket remains an enigma. It is impossible to say how closely this portrait at Canterbury resembles him. The one clue to its accuracy is the realistic representation of the mitre.

The commercial advantages of the Becket cult were exploited by the shopkeepers of Canterbury. This pewter souvenir badge was one of many variations of the martyr's portrait sold to pilgrims in Mercery Lane during the thirteenth and fourteenth centuries.

This Canterbury medallion depicts pilgrims worshipping at Becket's tomb in its original resting place in the crypt. The later shrine was lavishly decorated, gold apparently being the least valuable adornment.

The revival of Bobby of Rochester is one of the many miracles attributed to Becket and shown in the medallion windows of the Trinity Chapel. Bobby, a disobedient child, drowns in the River Medway while throwing stones at frogs. His parents visit Becket's tomb with the corpse, which is daubed with the martyr's blood and revives.

Fortunate indeed were the churches of the Middle Ages which could boast relics, saints and martyrs of their own, and enough miracles to fill a stained-glass window; they would never be short of pilgrims, glory and profit.

In England, Thomas Becket, Archbishop of Canterbury, provided the cathedral with its famous martyr, and a rapid succession of miracles. These miracles are depicted and enshrined in windows of the Trinity Chapel, where the gold- and jewel-encrusted shrine of St Thomas stood until 1538, when it was dismantled and removed by Henry VIII.

Thomas Becket, once the intimate friend and Chancellor of Henry II, incurred the enmity of the king when, as archbishop, he uncompromisingly upheld the rights of the Church against those of the Crown. For this he suffered death. Three years after his murder, Becket was canonized, such was already the reputation of his posthumous miracles.

Eight of the twelve windows in the chapel—the miracle windows—are of thirteenth-century glass. They are an unrivalled record of English dress and furniture of the period and a revelation of the medieval mind. The people for whom the saint is depicted as working miracles range through all classes of society—from Louis VII of France to peasants and workmen; the gamut of miracles runs from curing toothache to revival from the dead.

There is, for example, immortalized in these windows Adam the Forester, who was shot by a poacher's arrow and healed by St Thomas's water, a mixture of water and the blood that flowed from the murdered Becket. A carpenter cuts his leg with an axe and is healed when St Thomas appears to him in a dream. A farm labourer contracts leprosy and is cured as he kneels before the tomb in prayer. Perhaps naïve now, but not then, for an implicit faith in relics and miracles was a hallmark of medieval society.

Another interesting group of thirteenth-century windows at Canterbury are the so-called Poor Man's Bible windows. Also known as typological, or type and antitype windows, only three remain of the original twelve. The contrasting of a scene from the New Testament (the antitype) with one or more from the Old Testament (the type) was a popular device in medieval manuscripts, and this concept was widely translated into stained glass. In one of the Canterbury windows, for example, there is the child Christ on Mary's knee, adored by the Magi, who bear gifts. This is contrasted on one side by Joseph being offered gifts of money by Egyptian subjects, and on the other side by the Queen of Sheba bringing gifts to Solomon.

From the same period, in the north transept at York Minster, is a group of five giant grisaille lancets. Charles Dickens, whose imagination was as rich as the richest medieval stained glass, wrote an entirely fictitious account of why the window was called the Five Sisters. According to his story a tapestry created by five sisters was copied in stained glass as a memorial on the tragic death of the youngest.

The window's more recent history is far stranger. It was removed for safety during the First World War, and needed releading before it could be replaced. But York had neither the lead nor the money. In 1924, however, excavations at Rievaulx Abbey in Yorkshire unearthed lead which had been buried since the dissolution of the monastery in 1539. The money still needed for the releading was raised as the result of a vision a York woman experienced in the minster. One evening she was beckoned by her two long-dead young sisters towards the empty window. As that vision faded she saw another; five women busy with their needlework in a garden (as in the Dickens story). The idea came to her that restoring the window could be a memorial to the women of the British Empire who had died in the war. Within a few weeks thirty thousand women had responded to her appeal and the money was raised. In 1925 the window was back in place, cleaned and restored—a medieval glazier would have made a miracle window out of that.

Grisaille glass flourished in thirteenth-century England. Examples can be seen in Lincoln and Salisbury cathedrals, but it is at York Minster that the world's largest expanse—and England's finest example—of grisaille glass can be seen. From a distance, this vast five-light window, known as the Five Sisters, appears as a shimmering mass of greyish green. On closer inspection, however, the window reveals a delicate network of brown-painted foliage and ornamental patterns of coloured glass, as in the detail above.

THE FOURTEENTH CENTURY
The Age of Turmoil and Innovation

Europe had emerged from the Dark Ages in turmoil and was once more plunged into crisis as the Middle Ages drew to an end. There were natural disasters on a grand scale: the hard winters and floods that opened the century; the great famine of 1315 to 1317, which resulted in affluent cities like Ypres losing one-fifth of their inhabitants; the Black Death of 1348 to 1350, which struck again after six hundred years and wiped out one-third of the continent's population. There were man-made disasters, too: England embarked on a war with France that was to continue intermittently for one hundred years; agriculture and trade withered; inflation was rampant; great Italian banking houses crashed, including that of the Bardis, whose network of twenty-four banks had stretched from London to Jerusalem and Constantinople.

All Europe suffered to some degree, but France was the greatest victim. At the beginning of the fourteenth century she had been the most civilized and cultured nation in Christendom, but, afflicted with a degenerate and ineffectual feudal nobility and an unworkable fiscal system, she was ill-equipped to withstand the agony of being the battlefield in the war with England. Because the war was not being waged on English soil its effects on England were minimal, and the arts, including stained glass, flourished.

Technical advances as well as history affected the development of stained glass in the fourteenth century. The most valuable discovery, of silver stain, was accidental. One apocryphal version of the story is that a silver button, which fell from a glazier's tunic on to some glass, turned the glass yellow during firing. The discovery of silver stain, or silver oxide, made it possible for the glazier to add various shades of yellow, from pale lemon to deepest orange, to a piece of glass. One result was the reduction of the amount of leading needed in a window. If the glazier wished to add a halo around a face, for example, he could now stain it directly on to the one piece of glass, instead of leading it in separately. Silver stain was also used to enrich the decorative patterns of grisaille glass. Early in the fourteenth century, the French quickly adopted the method and the English shortly followed suit, but it did not come into general use in Germany until mid-century. By the end of the century, however, silver stain was being used to enliven windows in innumerable ways everywhere.

Another innovation, which gave a wider and brighter range of colours, was *verre doublé*, or flashed glass. This technique involved coating one colour with another, when the glass was still molten, to produce a third colour or a clearer colour. Thus, for example, green could be made by coating blue on yellow, and clear glass coated with ruby produced a brighter, less dense red.

A further refinement of the stained-glass-painter's skill was the introduction, in about 1380, of the stippling technique, which creates minute dots on a drying wash of paint, thus making possible a greater variety of shading—a particularly valuable innovation for the delineation of features.

The fourteenth century was notable for the divergent paths taken by glaziers in different countries. England turned from flowing, or Decorated, architecture, to the straitjacket of Perpendicular and this imposed new approaches to stained-glass windows. France used more grisaille, while England, where grisaille had been popular in the thirteenth century, was using more colour. Germany still preferred the deeper colours of earlier centuries, and even its grisaille was richly colourful, as in the windows of the abbey church of Altenberg. In both French and English windows, canopies, the light-admitting, ornamental architecture designs enframing figures, grew taller. But the greater areas of pale, sometimes colourless, glass which resulted were brightened by the use of yellow stain.

Even though France had fallen from the artistic heights of the thirteenth century, there is some fine French glass from this period, especially in Normandy, in the cathedral at Evreux and in the Church of St Ouen in Rouen, which had a large and famous stained-glass workshop from early in the fourteenth century. The windows of St Ouen are excellent examples of the French trend towards lighter interiors through the use of canopies and grisaille. Figures of patriarchs, apostles, saints and ecclesiastics stand under great architectural canopies which are infested with imaginary animals. The colours throughout the windows are pale, and silvery white is dominant.

At Evreux the earlier canopies are fanciful and decorative, and there is no attempt at realism or perspective. This style changed towards the end of the century, a change which is particularly noticeable in some of the choir windows. Two, donated by Bernard Cariti, Bishop of Evreux from 1376 to 1383, are almost fifteenth century in style. Not only are the vaults above the figures shown in perspective but also the chequered floor on which they stand. As in all the choir windows dating from the late fourteenth century, the figures are highly realistic in their portrayal and the faces have great individuality. Even the traditional border is replaced by realistic architecture.

One device which was used to make the interiors of buildings lighter without making the windows dull was to have a band of coloured glass across the entire window. The rest of the window lights were glazed with quarry glass, perhaps enriched with coloured borders and decorative coloured bosses. Such windows at St Ouen and Evreux were matched by a similar technique in the chapel of Merton College in Oxford.

In the fourteenth century the figures of donors spread like a rash through the windows of Europe, a trend which Merton and Evreux again had in common. At Merton one donor is depicted twenty-four times, while at Evreux window after window is distinguished by the portrayal of different ecclesiastical or aristocratic donors. One of the most charming is that of Canon Raoul de Ferrières, who kneels under a canopy, holding for the Virgin's inspection a model of his gift window. In the adjoining light the tall, graceful Virgin is suckling her child. Although the canopies above the figures are almost the same height, the Virgin is, of course, twice as tall as her devoted supplicant, the canon.

This was still a Gothic century, but the first light of the Renaissance was beginning to appear. One indication was the attempt to show volume and spatial depth through linear perspective and modelling. It originated in Italian painting and, spreading north of the Alps, appeared first in stained glass in the Habsburg monastery at Königsfelden, near Zurich.

There was, mirrored in stained glass, another, clearer, portent of the changing outlook which was to mark the end of the Middle Ages and the birth of the Renaissance. For centuries medieval art had been anonymous, reflecting a collective rather than an individual outlook. But in the fourteenth century, artists, including glaziers, began to shed their anonymity. An age of individualism was at hand.

Tiered arcs of vibrant colour sweep across the All Saints window in the Chapel of St John in Cologne Cathedral. Glazed between 1315 and 1320 by the anonymous "Master of the choir chapel windows", it portrays a heavenly hierarchy of saints and angels, the top of the saints' niches distinguished by trefoil moulding, the angels' by a cinquefoil. Each of the eight tiers, with their alternating red and blue backgrounds, contains eight figures, eight being a symbol of heavenly harmony and justice. Martyrs are depicted in the two lower tiers, and above them, in ascending order, are confessors, kings, bishops, prophets, popes and apostles. At the bottom of the window is the coat of arms of the donor.

FOURTEENTH-CENTURY ENGLAND

York – City of Stained Glass

The city of York is a living museum of seven centuries of stained glass. The tradition of glazed church windows in York is older still for, according to his biographer, St Wilfrid, Archbishop of York, had the windows of his church glazed in the late seventh century. By the eighth century, York's cathedral school and library were renowned; and by the time of the Norman Conquest the city was second only to London in population.

The wealth of medieval architecture and stained glass is the legacy of York's commercial success in the Middle Ages, especially as the centre of a thriving wool trade, which continued to flourish even when other commerce was flagging. The city lies on the River Ouse, a natural outlet to the continent for Yorkshire merchants and their wool. The traffic was two-way, stained glass, which was not then made in England, being imported from the Low Countries.

In the later Middle Ages, York had a number of thriving firms of glass-painters. Glaziers had sufficient standing for many of them to be given the privileged title of freeman—a hundred freemen are recorded between 1313 and 1540—and some became prominent in civic life. The work of the York school of glass-painters extended far beyond the city's churches and cathedral, but there is enough in York itself to satisfy—and even to satiate. The quantity is vast, the quality variable, but much of the glass is of outstanding artistic merit. It can be found not only in the minster but in many churches, including All Saints', North Street, Holy Trinity, Micklegate, St Denys and St Martin-le-Grand.

The stained glass in the minster is a lesson in itself. If the fourteenth-century glass, for example the Great West window of 1335, is compared with that of the early fifteenth century, such as the St William and St Cuthbert windows, the differences are immediately obvious between the Decorated Gothic style and Perpendicular Gothic. In the Decorated period, broad windows were divided by slim mullions into several lights surmounted by tracery. In the Perpendicular period the mullions continued right into the tracery, dividing the window by long vertical strips.

Among the outstanding fourteenth-century stained glass in York Minster the Heraldic window is notable for its alternation of coloured and grisaille panels, its wealth of royal armorials and heraldic borders and its use, perhaps for the first time in England, of silver stain.

The Great West window, which is fifty-four feet high by twenty-five feet, has eight lights containing three rows of canopied panels showing archbishops and apostles and above them the Annunciation, Nativity, Resurrection and Ascension. The window is made doubly effective by the exuberance of its curvilinear tracery, the design of which embraces a stylized heart, popularly known as the heart of Yorkshire.

The Bell Founders' window depicts its donor, Richard Tunnoc, who lived in Stonegate, the traditional street of both the glass-painters and the founders, giving a bell to St William. There are scenes of workmen in contemporary dress shaping and casting a bell. Bells in the canopies and bells in the borders are interspersed with monkeys playing musical instruments.

York glaziers had a fondness for portraying local scenes and customs; indeed, their whole outlook had a strongly secular and regional bent. There are borders in the minster, for example, which show a squire setting off hunting for stags. The glaziers revelled, too, in the lives and miracles of the saints, especially those who came from the North. They were also thoroughly at home with the grotesque and the macabre, including animal funerals, an old theme in art. Various mourning animals are sculpted in Strasbourg Cathedral, and the East Anglian Gorleston Psalter, of the early thirteenth century, has an incongruously jolly funeral procession of rabbits. Borders in York Minster illustrate a funeral procession of monkeys. Four monkeys carry the corpse, another bears a cross and another the bell, and a cock reads the lesson from a lectern.

The Great East window, seventy-six feet high by thirty-two feet, makes up for the lack of biblical scenes elsewhere in the minster. Below the 161 tracery panels of angels, patriarchs, prophets and saints are twenty-seven panels, each three feet square, of Old Testament scenes, beginning with the first day of Creation and ending with the death of Absalom. Then follow nine rows of panels illustrating eighty-one scenes of dire prophecy and doom from the *Revelation of St John*, a massive development of the Apocalypse theme. In the two bottom rows is the kneeling donor, Bishop Skirlaw of Durham, flanked by English kings, saints and archbishops. Without binoculars it is impossible to see any details of individual scenes, so the medieval worshipper is unlikely to have learned much from them. But, like the modern visitor, he was probably overwhelmed by the total effect of this wall of coloured light.

The Great East window was not the work of a York man. John Thornton was brought from Coventry to make it, perhaps because all the experienced York glaziers capable of undertaking it had died from the Black Death. He and his team completed the work in three years, as he promised, and although he cannot with certainty be credited with any other windows in York his influence was seminal. He revitalized the flagging York school, and the first effects of this are obvious in the minster in the slender, towering St William and St Cuthbert windows.

St William, the most minimal of saints, scarcely deserves such a window. William Fitzherbert was undisputed Archbishop of York for a month, a week of which he spent dying, at the end of a life noted more for its quarrelsomeness than for its holiness. But York needed a saint. It could scarcely have hoped to outdo the attraction of St Thomas of Canterbury, but at least it wanted to be able to compete with the saints who drew crowds of pilgrims to Beverley, Durham and Lincoln cathedrals. An outbreak of posthumous miracles finally persuaded the Pope to canonize the archbishop. Some of the countless miracles recorded in the window are as curious as those in the St Thomas windows at Canterbury: a boy cured after swallowing a frog; a man healed after being injured by a stone falling on his head; a man brought back to life after falling off a ladder. However, it was no miracle but simple fact that his canonization achieved its purpose—to attract both pilgrims and prosperity to the minster and the city of York.

Animals, notably in the Middle Ages, were used as a device to mock the foibles and follies of human beings. Apes in particular, traditionally associated with heresy and paganism, came to represent man's imitative nature and his foolish vanity, as in the bestiary illustration above. The monkeys' funeral, below, in a border of one of York Minster's nave windows, parodies the legend of the Burial of the Virgin, a popular feature of York mystery plays, which flourished in the fourteenth century.

THE GREAT EAST WINDOW

Dominating the easternmost end of the Lady Chapel of York Minster is one of the world's largest single expanses of ancient stained glass—the Great East window. The glazing of this vast wall of glass took, amazingly, only the three years from 1405 to 1408. It was the work of John Thornton of Coventry, who received the then handsome sum of fifty-six pounds for his labours.

The *Book of Revelation* in the hand of God at the apex of the tracery establishes the theme of York Minster's Great East window—*Ego Sum Alpha et Omega*—I am the Beginning and the End. The heavenly host in the tracery lights surmounts illustrations of the omnipotence of God as seen in his interventions on Earth. Three rows of panels depict such incidents from the Old Testament. Below these, in nine rows of panels, scenes from the Apocalypse, in the final book of the New Testament, are illustrated with great artistic power. Figures of ecclesiastics and kings are portrayed in the bottom panels.

- Heavenly host
- Old Testament scenes
- Scenes from the Apocalypse
- Ecclesiastics and kings

1 Birds and fishes of the fifth day of Creation.

2 Adam and Eve with the human-headed serpent.

3 Sounding of the fifth trumpet heralding locusts and scorpions.

4 The leopard-like beast from the sea makes war on the saints.

5 The casting of the Lost into the lake of fire.

6 King Aurelius, Ambrosius Lucius and King Arthur.

FOURTEENTH-CENTURY ENGLAND

The Medieval Minster

York Minster, with its one hundred and thirty stained-glass windows, contains the largest collection of medieval glass in England. There is some which dates back as far as the twelfth and thirteenth centuries, including the Five Sisters window in grisaille. But the most glorious windows are richly coloured, created either in the Decorated style of the early fourteenth century or in the mid-fifteenth-century Perpendicular style. The windows at the western and eastern ends of the minster are vast and spectacular, and there is great beauty and humour in many of the smaller windows. There have been frequent restorations—some misguided and some praiseworthy—but the essence of the Middle Ages remains and enchants.

Small figures, perched on ledges or standing amidst pillars and pinnacles, are common in York canopy windows. They appeared in the early fourteenth century in the Heraldic window as royal and aristocratic persons, suitably clad in costumes magnificently embroidered with heraldry. Predictably, angels often filled these architectural niches, but, in the fifteenth century, they were succeeded by curious old men with beards and caps. The Wolveden window, in the choir, is infested with these dwarf-like figures.

The five identical lancets of the thirteenth-century Five Sisters window, which is over fifty feet high, are composed of more than one hundred thousand pieces of glass. Touches of red, yellow and blue, which punctuate the subdued colour of the grisaille, are echoed by a bright twelfth-century panel at the bottom of the central lancet. Believed to be one of the earliest pieces of English stained glass, this panel shows the prophet Habakkuk being lowered by an angel into the lions' den and ministering to the prophet Daniel.

Fines, forcibly extracted from the sinners of York by eleven professional punishers, known as penancers, paid for a window in the north aisle of the nave. In the left-hand light a penancer whips a wrongdoer, while in the border a churchman empties the penalty money from a bag.

North aisle

 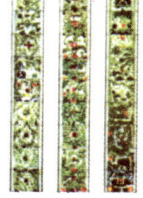

North transept

Unlike Chartres, York was not built with the donations of artisans. Although most of the windows were donated by ecclesiastics, the Bell Founders' window was the gift of Richard Tunnoc, a wealthy founder, who advertised his trade by having bells depicted in the border.

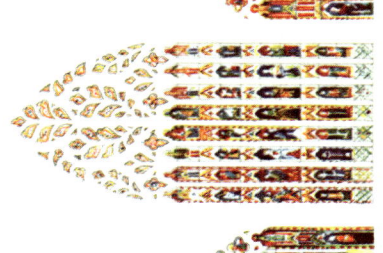

Nave

 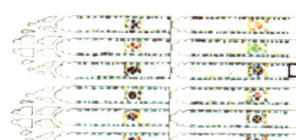

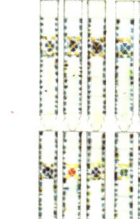

Strikingly delineated by delicately coloured glass, the complex, curvilinear patterns of the Great West window's tracery incorporate the design of a heart.

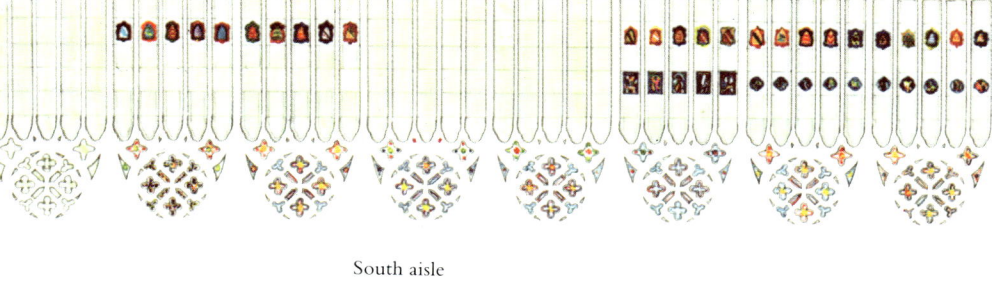

South aisle

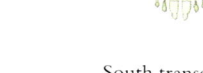

South transept

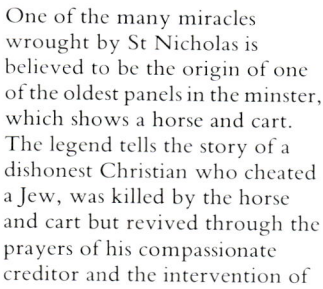

One of the many miracles wrought by St Nicholas is believed to be the origin of one of the oldest panels in the minster, which shows a horse and cart. The legend tells the story of a dishonest Christian who cheated a Jew, was killed by the horse and cart but revived through the prayers of his compassionate creditor and the intervention of the spirit of St Nicholas.

The red rose of Lancaster and the white rose of York are symbolically combined in the outer medallions of the south transept rose window. This window is believed to commemorate the important marriage, in 1486, between the Lancastrian King Henry VII and Elizabeth of York, which finally united the warring houses of York and Lancaster.

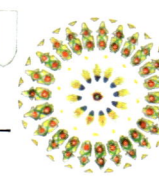

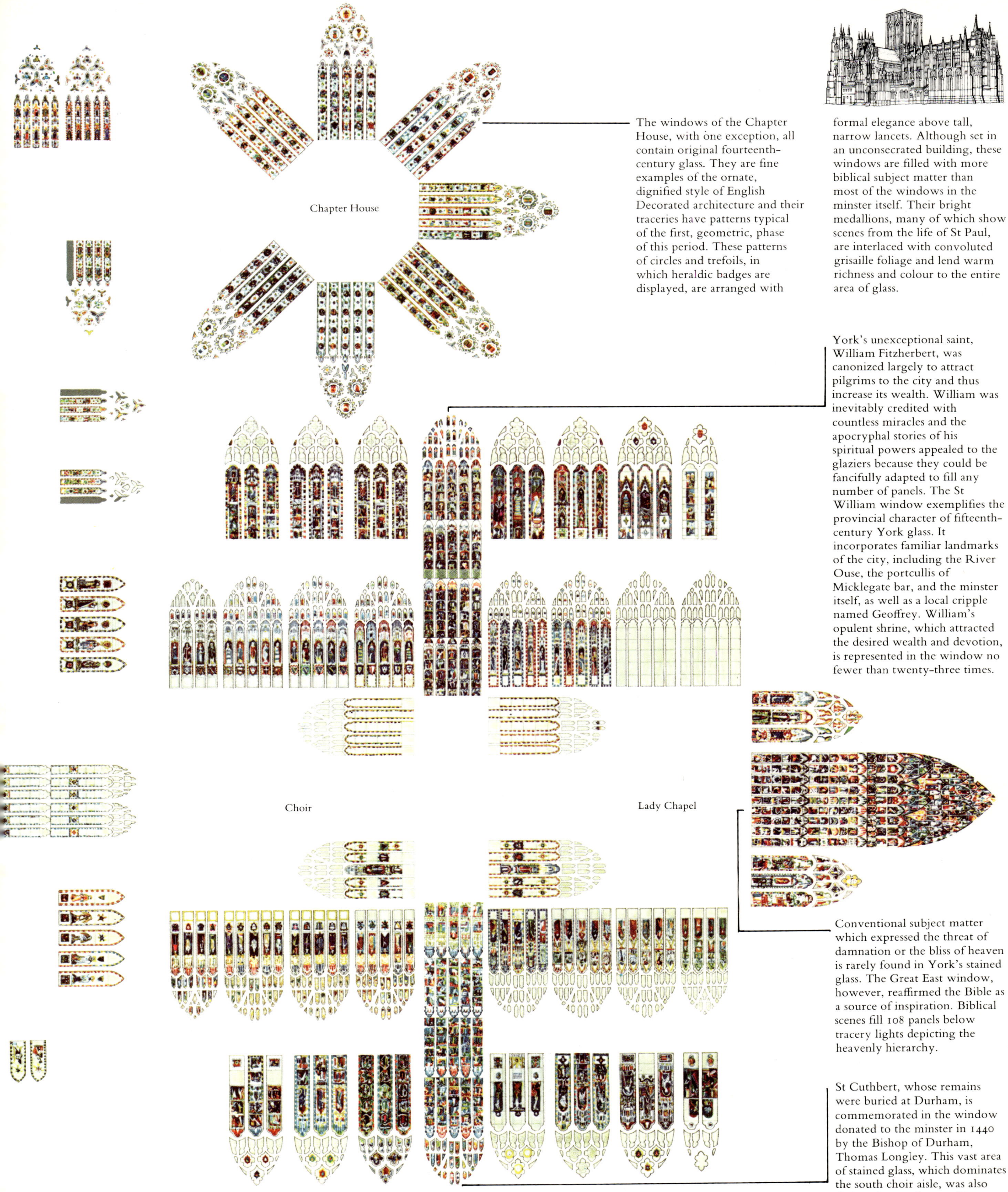

Chapter House

The windows of the Chapter House, with one exception, all contain original fourteenth-century glass. They are fine examples of the ornate, dignified style of English Decorated architecture and their traceries have patterns typical of the first, geometric, phase of this period. These patterns of circles and trefoils, in which heraldic badges are displayed, are arranged with formal elegance above tall, narrow lancets. Although set in an unconsecrated building, these windows are filled with more biblical subject matter than most of the windows in the minster itself. Their bright medallions, many of which show scenes from the life of St Paul, are interlaced with convoluted grisaille foliage and lend warm richness and colour to the entire area of glass.

York's unexceptional saint, William Fitzherbert, was canonized largely to attract pilgrims to the city and thus increase its wealth. William was inevitably credited with countless miracles and the apocryphal stories of his spiritual powers appealed to the glaziers because they could be fancifully adapted to fill any number of panels. The St William window exemplifies the provincial character of fifteenth-century York glass. It incorporates familiar landmarks of the city, including the River Ouse, the portcullis of Micklegate bar, and the minster itself, as well as a local cripple named Geoffrey. William's opulent shrine, which attracted the desired wealth and devotion, is represented in the window no fewer than twenty-three times.

Choir

Lady Chapel

Conventional subject matter which expressed the threat of damnation or the bliss of heaven is rarely found in York's stained glass. The Great East window, however, reaffirmed the Bible as a source of inspiration. Biblical scenes fill 108 panels below tracery lights depicting the heavenly hierarchy.

St Cuthbert, whose remains were buried at Durham, is commemorated in the window donated to the minster in 1440 by the Bishop of Durham, Thomas Longley. This vast area of stained glass, which dominates the south choir aisle, was also designed as a tribute to Henry VI, the ruling Lancastrian monarch and a devotee of St Cuthbert. The window became a political embarrassment when the Yorkist king, Edward IV, visited the city in 1471.

Witty little drawings of birds and animals neatly fill the diamond-shaped quarries in the south wall of the Zouche Chapel. Depicted with the accurate simplicity of cartoons, they include a bird stalking a spider, a procession of monkeys and a bear with its head stuck in a beehive.

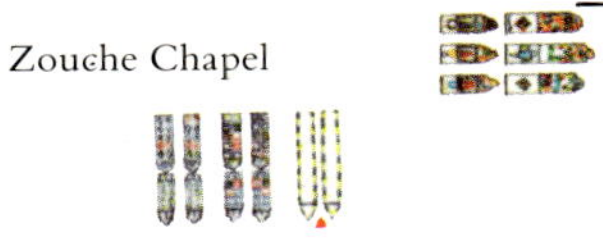

Zouche Chapel

In the east window of the chapel donated by the eponymous Archbishop Zouche are panels from the late fifteenth century in which two archbishops pay homage to King Henry VI.

FOURTEENTH-CENTURY ENGLAND

The Flowering of a Tradition

Fourteenth-century England was Chaucer's England. Looked at in one way, those one hundred years appear as an era of effete, extravagant and stupid kings, waging war on France, menaced by the marauding Scots and engaged in a see-saw struggle for power with the feudal barons. The majority of the population resented the grasping nobility and the luxuriously corrupt hierarchy of the Church, and the hatred erupted in the Peasants' Revolt and the Lollard movement. Above all, it was the time of the Black Death, which wiped out half of the country's four million inhabitants. But there were two fourteenth centuries. The other was one of the most brilliant in the history of English architecture and many of the visual arts, notably illuminated manuscripts, architectural sculpture and stained glass.

Once more, in this century, glaziers had to adapt themselves to a change in architectural style. From the single Romanesque, or Norman, windows of the twelfth century they had adjusted, during the late thirteenth and early fourteenth centuries, to the larger windows, divided by mullions, of the Decorated period. They were then faced with the elongated windows of the Perpendicular period, which lasted until early in the sixteenth century.

These developments are exemplified by the tracery of the windows. At the start of the Decorated period, usually defined as lasting from 1290 to 1350, the tracery, known as geometric, consisted of simple circles or foiled circles. Then tracery became curvilinear and extremely intricate. But, when the Decorated style reached heights of extravagance, a reaction set in and the more severe Perpendicular style emerged. In Perpendicular windows the mullions were carried up into the tracery, which became straight-sided panels, matching the main lights below.

In Gloucester Cathedral there is a prime and early example of a Perpendicular window, a development of a style which originated at St Stephen's Chapel, Westminster. The cathedral (still then an abbey) had reaped the rewards of an act of Christian charity. In 1327 it had provided a resting place, when no other abbey would, for the corpse of the murdered King Edward II. The tomb of this pseudo saint immediately began to attract pilgrims and with their offerings much of the cathedral was rebuilt, including, in about 1350, the Great East window, a spectacular combination of architecture and glass.

This window, more than seventy feet high and thirty-eight feet wide, has two great stone mullions running to the arch. The rest of the stonework provides a grid of panels and there is only a minimum of tracery. The subject of the window is the Coronation of the Virgin. She is attended by apostles and saints, many of whom stand in the exaggerated S pose typical of the period. The silvery canopies above them, illustrating the cathedral's architecture, are slim and tall. There is an imaginative diversity of foliage—tripartite leaves, heart-shaped leaves and berries. Below the figures is a series of roundels and heraldic shields. Many of the arms are of men who fought at Crécy, an early English victory in the Hundred Years' War.

Gloucester Cathedral was ahead of its time in soaring into Perpendicular, and in many parts of the country the Decorated style remained until late in the fourteenth century. Jesse Tree windows were among the most characteristic windows of the Decorated period and they changed little during the century. The Golden window of Wells Cathedral, dominated by bright yellows and olive greens, is one of the most remarkable.

Canopied figure windows were also popular during the Decorated period, and in the Perpendicular period they became almost universal. The figures beneath the canopies gradually became larger and more graceful, the features were more meticulously drawn and the robes were looser and more flowing. When canopies were first introduced, they were restrained, but later they became lofty and

A small figure, whose face is barely discernible, plays a stick and ball game in a fourteenth-century roundel at the bottom of the Great East window in Gloucester Cathedral. The player is controversially called the golfer, although the game of golf is not known to have existed before the fifteenth century. If the name is correct, this stained glass may well be the earliest evidence of golf.

Christ and angels with censers, candles and instruments of the Passion are ingeniously arranged within a pyramid of trefoiled tracery in the fourteenth-century east window of Wells Cathedral's Lady Chapel, above. In the lancets, canopies enshrine Old Testament figures, Virgin and Child and two serpents, one of which is a human-headed tempter, the other a brass image made by Moses to cure the snake-bitten Israelites.

90

elaborate, as at Tewkesbury Abbey. But even these cannot match the fantastic canopies above two tiers of standing figures in the antechapel windows at New College, Oxford. Although these windows were made by the glass-painter Thomas of Oxford, German influence may have been at work here. The canopies have "pepper pot" turrets, profuse battlements and are enriched with yellow stain. Thomas of Oxford also glazed the original Tree of Jesse window at Winchester, and included in it a kneeling self-portrait. Thomas was a man of substance, but nevertheless it was unusual for a glass-painter to be represented in a window during his lifetime.

Not so with the donors, who had no such modesty. Henry de Mamesfeld, Fellow of Merton College, Chancellor of Oxford University in 1311, Dean of Lincoln Cathedral in 1315, and donor of the Merton windows, is represented in them, sometimes clean-shaven, sometimes bearded, no fewer than twenty-four times. The windows themselves are an example of a type of window that became common during the fourteenth century—a band of canopied figures in richly coloured glass set off against grisaille glass decorated with naturalistic foliage.

Eleanor de Clare was another famous donor. She gave windows in the east end of Tewkesbury Abbey in memory of her murdered husband Hugh le Despenser. Not only are armoured knights of the De Clare and Le Despenser families given lavish pictorial treatment, but Eleanor herself is shown kneeling and naked in the east window.

The fourteenth century was a time of rapid transition. By the end of it, the English had evolved a style of architecture to which they were to cling for nearly a hundred and fifty years. By this time, too, the Cathedral Age was over in England; the era of the parish church was beginning.

The graceful, humanized figure of the Virgin, depicted dandling the infant Christ, in the east window of Eaton Bishop Church, Herefordshire, is characteristic of fourteenth-century English stained glass at its most original and beautiful. The Virgin's figure no longer seems stiff and awkward, as in earlier windows, yet it is still boldly simplified and stylized. The appearance of suppleness is created by the relaxed, S-shaped pose. Natural details and lively, realistic facial expressions add charm and individuality to the scene. Above the figures, in an upper part of the window, singing birds perch on the topmost pinnacles of the canopy.

THE OXFORD COLLEGES

Merton College, established in 1270 by the Bishop of Rochester, Walter de Merton, above, contributed enormously to the scientific and spiritual pre-eminence achieved by Oxford University during the fourteenth century. The windows of Merton College Chapel, right, are glazed with broad bands of rich colour and limpid grisaille.

William of Wykeham, Bishop of Winchester, above, founded New College, Oxford, originally Seinte Marie College, in 1379. The antechapel, built in the prevailing Perpendicular style, was glazed between 1393 and 1404 by Thomas of Oxford, one of England's earliest identifiable glaziers. His figure of Moses is shown right.

Henry de Mamesfeld, Chancellor of Oxford University and, later, Dean of Lincoln, is the first named donor to be portrayed in English stained glass. He appears more than twenty times in the windows which he donated to Merton College Chapel between about 1298 and 1311. In all the three-light windows except one, he is shown kneeling on either side of a prophet, left. Latin scrolls, which, translated, read "Henry de Mamesfeld ordered me to be made", emphasize his generosity.

91

FOURTEENTH-CENTURY ALSACE

Cultural Crossroads

Apostles are depicted beneath fantastic, slender spires in the tall, fourteenth-century windows in the St Catherine Chapel. The pinnacled canopies in grisaille glitter against diapered backgrounds of red and blue, which show the influence of the stained glass of neighbouring France.

The first city of Strasbourg was Celtic. It was conquered by the Romans in the first century, destroyed by the Huns in the fifth century and, rebuilt, was annexed by the Franks (then neither Germans nor French). Four centuries later Strasbourg was parcelled out to the Eastern Franks (who were to become the Germans). In 923, it was integrated into the Holy Roman Empire and then, in 1205, it became a Free Imperial City, subject to no authority except that of the emperor or the German king. It was taken over by Protestantism in the fifteenth century, became Catholic and French in 1681, was captured by the Germans in 1870, regained by the French in 1918, occupied by the Germans in the Second World War and bombed by the Allies.

Strasbourg is the city that can boast one of Europe's most dazzling cathedrals, a perfect fusion of French and German influence. The rebuilding of the splendid old cathedral, which in 1176 was finally razed to the ground after many fires, began in late Romanesque style, but after half a century the architecture suddenly changed to French Gothic. The oldest stained-glass panels in the present cathedral date from the Romanesque phase of the rebuilding. They are typically Germanic and show strong Byzantine influence. Two, which date from about 1200, portray figures of John the Baptist and John the Evangelist in a style that flourished in monastery workshops of the Upper Rhine and Lake Constance. The figures are statuesque and angular, and delicate shades of green and blue and also white predominate.

The figures are livelier and the gestures more varied in three medallion panels of about the same period, which depict the Judgement of Solomon. Another, later Judgement of Solomon window provides a dramatic contrast, with its four tall lancets each containing a figure under an enormous canopy. The difference in style seems far greater than the time—one hundred and fifty years—that separates the windows. Here the influence is unmistakably French.

A progression from Romanesque to Gothic style can be traced in the windows of German kings, from the eighth-century Pepin the Short (the father of Charlemagne) to the thirteenth-century Rudolf of Habsburg. Now in the Musée de l'Oeuvre Notre-Dame in Strasbourg, one of the earliest of these windows, glazed at the end of the twelfth century, is believed to portray Charlemagne. The figure is shown seated, in sumptuous cloak, holding orb and sceptre —a monumental, two-dimensional Byzantine figure. He stares fixedly ahead of him, for the glazier leaded around the eyes to make them more prominent; this window is one of the earliest examples of this device. There is a touch of realism, unusual in Romanesque, in a king window dating from about the mid-thirteenth century. It depicts Conrad II with his son, the future Henry the Black: the boy is shown with a squint, a bent nose and a lopsided mouth. Other king windows date from the fourteenth century. Although the figures themselves remain Byzantine and some Romanesque influence persists, increasingly Gothic features creep in.

The cathedral suffered yet another fire in 1298 and many windows were destroyed. Those which replaced them represent the second main period of Alsatian stained glass. The windows of St Catherine's Chapel, built between 1331 and 1332, belong to this phase. Glazed in the middle of the fourteenth century, they are generally credited to Johannes von Kirchheim, the only contemporary glass-painter who worked for Strasbourg Cathedral to be identified. His name notwithstanding, the six tall windows are basically French. They depict the apostles, each standing under an immense canopy three or more times his height. The canopies, in grisaille glass against alternating backgrounds of blue and red, are two-dimensional, but the pedestals on which the apostles stand are seen partly in perspective. It was not until the early part of the fifteenth century, with the spread of Italian influence via the Habsburg Chapel at Königsfelden in Switzerland, that the art of

MASTERPIECES OF GOTHIC SCULPTURE

Female figures representing Church and Synagogue, below, on the south portal of Strasbourg Cathedral are copies of statues which are now in the Musée de l'Oeuvre Notre-Dame. The exterior arcade, right, surmounting the web-like west rose, minutely follows the architectural drawing, below right, which was done by Erwin von Steinbach in 1276.

Crowned figure representing the enlightened Church.

Blindfolded figure representing the unenlightened Synagogue.

perspective was mastered at Strasbourg. There are brilliant examples of perspective in the cathedral cloister windows, which were originally in the city's Dominican Church.

In striking contrast to the windows in the St Catherine Chapel are those in the St Lawrence Chapel, on the opposite side of the nave. Two windows, showing scenes from the Life and Passion of Christ, were also in the Dominican Church, and have been in the cathedral only since the 1830s. In design and colour they are as German as the St Catherine Chapel windows are French.

The stained glass in the south aisle was renewed in the fourteenth century, the twelfth-century prophets making way for windows depicting scenes from the lives of the Virgin Mary and Christ. Some of the windows are so crowded with people as to be chaotic, but two others are simpler and more effective. These are the Last Judgement window and the adjoining Misericord window, in which Christ appears cold, hungry, thirsty, sick and imprisoned, watched compassionately from the borders by tiny angels. The window, glazed in 1325, is noteworthy for its use of silver stain, still rare at this time in Germany.

A favourite medieval device was to emphasize a moral by contrasting two ideas, and it was used throughout the visual arts. Strasbourg has a fragment of a window depicting the Battle of the Virtues and Vices, a concept that goes back to the fifth century. In the window the Virtues are shown as gentle young women wearing crowns and elegant robes, who are in the rather barbarous act of piercing the Vices—ordinary women in their everyday clothes and bonnets—with lances.

From century to century, the influences and ideas which Strasbourg received from the rest of Europe, above all from France and Germany, were transmuted into something proudly Strasbourgeois. But then nothing less could be expected of a city which maintained its identity under so many different rulers.

Scenes from Christ's life after death, in the St Lawrence Chapel, incorporate the greens, reds and yellows which often distinguish German stained glass. Christ's Entombment and descent into hell are depicted beneath leaf-like medallions, in which he sits in majesty, above.

A rose and rosettes designed with patterns of petals and circles surmount a Last Judgement window in the south porch. In the top row, beneath trios of angels who seem to swim downwards, St Catherine and Mary kneel before Christ. Below are pairs of apostles and figures doing good works.

FOURTEENTH-CENTURY ITALY

A Change of Direction

Built spectacularly on a hill overlooking the Tuscan plain, the vast, two-level church of San Francesco, Assisi, left, is the burial place of St Francis. Both upper and lower churches, built between 1228 and 1253, are decorated with frescoes and stained-glass windows, many of which were inspired by the life of St Francis, whose humanity and lack of pious pomp contributed significantly to the ideas of Renaissance artists.

The art of stained glass took root later in Italy and flowered and faded more quickly than it did in France, England and Germany. Moreover, when the art finally made its way across the Alps, it quickly developed a style of its own. There were many reasons for this. First, the brightness of the Italian sun had two easily observable effects. Grisaille was not in general use as it was in England, where it helped to compensate for darker northern skies. Nor are Italian windows overwhelmed by canopies, another English and French device for admitting more light. Instead, the Italians used architectural features as an integral part of their windows, and they depicted them in colour instead of clear glass. But the basic reason that Italian glass looks so different is that, even from its inception, it was more a painter's art than the glazier's art that it was throughout northern Europe.

It is not surprising that the early stained glass in Italy, in the two basilicas of San Francesco in Assisi, was created by German glaziers, since they not only knew the art but shared with the Italians a taste for rich colour. Their windows are also an appropriate tribute to St Francis, for it was the humanity of his teachings that helped to introduce a naturalism into Western art, thus bringing about a decisive break with the stylized Byzantine tradition.

Born to wealth, St Francis was the leading playboy among the youth of Assisi until he was converted by spiritual visions in his early twenties. He gave up his possessions and, founding the Franciscan order, spent most of the rest of his life as a travelling preacher. The Church of San Francesco

St Anthony, patron saint of Padua, where he died in 1231, was a Franciscan friar and a great preacher. According to legend, while walking alone along the sea-shore he preached to the fishes for want of another audience. This story is depicted in two left-hand panels of the fourteenth-century window, right, in the Chapel of St Anthony in the lower basilica of San Francesco. The four-light window is the work of two glaziers. On the left, figures occupy central positions against relatively flat backgrounds, while on the right side the figures are visually of equal importance to the surrounding architecture, which is drawn in perspective.

The Flight into Egypt, one of Giotto's fourteenth-century frescoes in the lower basilica of San Francesco at Assisi, demonstrates the revolutionary realism of this Florentine painter, who freed art from its frozen, medieval stylization.

ARTISTIC OPULENCE

Sumptuous frescoes and stained glass decorate Santa Croce in Florence, below, another fourteenth-century painters' church. Giotto decorated four chapels in this spacious church, which was built in the Florentine Gothic style, and two frescoes remain. The one in the Bardi Chapel, portraying episodes from the life of St Francis, is reminiscent of the style of the frescoes attributed to Giotto at Assisi. The frescoes and stained glass were probably conceived to complement each other, both in the Bardi and the Tosinghi-Spinelli chapels, as part of the overall scheme for the glorification of St Francis. In the windows, monumental saints, exemplified by the figure, right, from the Baroncelli Chapel, stand beneath simple Gothic arches, an idea carried through from the frescoes.

was built, two years after his death, to house his remains.

The upper basilica was built in French Gothic style, but many of the basically Romanesque windows are the work of German glaziers of the mid-thirteenth century. Those of the late thirteenth century reflect current French Gothic taste. Some of the surviving windows honour St Francis.

Two Florentine and two Sienese painters created artistic landmarks in the change from Byzantine Romanesque to an Italian Gothic style. Giovanni Cimabue (c. 1240–1302) worked in a fundamentally Byzantine style, but his frescoes in the upper and lower basilicas at Assisi, especially of the Crucifixion, have tremendous emotional power. He is said to have been Giotto's master. Giotto, however, soon broke from the two-dimensional Byzantine style and developed in his work a naturalism that was then revolutionary. Through the influence of Giotto and two Sienese artists—Duccio and his more obviously French Gothic follower, Simone Martini—glass-painters turned to representing volume and depth by means of modelling and perspective. At Assisi these developments can be seen in the Giotto frescoes and the Giottoesque windows and, even more strikingly, in some of the St Anthony windows.

Italian glass-painters could never have achieved the same effect as the French, English and German glaziers of this period, for the Italians were wedded to painted walls. Therefore, Gothic architecture, which created large areas of window, was never taken seriously in Italy. However, even if the Italian cathedrals and churches of the fourteenth century are not "true" Gothic to northern eyes, in the course of their decoration many masterpieces were produced in what can be described as Gothic–Renaissance style. The growth of this style can be traced in the development of the eye window, or *occhio*. While in the north tracery was an integral part of the design of circular windows, in Italy there was often no stone tracery and only the minimum of iron armature that was needed for support. These eye windows are, in fact, circular paintings transferred to glass and many famous painters showed unusual skill in adapting scenes to the shape.

In the façade of Santa Maria Novella in Florence there is a magnificent *occhio* by Andrea da Firenze. The centre scene shows the Coronation of the Virgin, the two solemn figures in complete contrast to the music-making angels who encircle them. This joyful window, rich in movement and colour, is truly Italian. In this form, there was nothing to be learned from the north. Indeed, when enthusiasm for Gothic started to ebb, it was the Italians who began to influence the northern style.

According to legend, while St Anthony was preaching to the Franciscans at Arles in Provence, St Francis, who was unable to attend in person, appeared to his friars in a vision. The Apparition at Arles is illustrated with perspective in two right-hand panels, one of which is shown left, of the fourteenth-century window in St Anthony's Chapel in the lower basilica of San Francesco. St Francis is depicted floating off the ground with arms outstretched like those of the crucified Christ. The stigmata on his hands are visible.

Memorial to a Murdered King

One of the most powerful and often hated dynasties in Europe, the Habsburgs are commemorated by eleven magnificent stained-glass windows in the deserted church of the ruined monastery of Königsfelden, to the northwest of Zurich. Their name deriving from the castle of Habichtsburg, meaning hawk's castle, in the Swiss Aargau, the Habsburgs had by the thirteenth century firmly established their overlordship in parts of Alsace, Switzerland, Austria and Styria. In 1273 their power and status were augmented by the coronation of Count Rudolf IV of Habsburg as Rudolf I of Germany.

In 1308, on the site of the monastery, King Albert, son of Rudolf, was murdered by his nephew. His devoted widow, Elisabeth, built a hermitage there, for God and his saints and "for the salvation of King Albert and all his forefathers", and his daughter, Agnes, who succeeded Elisabeth as queen, enlarged it. Thereafter its fortunes declined. It fell into the hands of the Swiss, and when the monastery was dissolved in 1528 it became a hospital and mental asylum. In the nineteenth century the original buildings were largely demolished. Only the empty church, altarless and denuded of its Habsburg tombs, remains.

Not all the glass in the towering windows has survived; indeed, considering all the vicissitudes the building has undergone, it is surprising that any still exists. Seven windows were originally dedicated to four generations of Habsburgs, who were depicted kneeling in prayer beside their coats of arms. Only four panels remain. The eleven windows in the choir have fared better and about two-thirds of the glass is original. A harmonious colour scheme runs through all the windows. Against the red and blue backgrounds the scenes are depicted in rich tones of reds, yellows, violets and greens. In some of the windows canopied figures stand side by side in separate lancets; in others the scenes portrayed in medallions are spread across the whole window. The effect in both is equally dramatic.

The three windows in the apse are in praise of Christ. The subjects range from the Annunciation and Birth of Christ in the window of the north wall to the Passion in the east wall window and the Resurrection and the coming of the Holy Ghost in the south wall window. These three windows are flanked by four on each side of the choir devoted to the Virgin Mary, the apostles and saints, including St Anne, St Catherine and St Clare. The donors—children or close relatives of the murdered king—are depicted in panels of five of the windows.

Although more than one glazier was involved, the windows themselves are evidence that there was one brilliant and original master, who became more confident as he designed his way around the church. The Passion window was probably the first to be completed and here the attempt to show perspective in the sarcophagus in the Entombment scene produces the idiosyncratic result that the arches are seen from the left, but the corbels above them are seen from the right. The background of the Italian-style buildings in the late and masterly St Anne window shows that, by the time the glazier had reached this window, a great advance in the use of perspective had been made.

The identity of the glazier responsible for the windows is unknown, and there is much speculation about the origin of the suggestion of depth in space in stained glass from which it had previously been absent. The obvious source for this daring innovation was Italian painting, for the influence of Florentine and Sienese art had already been established in the Habsburg city of Vienna.

It is perhaps ironic that such a beautiful monument to the Habsburgs survives in a country whose people had, by the fifteenth century, thrown off the Habsburg yoke, a monument which is a landmark in the story of stained glass.

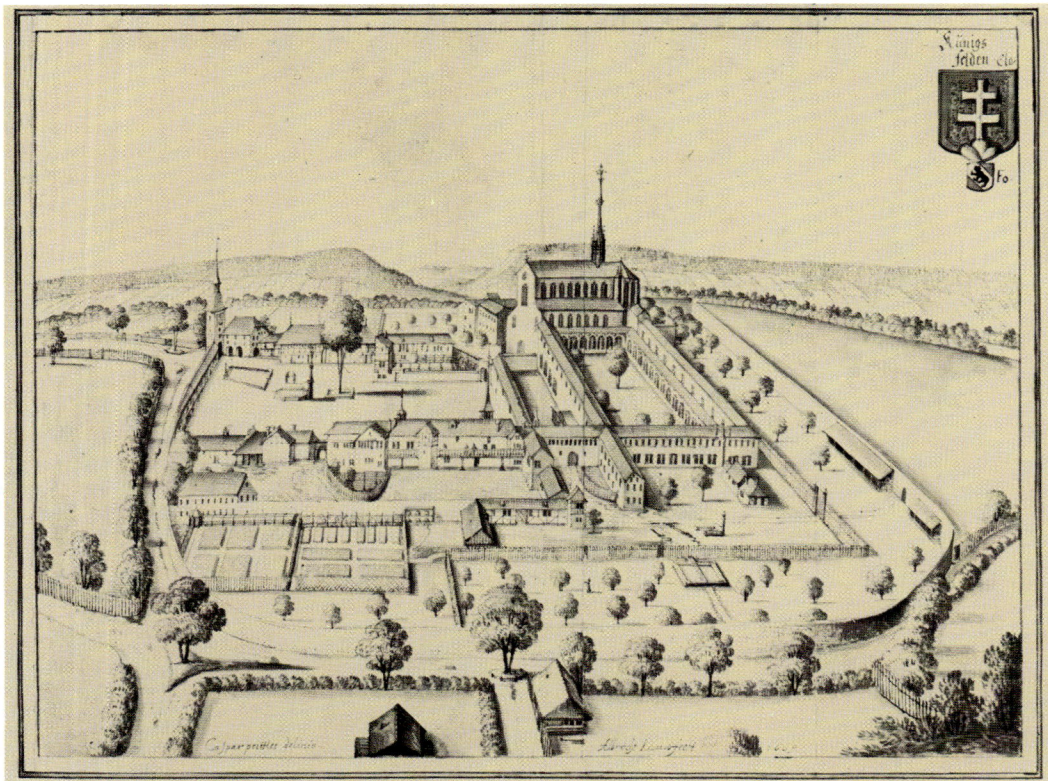

Built to commemorate the Habsburg king, Albert I, the shrine at Königsfelden became a monastery. The original buildings, later converted into a hospital, are shown in this seventeenth-century illustration.

Perspective first appeared in stained glass north of the Alps in the fourteenth-century windows at Königsfelden. In the Laying in the Tomb scene, left, from the Passion window, the artist marred the spatial depth, which was suggested by the arches of the sarcophagus, by incongruously pointing the corbels above them in the opposite direction. Perspective is far more convincingly represented by the Italianate architecture in the later St Anne window, above.

The Pinnacle of Perfection

One of the finest expressions of Gothic architecture in Germany, built between 1250 and 1320, the tower of Freiburg Cathedral with its delicately traceried spire soars to a height of 377 feet.

Germany may have started late in the pursuit of Gothic architecture, but she certainly made up for it during the fourteenth century as her Gothic became more and more Gothic. The Gothic style did not stand still anywhere; that would have been a contradiction of its very character, for experiment was the basis of its existence. Late Gothic architecture did not have the directness of early Gothic, but it was, perhaps, the richness of medieval imagination, rather than decadence, that pushed the style to its ultimate limits. In France, the flamboyant Gothic emerged. England produced her own Perpendicular Gothic. In Germany, the corresponding exploitation of space, verticality and feeling of movement was labelled *Sondergotik*. The glaziers in each country had, of course, to adjust to these changes of architectural style evolved by the master masons.

The Parlers were a powerful family of master masons. In the fourteenth century they, or their pupils, had a hand in the building of many of the major churches throughout Germanic Europe. They, more than any other architects, were responsible for the *Sondergotik* style. Although the Parlers did not design or glaze any stained-glass windows, their influence on buildings and sculpture affected window design and led to a revival of narrative windows.

The influence of the Parler family began with Heinrich, who established his reputation at Cologne. His sons, the famous Peter and Johann, his grandson Wenzel, and other members of the family by birth or marriage were involved in building many cathedrals, including Cologne, Prague, Ulm, Freiburg and Milan, as well as countless churches.

Germany is rich in fourteenth-century stained glass. Its outstanding quality, the warmth of its colours, in which greens, yellows and reds predominate, is unmatched anywhere in northern Europe. It was, indeed, their use of rich colours that made German glaziers so welcome in both Italy and Spain.

Grisaille glass was not used extensively, but when it was it, too, had a curious warmth. The Germans distributed clear glass differently from the English and the French. They glazed the lower part of a window with richly coloured glass and put grisaille above it. Later, to add interest, the grisaille section of the window was designed in geometric patterns. A further development was to give the top of the coloured band a decorative edging which gradually tapered off into the clear glass above, thus counteracting the abrupt division between coloured and clear glass. Grisaille may not have been used in this way in order to admit more light. In German fourteenth-century buildings, many windows were much taller than those of previous centuries, making glazing more costly, and narrower, making designing more difficult. Both these problems could be solved by dividing the window into plain and coloured glass.

German glass-painters of the fourteenth century were as fortunate as the English in having so many Gothic cathedrals of outstanding beauty waiting to be glazed. Among them were the cathedrals at Freiburg, Regensburg and Erfurt, and the churches of St Dionysius and St Mary at Esslingen. With at least six stained-glass workshops busy at one period during the fourteenth century, Esslingen was the most important stained-glass centre in Swabia. St Dionysius, the oldest church in the city, was begun in late Romanesque style, but changed to Gothic architecture as the building continued through much of the century. The lofty windows of the choir have over-life-size figures and a wide range of medallions, from simple circles to intricate foliated shapes.

Subjects of the windows include the Life of Christ, martyrs, wise and foolish virgins and Poor Man's Bible scenes. Plato and Aristotle find a place among the martyrs and virgins, evidence of the interest in Greek philosophy in the late Middle Ages. (Their rediscovery was a mixed blessing, for one effect was to inhibit the roving imagination of the medieval mind and to encourage the growing arid scholasticism.) Besides the Greeks, other intruders in the glass are birds; in one window there are flocks of them, green and grey, perched on a green and yellow tree. In

Christ, the Man of Sorrows, is portrayed with the elegant simplicity typical of the early fourteenth century in this tracery rosette from the bakers' window in Freiburg Cathedral. Surrounding Christ are the instruments of his Passion.

Adorned with a red halo, rather than the more usual golden one, the Virgin embraces Elizabeth in this Visitation scene from the smiths' window in Freiburg Cathedral. The central pillar suggests that an arch once surmounted the figures.

FOURTEENTH-CENTURY GERMANY

The Pinnacle of Perfection

St Mary's Church in Esslingen there are even more birds, brightly coloured and swallow-tailed and formally perched in pairs. From about the middle of the fourteenth century Heinrich Parler was involved in the building of this church, and many of its windows—which are later than those of St Dionysius and belong to the best Esslingen period—are the narrative scenes which the Parlers brought back into favour.

Nowhere is the Parlers' influence more evident than at Erfurt, now in East Germany, which had no local tradition or stained-glass school. The cathedral there had one of the most extensive programmes of narrative windows in all medieval Germany—640 panels. The choir's tall, slim windows, still with most of their late fourteenth-century and early fifteenth-century glass, are outstanding for their warm colouring, boldness of design and imaginative detail. The predominant colours are a mellow blending of green, yellow, yellow-brown and red. The design of the glass permits tiers of narrative scenes to stretch across the four lancets of the windows, ignoring the mullions. In the architectural framework which divides the scenes, there is an endless variety of detail, including little people peeping at what is happening below.

Freiburg was still a town of no importance when, towards the end of the twelfth century, it embarked on building an ambitious minster about which even a wealthy city might have had second thoughts. Funds soon ran out, and by the time building began again, in the middle of the thirteenth century, the Gothic style had arrived and it took over where Romanesque had left off.

The first Gothic windows are in the façade of the north transept. They were glazed by a Strasbourg-trained workshop, which established itself in Freiburg and next glazed the windows at the eastern end of the south aisle. The windows at the western end of the aisle were not glazed until the mid-fourteenth century, and by then the Freiburg school had developed a style of its own. Many of these windows were given by guilds—wine-growers, shoemakers, shopkeepers, bakers, smiths and even miners.

One of the famous fourteenth-century windows at Freiburg is of Christ on the Cross with the "pelican in her piety" above. The pelican as a symbol of Christ as Redeemer appears often in late medieval art, although it was most popular during the Renaissance. It has its roots in the folklore notion that the pelican feeds its young with blood drawn from her own breast, an illusion presumably created by the reddish tinge of her breast feathers and the red tip of her beak.

Regensburg also had a glass workshop of its own and in the fourteenth century it was understandably receptive to Western influences, since the city lay on the great trade

In accordance with the popular symbolic convention of the fourteenth century, the infant Christ rests not in the customary manger but upon an altarpiece adorned with Gothic windows in this Nativity scene from the Poor Man's Bible window in St Mary's Church, Esslingen. The altar is an allusion to Christ's supreme sacrifice.

THE MASTER MASONS

The most famous of all German masons in the fourteenth century, the Parlers exerted a seminal influence on late German Gothic architecture and sculpture. They worked mainly in South Germany and Bohemia, notably in Prague. The new realism introduced into sculpture by the Parlers is evinced by the self-portrait of Peter, left, in the triforium of Prague Cathedral.

The magnificent choir of Prague Cathedral, with its radiating *chevet* and pinnacled flying buttresses, bears eloquent testimony to the genius of its creator, Peter Parler.

One of the numerous churches on which the Parlers worked, the Church of St Mary, Esslingen, right, is a masterpiece of German Gothic, both in its architecture and its sculpture.

route between eastern and western Europe. For centuries Regensburg had been a city of kings, dukes and bishops, and its political importance was matched by its cultural reputation. The first cathedral dated from the eighth century and it was replaced by an early Romanesque building at the beginning of the eleventh century. After a typically medieval record of fires and reconstruction, the Romanesque cathedral was finally consumed by flames in 1273 and was then rebuilt in High Gothic style.

The cathedral, not particularly outstanding architecturally, is oddly satisfying emotionally, in part because of the abundance of medieval stained glass, some of which survived from the Romanesque cathedral. In this kaleidoscope of colour the feeling of warmth is created by the characteristically German greens, rich oranges and yellows.

How broad was the glaziers' range of colours and how it was used can well be seen in the windows of the choir. In the depiction of the Birth of Jesus, the manger is a light green against a dark blue background. For the Resurrection and the Coronation of the Virgin, subdued olive green and light blue contrast with dark blue backgrounds lit with golden stars. God the Father, within a white frame on a red background, is supported by angels with warm brown wings and red haloes.

Individually and as an ensemble, the choir windows at Regensburg exemplify the pinnacle of perfection reached by German glazing in the fourteenth century. This level of excellence was to persist into the fifteenth century, for, in Germany, unlike much of Europe, the end of the fourteenth century brought no waning of Gothic inspiration.

Popularly regarded as the "interpreter of St Peter", St Mark is often depicted writing. Originally in Erfurt Cathedral, the panel below is now in the Bavarian National Museum.

Resplendent in richly coloured green and red robes, and in his left hand holding his emblem, a key, this majestic St Peter is one of a series of saints depicted in Regensburg Cathedral.

THE FIFTEENTH CENTURY
The Age of Transition

According to taste, the fifteenth century can be labelled the twilight of the Middle Ages or the dawn of the Renaissance. Either as twilight or as dawn it was prolonged. Medieval man did not die and overnight be reborn Renaissance, and in many parts of Europe medieval outlooks persisted into the sixteenth century. The early signs of a new humanism which appear in works of art reflect the attitudes of only a small élite; the mass of people had not changed.

But no matter what its label, this was an age of extravagant emotions. As Professor Johan Huizinga summed it up in *The Waning of the Middle Ages*, published in 1924: "So violent and motley was life, that it bore the mixed smell of blood and roses. The men of that time always oscillate between the fear of hell and the most naïve joy, between cruelty and tenderness, between harsh asceticism and insane attachments to the delights of the world, between hatred and goodness, always running to extremes."

Lacking only the Black Death, the fifteenth-century scenario, with its background of warfare, was similar to that of the fourteenth century. A martyr came to the rescue of France. The peasant Joan of Arc, by being burned to death by the English as a heretic and witch, became a patriotic symbol that helped the French to rid their country, except Calais, of the English after a hundred years' fighting. England emerged defeated but unbowed from that bloody war-cum-tournament, only to plunge immediately into her own Wars of the Roses. In Italy, the first half of the century was wasted in fighting between the Duchy of Milan and her rivals, the republics of Venice and Florence, but the artistic brilliance of the second half made up for those lost years. The Great Schism, which for nearly forty years had split the Roman Church into two camps, each with a Pope, was healed in 1417, but in Bohemia the religious wars which were the prelude to the Reformation were beginning. In Spain throughout the Middle Ages two civilizations—Muslim and Christian—struggled for ascendancy, and it was not until the end of the fifteenth century that the Christians emerged supreme.

Hardly surprisingly, an undercurrent of pessimism ran through the century. Yet many of the arts flourished, not only in Italy and Flanders, but in Germany, England and even in France. The impetus of previous centuries had been lost and was replaced by a grandiloquent elaboration of old ideas—ideas no longer living but lying in state. Even so, the naturalism associated with humanism began to creep in, long before the spirit of humanism became the new driving force.

There was certainly no danger of the arts languishing through lack of money. The fifteenth century was a time of prosperity, based on capital, trade, profit and usury. The affluence did not seep far down in society, but from the point of view of art that did not matter, for it was the merchants and bankers, not the poor, who were its patrons. Previously, patronage had largely been provided by royalty and the Church. Now they were joined by bankers and entrepreneurs.

One of the most famous of all fifteenth-century entrepreneurs, Christopher Columbus, wrote: "Gold is an excellent thing. When one has it, one does all one wants in the world, even to leading souls into Paradise." Among those who could lay their hands on this excellent commodity were Jacques Coeur, financier to Charles VII, King of France; the Medicis, all-powerful in Florence; the Fuggers, leading merchant bankers in Germany; and Sir Richard (Dick) Whittington in London, who even had to lend seven thousand pounds to the straitened King Henry IV for his daughter's wedding trousseau. The merchant bankers, many of them working closely with the Church, which had come to accept usury, collected not only gold but art and artists as well. The art of Italy and of the Netherlands, in particular, was founded on the wealth of their independent cities and by mid-century Italian and Flemish influences began to have a profound effect on stained glass.

For the first three decades of the fifteenth century, stained glass continued to be created in the elegant, mannered Gothic style developed at the end of the fourteenth century. This style was matched in contemporary miniature painting and reflected the courtly extravagance of the time. (Looking at the Middle Ages through stained glass often makes them appear rosier than they indeed were for most of the population.) There are examples of such mannered windows throughout Europe—in France in the cathedrals of Bourges, Le Mans and Evreux; in Germany in the Besserer Chapel of Ulm Cathedral; and in England in the Beauchamp Chapel of St Mary's Church in Warwick.

But from 1430 the style of Flemish painting, above all of Jan van Eyck, vitally changed the approach of glass-painters. Van Eyck was the master (or the slave) of detail. The realism he achieved in his painting owed nothing to the Classical realism of the Italians; it was a product of his native medieval Flemish soil. But it was impossible for a glazier, using the current techniques, to translate this much-admired, painstaking realism into stained glass. Instead of making a picture in glass, with the lead an integral part of the design, he began to paint pictures on glass, ignoring rather than utilizing the lead lines. Thus began the decline of traditional stained glass, as it changed into an imitation of fresco and easel painting, which eventually destroyed the essential quality of coloured glass—its translucency. This trend became all the more established because Italian and Flemish painters and sculptors, including Ghiberti, Donatello, Van Eyck and Van der Weyden, often designed windows.

Other significant trends in the fifteenth century were the increasing choice of secular subjects for church windows and the greater use of stained glass in domestic buildings. There is, in fact, evidence of stained glass in palaces and in the living quarters of monasteries from early in the thirteenth century, but it was only in the fifteenth century that it became widespread in secular buildings. Stained glass was expensive, but since it was removable it could be looked at and enjoyed, and considered a portable asset.

Since domestic windows had to let in maximum light they were not made with the rich colouring of church windows. The greater part of each window was, therefore, usually glazed with quarries, diamond-shaped panels, but with some decoration, which most frequently was heraldic. Circles of glass, roundels, were also popular, and a favourite subject among both English and French was the labours of the months. Another popular theme was the Nine Worthy Conquerors. The nine were composed of three biblical figures, three Classical figures and three Christian knights.

Because the scale of windows in a domestic setting was small, painted quarries could be more effective there than in a church. Most of them have been lost, but, ironically, some are preserved in church windows. One at Yarnton Church in Oxfordshire has obviously come from an inn; it shows a bird holding a tankard in its claw and the inscription reads: "Who blamyth this ale."

It was fortunate that the trend towards greater realism, reflected in both secular and ecclesiastical glass, did not coincide with but followed the great age of cathedral building. Church windows throughout France, England and Germany were already filled with masterpieces of a medieval art form which, while it gained inspiration from other visual arts, never had need to imitate them.

While angels tear up the thatched stable roof to admit the starlight, the Virgin, in this panel from the east window of St Peter Mancroft, Norwich, displays the infant Christ to the kneeling Magi, who are depicted in the adjoining panel. Joseph sits in a squat, round-backed chair which is also included in the Nativity scene in the same window.

FIFTEENTH-CENTURY FLANDERS

Birth of the Flemish Tradition

A bearded fuller and his apprentice are depicted in one of the two draper panels in the Church of St Martin, Halle. The simple figures and the bulky apparatus of their work stand out against the glowing ruby background and the rich blue of the cloth. The spindle in the left-hand corner is a symbol of their trade. The two panels, probably donated by the drapers of Brussels, show a strong French influence in their stylized elegance.

The fifteenth century was a heyday for the arts in the Low Countries. Six centuries had passed since the Norse invasions and in that time the land which is now Holland, Belgium and Luxembourg developed into one of the great trading centres of Europe. At its heart was Flanders, which had evolved into a powerful, autonomous commercial and financial territory under a dynasty of counts.

The financial wealth of the Low Countries came from wool, but its richness in the arts owed much to the influence of the House of Burgundy. Vengeful, ambitious, flamboyant, luxury-loving Philip the Good, Duke of Burgundy from 1419 to 1467, was head of the first union of the Low Countries since Charlemagne, a union which included Burgundy, Flanders, Artois, Brabant, Luxembourg, Holland, Zeeland, Friesland and Hainault. He was a lavish patron of the arts and artists, particularly of Jan van Eyck, the great Flemish painter. Van Eyck was the Duke's court painter, *valet de chambre* and emissary extraordinary, involved on secret journeys "to distant places of which no mention is to be made". He went to Portugal, on one of the journeys which could be mentioned, with the mission of negotiating the marriage of Philip to Isabella of Portugal and to paint Isabella's portrait.

Although Flemish art reached its zenith under Burgundian rule in the late Gothic period, French influence had been at work much earlier. Because of proximity to France the Gothic style of architecture was adopted far sooner in the southern Netherlands than in the northern, where, as in neighbouring Germany, Romanesque prevailed longer.

In the architecture of the cathedral at Tournai in Belgium there is a remarkable contrast between the twelfth-century Romanesque nave and towers and the spacious Gothic choir of the mid-thirteenth century. There are two groups of interesting fifteenth-century windows, now in the transepts, which record how the original cathedral acquired its wealth, as a result of regicide and the diplomacy of a bishop. Towards the end of the sixth century the king of the western Frankish kingdom, Neustria, was Chilperic I, described by Gregory of Tours as the combined Herod and Nero of his time. Defeated in battle while trying to oust his brother Sigebert from the eastern kingdom, Austrasia, he took refuge with the Bishop of Tournai. But his wife, a persistent murderess, hired two assassins to kill Sigebert. Thereupon Chilperic usurped the throne and rewarded the bishop by granting the see the right to levy taxes. In seven vivid scenes the windows illustrate Sigebert's victory, Chilperic's flight, the Queen's plot, Sigebert's assassination while sleeping in his tent and Chilperic's granting of privileges to the bishop. Five panels above these narrative scenes, which show how the Church benefited from the Queen's wickedness, depict surpliced officials collecting tolls on the bridge over Tournai's River Scheldt and gathering taxes on merchandise in the market-place.

The other series of windows deals with another major event in the cathedral's history that occurred five centuries later. The annexing of the bishopric of Tournai to that of the nearby town of Noyon in the seventh century had been a source of resentment over the centuries. Ten crowded scenes in the north transept windows tell the story of the way in which Tournai regained its bishopric in the twelfth century, by sensibly enlisting the help of the formidable St Bernard of Clairvaux, whose influence with the Pope, Eugene III, was immense.

Both groups of windows are the early work of Arnt Nijmegen, also known as Arnoult de Nimègue and Artus

PHILIP THE GOOD

Powerful and influential, Philip the Good (his coat of arms is shown below), made the House of Burgundy a great power in fifteenth-century Europe. He ruled as Duke of Burgundy from 1419 to 1467. Through aggression and diplomacy he drew together the regions around Flanders to form a union of the Low Countries. He indulged in a luxurious court life and was an enthusiastic patron of the great artists of the day, commissioning many works of art. The Flemish painter Jan van Eyck was in his personal service.

Flanders was renowned for its tapestries in the fifteenth century. A detail from the third Unicorn tapestry, above, shows the influence of this craft on the contemporary stained glass in Tournai Cathedral, left. In one of the transept windows which illustrate historic events in the diocese, Bishop Anselm, mounted on a mule with the Canon of Noyon beside him, returns to Tournai from Rome. There the pope had reinstated Tournai, previously under the jurisdiction of Noyon, as a separate diocese and ordained Anselm as its bishop.

van Ort. At this time, his style was still essentially Gothic, although when he was working in Rouen only a few years later it had become Renaissance in character. While Nijmegen himself did not make all the windows at Tournai, the designs were his. Similarities can be detected between the High Gothic style of the windows and the tapestries for which Tournai was then noted and which rivalled even those of the famous centre of Arras. Under strict guild rules, tapestries had to be woven to the designs of painters and common traits were, therefore, almost inevitable.

In Flanders, even more than in the rest of northern Europe, guilds proliferated and became powerful during the fourteenth century. There was often great rivalry between them. In the woollen industry, the weavers and the fullers, who prepared the cloth, even resorted to massacring each other from time to time. Stained-glass artists, who originally belonged to other guilds concerned with the arts, gradually formed guilds of their own, thus increasing their prestige.

In the fifteenth century, guilds throughout the Low Countries were outstandingly generous donors of stained glass. In the spacious Gothic Church of St Martin in Halle there are two panels showing clothiers at work. These are all that survive of an early fifteenth-century window, which is thought to have been given by the drapers of Brussels. Two fullers prepare the cloth while an apprentice spins. The stylized simplicity of the figures and the machinery of their trade gives the workaday scene great elegance.

The radical change of style that took place in Flemish stained glass before the end of the century is exemplified by a window in the Church of St Gommaire, Lierre, depicting the Coronation of the Virgin. Although much restored, it is a masterpiece of medieval Belgian stained glass. The influence of Van der Weyden is unmistakable, above all in the expressive faces of the angels. Van der Weyden's painting of religious themes conveys an emotional involvement, which is totally different from the cool realism of Van Eyck.

The influence of Van Eyck and Van der Weyden and their followers spread like ripples in a pond throughout Europe. France, Germany, Spain, Portugal and Italy all felt their impact, which was not confined to painting but was absorbed by all the visual arts.

The levy and collection of taxes—a privilege granted the Bishop of Tournai by King Chilperic—are depicted in five transept windows in Tournai Cathedral. In the last of the series, above, a tax official visits a brewery where, in the background, workers make the beer and fill the vats. Full of vitality, the tax windows are the work of Arnt Nijmegen.

One of the most beautiful examples of medieval Belgian glass, this window at St Gommaire, Lierre, depicts the Coronation of the Virgin by God the Father and God the Son. The delicacy of the graceful figures in white glass is complemented by the richness of the background. The influence of the work of such fifteenth-century Flemish painters as Rogier van der Weyden, exemplified in the detail from Van der Weyden's Annunciation, above, is evident in the flowing draperies and in the expressive elegance of the Virgin.

FIFTEENTH-CENTURY FRANCE

Munificent Donors

A royal duke and an entrepreneur have to be credited with some of the finest fifteenth-century stained glass in Bourges Cathedral, indeed in the whole of France. Both men were larger than life, even medieval life. Jean, Duke of Berry, uncle of the French king, held court in his palace at Mehun-sur-Yèvre, near Bourges, surrounded by scholars and artists including the three Limbourg brothers, Pol, Jehannequin and Herman. They created illustrated manuscripts for the Duke, of which the most famous is the *Très Riches Heures*, and became so rich in the ducal service that they were able to lend money to their patron.

The courts drew in the artists like magnets, and there is no doubt that their art was influenced by the fact that their patrons were princes and noblemen. These Franco–Flemish artists spent their lives not in garrets but in palaces, and they probably had to pay for their comforts with more than a modicum of sycophancy. The environment in which they lived and worked gave to their paintings a courtly refinement, nowhere more evident than in the work of the famous miniaturists of the century.

Enterprising and ambitious, Jacques Coeur of Bourges, left, was not only a highly successful merchant but a key figure in fifteenth-century French politics. He eventually fell from favour and was exiled, but while he prospered he was a generous patron of the arts. He donated a window, detail right, to Bourges Cathedral and was sufficiently wealthy to have the windows of his home glazed with stained glass.

The Duke of Berry lived flamboyantly, but he was merely outstanding in an age of courtly extravagance. The other patron of Bourges, however, was formed in an entirely different mould. He was one of the new capitalists of the late Middle Ages. Jacques Coeur, born about 1395, was the son of a tradesman, probably a furrier or a tanner. From modest beginnings in the town of Montpellier, which had been brought to ruin in the Hundred Years' War, he acquired enormous wealth and power by finding ways of reviving the trade that France had lost as a result of the war.

He became a shipowner, exporting cloth and precious metals to the Levant and bringing back slaves from Africa and carpets, silks, scents and spices from Arabia and beyond. He was a mine-owner, banker, master of the King's Mint and, with the permission of the Pope, established a travel business, taking pilgrims to the Holy Land, with gun-running on the side to Egypt. For services to the French king, he was ennobled and his relatives and friends, doubtless as a result of Coeur's influence, were created bishops. Easy to bribe himself, he was adept at bribing others, among them the king and the king's mistress, Agnes Sorel. She was his undoing, for the king accused him of poisoning her, put him on trial, confiscated his wealth and imprisoned him. Whether or not the charge was justified is not certain. Coeur escaped and fled to Rome to the Pope, who gave him a fleet to sail off to fight the Turks. He died in Chios in Greece in 1456.

In the Annunciation window, which he gave to Bourges Cathedral shortly before his downfall, Coeur is curiously self-effacing, for neither he nor his wife is shown, but instead are represented by their patron saints, St James and St Catherine. The Annunciation scene, which ignores the mullions and stretches right across the window, is unusual in several ways. The Virgin, generally depicted expressing surprise at the angel's appearance and news, is here composedly reading her breviary. Moreover, the scene takes place not beneath a stylized canopy but in a sumptuous interior with realistic Gothic vaulting, painted in the French royal blue with a pattern of golden French fleurs-de-lys. A technical innovation is the use of abraded flashing in the damask background. The thin layer of blue fused on to red glass is worn away to create a mottled purple effect.

The meticulous detail in both the architectural features and clothing is probably the result of Flemish influence for this building up of endless detail to give an illusion of reality is the mark of Flemish painting of the period. It is also the hallmark of the illuminated manuscripts of the Limbourg brothers. There may in fact have been a two-way exchange of ideas between manuscripts and stained glass, for the brothers' subtle use of blue in their miniatures suggests the inspiration of stained glass.

Jacques Coeur was also one of the early patrons of secular stained glass, which became popular among the wealthy in the fifteenth century. In the magnificent residence, the Maison de Jacques Coeur (now the Hôtel de Ville), which he built for himself in Bourges, is a charming window of one of his merchant ships in full sail.

The Duke of Berry's legacies to the stained glass of Bourges are five four-light windows in the crypt, where he was buried. These were originally made for the ducal Ste Chapelle, now destroyed. The twenty lancets are filled with figures of apostles and prophets, clad in white and pink, on golden pedestals. The two central figures in each window stand beneath conventional canopies, but the outside pairs are seen peering through simulated pillars (a device also used by York glaziers). The Duke himself is represented in the glass by his coat of arms, supported by angels with pheasant-like wings and Medusa-like hair.

Two other famous donors of windows to Bourges Cathedral in the early fifteenth century were Simon Aligret, personal physician to the Duke, and Pierre Trousseau, who became Bishop of Poitiers. Many of the cathedral's windows show their donors kneeling alone, but the Trousseau window has his sister and two brothers as well. In a window

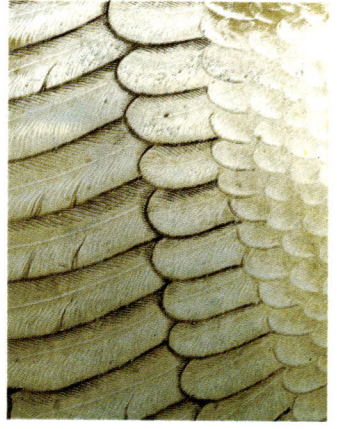

Secular splendour distinguishes the Bourges Annunciation window, detail top, which was donated by Jacques Coeur in the mid-fifteenth century. The angel Gabriel wears a magnificently embroidered robe and the blue vaulted ceiling of the Virgin's dwelling recalls a French royal apartment rather than a room in Nazareth. The courtly extravagance of the scene is tempered, however, by the detached, almost absent-minded facial expressions, whose serenity is reminiscent of figures in contemporary Flemish paintings. The minute attention to detail, also characteristic of Flemish art, is exemplified by the feathers of the angel's wings, detail above, in which even the barbs are clearly visible.

The signs of Leo, Virgo and Libra, detail above, and the nine other zodiacal symbols radiate around the upper half of the south rose, left, in Angers Cathedral. The window, glazed in the mid-fifteenth century, faces its counterpart in the north transept, in which labours of the months are shown. These labours were often juxtaposed with signs of the zodiac in Books of Hours, illuminated medieval prayer books. In the fifteenth-century *Bedford Hours*, Libra, right, is represented by a woman dressed in autumnal golden-brown balancing scales.

in the north transept at Le Mans the donor, Louis II of Anjou, appears with members of his family, and they are in much the same scale as the religious figures above them. Such family groups later grew in number to the point where room had to be found in the windows for several generations.

In the Church of Notre Dame, Semur-en-Auxois, the cloth-makers' guild abandoned all modesty and appropriated a whole window to itself in which no sacred element at all is depicted. There is a delicacy about the figures—and even about that of a butcher about to cleave the head of an ox in another guild window—which gives the panels the appearance of miniatures on glass.

There is some fine glass in Angers Cathedral which is typical of the fifteenth-century glazier's interest in non-religious subjects and shows a certain realism. Two mid-century rose windows in the transepts are by André Robin, whose work at the cathedral spanned half a century. The theme of the north transept window is one that was occasionally used by English glaziers, but is most unusual in France—the fifteen signs of the end of the world. In one medallion there is a scene depicting the resurrection of the dead—the corpses pushing open the covers of their tombs—and in the central panel of the window is Christ on the Day of Judgement. In the oddest contrast, the outer ring of medallions shows farmers engaged in the labours of the months—for example, cutting the hay or reaping the corn—as unconcerned as though the world would never end.

Robin's design for the south transept window similarly contrasts religious and secular subjects. The main theme is Christ in Majesty, but among the Elders of the Apocalypse and the inevitable angels are the signs of the zodiac.

Although secular subjects and some superficial realism were finding their way into French stained glass at the end of the fifteenth century, past styles of window design were still predominant, notably stylized figures standing under canopies, each figure in a separate lancet. True inventiveness was to return with the next century.

St Denis, martyr and patron saint of France, reputedly carried his severed head to its burial place in the Abbey Church of St Denis near Paris. This miraculous being, holding his detached head, is depicted in this detail from an early fifteenth-century window in Evreux Cathedral. He is commending the kneeling King of France, Charles VI, accurately portrayed on the left, to the Virgin. The figures, surmounted by the customary canopies, are drawn with the realism which is characteristic of the style of contemporary Burgundian miniaturists.

FIFTEENTH-CENTURY SPAIN
A Cosmopolitan Era

The art of medieval Spain has been described as "alluvial". But in fact all the rich cultural deposits left by the Moors, the French, the Italians, the Germans and the Flemings gradually underwent a metamorphosis and became part of the Spanish landscape. The Spaniards did not so much adopt each new style in architecture and art as have it inflicted upon them. Then, slowly, they adapted it.

Romanesque was brought to Spain by the Benedictine monks of Cluny in France who began to overrun the country in the eleventh century. The style travelled along the five-hundred-mile pilgrimage route, which ran from the French border to Santiago de Compostela. Here was the reputed resting place of the body of St James the Greater, brother of St John the Evangelist, which was miraculously transported from Jerusalem to this remote corner of north-west Spain. In the ninth century, the pilgrimage had been largely a local affair, but as a result of Benedictine propaganda the shrine became as important a pilgrim centre as Jerusalem or Rome and a Romanesque cathedral was built to house the body.

The Cistercians, who followed the Cluniacs, introduced the severe Gothic style of ecclesiastical architecture for which they were noted elsewhere in Europe. But the magnificent Gothic of the great cathedrals of France and England was late arriving in Spain, and the first cathedrals to be built in this style were the trio of Burgos, Toledo and León. The early part of Burgos, the first great Spanish cathedral, which was begun in 1220, was entirely in the French tradition. It was probably the same master builder Enrique who went on to build the cathedral of León, and there was scarcely anything Spanish about it except the soil on which it was built. Even Toledo can be recognized as French Gothic beneath its later Spanish encrustations.

Wherever Gothic put down roots in Spanish soil hybrids arose—magnificent as at Seville, or confused as at Avila. These hybrid buildings had in common fewer and smaller windows than the northern Gothic cathedrals with their walls of glass. And, although the stained glass in these Spanish Gothic cathedrals may be beautiful, the overall impact of the "French" cathedrals of León and Toledo is lacking. (Burgos lost much of its ancient glass during the Peninsular War in 1813, when the retreating French soldiery blew up a powder magazine.)

One of the most impressive ensembles of Spanish stained glass is that of León Cathedral, with its two hundred and thirty windows of nearly seven hundred and fifty panels. Some of the glass dates from the thirteenth century, little from the fourteenth and a plethora from the fifteenth century. Among the innumerable biblical scenes and the figures of saints, prophets and ecclesiastics, it is odd, and pleasant, to find a window filled with secular scenes of medieval life, but these belonged originally to a royal palace in León which was destroyed. These panels illustrate such cultural activities as writing books, painting miniatures, playing the viola and dancing to castanets. Sporting activities are also depicted and hunting is paramount, with the nobility in full pursuit of many species of wildlife.

The fifteenth century saw the start of an astonishing period of glory for Spain. For centuries it had been a collection of separate kingdoms—León, Castile, Aragon and Navarre—disputing with each other and the Moorish rulers of Granada. Gradually, by war and marriage, the kingdoms had been reduced to two—Aragon and Castile—and these were united when Ferdinand, heir to Aragon, married Isabella, future Queen of Castile. Under these two Catholic monarchs the Moors were finally driven from Spain.

The new era was built on the most cosmopolitan of foundations. Enterprising foreigners thrived under Spanish patronage. The Italian explorer Christopher Columbus, for example, was financed by Queen Isabella after he had unsuccessfully touted his intended expedition elsewhere.

The pattern in the visual arts was the same. In stained glass, schools existed with centres at, for example, Burgos, Barcelona and Seville, but in all of them foreign influence was dominant. At Burgos the glaziers included Flemings and Frenchmen; at León there were Flemings; at Barcelona the glaziers were Flemings, Germans, Frenchmen and Italians; and at Seville they were Flemings and Germans. Many of the glaziers were almost nomadic. Some glaziers' names, however, are particularly associated with one or two cathedrals.

Early in the century the most renowned craftsman, apart from those working at Toledo, was the Frenchman Juan de Arqr, who worked at León and Burgos. At the end of the century the most important name was Enrique Alemán. A German, he is credited with seventeen windows in Seville Cathedral, including the famous window of the Four Evangelists, often considered his most important work because of its masterly figures and imaginative use of colour. Some of the cartoons for this window were used again at Toledo, where he spent his last, extremely active years.

From wherever the glaziers came, their style of glazing underwent a change in the Spanish sun. The light was brighter than in the northern lands from which most of them had come and, therefore, the colours they began to use were more robust. Their painting became more florid and dramatic, and also (like the contradiction in the Spanish temperament) more melancholy. In addition they drew on the Moorish tradition of Spain; the influence of the non-figurative art of the Moors can be seen in the geometric patterns of the traceries and in backgrounds and borders.

By the end of the fifteenth century foreign glaziers were founding family dynasties of glass-painters; their roots were foreign but their fruits were Spanish. They had much brilliant work to do in the next century before the original impetus was killed by the growth of illiberalism in a Spain which had been both civilized and tolerant under the Moors.

THE UNIFICATION OF SPAIN

For hundreds of years a collection of separate kingdoms, shown on the map left, Spain emerged as a nation in the fifteenth century through the unification of its two most powerful kingdoms, Aragon and Castile. This alliance was achieved by the marriage of Ferdinand of Aragon to Isabella of Castile in 1469 and Ferdinand's accession to the throne of Aragon ten years later. The two monarchs, shown in details, right, from the painting *The Virgin of the Catholic Kings*, were also responsible for the expulsion of the Moors from Spain in 1492.

1 León 2 Castile 3 Aragon
4 Navarre 5 Granada

The sumptuously decorated apse at the east end of León Cathedral, left, epitomizes the exquisite extravagance of Gothic Spain. The high altar is enshrined by a golden altarpiece whose panels were painted in the fifteenth century by Nicolás Francés. With the exception of the thirteenth-century central lancets, the tall windows were glazed in the fourteenth century with two tiers of elongated apostles, detail below, whose figures are compressed by the narrow apertures.

Powerful, deep colours distinguish the windows of Barcelona Cathedral and pierce the gloom of its exceptionally dark interior. In the fifteenth-century window, above, which depicts the *Noli me Tangere* scene between Christ and Mary Magdalene, the figures are rounded and fleshy compared with the earlier stiffly awkward apostles in the León windows.

Colours which are unusually limited without being dingy characterize the fifteenth-century window known as Our Lady of Fortune in León Cathedral. The detail, left, shows a bishop kneeling beside his coat of arms, a cow's head. Like the giant image of the Virgin at which he is gazing, he is partially obscured by areas of dark brown and emerges mysteriously from the chequered background.

FIFTEENTH-CENTURY SPAIN

A Treasure-house of Spanish Art

Once a poor and humble monk, Jiménez de Cisneros, Archbishop of Toledo, was made Cardinal and Grand Inquisitor in 1507. Later, as Regent to Charles V he became one of the most influential statesmen of his day.

The glowing colours in this lancet in Toledo Cathedral typify fifteenth-century Spanish stained glass. The demure musician is one of five figures of angels and saints depicted in this window by Juan Dolfin, master glazier at Toledo from 1418 to 1427.

Toledo can boast the most spectacular cathedral, the most saintly saints, the most miraculous miracles and the most powerful bishops. To appreciate the city's history it is necessary to suspend disbelief.

Perched on a hill with the Tagus as its moat, Toledo was a vital stronghold for the Romans, for the Visigoths, who overran Spain in the fifth century, for the Moors, who conquered most of the country in the eighth century, and for the Christians, who retook it from the Moors in 1085. It was, indeed, the first city to be won back in the Reconquest, as it had been, in 587, one of the first cities of Spain to become Christian. By the seventh century it had gained a saint, Ildefonso, who is revered almost as much as St James of Compostela. His fame as Bishop of Toledo rests on his devastating rebuttal of doubts cast on the virginity of Mary, and on the miracles that followed.

The first miracle was the appearance at a church service of St Leocadia, dead for three hundred years. She emerged from her sepulchre, which had opened of its own accord, and before she returned to it Bishop Ildefonso had managed to acquire a relic, by severing a large piece of her veil with a sword. The following week the Virgin herself appeared at Matins, accompanied by angels who sang in the choir. After sitting attentively through the sermon, the Virgin presented the bishop with a chasuble made by angels, and then departed. The occasion is commemorated in a relief on the west front of the cathedral.

Under the Moors the cathedral was turned into a mosque, and it was not until the reconquest of Toledo that miracles began again. Several of the miracles centred on the bitter controversy aroused by replacing the Visigothic mass with the Gregorian. In combats arranged by the king to settle the issue, the pro-Gothic knight killed his opponent, and so did a pro-Gothic bull. For the final test both missals were thrown on to a fire; the Gregorian missal was consumed by the flames, the Gothic missal was untouched. It was to no avail—the Gothic mass was eventually abandoned, and the cathedral has a window depicting St Gregory's mass.

It was no miracle, but fanaticism and royal patronage that raised a peasant lad to be all-powerful Archbishop of Toledo in 1495. Jiménez de Cisneros had been the Queen's confessor and it was she who appointed him Prime Minister and Regent. But his name has gone down in history as the most dreaded Grand Inquisitor of the Spanish Inquisition.

In 1227, in place of the old Christian-Moorish building which had been destroyed in 1226, a new cathedral was begun, but it was not completed, inside and out, until the eighteenth century. Consequently, although the architecture of the building is basically inspired by French Gothic cathedrals, it is also part Renaissance and part Baroque in style, with great Moorish influence persisting.

The seventy-five stained-glass windows of Toledo Cathedral compete for attention with such extravagances as the elaborate sculptured choir enclosure, the stupendous carved altarpiece, and the florid *Trasparente*, a Baroque carved screen behind the main altar. The richness of the colour in the windows, however, complements the exuberance of the other works of art and, against all odds, the disparate creations of so many hands over five centuries achieve a curious unity.

The stained glass of Toledo is impressive. The three large roses are outstanding. The south transept window is a fully developed rose with sixteen petals. At the centre of the earlier rose in the north transept, which dates from the fourteenth century, is Christ on the Cross, a white figure against an almost totally red background. The other eighteen cusped circles that complete the window are predominantly blue. The six circles which encircle the Crucifixion depict St Mary and St John and four angels. Around them are twelve prophets, pointing inwards to Christ. The early fifteenth-century west rose is remarkable for its

tracery, which forms seven rings of different designs around the central eye, which contains not a figure but the insignia of a bishop.

Along the nave there are three horizontal bands of windows, a few of which are in clear glass. There are varying shapes of window in the topmost row in the clerestory. The windows in the walls of the aisles above the chapels form the second tier. These depict biblical scenes, starting with the expulsion of Adam and Eve from Paradise and working eastwards through the Old Testament. Although the design is the same on both sides of the nave, there is a striking difference in the colour of these windows. Five on the north

The west rose of Toledo Cathedral is noted for the intricate tracery which frames seven concentric rings of small, jewel-like lights of varying shapes and designs. Figures and heads are illustrated in some of the lights while others are filled with colourful abstract decorations. Within the central eye of the rose are the insignia of the cathedral's prelate, with the characteristic bishop's hat.

The cathedral and the Alcazar, originally a fortress, are the main landmarks of Toledo, which stands on a hill overlooking the River Tagus.

Geometria and Astrologia, below, are two of the eight figures representing arts and sciences, which is the theme of the brightly coloured lower tier of a large window in Toledo's south transept.

wall are predominantly a rich blue, while those on the south are of a lighter blue and a lively red. The bottom row is formed by the chapel windows—mainly clear glass on the north side and filled with New Testament scenes on the south.

Although the overall style of the stained glass at Toledo is unmistakably Spanish, foreign glaziers had worked there, as they had in the rest of Spain. When work on the windows in the cathedral began in 1418 the master glazier was Juán Dolfin, who was probably French. Ten years later he was succeeded by his assistant, Loys Coutin. From 1485 until his death in 1492 the master glazier was the German Enrique, probably the same Enrique who had worked at Seville. With his assistants he was responsible for twenty windows. The glass as well as the glaziers was imported, for Enrique's contract provided that he should "proceed to Flanders or any other part he may desire where good glass is to be found" and buy it there.

Toledo reached the height of its power during the fifteenth century, when from being the capital of Castile it became the seat of the court of Ferdinand and Isabella, the Catholic monarchs of a united Spain. But the arrogance of its archbishops grew to be more than Philip II could bear. In the sixteenth century he moved his court to Madrid, and the long slow decline of Toledo began.

FIFTEENTH-CENTURY SPAIN

Toledo – Cathedral of Soft Mysterious Light

Toledo Cathedral has seventy-five stained-glass windows, many of which date from the fifteenth and early sixteenth centuries. Although most of these glorious windows were made by French and German glaziers (using Flemish glass), they mark the emergence of a style which is unmistakably Spanish. The tiers of windows along the nave, the great windows of the transepts and the lancets and the eye windows of the apse are almost all filled with glass of an unusual richness, creating an overall effect that is dramatic and awe-inspiring. When Théophile Gautier, the French writer, visited Toledo in 1840 he was overwhelmed on entering the cathedral. In *Voyage in Spain* he wrote: "From windows where emeralds, sapphires and rubies sparkle, set in stone like jewels in a ring, there filters a soft, mysterious light that transports you to religious ecstasy."

Large and colourful, the nave clerestory windows, with four exceptions, each have a double tier of six lancets surmounted by tracery lights in varying designs. Figures of bishops, saints and apostles each stand beneath an elaborate canopy, which, in a uniquely Spanish style, has the space above the figure's head within the canopy filled with decorative detail.

The remaining four windows, at the west end of the nave, are in a similar style, but have an upper tier of three broad panels depicting figures within yellow frames. The windows on the north side of the nave are believed to be the work of the glaziers Pedro Bonifacio, Cristóbal and Friar Peter; and those on the south side the work of the German Enrique Alemán.

Episodes from the Old Testament are depicted in the aisle windows, which all have the same distinctive design. In each window of six lancets, against a decorative background, biblical scenes are framed in three circles, which cut across the mullions to the width of two lancets. Identical in design, the windows in the two aisles contrast dramatically in colour; the five north windows are sombre in deep blues and the six to the south vivid with a predominance of red.

Toledo's splendid fifteenth-century west rose has a concentric pattern rather than the radiating effect of earlier rose windows. The rose is not visible from the exterior because it is concealed by the narthex, or porch. No shadow of this, however, disturbs its brilliance inside the cathedral.

North aisle

 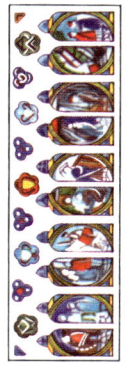 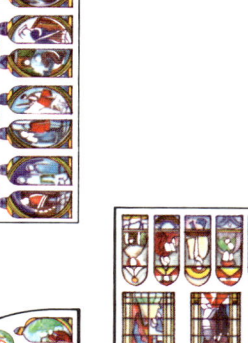

Nave

South aisle

The light to the chapels north of the nave is obscured by the cloisters built on to that side of the cathedral; consequently, with one exception, these windows have clear glass. The south chapels have interesting fifteenth-century windows depicting scenes of the Nativity, Pentecost and Epiphany. Believed to be the work of Pedro Bonifacio, the Nativity window is particularly beautiful.

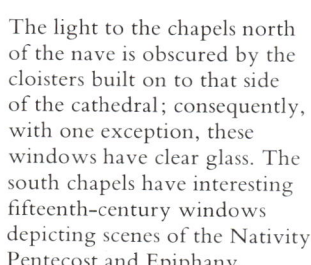    

One of Spain's most exquisite windows, the north rose, which dates from the fourteenth century, is among Toledo's earliest stained-glass windows. The Crucifixion is depicted at its centre and around it are six lights of St Mary, St John and four angels. In the outer ring of twelve lights are the twelve prophets. The blue tones of the eighteen lights accentuate the dramatic red and white of the central image.

The largest windows in Toledo Cathedral are those in the west walls of the transepts. They each have two tiers of lancets and are richly coloured with a wealth of sophisticated detail. Saints and bishops—including Jiménez, Archbishop of Toledo—are depicted in the upper tiers, below which are such subjects as heraldic shields, famous scholars and figures representing the Virtues and the arts and sciences. Although smaller and simple in style the vivid figure and canopy windows of the east walls are equally interesting and many are believed to date from the fourteenth century. Some of the windows may have been transferred from another church.

Choir

North transept

Apse

Ambulatory

South transept

Poised over the Door of the Lions is the sixteenth-century south rose, the work of Nicolás de Vergara.

Angels, saints and heraldic devices are shown in the apse clerestory windows, many of which are the work of Juan Dolfin. Eight colourful lights in two alternating ornamental designs adorn the walls of the ambulatory.

111

FIFTEENTH-CENTURY ENGLAND

Era of the Parish Church

Seven compassionate deeds known as the corporal acts of mercy were frequently illustrated in fifteenth-century stained glass. Giving drink to the thirsty, above, is one of six of these scenes which remain in a north aisle window of All Saints', North Street, York.

Richard Beauchamp, Earl of Warwick, bequeathed money to build the Beauchamp Chapel in St Mary's, Warwick. Sumptuous remains of the chapel's glass, including the figures, of c. 1447, of St Thomas Becket and St Alban, right, are in the east window. Richard was depicted in a contemporary manuscript, above, with the infant Henry VI and a model of another chapel he built.

Despite the Hundred Years' War and the Wars of the Roses, England was prosperous during the fifteenth century. The lasting evidence of this wealth is to be seen not only in her cathedrals and minsters, but also in the many parish churches and civic buildings of the period. The wool trade was particularly flourishing, and some of England's grandest and most beautiful parish churches are the so-called "wool" churches of such sheep-rearing areas as Norfolk, Suffolk, the Cotswolds and Yorkshire.

Local pride was far more genuinely involved in building the churches than it had been in the building of cathedrals and the money was given by all sections of the population. While the lord of the manor might himself build a church for the parish in which he lived, often the initiative came from the parishioners and the local guilds, who shared the cost by contributing money, livestock or labour.

York, which was a great wool centre, still has nineteen medieval parish churches. Although a few are disused, many are rich in stained glass; not surprisingly, since York was also famous for its stained-glass workshops. The most exciting fifteenth-century windows are in All Saints' Church, North Street. A particularly fine one, with most of its original glass, depicts the corporal acts of mercy, a popular medieval theme: six acts of mercy—feeding of the hungry, giving drink to the thirsty, clothing the naked, housing the stranger, visiting the sick and visiting the imprisoned— still survive, but the seventh, burying the dead, is missing.

Death dominates another of the church's famous windows, which is based on a poem written in the Northumbrian dialect by a Yorkshire recluse, Richard Rolle of Hampole. His output of writing was prodigious, but his best-known work was a poem called *The Pricke of Conscience*, which covered life, death, purgatory, doomsday, the pains of hell and the joys of heaven. The window concentrates on the last fifteen days of the world and most vividly evokes them. The superbly macabre scenes include monsters emerging from the sea and overrunning the land, the sea and trees on fire, earthquakes, and flames devouring everything on the last day.

There is also excellent fifteenth-century glass in the York churches of St Denys (in one of whose windows an angel is depicted with a barrel organ), St Martin le Grand, and Holy Trinity in Micklegate.

Norwich's thirty-two parish churches outnumber those of York, and St Peter Mancroft is the finest among them. Its most interesting stained glass is in the fifteenth-century east window, which is composed of forty-two Bible scenes. In a panel devoted to the Birth of Christ the East Anglian glazier, probably knowing only too well how the cold east winds of winter whistle over the Fens, thoughtfully provided the manger in Bethlehem with a brazier. In front of this a woman airs the swaddling clothes of the infant Jesus, while Joseph crouches by it in an armchair. Resident animals and visiting angels watch the unlikely scene.

One of the great "wool" churches of Suffolk is at Long Melford. Originally the windows were filled with glass given by the Cloptons, a wealthy local family, but much of this was destroyed in the sixteenth and seventeenth centuries. Many figures of the Cloptons and of other donors have survived, and are now in several windows in the lower part of the church. They reveal what clothes it was considered proper to wear when being depicted in stained-glass windows towards the end of the fifteenth century. The ladies' cloaks are embroidered with elaborate heraldic designs, some of which are the arms of the Cloptons. Their headdresses include the exaggerated butterfly styles popular during the reign of Edward IV, which consist of a white veil over a wire framework that stretches backwards from the head. The men wear heraldic tabards over plate armour, which was flexible enough to allow the knights to kneel, as was *de rigueur* for donors.

Figure windows were the most popular type of window in fifteenth-century England, as they were in the rest of Europe. To fill the long and narrow Perpendicular lancets the figures were tall, and the canopies above them were even taller. The poses were relaxed and the draperies flowing. The colours became lighter and brighter and, after the introduction of stipple shading in place of the earlier smear shading, the painting was more delicate.

An impression of what a multi-windowed parish church looked like in the fifteenth century can be gained not from a parish church but from the Priory Church of Great Malvern in Worcestershire. Soon after the rebuilding of the church was completed in 1460, its forty windows were filled with stained glass and a considerable amount remains. In the windows there is some dark blue, very little red and a lot of yellow and brown, as well as white. The overall effect is one of delicacy and brightness.

The Beauchamp Chapel in St Mary's, Warwick, must have been even more splendid in its prime. Richard Beauchamp, Earl of Warwick and captor of Joan of Arc, provided in his will for the building of the chapel. The king's glazier, John Prudde of Westminster, was contracted to provide the windows, and it was stipulated that he was to use only the best richly coloured foreign glass. John Prudde's lowest charge for glazing with quarry glass was eight and a half pence a foot, for simple figures his price was one shilling and two pence a foot, but for the Beauchamp windows he charged two shillings a foot. Giving value for money, however, he even glazed the notes of the hymn which the angels sing among the traceries. It is real plainsong and is still occasionally sung by mortals in the church. Feathered angels also play a whole range of musical instruments, including bagpipes. What remains of the glass that originally filled all the windows is now in the east window, a tantalizing legacy of the chapel's original magnificence.

The fifteenth century marked the end in England of the superlative years of medieval stained glass. The next two centuries were to see infinitely more masterpieces destroyed, in the name of religion, than were created.

Unlikely details and figures drawn to varying scales create a distinctive, charming and humorous Nativity scene in the fifteenth-century east window of St Peter Mancroft Church, Norwich. A small midwife warms clothes against a miniature brazier while a comparatively large figure of the Virgin is about to suckle the infant Christ. An aged-looking Joseph sits in a type of low, rounded armchair that is frequently seen in medieval illustrations of bedrooms. Two diminutive angels, one feathered and one wearing a dress, are ecstatic witnesses of the scene.

Long Melford Church, Suffolk, was built in the fifteenth century by John Clopton, a rich local clothier. Windows in the north aisle portray members of his family including, below, from left to right, Elizabeth, wife of Sir Walter Clopton, Sir Thomas Clopton and his wife Catherine.

Rich in symbolism, a small fifteenth-century panel in the Clopton Chantry Chapel in Long Melford Church, Suffolk, depicts a cruciform lily to which Christ is nailed. The theme of suffering is linked, through the image of the plant, to that of rebirth, and the Crucifixion of Christ is associated with the lily, symbol of purity and of the Virgin Mary.

Three rabbits, in the tiny fifteenth-century roundel, right, above the north door in Long Melford Church, Suffolk, are joined by three single ears, although each rabbit, when seen individually, appears to possess two ears. This strange image, which also appears in contemporary Devonshire wood-carvings, forms a triangle symbolizing the Trinity.

FIFTEENTH-CENTURY GERMANY

Master Glaziers in Merchant Cities

Lüneburg Town Hall boasts the earliest secular stained glass in Germany. Glazed in the first half of the fifteenth century, the windows depict nine German kings bearing shields emblazoned with their coats of arms, as in the detail above.

Many of the hallmarks of Peter Hemmel von Andlau's style can be seen in the detail, right, from the St Catherine window in St Guillaume's, Strasbourg. They include the blue brocade background, the careful modelling of the clothing and the convincing facial expressions—from the cruel leers of the torturers to the serenity of the virgin saint.

Peter Hemmel von Andlau, an unusually prolific German glass-painter of the fifteenth century, has been singularly unlucky in the way history has treated him. Until recently he was mistakenly identified as Hans Wild because of confusion over his monogram. Much of his work has been destroyed by fire or ruined by restoration. And experts writing about him, even while admitting the quality of his work, often seem resentful that he produced so much.

Von Andlau was born in Alsace in about 1420. He became a citizen of Strasbourg by marrying a wealthy widow there when he was still in his early twenties. This was an astute move, for as well as gaining a wife he acquired the workshop of her previous husband, who had been a painter. He also gained a stepdaughter, who married a painter, as did his own daughter, and father, sons and sons-in-law all worked together in the workshop. Later four other independent glass-painters became involved in the concern, which with "the Strasbourg style" established an international reputation.

Although master glaziers of the Middle Ages were notoriously peripatetic, Von Andlau's workshop was firmly based in Strasbourg. There he and his workshop made windows for cathedrals and churches in Strasbourg, Ulm, Nuremberg, Augsburg, Tübingen, Munich, Salzburg, Frankfurt, Freiburg, Metz and, possibly, Milan. Von Andlau's windows developed an undoubted sameness, both in subjects—the most recurrent were the Virgin Mary's life and the Tree of Jesse—and in treatment, although different coats of arms and donors added a touch of variety. None the less, at its best his work is better than any other German glass of the second half of the century.

In Ulm Minster two windows, dating from about 1480, which have escaped restoration and significant damage, demonstrate the quality of his Strasbourg style. One is the shopkeepers' window, named after the donors' guild, which depicts scenes from the life of Christ. It includes a Jesse Tree with elaborately formal branches and leaves enfolding twelve prophets and kings, among them David playing a harp. The adjoining window, the Ratsfenster,

Botanical detail abounds in the windows of Peter Hemmel von Andlau. In the detail, left, originally in Strasbourg Cathedral and now in the cathedral museum, Adam stands against a typically elaborate background of delicately painted foliage and wild flowers.

Regional gastronomic preferences prevail over biblical tradition in the Last Supper window in the Wiesenkirche at Soest in Westphalia to produce a singular menu—a boar's head, detail above, and, in the adjoining lancet, pumpernickel. The window, in which the extensive use of yellow stain heightens the naturalistic effect, is a high point of Westphalian stained glass.

donated by the city council, continues these scenes on backgrounds of blue and red under the elaborate gold and silver canopies which were almost Von Andlau's trademark. His beautiful figures strike no poses, but stand gracefully and naturally. He filled his windows with realistic plants and flowers and lovingly drawn animals—a calf and a sheep watching the infant Jesus sucking his thumb in the manger; white hares playing at the feet of the Virgin in a Visitation scene. The colours, especially the blues and reds, are brilliant.

Ulm Minster itself is yet another monument to civic pride. Work on it began in 1377 under Heinrich Parler, founder of that dynasty of master builders, and two younger Parlers continued it. Ulrich von Ensingen made it wider and a successor, Matthäus Böblinger, made the tower taller, but without ensuring that the foundations were strong enough. After signs of collapse occasioned a conference of twenty-eight master builders, that oversight was rectified. A further blow to the minster was that Ulm became Protestant in 1530 and more than sixty altars and many works of art were destroyed. The building, not completed until 1890, is today the city's Lutheran parish church, and not the Catholic cathedral the medieval burghers had envisioned.

There is excellent glass besides Von Andlau's in the minster. The oldest is in the choir—the two tall windows devoted to the lives of the Virgin Mary and of her legendary mother St Anne portrayed against a dominating background of fantastic architecture. The Ackers, an Ulm family of painters, are believed to have designed these windows, as well as the St John windows in the choir.

The most talented member of the Acker family, Hans von Ulm, glazed the windows in the minster's exquisite, tiny Besserer Chapel, which was designed by Ulrich von Ensingen and named after the family which paid for it. The smallness of the chapel is in extreme contrast to the vastness of the minster's nave. Its windows are marvellous, a conglomeration of small but clear biblical scenes that have a curious air of sophisticated innocence. The panel showing the return of the dove to the ark is an example.

Noah emerges from what looks like the chimney of a small red-roofed doll's house built on the deck of the ark and greets the astonished bird, while his children gaze out of the windows over the grey sea. Above the scene are two lions, one grinning and the other scowling like an irate, moustached colonel. A small piece of dry land at the bottom of the panel adds a kind of footnote to the story, explaining why the raven did not return to the ark—it had caught a rabbit.

The prodigious detail in many of the chapel's windows never dominates the scene, even in the crowded Day of Resurrection window. The bottom panels depict the dead rising from their tombs and being separated into the blessed and the damned. Above is a row of about thirty kneeling donors, and at the top is Christ against a flame red background, while angels swirl in the tracery. The Gothic genius may have been dying elsewhere in Europe, but it was certainly alive here.

THE RIVAL MINSTER

Planned to surpass the minsters of Freiburg and Strasbourg, Ulm Minster was the work of many master masons, including Ulrich von Ensingen, who designed the massive west tower—a perfect expression of civic pride. He also designed the tiny Besserer Chapel, between the ambulatory and the east end of the nave, which was donated by the Ulm merchant, Eitel Besserer, right.

The dove returns to Noah bearing an olive branch—a sign that the flood is subsiding and God's wrath appeased—in the panel, above, from a window in the Besserer Chapel by Hans Acker. There are interesting parallels with—and differences from—the thirteenth-century manuscript, right. For example, although the arks differ, the waves in both are vigorously indicated according to the same stylized conventions.

FIFTEENTH-CENTURY GERMANY

Nuremberg–the Venice of the North

The richness of its stained glass was an excellent indication of the prosperity of a city or town in the Middle Ages. Chartres, York and Florence are typical of French, English and Italian cities that acquired their wealth of stained glass when their merchant classes were at their most affluent. In Germany the pattern was the same, as evidenced by the wealthy merchant cities of Lübeck, Ulm and Nuremberg. All the ancient glass in Lübeck's cathedral and parish church is lost, but twenty-five panels remain from the Dominican Church and they are enough to suggest that Lübeck glass must have been among the best in Germany. (Indeed the Florentines sent to Lübeck for help with their church glazing.) Nuremberg and Ulm have, however, been more fortunate, for much of their ancient glass remains.

Nuremberg had a long struggle for independence, notably from the claims, in the eleventh and twelfth centuries, of Bavarian and Frankish dukes. In the thirteenth century it achieved its status as a Free Imperial City from Frederick II, the Holy Roman Emperor. Nuremberg then flourished, commercially and artistically, and by the fifteenth century it had gained an international reputation such as few cities had; Italians were given to describing it as either the Venice or the Florence of the North. It was famous for its goldsmiths, sculptors and painters, its meistersinger and church musicians. In the eleventh century people flocked to Nuremberg to the tomb of Franconia's

In vivid and minute detail the late fifteenth-century window, left, in the choir of St Lorenz, Nuremberg, depicts scenes of the exodus of the Israelites from Egypt. So literal was the unknown artist's interpretation of the story that he glazed the Red Sea in red. In the panel above, the men wear the pointed yellow hats characteristic of medieval Jewish dress. Known as the Rieterfenster, the window was donated by the Rieters, a wealthy Nuremberg family.

St Sebaldus; from the fourteenth century the attraction was the Imperial jewels, which had been transferred there. And these pilgrimages contributed to the city's prosperity.

The building of the Church of St Lorenz was begun towards the end of the thirteenth century and it took two hundred years to complete. Although at times there seems to have been a shortage of money for the main building work, there was no lack of people willing to donate altarpieces, carvings and windows, and even to furnish whole chapels. Among the first donors was Emperor Ludwig the Bavarian; his gift, in the early fourteenth century, was the bones of Deocarus, Confessor to Charles the Great. The Emperor Frederick III, a devotee of botany, alchemy and astrology, and his wife Eleanor of Portugal gave the central window in the choir, and are commemorated in it. Members of the city council, which had initiated the building of the church, were generous in their gifts and were as generously acknowledged in plaques and windows. The names of many famous Nuremberg families appear in the church and many of the windows are commonly referred to by the names of their donors.

Almost all the original windows of the choir of St Lorenz are intact. Glazing began even before the choir was half built and, after an interval when no work was done, was completed soon after 1480. The windows have no overall theme, and some of the subjects chosen for them—presumably by the donors—are distinctly unusual. The Rieter window, for example, has Exodus scenes, while for the Hirsvogel window (damaged in the Second World War, but restored) the choice was the life of St Sixtus, an early Pope. And in the Kunhofer window, named after the scholarly Dr Konrad Kunhofer, once rector of the church, the visions of a monastery shepherd are depicted.

A number of glaziers worked at Nuremberg. An itinerant workshop, connected with Peter Parler's guild, glazed two windows at St Lorenz, nine at St Sebald's and one at St Martha's. In St Lorenz there is a Tree of Jesse window by Peter Hemmel von Andlau; the tree grows from Jesse's breast instead of, as was traditional, from his loins. Most of the windows, however, were done by a local workshop under the aegis of Michael Wolgemut, the Nuremberg painter and engraver. Among his apprentices was Albrecht Dürer.

As in previous centuries there were considerable variations in stained-glass style in different regions of the country and workshops flourished throughout Germany, from Stendal in the east to Cologne in the west and Lüneburg in the north. Stendal had its day in the middle of the century, when it was the magnet for German glaziers who wanted to work on the many windows of the cathedral. More than one thousand panels still survive. In marked contrast, only three fifteenth-century windows survive in Cologne Cathedral—the two windows of the Life of Christ in the Chapel of the Holy Sacrament and the Chair of Mercy window in the north transept. All three belonged originally to other Cologne churches. The influence of the contemporary Cologne school of painting is detectable in such details as hands and faces, and Flemish influence is apparent in the landscaped backgrounds in the Life of Christ windows.

During the course of the century, Flemish-influenced realism filtered in everywhere, despite regional differences, but not always at the same rate. Landscapes began to take the place of purely ornamental backgrounds. Buildings were drawn in perspective. Ladies and gentlemen of aristocratic mien were joined by commoners with crooked noses.

But there were far greater changes to come, for at the end of the century Dürer returned from Italy and began his work as pioneer of a new art, which was to have a vital influence not only in his native Germany but over much of northern Europe.

Surrounded by forest, as in the early sixteenth-century painting, above, the walled city of Nuremberg was one of the most prosperous cities in fifteenth-century Germany. It was also renowned for its craftsmanship and the first globe and pocket watch were produced by citizens of Nuremberg. The globe, right, with its erroneous delineation of America, was made in 1492 by the geographer and traveller Martin Behaim, and the watch, far right, by Peter Henlein. Both are now in the Germanisches National-Museum, Nuremberg.

St Lorenz is rich in wood, stone, clay and marble sculpture created by such masters as Veit Stoss, Peter Vischer and Adam Krafft. At the base of the elaborately sculpted sandstone tabernacle in the choir, Krafft depicted himself and his associates. His self-portrait, above, expresses both humility and a sense of dignity.

One of the most beautiful and joyous of all the artistic treasures of St Lorenz, this gilded limewood Annunciation by Veit Stoss is suspended, like an enormous wreath, from a choir arch. Mary and the angel Gabriel are surrounded by a garland of roses in which are set seven medallions showing scenes from the life of Mary.

FIFTEENTH-CENTURY ITALY

The Renaissance City

Uccello's Resurrection, above left, and Del Castagno's Deposition, above, two of the glazed *occhi* in the dome of Florence Cathedral.

Donatello, the great fifteenth-century sculptor, carved this majestic lion, now in the Bargello Museum, to symbolize the power and dignity of Florence. The lion holds a shield upon which is a lily, the city's emblem. Surrounded by blossoms in springtime, Florence is known as the city of the flower.

For much of its history Florence had been one of the leading cities of Italy; indeed, when the Romans established themselves there the name they gave it—Florentia, meaning riches—was significant. After the Roman occupation it was captured successively by the Ostrogoths, the Byzantines, the Goths, the Lombards and the Franks. But in the thirteenth century the city gained its independence and its economic and cultural life began to revive. By the end of the century the leading members of the Florentine Commune, the city republic, were impelled to build a cathedral worthy of the new Florence. Work, begun confidently in 1300, continued only spasmodically against a background of war and civil strife which involved the two factions of the nobility, the Guelphs and Ghibellines, the increasingly powerful guilds and the workers. As a result of the interruptions in the building of the cathedral, its architecture is neither Romanesque nor early Renaissance, and not so much Gothic as the negation of it.

When, in the second decade of the fifteenth century, the time came to erect the cathedral's giant cupola—almost 140 feet in diameter—nobody had worked out how it was to be done. The width at the base was too great to support centering—the horizontal beam and the wooden structure built upon it, which facilitated the construction of arches and domes. Furthermore, the thrusts and weight of the dome had to be withstood without the reinforcements of flying buttresses. Filippo Brunelleschi, goldsmith, sculptor and architect, who had studied the Ancient Roman methods of construction, came to the rescue with a design for a pointed dome, whose side thrusts would be less than those of a hemisphere. The idea was at first scorned, but it was later accepted and the dome was completed in fourteen years. It was built in horizontal stages, which obviated the need for centering, and bricks, which were lighter than stone, were used for the upper part. Florence was fortunate that Brunelleschi continued working in the city, for he also designed the churches of Santo Spirito and San Lorenzo and the Pitti and Quaratesi palaces. His influence continued to be felt throughout Italian architecture for two centuries.

The cathedral of Florence has eleven *occhi*, or eye windows, ten of which contain stained glass designed by leading fifteenth-century artists. The three on the west façade were designed by Lorenzo Ghiberti, beginning with the large one in the centre—the Assumption of the Virgin—which was completed in 1405. The Virgin is surrounded by music-making angels whose wings tail off into lobster-like claws, giving an extraordinary feeling of movement. The background is a rich blue, which deepens towards the centre. Busts of apostles and prophets in a formal and elaborate border encircle the scene. The smaller windows at each side, made ten years later, depict the enthronement of St Lawrence and St Stephen.

When the building of the cupola was completed, Ghiberti began to design the stained glass for its eye windows. But his first design, for the window of the Coronation of the Virgin, was rejected, and Donatello was entrusted with it instead. He achieved neither the boldness nor the delicacy of Ghiberti's three west windows. The two painters Uccello and Del Castagno, commissioned to complete the eye windows of the cupola, were infinitely more successful, although neither had ever worked in the medium before. Uccello designed three windows, one of which has disappeared. The other two—the Resurrection of Christ and a very beautiful Nativity—show a remarkable ability to introduce touches of realism into biblical subjects. Uccello also admirably managed to translate into stained glass the pure colouring of his paintings. Andrea del Castagno produced one boldly designed eye window which depicts Christ brought down from the Cross.

The three remaining eye windows in the cupola are the mature work of Ghiberti. The Ascension and the Prayer in the Garden were finished in 1444 and the Presentation in the Temple in 1445. The Gethsemane scene is a magnificently balanced composition showing the kneeling Christ and a group of sleeping disciples against a background of trees and the buildings of Jerusalem.

Besides his six eye windows, Ghiberti certainly designed

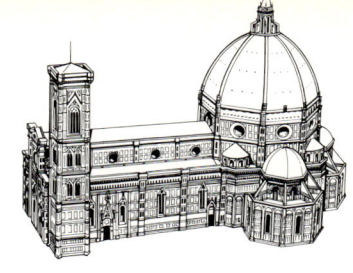

Ghiberti's Presentation in the Temple, above, and Prayer in the Garden, above right, both in the cathedral dome.

eleven and probably seventeen windows in the apse and chapels. Prophets and saints depicted in these windows are on a majestic scale and depend for their impact on their boldness of design and brilliance of colouring. The riot of colour has been contrived by dressing the figures in the most extravagant clothing—an Italian conception of Oriental apparel. Even the architectural details are full of colour and the borders are equally rich.

As well as the cathedral, Florence has several churches with beautiful glass of the fifteenth century. Among the subjects of the richly coloured windows of the Church of Orsanmichele are twelve episodes representing the miracles of the Virgin Mary, a rare theme for that period. One story is of a Pope who, feeling lustful after being kissed on the hand by a woman he had once loved, cut off his hand; but while he was sleeping the Virgin put it back.

In two other churches, two famous painters of Florentine frescoes—Domenico Ghirlandajo and Pietro Perugino—showed themselves equally brilliant in glass-painting. The Pentecost eye window of Santo Spirito, Brunelleschi's most beautiful church, was executed by Perugino in deep but most vivid colours. Equally full of colour, but lighter and brighter, are Ghirlandajo's three windows in the apse of Santa Maria Novella, where he had already painted the frescoes. Some are figure windows of saints, but the liveliest depicts the Circumcision.

Florence at the beginning of the fifteenth century was in the grip of an oligarchy of the major guilds; at the end of the century the city had, to its advantage, been taken over by the Medici family, whose members were bankers, merchants and generous patrons of the arts. It is not surprising that with Medici money and the genius of such Florentines as Botticelli, Leonardo da Vinci, Brunelleschi, Donatello, Ghiberti, Michelangelo and Machiavelli the city was in the vanguard of the Italian Renaissance and that it became the centre of fifteenth-century Italian art, rich in masterpieces of fresco-painting, sculpture and stained glass.

PATRONS OF THE ARTS

The illustrious family of Medici ascended to power in fifteenth-century Florence because of their political astuteness and the enormous wealth which Giovanni de Medici, a banker and moneylender, had amassed in the late fourteenth century. The Medici were generous sponsors of artists and scholars whose achievements made Florence the centre of the Italian Renaissance. Lorenzo, the resplendent great grandson of Giovanni and the grandson of Cosimo, exercised the greatest influence of all the Medici on Italian art.

Cosimo de Medici, the patron of such artists as Donatello and Brunelleschi.

Lorenzo, who was called *The Magnificent*, was a friend and a patron of artists.

In 1402, the sculptor, architect and stained-glass artist Lorenzo Ghiberti won a competition to design the doors of the Florentine baptistery. His self-portrait, left, is depicted in bronze relief, as are narrative Old Testament scenes, detail above, on the ten-panelled east door, which Michelangelo referred to as the Gate of Paradise.

FIFTEENTH-CENTURY ITALY

The Artists' Cathedral

With its splendid, sumptuously coloured windows, the cathedral of Florence is an astonishing amalgam of artistic skills. Completed in two stages in the first half of the fifteenth century the windows are largely the inspiration of four men. Foremost among them was Lorenzo Ghiberti, who designed more than half the windows, including six of the magnificent *occhi*, or eyes. He was a goldsmith, a worker in bronze, a sculptor, a painter and an architect. Donatello, the father of modern sculpture, contributed one window to the cathedral as well as statues and the joyful bas reliefs for the singing galleries. Paolo Uccello and Andrea del Castagno painted frescoes for the cathedral and designed eye windows in the cupola—their first venture into stained glass. This spectrum of talent was enhanced by the superb craftsmanship of the many glaziers who executed the designs. This is truly an artists' cathedral.

Lorenzo Ghiberti devised a unified scheme for the two tiers of windows for the apse and its chapels. Each of the upper lancets is filled by two pairs of prophets, while below, in all except two of the chapel windows, two small saints are surmounted by a larger one. Although Ghiberti is not known to have been responsible for the design of every window, his influence is obvious throughout. The stylistic difference between the upper and the lower lancets is dictated by distance. The towering figures of the prophets have a simplicity of design which conveys form and space. Because of their proximity, the saints in the chapel windows are depicted in greater detail. The figures on both levels display none of the rigid archaism of previous styles. Unlike the thirteenth-century Chartres prophets, for example, they appear elegantly relaxed, and instead of being separated by niches are turned slightly towards each other. The exotic intensity of colour of their flamboyant costumes is heightened by the deep blue backgrounds and geometric borders, which resemble mosaics.

North aisle

The Italian round windows known as *occhi*, or eyes, are usually uninterrupted by the patterns of stone tracery which fill the conventional rose windows of Europe. Compared with the radiating and rotating effect of the rose windows, these circles of glass, divided only by vertical and horizontal bars, create an impression of peaceful balance, which suggests the Renaissance rather than the Gothic spirit.

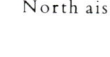

Nave

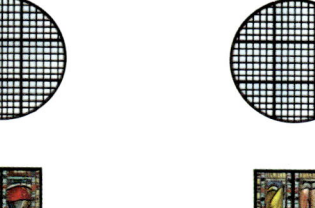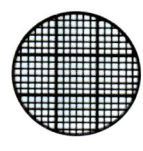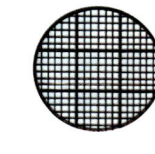

South aisle

The three *occhi* in the west façade were designed by the Florentine sculptor Lorenzo Ghiberti, who successfully adapted his skills to the medium of stained glass. The central *occhio*, the first to be completed, depicts the Assumption of the Virgin and is similar yet superior in style to Andrea di Bonaiuto's Coronation of the Virgin window in the Florentine Church of Santa Maria Novella. Ghiberti's window achieves lyrical brilliance in its rhythmic, exuberant composition of flying angels carrying the Virgin's embroidered robe. A domed sky, created by the deepening blue in the centre of the window, was clearly influenced by the painter Nardo di Cione. The intensity of the blue enhances the red of the angels' wings and the gold of their haloes and hair.

The two smaller *occhi* in the west façade were designed by Lorenzo Ghiberti ten years after he completed the central eye window, to which they are stylistically related. Wearing flowered mantles, St Stephen in the north eye and St Lawrence in the south eye are enthroned against blue backgrounds and are attended by angels with brightly coloured wings.

A change of plan during the construction of the nave led to an apparent contradiction between the interior and the exterior of the cathedral. Each wall of the nave appears to contain four glazed lancets when seen from the inside and six when seen from the outside. In reality, however, only the two easterly lancets on each side are filled with stained glass. Four of the six windows which are seen on each side of the exterior are a convincing architectural trick, for behind them there are two simulated lancets filled with mosaics, which are ingeniously made to look like stained glass. To harmonize with the mosaics, the two real stained-glass windows on each side of the nave are designed in muted tones, which are sombre in comparison with the pure, brilliant colour of the glass throughout the rest of the cathedral. In each of the four lancets six saints, paired on three levels, stand under elaborate canopies. These windows are rare examples of the use of a canopy in a country where, because of the strong sunlight, this light-admitting device was seldom necessary.

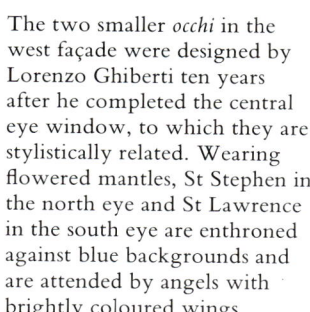

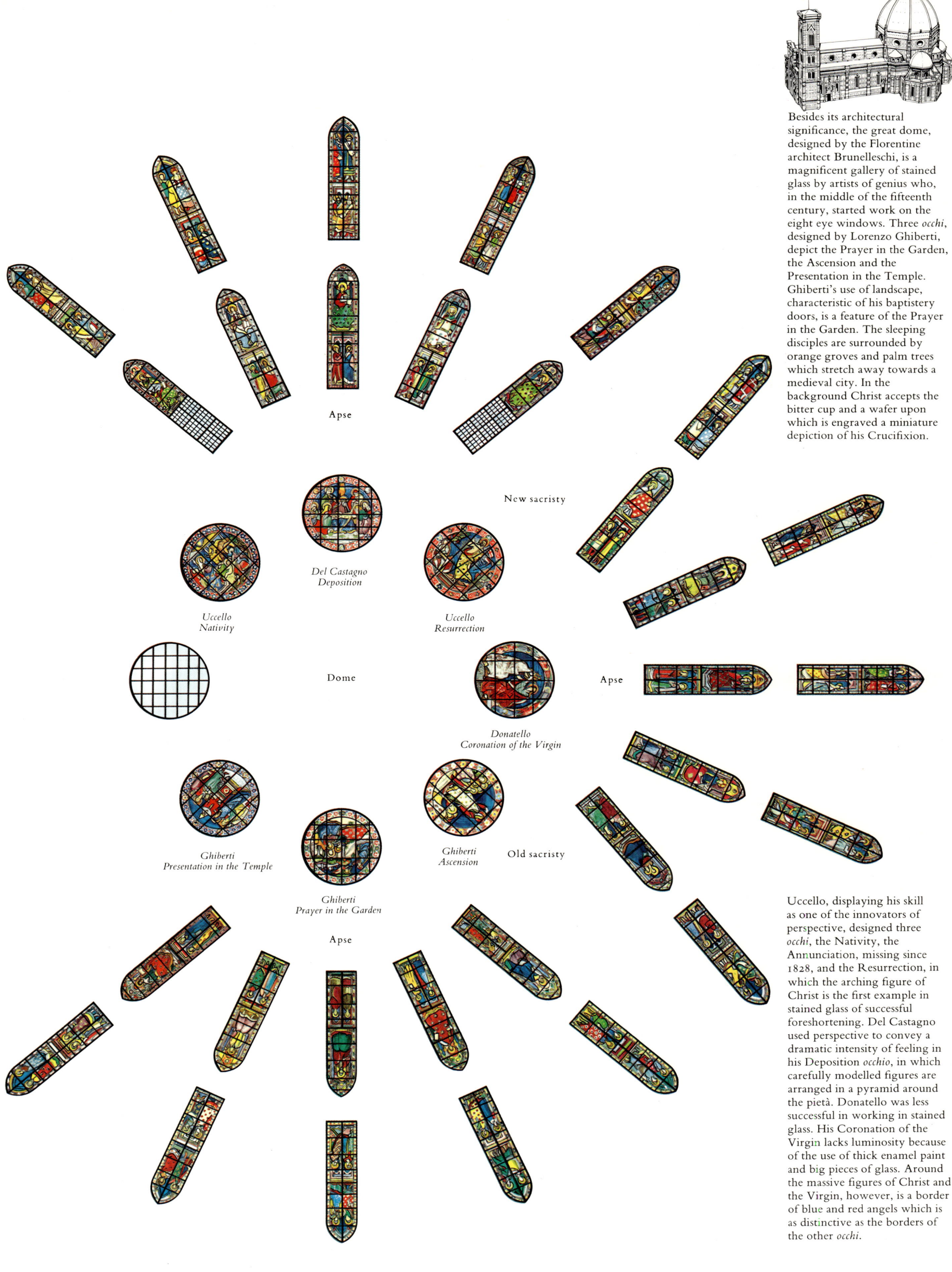

Besides its architectural significance, the great dome, designed by the Florentine architect Brunelleschi, is a magnificent gallery of stained glass by artists of genius who, in the middle of the fifteenth century, started work on the eight eye windows. Three *occhi*, designed by Lorenzo Ghiberti, depict the Prayer in the Garden, the Ascension and the Presentation in the Temple. Ghiberti's use of landscape, characteristic of his baptistery doors, is a feature of the Prayer in the Garden. The sleeping disciples are surrounded by orange groves and palm trees which stretch away towards a medieval city. In the background Christ accepts the bitter cup and a wafer upon which is engraved a miniature depiction of his Crucifixion.

Uccello, displaying his skill as one of the innovators of perspective, designed three *occhi*, the Nativity, the Annunciation, missing since 1828, and the Resurrection, in which the arching figure of Christ is the first example in stained glass of successful foreshortening. Del Castagno used perspective to convey a dramatic intensity of feeling in his Deposition *occhio*, in which carefully modelled figures are arranged in a pyramid around the pietà. Donatello was less successful in working in stained glass. His Coronation of the Virgin lacks luminosity because of the use of thick enamel paint and big pieces of glass. Around the massive figures of Christ and the Virgin, however, is a border of blue and red angels which is as distinctive as the borders of the other *occhi*.

121

FIFTEENTH-CENTURY ITALY

Milan the Magnificent

Just as Florence had its Renaissance patrons in the Medicis, so Milan had its patrons in the Visconti and the Sforza families. The noble family of the Viscontis (their name meaning viscounts) established, in the early fourteenth century, a supremacy which inaugurated one hundred and fifty years of tyranny, prosperity and ostentatious patronage of the arts. It was under the ambitious Gian Galeazzo Visconti, who ousted his uncle to gain total control of Milan, that in 1387 the city embarked on building a cathedral that was intended to outshine all others.

The last of the Viscontis, the effete Filippo Maria, was succeeded by his son-in-law, Francesco Sforza, who continued the work on the cathedral. His successor, Galeazzo Maria, who was assassinated after a ten-year rule characterized by violent despotism and debauchery, was succeeded by a son and he, in the Visconti tradition, was usurped in 1481 by Ludovico, his uncle. An artist, a writer, an economist, an agriculturist and a generous patron of Renaissance art and artists, Ludovico became totally involved in the building of Milan Cathedral. However, when he died, a prisoner of King Louis XII of France, only the choir and the transepts had been completed. The nave was not completed until the nineteenth century and even today all the details of the building are not finished.

From the start the building of the cathedral was fraught with problems. The numerous foreign architects who were consulted thought in terms of Gothic architecture, while the Italians, although talking of a Gothic cathedral, were thinking along Classical lines. Furious arguments ensued, and none of the foreign consultants stayed long. The great German master builder Heinrich Parler was engaged and dismissed. Von Ensingen came from Ulm and departed after six months. French advisers under the direction of Jean Mignot survived for a year. They need hardly have gone to Milan in the first place, for the Italians continued in their own way, building a cathedral which, according to the Gothic experts, was architecturally unsound (although for five hundred years it has survived).

Considered the leading Lombard artist of the fifteenth century, Vincenzo Foppa was responsible for the design of the New Testament windows in the apse of Milan Cathedral. This Annunciation panel demonstrates a similarity in style to the work of Foppa's contemporary, Sandro Botticelli.

Patron of the arts, unscrupulous diplomat yet dedicated to his people, Gian Galeazzo Visconti created in Milan a state to rival the wealth and power of Florence and Venice, which was exemplified in his new cathedral.

Black enamel paint has been skilfully used, particularly in the unfinished top part of the tower and the figures working on it, to create an atmosphere of foreboding in this Tower of Babel panel. Originally in the cathedral, the panel is now in the cathedral museum.

The result is magnificent. The cathedral is vast, and, among the great medieval cathedrals, second only in size to Seville. Uniquely, it gives the impression of being flamboyantly Gothic while denying basic Gothic design—vertical lines, for example, are deliberately broken.

Although the windows of the nave are tall and narrow, three windows in the apse are both tall and exceptionally broad, together making the largest window area in Italy and possibly in Europe. Each window has twelve lancets, crossed by a transom, and each lancet contains ten or eleven scenes. The left-hand window was devoted to the Old Testament, the centre window to episodes from the Apocalypse and the right-hand window to the New Testament. Little remains of the glass from the early fifteenth century, but much has survived from the second half, although it was murderously restored in the nineteenth century.

Unusually for Italian cathedrals, some of the windows were donated by corporations and guilds and were dedicated to the patron saints of the relevant trades or professions. The St Eligius window, for example, was given by the Corporation of Goldsmiths, the St John of Damascus window by the Corporation of Apothecaries and the St John the Evangelist window by the College of Notaries.

Among the many fine glass-painters who worked on the cathedral's windows in the fifteenth century are Cristoforo de Mottis, whose window with stories from the Gospel of St John is virtually intact; Nicolò da Varallo, who painted the windows dedicated to St Eligius and St John of Damascus, and Vincenzo Foppa, who worked on New Testament scenes. His Annunciation, Last Supper and large, spectacular Crucifixion are particularly arresting.

Stained glass was essentially a northern Italian art form. Besides Milan and Florence, other towns and cities in the north, such as Bologna, had flourishing stained-glass workshops and between them the painter-designers and the glaziers of northern Italy produced in the fifteenth century a wealth of glass that compensated magnificently for the paucity of Italian glass in the previous centuries.

The Corporation of Goldsmiths donated the windows, by Nicolò da Varallo, depicting stories of the life of St Eligius, their patron saint. This panel showing the infant saint receiving his first bath reveals Varallo's concern with details of everyday life.

Known as "the Moor" because of his dark complexion, Ludovico Sforza, right, was the son of Francesco, the soldier and the first of the Sforza dukes of Milan. A ruthless ruler, Ludovico was, however, lavish in his patronage of artists, including Leonardo da Vinci.

One of Milan's greatest fifteenth-century glaziers, Cristoforo de Mottis created the St John the Evangelist window. This panel shows the saint exhorting youths to work. The use of perspective in the architecture and the green hills are typical of the work of the Lombard masters.

THE SIXTEENTH CENTURY
The Age of Decline

The medieval art of stained glass was an offspring of the Catholic Church. It was born in northern Europe in the eleventh century, spent a magnificent youth there during the great Cathedral Age, travelled widely in southern Europe as it matured, and died in the sixteenth century, slowly poisoned by the Renaissance and, finally, stabbed in the back by the Reformation. Because medieval glass was so much a Catholic art it was particularly vulnerable during the sixteenth-century religious upheavals that tore Christendom apart. The windows which, with their stories of the Bible and the saints and their miracles, were a source of inspiration to devout Catholics were considered expressions of rank idolatry and superstition by the Protestants.

It was in England and the Netherlands that the reaction to Catholic doctrine and practices was most violent, and the destruction of church art treasures most widespread. In England all the religious houses which had been closed as a result of Henry VIII's suppression of the monasteries in the 1530s began to fall into decay. Laws were passed for the destruction of all church paintings and windows which showed "feigned miracles, pilgrimages, idolatry, and superstition".

In the Netherlands, in 1566, Calvinists, who were among the main targets of the Inquisition there, attacked churches all over the country and smashed the art treasures which they regarded as idolatrous. Painters themselves were among the Flemish iconoclasts. In Germany, Lutheranism made religion the main preoccupation of the nation and the previously flourishing arts began to stagnate.

As far as stained glass was concerned, the destruction of existing windows was not the only consequence of the Reformation. Wherever Protestantism established itself, religious imagery was almost completely ignored in new church windows and was replaced by heraldry and historical themes. The most striking example of this within one church is in St John's at Gouda in the Netherlands. Twenty-two Catholic windows, filled with religious scenes and royal and ecclesiastical donors, had been completed when the town of Gouda rose in revolt and became Calvinist. Some twenty years elapsed before the first Protestant window was made, and it consisted entirely of coats of arms. And most of the windows which followed depicted, sometimes with biblical parallels, episodes associated with the liberation of Holland from Spain and from Catholicism.

During the sixteenth century, France and Spain, both still Catholic, had a period of prolific brilliance in glass-painting, which in Spain continued into the next century. In France, however, the art had died by the end of the century. Here, the Reformation was not to blame, even though the country had been through fifty years of religious wars; stained glass in France perished from a surfeit of stylization without inspiration. Neither can the Reformation be held responsible for the death of the medieval art in Italy, for there was really no place for stained glass in a country so genuinely steeped in Renaissance ideals and Renaissance architecture.

By introducing into stained glass greater naturalism and more realism through the use of perspective, and by imbuing the people depicted with more individualized features, the Italian style at first infused new life into an art which had become too static. But it became anomalous when the laws of painting replaced those of stained glass. The essence of stained-glass artistry, the creation of a design by the use of separate pieces of coloured glass held between leads, was lost when paintings were imitated, larger pieces of glass were used and the leading was disregarded.

It was in part the discovery of new techniques which made the change possible. Although the introduction of silver stain in the fourteenth century was the first major step to painting on glass, it would not of itself have ousted the old approach. But the extended use of enamel paints during the latter part of the sixteenth century made the change, and the decline, inevitable. For centuries only dark enamel had been used to paint such details as facial features on to glass. But when new enamels were introduced—brown, red, cobalt blue, green and purple—glaziers could paint various colours on a single piece of glass and then fix them by firing. Glass painted in this way lost much of its translucent brilliance and in time, too, bits of the enamel peeled off. French, Dutch and Swiss glaziers exploited this new technique to the full, but the Spanish were far more circumspect in the use of enamels, which is one of the reasons that the quality of stained glass deteriorated more slowly in Spain than it did elsewhere.

Protestant objections to religious imagery in stained glass and the development of the enamelling technique combined to make popular a new genre of glass-painting—small panels for secular use. A craze for giving such panels as gifts began in Switzerland late in the fifteenth century, and the practice did not die out until the end of the seventeenth century. The occasions that were used for giving a panel were many—from a great civic occasion to a family wedding. At the beginning the panels were mainly heraldic, bearing the arms of the donor, whether an individual or a group, such as a town council or guild. Later the figures of the donors began to appear in the windows and then their wives and children, until heraldry was very much in second place. Friezes were introduced at the top of the panel. They illustrated religious and historical scenes and inevitably included the legendary Swiss tyrant killer, William Tell.

Holbein the Younger was among the artist-designers of panels and through his influence the Gothic architectural frameworks which originally surrounded such pictures were replaced by Renaissance architecture and vegetation. Elaborate scrolls and buildings in perspective were later variations in framework design. The character of the panel had altered with the introduction of Renaissance decoration, but it was changed even more by use of the wider range of enamels. Intricate designs on clear glass were now quite simple to achieve, and many were extremely attractive.

Panel-painting spread from Switzerland to southern Germany, where Augsburg and Nuremberg were the main centres of production, and then throughout the Rhineland. In Germany the subjects were mainly religious, even when they were intended for secular buildings. As in Switzerland famous artists were eager to provide designs.

In the Netherlands, production of small panel paintings began late in the fifteenth century and continued on an enormous scale for almost two hundred years. Although the style of these panels differed from that of the Swiss, their historical development was similar—from purely Gothic, through a combination of Gothic and Renaissance, to purely Renaissance, and from painting with dark enamel and silver stain to the use of a spectrum of coloured enamels. The popularity of panels spread to England and France, but painting them never became the major industry that it was in Switzerland, Germany and the Netherlands; nor were the skills as great.

Goethe considered the Swiss panels the highest achievement of stained glass—although in his time they had already gone out of fashion except among collectors. Although few connoisseurs of stained glass would agree with Goethe, this branch of glass-painting certainly did help to prevent the art from completely languishing in the seventeenth and eighteenth centuries.

Catholic monks and bishops, fed into a "priest grinder" by Protestant grotesques, are transformed into writhing, hideous creatures in this sixteenth-century Swiss panel, which is now in the National Museum, Zurich. This satirical panel, in which both sides of the Reformation are viewed with equal distaste, is signed and dated by its artist, Hans Jacob Kilchsperger.

SIXTEENTH-CENTURY NETHERLANDS

Versatile Artists of the Flemish Renaissance

During most of the sixteenth century there was savage religious persecution in the Netherlands. Both Charles V and his son, Philip II, were determined to uproot the Protestant heresy from their dominions, even if it involved the most Draconian measures. In the six years from 1567 to 1573 the Duke of Alba and his Council of Blood killed eighteen thousand men and women—and boasted of it—and forced one hundred thousand more to emigrate to England. In the end the stubborn Habsburgs succeeded in keeping Flanders Catholic and lost the northern provinces, the Protestant Dutch Republic.

And yet this fearful century was remarkable for its painting. The level of achievement was exceptionally high, even in the work of those who were not great masters. Moreover, artists were not exclusively painters on canvas, but worked in tapestry and in stained glass, too. Bernard van Orley, for example, went to Rome at the beginning of the sixteenth century and studied under Raphael. When he returned to Brussels he was appointed court painter and spent the rest of his thoroughly busy life painting pictures and portraits and designing tapestries and, increasingly as he grew older, stained glass. He was competent rather than inspired, but he did produce a major work in his large Charles V window in Brussels Cathedral. In this window the emperor and his wife are almost lost beneath the enormous and elaborate arch under which they stand. The whole composition is completely in the spirit of the Italian Renaissance, an effective combination of grisaille, silver stain and a few striking colours.

One of Van Orley's pupils was Pieter Coecke van Aelst, a painter, an architect and a writer as well as a designer of stained glass and tapestry. Like his master he was not a genius, but he has been credited with the brilliantly multi-coloured and opulently Renaissance Counts of Holland window in the Church of St Catherine at Hoogstraten.

A particular darling of the court, who even managed to save his son from a ten-year sentence in the galleys for heresy, Michiel Coxcie was another pupil of Van Orley's who became famous and rich as a painter and as a designer of tapestry and glass. During a long life his output was prodigious. At the age of ninety-two, while he was restoring a painting in Antwerp, he fell off a ladder and was killed.

Unlike Van Orley and his two pupils, all of whom designed in a style which was essentially that of the Italian Renaissance, Nicolas Rombouts, one of the glass-painters most in demand at the beginning of the century, continued some Gothic traditions, such as architectural and heraldic details, even after he had largely turned to the Italian style. He designed windows in Antwerp and Mons and is believed to have been the designer of the series of Royal windows in the Church of St Gommaire, Lierre.

Arnt Nijmegen, whose windows at Tournai Cathedral at the end of the fifteenth century were still in the Gothic style, had been converted to Italian Renaissance before he returned to Antwerp from France in 1513, although he remained more of a true glass-painter than most who worked in this style. His work of this period survives only abroad, notably in Lichfield Cathedral and St George's, Hanover Square, London. Scarcely anything remains in Belgium of the windows glazed by Dirck Vellert, only one of a host of Flemish glass-painters who worked abroad—in Spain, Portugal, Italy and France, as well as in England. He designed many of the windows in King's College Chapel, Cambridge.

In this period, as in the fifteenth century, contemporary painting influenced Flemish stained glass. This is best seen in pictorial windows, in which relaxed human beings, with individualities of their own, each play a part in the action of the scene. There are often, too, a landscape background, ornate architectural frameworks and much heraldry. In the windows depicting royal or noble donors—which the glaziers were frequently called upon to produce—the style tends to be stiffer. While the windows may still be a brilliant show of colour, achieved by clothing the figures in the sumptuous costumes of the time, the character of the people was lost because the artists followed the convention of court portraits that demanded formal magnificence.

Flemish artists also designed stained glass for private houses, which became as fashionable in the Netherlands as elsewhere in Europe. Roundels, small panes of white glass painted in black enamel and silver stain, were especially popular from the late fifteenth century. Two leading Antwerp designers of roundels were Dirck Vellert, who also painted some himself, and Pieter Coecke, who used an exaggerated Italian style. Because the roundels were small and were usually at eye level, the designs could be quite intricate. Many seem to have been copied from illustrated manuscripts or engravings. They were at their best early in the sixteenth century.

Indeed, in all types of stained glass there was a gradual decline in quality and quantity during the second part of the sixteenth century. The outstanding exception was the ensemble of windows of St John's, Gouda, in the rebellious northern provinces, soon to become an independent Holland. Here, the Crabeth brothers, Dirck and Wouter, glazed fourteen of the windows, one of the sixteenth century's greatest achievements in stained glass anywhere.

The legendary birth of St Nicholas is depicted in this early sixteenth-century stained-glass panel which is now in the Victoria and Albert Museum, London. In accordance with tradition, the saint is shown in his bath standing up in prayer on the day of his birth. Designed by the artist Jacob Cornelisz of Amsterdam, this striking composition was clearly influenced by the precise and realistic interiors so characteristic of Flemish painting.

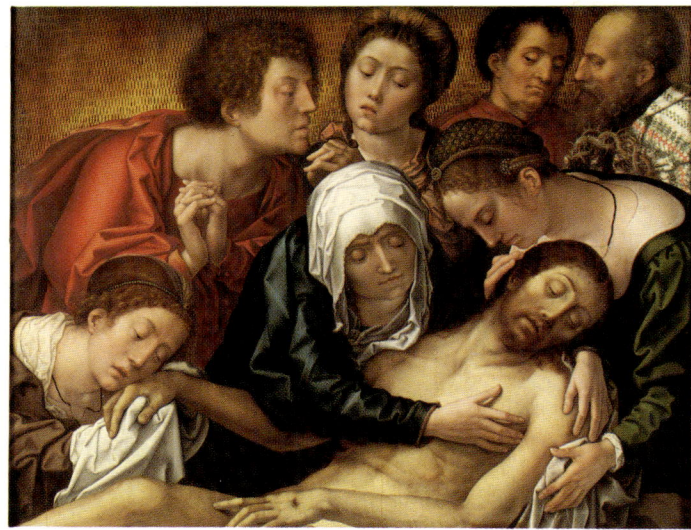

Bernard van Orley, whose paintings include *Joseph of Arimathaea*, above, designed the Charles V window, below, in Brussels Cathedral. Dominated by Classical architecture and ornament, it was the first Flemish stained glass to be wholly Renaissance in style.

The Blinding of Elymas, right, is one of the Raphael cartoons for the Sistine Chapel tapestries, which were woven in Brussels between 1516 and 1519. Widely seen in Flanders, Raphael's work strongly influenced the transition of Flemish stained glass from Gothic to Renaissance.

SIXTEENTH-CENTURY NETHERLANDS

The Church that Changed its Religion

Wouter Crabeth was, like his brother, a great stained-glass artist. His finest work is in St John's in his native Gouda. Believed to have travelled in Italy, he was influenced by the Renaissance style.

Dirck, the elder Crabeth brother, studied painting under Cornelis Ketal and was influenced by the work of Dürer and Jean Cousin. His glass has a memorable grandeur, typified by his windows at Gouda.

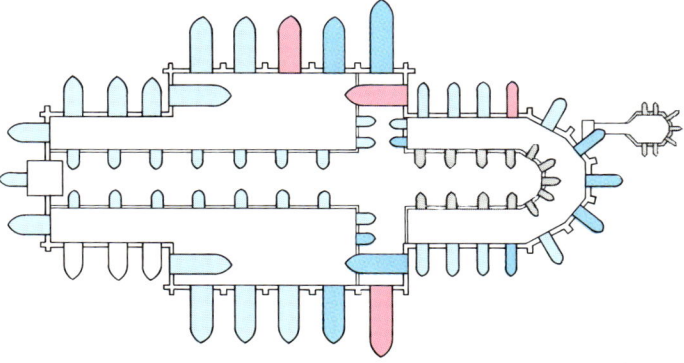

The Church of St John was raised on the site of a thirteenth-century church which had been destroyed by fire in 1552. One of the longest churches in Holland, it is situated at the heart of Gouda. The simple interior with its wooden vaulting is dominated by the finest sixteenth-century glass in the Netherlands.

- ☐ Early sixteenth century
- ☐ Dirck Crabeth (c.1555–70)
- ☐ Wouter Crabeth (c.1555–70)
- ☐ Late sixteenth century
- ☐ Twentieth century

The first Gouda window, the Baptism of Jesus, right, was made in 1555 by Dirck Crabeth. The donor of this stunning pictorial glass was George van Egmond, Bishop of Utrecht, who is portrayed with his patron saint, Martin, in the lower half of the window. Originally the bishop was kneeling before a representation of the Holy Trinity, which was removed during the Reformation. In the upper half of the window Jesus and John the Baptist are depicted on the banks of the Jordan surrounded by spectators. The cartoon of the two major figures is shown left. At the head of the window is the dramatic seated figure of God the Father blessing his Son; God's image was replaced with yellow glass by the Protestants, but was later restored. The figures in these scenes are beautifully composed—attesting to Dirck Crabeth's skill as a painter and glazier.

128

The architecture and stained glass of some cathedrals changed from the Romanesque to the Gothic style while the cathedrals were being built and glazed. The style of some changed from Gothic to Renaissance. But in the course of its building the Church of St John at Gouda in Holland changed the form of its religion. The finest sixteenth-century stained glass in the Netherlands thus consists of twenty-two Catholic windows and nine Protestant windows.

When the original church was struck by lightning and burned down in 1552, the citizens of Gouda rebuilt ambitiously—a vast, gaunt, galleon-like building more than three hundred feet long. There were thirty-one major windows, some of them sixty feet tall, and thirty-three smaller windows to be glazed with stained glass. Donors were sought among royalty, nobility and clergy. The donors of the first three windows were high ecclesiastics. These windows were designed and made by Dirck Crabeth, the elder of the two famous brothers who, over the next sixteen years, were responsible for fourteen of the church's large windows.

Curiously little is known of the personal life of the two Crabeths, Dirck and Wouter, and even less of their method of work, for they left behind a reputation for never talking about their craft to anyone for fear they would give away secrets. Their father, known as Pieter the Cripple, is variously described as a glass-stainer and as the market sweeper of Gouda. Dirck and Wouter spent most of their lives creating stained glass in Gouda, having learned the art, it is said, from monks. Both may have visited Paris, but only Wouter is believed to have been to Italy. Facts about other influences on their art are equally scanty. Dirck knew the Gouda painter Cornelis Ketal, who spent some years in France and England out of the reach of the Inquisition (and devoted the last years of his life to learning to paint with his feet). Wouter knew the Antwerp painter Frans Floris (who spent his declining years being carried drunk to bed by his pupils). Dirck was obviously influenced by the work of Dürer and Wouter by that of Raphael. Dirck never married, but Wouter did, and his descendants, some of them republican-party supporters, were active in public life into the eighteenth century.

The earliest window, which stands in the centre of the apse, depicts Jesus being baptized by St John, the patron saint of the church. One of the flanking windows shows John preaching by the banks of the Jordan—a very Dutch-looking river—and the other is of Jesus preaching there. The donors take up more than a third of each window, and in the panel in which the Provost of Utrecht appears with his patron saint, St Vincent, there are also the flames in which the saint met his death, the hook with which he was tortured and the millstone that was tied to him when he was thrown into the sea—an unintentionally ironic scene at a time when the Inquisition was so active in creating martyrs among the ever-growing number of Dutch Calvinists.

Wouter made his first window in 1561. It shows the Queen of Sheba being received by Solomon. When Dirck heard that his brother had undertaken this theme he reportedly said, "Oh, the conceit of these youngsters! They fancy themselves equal to anything."

One of the sixty-foot-tall windows done by Dirck depicts the Last Supper in the lower half. The donor, Philip II, described in the inscription as the "father of the country, and most clement and religious prince", is shown kneeling with his English queen, Mary Tudor. The donor is missing from Dirck's striking window of the Purification of the Temple. It was given by Prince William of Orange in 1561, but by the time it was finished, almost eight years later, William was in open revolt against the clement Philip and had thought it politic to go into exile. He was, therefore, exiled from the window as well. Prince William, soon to declare himself a Calvinist, must have considered the Purification theme a suitable one for his window, just as the fishmongers of Gouda must have done when they gave the Jonah and the Whale window and the butchers when they chose Balaam and the Ass for their donation.

In 1571 Dirck made his last window, which depicts one of the most bloodthirsty scenes of the Apocrypha—Judith with the head of Holofernes, the commander of the besieging Assyrian army, whom she had slain while he lay drunk in his tent. Not only was this Dirck's last window, but it was the last of the Catholic windows, for in 1572 Gouda, along with Rotterdam and Flushing, rose in revolt against Philip and the Inquisition. Although no windows were destroyed in their entirety, certain images offensive to Protestant doctrines were removed, such as representations of God the Father and the Trinity.

By 1581 the Dutch Republic had been established, but it was 1593 before the Protestants resumed the glazing programme, and 1603 before it was completed. The first Protestant window was of coats of arms, but this was soon followed by windows associated with the fight for freedom. In the Freedom of Conscience window, Liberty of Conscience drives her triumphal chariot over Tyranny. The Relief of Samaria is paired with the Relief of Leyden, in type and antitype style. There William of Orange does at last appear, and in the foreground, giving orders for the relief of Leyden and liberation from Spain.

These windows were joined, 344 years later, by another Liberation window, to commemorate the end of the Nazi occupation of Holland.

The reception of the Queen of Sheba by King Solomon is the exotic subject of Wouter Crabeth's first window for St John's Church, Gouda, in 1561. Wouter excelled in the treatment of architectural background and perspective. The window is lively in colour with a wealth of such detail as the ornate regal foot, below, and there is a decidedly Renaissance air in the features and draperies.

SIXTEENTH-CENTURY NETHERLANDS

History in Stained Glass

Stained-glass windows in sixteenth-century Flanders were crowded with donors. After room had been found for the donors themselves, their wives or husbands, their ancestors or descendants, their patron saints and a considerable amount of impressive Renaissance architecture, there was often little room left in the windows for any religious scenes. There was certainly no space for tall standing figures of biblical characters or saints. In their place many artists chose to portray the Last Supper with the twelve seated apostles spread across the width of the window.

The figures in Flemish windows are kings, queens, princes, dukes and prelates. Inevitably, those most in evidence are Emperor Maximilian I, "the last of the knights", his beautiful and pleasure-loving son, Philip I, King of Castile, his half-witted daughter-in-law, Joanna of Castile, her parents, Ferdinand and Isabella, the Catholic monarchs of Spain, and their grandson, Charles V. These were the main dramatis personae in the story of squalid and tragic political intrigue, with frequent interventions by fate, a story that was to affect the whole future of Europe. Indeed, the Royal windows of Flanders are a picture book of a century of history.

Maximilian and Ferdinand, as part of a peace negotiation, had arranged their children's marriage. Maximilian's son Philip was nineteen and Ferdinand's daughter Joanna was sixteen when their marriage eventually took place in the Church of St Gommaire, Lierre, where above the altar they still live on in stained glass. Neither Joanna nor Philip liked the rigidity and demanding life of the Spanish court, and when Philip could no longer endure it, he returned to the Netherlands alone, leaving behind a moody and neurotically passionate Joanna. When she finally escaped her mother's surveillance and followed her husband to Brussels she found him involved in an affair with a lady of the court. Enraged with jealousy, she assaulted Philip's mistress, frequently gave way to screaming and refused to eat. After Isabella's death, Philip and Ferdinand, disputing which of them was to rule Spain, were agreed that it was not to be Joanna, whom they sought to have declared mad. However, whether or not she was insane before, Joanna was certainly driven mad by the sudden and mysterious death of Philip at the age of only twenty-eight. It was said that she carried her husband's corpse with her on her travels. In 1509 she was sent to Tordesillas in northern Spain where, deprived of her children, she remained under guard until her death at the age of seventy-six.

There is no hint of this personal misery in the stately figures of Joanna and Philip as they appear in the windows of the minute Chapelle de Bourgogne in St Lierre, Antwerp (the chapel which was prepared for them after their marriage); in the Cathedral of Notre Dame at Antwerp; or in a window now in the Victoria and Albert Museum in London, which came from the Chapel of the Holy Blood in Bruges.

The life of their son Charles was equally tragic. He was six when he lost his father but gained the Netherlands. When he was sixteen, Ferdinand, his maternal grandfather, died and he inherited Castile, its American possessions and Aragon, Catalonia, Sicily, Sardinia, Naples and part of North Africa. He was nineteen when Maximilian, his paternal grandfather, died, leaving him Austria, Tyrol and parts of southern Germany. His chancellor was scarcely exaggerating when he then told him, "God has set you on the path towards a world monarchy." There were many who came to regret this act of God before Charles abdicated in 1555 (the year of his mother's death), crippled with gout and tortured by his failure to keep his empire intact and Catholic. Born a Fleming, he died a recluse in a Spanish monastery in 1557.

Charles is depicted in many windows in Belgian churches. He can be seen as a child, with his brother Ferdinand, in the churches of St Gommaire, Lierre, and St Waudru, Mons. As an adult, always wearing the collar of the Order of the Golden Fleece, he is portrayed in windows in, for example, St Catherine's Church, Hoogstraten, and the cathedrals of Brussels and Tournai. In one window in Malines Cathedral that was destroyed, probably during the French Revolution, no fewer than forty ancestors of Charles V and their coats of arms were depicted. Charles himself appeared as a child with a family group.

The Flemish nobility was as ostentatious as royalty in its windows. In a Last Supper scene in Antwerp Cathedral the donor, Engelbert II, who was governor of the Low Countries under Philip the Fair, is prominently portrayed as an onlooker. The sixteenth-century Church of St Catherine at Hoogstraten was built by the Lalaing family, the local aristocracy, and they have six windows devoted entirely to themselves, their wives, their patron saints and their coats of arms. The only intruders are fat-thighed cherubs.

A glorious portrait gallery, the five Royal windows in the apse of St Gommaire, Lierre, three of which are shown above, depict the Emperor Maximilian and other members of the Habsburg family. Each window portrays two religious figures, some of whom are the patron saints of the two royal personages in the central sections beneath them. In the lower part of each window the coats of arms of the donors and their dominions are particularly well executed. Installed in the church in 1519, the five windows are attributed to the glazier Nicolas Rombouts.

In three windows at St Gommaire, ecclesiastical donors and their patron saints appear as part of the religious scene. Arnold Streyters, Abbot of Tongerlo, accompanied by St Jerome dressed as a cardinal, watches the Crown of Thorns being placed on the head of Christ. Denis van Zeverdonck, Abbot of Villers, gazes with St Denis at Christ on the Cross. Marcus Cruyt, Abbot of St Bernard sur l'Escaut, and his patron saint, Mark, are witnesses as Christ is brought down from the Cross.

But for conspicuous donation nobody could rival the Adornes family who, in Bruges, built a church, based on the plan of the Church of the Holy Sepulchre in Jerusalem, and devoted all six windows to generations of their family with patron saints and coats of arms. All vestiges of modesty had been cast aside in the service of the paramount aim—to proclaim the wealth, lineage and munificence of the donors. By contrast, the church itself is a mere thirty feet wide by forty feet long.

THE HISTORY-MAKERS

Eight great men in the history of the Netherlands are portrayed in the lower half of the States of Holland window in St Catherine's Church, Hoogstraten. The four above are, from left to right, Philip the Good, Duke of Burgundy, Emperor Maximilian, Philip, King of Castile and son of Maximilian, and his son, Charles V, Holy Roman Emperor. All once held the title of Count of Holland and are shown with the coat of arms of Holland.

The illegitimate daughter of Charles V, Margaret of Parma, right, in a window by Wouter Crabeth in St John's Church, Gouda, was brought up in Brussels and married the Duke of Parma. Her half-brother Philip II, King of Spain, appointed her Governor of the Netherlands in 1559 and she became his pawn in the struggle against Spanish rule.

William of Orange, the first stadtholder, or governor, of the Dutch republic, was one of the leaders of the revolt against Philip II of Spain and his persecution of the Protestants. His portrait, above, is in the Relief of Leyden window in St John's, Gouda.

Philip II of Spain and his wife, Mary Tudor, Queen of England, are depicted, left, in a window in St John's, Gouda, by Dirck Crabeth. A member of the Habsburg family, Philip was a tenacious and hardworking ruler dedicated to defending the Catholic faith against Protestantism.

SIXTEENTH-CENTURY SPAIN

The Golden Age of Spanish Glass

St Juliana of Nicomedia, above, leads the vanquished devil, who tried to tempt her. This martyred saint is represented in a window by Diego de Santillana, in León Cathedral.

Marked as it was by recurrent wars with France, by uprisings within the Empire—of the Protestants in Flanders and the Moriscoes in Spain—by the horrors of the Inquisition and by the humiliating destruction of the "invincible" Armada by England, the sixteenth century in Spain hardly seems to merit being called a Golden Age. Yet, culturally, it most certainly was.

During this period there were such outstanding scholars as Luis de León, religious leaders like Loyola and such writers as Lope de Vega and Cervantes. But the painters outshone them all. While many of the great artists of the end of the century, including Ribera, Murillo and Velasquez, were Spanish by birth, the artists of the early part of the century were almost exclusively Flemish or Dutch. They had absorbed the Renaissance style from Italy, given it Flemish interpretations and adapted it further when they were working in Spain.

Stained-glass artists may well have been the first to introduce the Renaissance style to Spain and, in the middle of the century, they had many windows to glaze. The new Gothic cathedrals of Segovia and Salamanca and the Renaissance cathedral of Granada all had great expanses of glass. In the cathedrals of Seville, Toledo and Avila, too, there were many windows still to be glazed.

It was at Seville that two brothers, Arnao de Vergara and Arnao de Flandes, did most to create a new style in Spanish stained glass. Whereas the style of the fifteenth-century windows at Seville glazed by Enrique Alemán was that of Flemish realism, De Vergara's first windows at Seville, glazed after 1525, display a mixture of Flemish and Italian influences. In those glazed after his brother had joined him the influence of Raphael is paramount. This new style was continued by the Arnaos' successors at Seville, Carlos de Brujas and Vicente Menardo.

A particularly interesting window by Arnao de Vergara is dedicated to St Sebastian. It shows the saint standing majestically under equally majestic Renaissance architecture. He wears a tabard and doublet and beneath his halo is a cap with the crespinette fashionable in Spain in about 1530. He carries sword, sceptre and arrow, and also sports a beard, making him look suspiciously like Charles V.

From the outset, Arnao de Flandes was more confidently a Renaissance painter than his brother had been. He worked in Seville Cathedral over a period of twenty-three years, but his windows never became stereotyped. Among them is a series of figures of saints glazed between 1543 and 1552. These continue the fifteenth-century series done by Enrique Alemán, but the style has changed to High Renaissance with an abundance of Classical ornament and architectural detail and firmly drawn figures with powerfully expressive, individualized features. When he had finished his saints, Arnao embarked on a series of windows illustrating the life of Christ, but these, completed within only four years, are less impressive; the quality suffered from the speed with which they were executed.

Although the Arnao brothers worked in the cathedral for many years their relations with the Cathedral Chapter were not always smooth and undoubtedly exemplified some of the problems that beset contemporary glaziers. In their contract in 1534 each brother undertook to make four windows a year. Two years later they complained that for four months they had not been paid the ducat a day due to them, and they could not fulfil their quota of work because the Chapter could not decide what story it wanted the glaziers to illustrate. Later, Arnao de Vergara was told to stop work, was paid off and went to Granada for a short time.

In 1552 Arnao de Flandes asked for an increase in pay because the cost of everything had doubled—the wealth pouring into Spain from her new American possessions was creating problems of inflation. The request was granted—and benefited not only Arnao, but also De Brujas and Menardo, who received the same salary as Arnao.

Divided into two sections representing heaven and earth, this circular window, left, in Seville Cathedral depicts the Ascension. It was designed by the two Arnao brothers, whose style marked a high point of of Sevillian stained glass.

Flemish stained-glass artists were equally active in other parts of Spain—in Segovia, Salamanca, Granada and Toledo. Segovia and Salamanca were the last great Gothic cathedrals of Spain, built at a time when Gothic architecture was all but extinct. A grand plan was drawn up for the ninety-two windows at Segovia and various artists were then commissioned to execute individual windows. Some were done by Nicolas de Holanda, Arnao de Vergara and Nicolas de Vergara the Elder and some were brought from Antwerp. The Cathedral Chapter at Salamanca, finding the glazing of the cathedral expensive, looked to Flanders for cheaper glass and labour, as well as employing the peripatetic Flemish glaziers Alberto de Holanda and his son Nicolas, who also worked at Avila.

Granada was the other great Spanish cathedral of the century, and although it is a Renaissance building it has more than forty windows richly glazed in excellent Renaissance style. Again, some of the windows were brought from Flanders, but Teodoro of Holland and Jean de Campin, sometimes working from cartoons by the painter, sculptor and architect Diego de Siloe, created most of them.

Spain shared with Italy a fondness for large round windows unbroken by the tracery of the rose. Among such *ojos de buey*, or bull's-eyes, as they were known in Spain, that done by the Arnao brothers in Seville—the Annunciation—is particularly fine. In Toledo Cathedral, too, there are many windows which show how Flemish-Spanish glaziers of the late fifteenth and early sixteenth centuries could adapt a scene to this circular shape. They ignored the mullions, carried the circle across two lights of a window and, to emphasize its roundness, surrounded it with a narrow band of glass in a distinctive colour.

The glorious era of painting continued in Spain through the first half of the seventeenth century. But by then cathedral building was at an end and with it the major work of the glass-painters.

Biblical scenes in the aisle windows of Toledo Cathedral are within circular medallions whose shape is a deliberate counterpoint of the lancets' verticality. The sequence begins at the southwest corner with Adam and Eve, above.

Gold, deep red and royal blue are judiciously combined to give an effect of extraordinary richness in a sixteenth-century window, right, in Seville Cathedral. The artist, Arnao de Vergara, signed his monogram below the regal figure of St Sebastian, who resembles Charles V. Within the window's Moorish arch, God, who looks down at the saint, makes a gesture of blessing. The filigree decoration of St Sebastian's extravagant niche is similar to the convoluted carving resembling *plateria*, Spanish silverwork, which distinguished sixteenth-century Spanish architecture. This ornamentation is exemplified by the façade of Salamanca University, above.

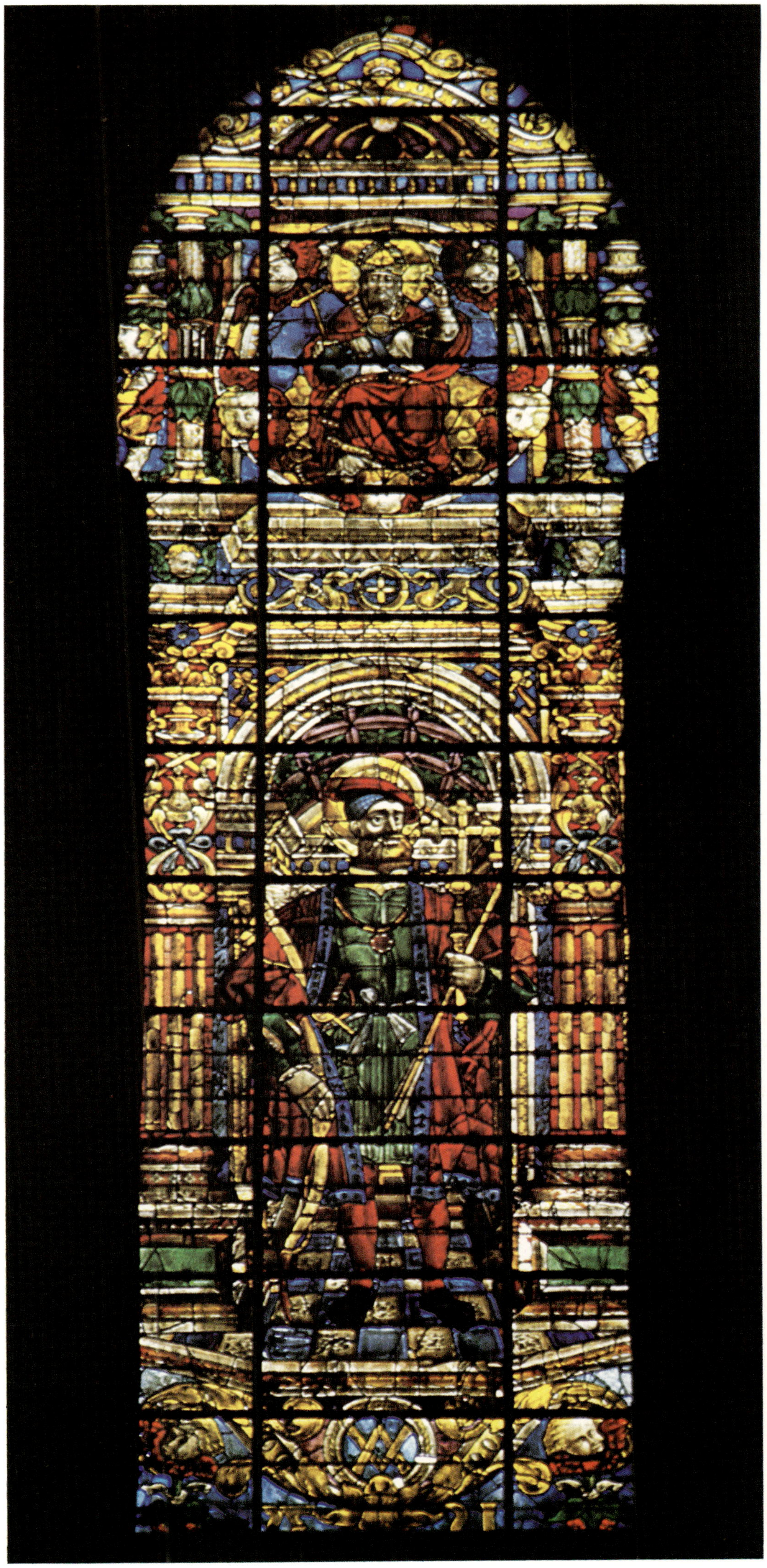

133

SIXTEENTH-CENTURY ENGLAND

Death of a Native Tradition

The cautious calculating nature of the Lancastrian King Henry VII, founder of the Tudor dynasty, is suggested in this portrait, painted in 1505, in the National Portrait Gallery, London. Through his marriage to Elizabeth of York, Henry united the rival families of York and Lancaster and restored peace to England. He encouraged trade, especially with Flanders, and, as a keen patron of the arts, was responsible for importing German and Flemish glaziers who were influenced by the Renaissance aesthetics. He donated the money for the windows of King's College Chapel, Cambridge.

Surmounting the Perpendicular stained-glass windows and spanning the tall, narrow chapel of King's College, Cambridge, is the finest example of English fan vaulting, designed in the early sixteenth century by John Wastell of Bury St Edmunds. Each fan is a concave cone of stone supported by equidistant ribs of equal lengths which radiate from the same point. The vault's web-like pattern is completed by decorative horizontal ribs bordered by tracery.

Between them the Renaissance and the Reformation precipitated the demise of medieval stained glass in England. The Renaissance style, at least in its outward forms, was imported to England from the Continent in the first half of the sixteenth century. But just as the spirit behind the Gothic style never took root in Italy, so Renaissance thinking remained alien to the English mind. The noteworthy Renaissance glass in sixteenth-century England was, therefore, created by foreigners and they were painters on glass rather than the painters in or with glass that English medieval master glaziers had been.

It was largely due to Henry VII that English glass-painting during the Renaissance period was dominated by Flemings and Germans and their interpretation of the new Italian style. During the second half of the fifteenth century, increased political and trading links between England and Flanders had led to an influx of Flemish artists and glaziers, and it was this trend which was reinforced by the predilections for Flemish art of Henry VII and his court. The glaziers settled in Southwark, outside the jurisdiction of the City, where aliens were forbidden to employ other alien workers. But Southwark had been a centre of English glass-painters since the thirteenth century and the natives bitterly resented this stream of immigrants. For almost fifty years there were endless disputes between them and the London Guild of Glaziers and Painters on Glass, but the Flemings enjoyed the advantage of the patronage of both Henry VII and Henry VIII.

Although the Flemings and Germans were concentrated in Southwark, their work and their influence can be seen in many parts of the country. The prime example is King's College Chapel, Cambridge. The building itself, completed in 1515, is magnificently Gothic. The stonework takes up only one-third of the wall area and when the sun falls on it through the multicoloured glass even that seems an extension of the twenty-six immense windows. In his sonnet on King's College Chapel, William Wordsworth wrote the "... stonework glimmers, dyed in the soft chequerings of a sleepy light". The earliest glass, which dates from 1515 to 1517, is largely Gothic in style, but the major part, done between 1526 and 1531, is unmistakably Renaissance, with only a few lingering traces of Gothic.

Many of the windows were designed by the Antwerp painter and engraver Dirck Vellert, the only designer whose identity is certain. The first glazier, and the first foreigner to be appointed King's Glazier, in 1505, was Barnard Flower, from the Netherlands or Germany. Galyon Hone, Dutch-born and Flemish-taught, succeeded Flower as King's Glazier and from 1526 to 1531 he worked on the chapel windows with his many apprentices. Of the other

Designed by Dirck Vellert, a Fleming, and glazed by Galyon Hone, a Dutchman, who is believed to have trained in Flanders, these heads of St Barnabas and St Paul, from a window in King's College Chapel, exemplify the vigorous realism of sixteenth-century Flemish art.

glaziers Symond Symondes may have been English; Richard Bownde and Thomas Reve were Londoners; and Francis Williamson and James Nicholson were foreign. Nicholson was in fact extremely versatile. After working at King's College Chapel, he was employed by Cardinal Wolsey at Oxford. In about 1530, the time of Wolsey's arrest and death, Nicholson became interested in the new Lutheran doctrines and turned from glass-painting to printing, publishing translations of the Bible as well as several works which were considered heretical.

Besides King's College Chapel the hand of Flemings can be seen in pictorial windows elsewhere in England: at Fairford Church in Gloucestershire (but notable more for the quantity than the quality of its glass) and in the richly coloured and lively window depicting eight miracles of St Nicholas at Hillesden Church in Buckinghamshire.

In general, this Flemish Renaissance influence brought much greater realism into stained glass. Such artificial conventions as canopies tended to disappear, to be replaced by landscapes and buildings that showed great concern for perspective. The people depicted looked more like ordinary people, a development condemned as "aesthetic decadence" by Westlake, that great and thoroughly Victorian historian of stained glass. "The general characteristic", he wrote, "was coarseness. The men are huge limbed as dray horses, whilst the women seem fat and puffy, as though they had neglected healthy exercise or intelligent application of any kind." Moreover, the clothes they wore were "full and large, probably from the habit of wearing thicker materials and a greater amount of underclothing".

The Renaissance style scarcely had a chance to establish itself in England before it was overtaken by the Reformation. The first stained glass to be destroyed was in the monasteries. Soon after Henry VIII's break with Rome in 1534 the so-called Dissolution of the monasteries and other religious houses began. There were then more than eight hundred of them and the first to go were the small ones. The pretext

THE SECULAR VOGUE

Much sixteenth-century stained glass was inspired by the safely secular subject of heraldry. Typical is the crowned red rose, below, a badge of the Tudors, now in the Victoria and Albert Museum, London.

Family coats of arms proliferated in churches and private homes in the sixteenth century. Dated 1550, the coat of arms of the Beckingham family is represented in a window in St Mary's Church at Bishopsbourne in Kent.

The surname of John Islip, an abbot of Westminster, is visualized on a sixteenth-century quarry, above, from Westminster Abbey, now in the Burrell Collection, Glasgow. Between the eye and the word slip, a man who might well be saying "I slip" falls from a tree.

given in the Suppression Act was that they had become centres of "manifest sin, vicious, carnal and abominable living", which was probably true of only a minority. The real reason was that the king needed money, and the assets of the monasteries were destined for the Crown. Next the larger monasteries were destroyed and by 1540 none was left. The lead from the roofs and windows was melted down (some to be used as shot) and the buildings, unprotected from the weather, fell into ruins.

Coinciding with the suppression of the monasteries was a bitter campaign against shrines and relics, which were said to encourage idolatry and superstitious practices, and this led to the ending of pilgrimages. The nation became more secular and the church poorer. In 1547 churches were ordered to "take away, utterly extinct, and destroy all shrines, coverings of shrines, all tables, candlesticks, trindles or rolls of wax, pictures, paintings, and all other monuments of feigned miracles, pilgrimages, idolatry and superstition; so that there remain no memory of the same in walls, glass windows or elsewhere". As a result, many windows were destroyed. But many survived because of a later royal proclamation protecting "monuments of antiquity", especially stained-glass windows. A few windows were saved by being taken down and hidden.

The art of stained glass survived during the second half of the sixteenth century only because glaziers, English and foreign, turned to creating stained glass without religious imagery. This secular glass consisted largely of quarries, painted with flowers, animals and, above all, birds engaged in all kinds of human as well as avian activities. Although comparatively few remain, numerous heraldic windows were made for churches as well as for private houses. For, while religious imagery was illegal or suspect, heraldry continued to be a safe and popular subject. Its character changed, however, during the century. Increasingly enamels came into use for painting elaborate coats of arms, with much grotesquerie, on clear glass.

Thus, in the sixteenth century, the great English medieval tradition of stained glass finally came to its end—first with a whimper during the Renaissance and then with a bang as a result of the Reformation.

Flemish glaziers were responsible for the detailed window in Hillesden Church, Buckinghamshire, depicting the miracles of St Nicholas. In the panel left, repentant thieves return stolen gold to its rightful Jewish owner. The legend, which ends with this scene of reconciliation, concerns a Jew who seeks to protect his possessions by stealing an image of St Nicholas from a church and invoking its power to watch over his home. When the Jew finds that his house has been robbed, he attacks the effigy in a rage and the thieves have a vision of the wounded, bleeding saint, who tells them to restore the stolen goods. Upon receiving them the Jew is converted to Christianity.

SIXTEENTH-CENTURY GERMANY

Art of Painters

Albrecht Dürer, whose humanistic self-portrait is shown left, was Germany's most important Renaissance artist and a major influence on sixteenth-century European stained glass. Without rejecting the individualism of northern, medieval tradition, Dürer's work assimilated the objectivity and naturalism of Italian art. His dictum that "art is hidden in nature" is reflected in his engravings, drawings and woodcuts, in which even the allegorical and legendary subjects are represented with meticulous realism.

Samson slaying the lion, above, a Dürer woodcut, was obviously copied by the sixteenth-century German glazier of the panel, right, now in St Mary's Church, Patrixbourne, Kent. Inspired by Dürer's naturalism, the glazier reproduced many of the details of the original landscape, including the flowers, the leaves, the rocks and the city in the background. The thick fur of the beautiful golden lion successfully combines the glazier's use of colour with the artist's form.

The sixteenth century began auspiciously for the arts in Germany. Since the invention of printing in the previous century Germany had become renowned throughout Europe for her fine books, her painting, engraving, sculpture and carving. And, encouraged by the chivalrous and handsome Emperor Maximilian I, the arts flourished. The Church, however, was corrupted by its immense wealth and its degenerate hierarchy. As Martin Luther's campaign to reform it grew more intense during the sixteenth century, the German people became more involved in religion than in the arts.

It is ironic that the Reformation in Germany was sparked off by a practice of the Catholic Church which had played a great part in financing the Cathedral Age and its splendid stained glass. This was the sale of indulgences, whereby the faithful gave money for the remittance of their sins. An unfailing source of income for the Church, its abuse had long been a scandal. For Luther, the breaking point came with the widespread sale of indulgences, authorized by Pope Leo X, to finance the building of the new St Peter's in Rome. In protest he nailed his ninety-five theses on a church door in Wittenberg, thereby inaugurating a hundred years of religious strife in Europe.

The start of the Reformation also marked the end of Germany's long attachment to the Gothic style of art and architecture. New influences were at work, mainly of Flemish and Italian origin, and by the end of the century the style of glass-painting had radically changed. But it was a German artist, Albrecht Dürer, who was in major part responsible for initiating the change. The son of a competent but not especially successful Hungarian goldsmith, he was born in Nuremberg in 1471 and was destined to become the greatest of the city's talented sons. After completing his apprenticeship with the painter and engraver Michael Wolgemut and travelling widely in Germany, Dürer made his first journey to Italy in 1494. There he became thoroughly imbued with the concepts of the Italian Renaissance, which his art was to spread throughout northern Europe.

When he died, at the age of fifty-seven, he left nearly a thousand drawings, two hundred woodcuts and more than a hundred copperplate engravings. His writings included *Treatise on Fortifications* and *Treatise on Human Proportions*. In his early years Dürer was greatly interested in stained glass and he designed a number of windows, including one for the Schmidtmayer Chapel of St Lorenz, Nuremberg. But his indirect influence was far more important, for in churches throughout Europe there are sixteenth-century stained-glass windows which have been inspired by, or blatantly copied from, Dürer's woodcuts and engravings.

Dürer's influence was also exerted through his pupils. The most brilliant was Hans Baldung Grien, court painter, designer of stained glass and of textiles. Later in life he produced beautiful woodcuts, which were often sensual and erotic. His greatest achievement was the high altar in Freiburg Minster. While he was working on the altar he

Like his teacher, Dürer, the Alsatian artist Hans Baldung Grien combined masterly draughtsmanship with depictions of intense emotion or gruesome allegorical subject matter. A suitably emotive subject, Mary weeping below the Cross, left, is part of a window which was designed by Baldung Grien and executed by the glazier Hans Gitschmann von Ropstein. Removed from its original place in Freiburg Cathedral, it is now in the city's Augustiner Museum. A drawing by Baldung Grien, far left, in the Musée de l'Oeuvre Notre Dame, Strasbourg, shows Doubting Thomas touching the wound in Christ's side.

also did cartoons for windows of the choir, which were executed by Hans Gitschmann von Ropstein, a colleague of the Strasbourg master glazier Peter Hemmel von Andlau. Yet only a few decades after these windows were completed in 1528 all the minster windows began to show signs of neglect, caused by lack of expert attention, which in turn was the result of the dwindling interest in stained glass.

Hans von Kulmbach, another of Dürer's pupils, was a highly original painter who portrayed his subjects with a deep humanity. He designed two striking windows in the choir of St Sebald's in Nuremberg which were made in the workshop of the master glazier Veit Hirsvogel. One is the Maximilian window, which includes the figures of the emperor and his first wife, Mary of Burgundy, their beautiful son Philip and his mad widow Joanna, victims of high politics and deep tragedy.

As in Nuremberg, the influence of contemporary painting was paramount in the windows glazed by the workshops in Cologne, the other most prolific stained-glass centre in sixteenth-century Germany. Two of the city's archbishops and a count gave the five picture windows in the north aisle of the cathedral, which date from about 1508. Three of them have the Virgin Mary as their main character, and she appears in the other two windows as well. It is interesting to compare the thirteenth-century Bible window scene of the Adoration of the Magi in the Chapel of the Magi with that of the early sixteenth-century Magi window in the north aisle. The early monumental simplicity has gone and the scene, which stretches across three lights, ignoring the mullions, has become theatrical, courtly and colourful. But, in fact, the comparison is hardly of like with like, for these sixteenth-century windows are imitations of painting, and all the rich detail, the perspective and the colour are achieved by the techniques not of the glazier but of the painter.

The Annunciation window, left, in the Tucher Museum, Nuremberg, was designed by the painter Hans von Kulmbach, one of Dürer's most famous pupils, who was also fortunate enough to receive the patronage of the Tuchers, the wealthiest family in sixteenth-century Nuremberg. Von Kulmbach's contented young Virgin, surrounded by the conventional symbols of lily, dove and aureole, contrasts with Hans Baldung Grien's sorrowful figure above, although the hands of both Virgins are similarly modelled.

An amusing scene, delicately drawn in the style of the engraver J. A. Ducereau, is depicted on glass now in Darmstadt Museum.

SIXTEENTH-CENTURY FRANCE

Masterpieces of the Renaissance

France was as beset with troubles in the sixteenth century as Spain. Indeed, for more than half of the century, these two great Catholic powers were at war with each other. For France the last fifty years were particularly disastrous. Henry II, who was ruled by his mistress, Diane de Poitiers, was succeeded by his three sons, Francis II, who was sick, Charles IX, who was neurotic, and Henry III, who was degenerate. But it was their mother, Catherine de Medici, who ruled France. Perhaps the only admirable thing about her was her interest in the arts—particularly painting and literature—and her impeccable taste. Under this fat, gluttonous, revengeful, doting mother, France entered into the civil religious wars with the Huguenots that lasted to the end of the century. Catherine herself helped to engineer the Massacre of St Bartholomew, in which thousands of Protestants in Paris and in the provinces were killed.

Yet despite the upheavals, in Catholic France, as in Catholic Spain, stained glass flourished. Not since the thirteenth century had so much been produced. But there was a difference. Whereas in the thirteenth century the native style of French stained glass influenced styles abroad, the glass of sixteenth-century France showed strong evidence of Italian and Flemish influences.

At the end of the fifteenth century the French King Charles VIII and his army had brought back from Italy first-hand knowledge of the Italian Renaissance, and this was soon reflected in French architecture—in the royal châteaux of the Loire and the bishop's palace at Gaillon in northern France. Architectural details in stained glass also changed; the Perpendicular canopies of the previous century were replaced by the Classical shell-shaped niches beloved by the Italians.

Flemish styles were introduced into France by Arnoult de Nimègue, a Flemish stained-glass artist who came to Rouen from Tournai in 1502. Confusingly, he sometimes signed his name as Arnouldt de la Pointe on windows in Normandy and was known as Artus van Ort or Arnt Nijmegen in Flanders. In Tournai Cathedral, at the close of the fifteenth century, he had glazed the historical windows in Gothic style. In Normandy he launched into Renaissance forms and combined them with medieval iconography. His large Tree of Jesse in the Church of St Godard, Rouen, bears great figures of the prophets and the kings of Judah which are reminiscent of the early Dürer woodcuts, *The Apocalypse* and *The Passion*. The figures stand in shell-shaped niches and the pillars are covered with a variety of Renaissance ornaments.

De Nimègue also designed eight stylish windows in the Church of St Ouen, Rouen, depicting legends of various saints, including the thirteenth-century Elisabeth of Hungary, a prodigy among saints. She was affianced at the age of four, married at fourteen, spent most of her adolescence in prayer and almsgiving, was widowed at twenty, when her husband Louis IV was killed on a Crusade, and died at twenty-four, a paragon of good works and mortification. She was canonized four years later.

In 1513 De Nimègue returned to Flanders, but he still maintained contact with the Normandy schools of glass-painters, which he had profoundly influenced. From

Exotic portraits of sixteenth-century dignitaries and a self-portrait of the artist, Engrand le Prince, represent Christ's ancestors in the vivid Jesse Tree window in the Church of St Etienne, Beauvais. Yellow stain, applied with the skill which distinguishes Le Prince's work, creates the luminous golden robes, jewels and sceptres, the artist's hair and beard and the ornate grotto in which Jesse sleeps. King Solomon, who "in all his glory" was inferior to the lilies of the field, is depicted in the centre of the window as a corrupt-looking, wizened old man. Ironically, a shining white lily containing the Virgin and Child blossoms at the top of the window in the heart-shaped tracery light.

138

Antwerp, in about 1520, he sent the window of the Three Marys to the Church of Notre Dame of Louviers, and until the middle of the century he also provided cartoons for his pupils in Normandy.

Another determining influence upon Normandy glass in the early part of the century was the famous workshop in Beauvais of the Le Prince brothers—Engrand, Jean, Nicolas and Pierre. Netherlandish influences are apparent in their work, particularly in the windows done by Engrand, which also show an affinity with Dürer's later work. Of this brilliant family Engrand was the genius, but nothing is known of his life except from his windows, and from his tombstone the year of his death—1531. However, he included a self-portrait in his unusual Tree of Jesse window in the Church of St Etienne, Beauvais. Christ's ancestors, their faces suspiciously like those of sixteenth-century French kings, appear like flowers on the tree. Among them is Engrand, whose sleeve bears the initials ENGR. His wavy golden hair and curly beard and his golden tunic gave Engrand an opportunity to show how brilliantly he could use yellow stain, for just as Arnoult de Nimègue was addicted to the use of blood red, so Engrand le Prince was to gold. Adjoining him in the window is King Solomon, a toothless old man, and his intricately embroidered clothes and ornate head-gear show another aspect of Engrand's perfectionist skill—his infinite care with multicoloured details.

There are other beautiful windows by the Le Prince family in the Church of St Etienne and elsewhere in Normandy, in Paris and in Montmorency. The most dramatic is the Chariot window, made for the Church of St Vincent in Rouen and now in the Musée de Rouen. This large window, the joint work of Engrand and Jean le Prince, depicts the triumph of the Virgin Mary over original sin through the Birth of Christ. In the upper part of the window, devoted to the Triumph of Innocence, Adam and Eve help the two Virtues, Faith and Fortitude, to pull the chariot, while in the lower part, in which the Devil is triumphant, Adam and Eve walk in chains ahead of the chariot. (So unrealistically realistic and detailed are the backgrounds that Adam and Eve are walking past the bridge and cathedral of Rouen.) Whereas the medieval glass-painter at Strasbourg Cathedral had made the Virtues beautiful women and the Vices ordinary plain women, the Le Prince family, influenced by Renaissance painters, took the opposite point of view and made the women who represent the seven deadly sins—for example, Gluttony on a pig and Pride on a lion—temptingly beautiful. The influence of the Le Prince family was widespread for some thirty years. Outside the family circle, Romain Buron, Engrand's most talented follower, was responsible for many of the best of the superb Renaissance windows in Ste Foy at Conches.

Troyes, an influential glass centre early in the century, was rivalled later by Châlons-sur-Marne, where Mathieu Bléville emerged as the leading stained-glass artist. He executed some fine windows at the church of Notre-Dame-en-Vaux in Châlons. The most memorable is a crowded and violent battle scene showing the legendary appearance of St James, the brother of John, during the fighting at the battle of Clavijo to urge on the Spaniards against the Moors. Bléville's signature is on one of the horses. Although he was an excellent draughtsman with a sharp eye for detail, his exuberant style was outmoded by the cold elegance of the Renaissance windows. After the middle of the century, Troyes became a centre of delicately coloured enamelled and engraved glass, and deep Gothic colours were finally abandoned.

The city of Metz was, like Strasbourg, alternately possessed by Germans and French. Converted to Christianity in the third century, it was captured by the Franks in the sixth century and became a seat of Merovingian kings. It became a Free Imperial City in the thirteenth century, but

DISTINGUISHED PATRONS OF FRANCE

The Renaissance château of Chantilly, above, belonged in the sixteenth century to the illustrious House of Montmorency. Anne, a distinguished soldier and patron of stained glass, is immortalized with his large family in windows of the chapels at Ecouen and Chantilly and in the Church of St Martin, Montmorency, founded by his father, Guillaume, in 1523.

Guillaume de Montmorency
1452–1531

Anne de Montmorency
1493–1567

Rabbits with exquisitely painted fur sit among flowers, below, at the feet of the Virgin in a window in St Martin's Church, Montmorency. The window is signed by the Beauvais artist Engrand le Prince.

Cupid, popular in Renaissance art, embraces Psyche, left, the maiden whom he bewitched. This scene, painted in enamel by a pupil of Raphael, is one of forty-four panels in the château of Chantilly depicting the couple's legendary exploits.

SIXTEENTH-CENTURY FRANCE

Masterpieces of the Renaissance

in 1552 it reverted to France. The stained glass, which dates from the thirteenth to the twentieth century, in the massive Cathedral of St Etienne reflects the double nature of the city's history.

The vast and magnificent windows done in the first half of the sixteenth century were created by a glazier who had not been led astray, as had so many of his contemporaries, into painting on glass and who still largely remained loyal to the late Gothic style. He was the Alsatian Valentin Busch, who came to Metz from Strasbourg when the iconoclasm of the Reformation was making life uncomfortable for glaziers; even workshops were being spied upon to be sure that images of the Virgin Mary were not lurking there. Little is known of Busch's early life, but the evidence of his windows suggests that he had travelled in Italy, even if he had not been totally seduced by Italian style and still preferred large single figures to landscapes. In 1520 he was appointed official glazier to Metz Cathedral, and spent the rest of his life working on windows in the cathedral's choir and transepts and in other churches in the city.

In the windows he did for the cathedral it is obvious that Busch's great talent lay in portraying figures, whether the early busts of the fathers of the Church in the south transept tracery or the monumental figures of rows of saints in the main part of the windows. The dramatic impact was built up by a masterly use of detail, especially in the clothing. For example, on the copes of bishop saints in south transept windows, the figures of other saints are delineated in finely executed embroidery.

Although Busch's approach to stained glass was fundamentally medieval in its rejection of the technique of painting, and his style was late Gothic, Renaissance influences are apparent in his work. The faces of his saints tend to be shown as very human Renaissance flesh. His decoration is rich in Renaissance motifs—the shell niches and exotic vegetation—while retaining the damask and architectural backgrounds of the Peter Hemmel von Andlau school. Busch had a pleasant comic touch worthy of the medieval painter, but executed in Renaissance style. Competing with the bishops in the south transept window, for example, are countless instrument-playing cherubs performing acrobatic feats among the foliage and the architecture.

Busch died in 1541, working almost to the end with undiminished skill. Most of the windows he did for other Metz churches have been destroyed. He left behind him no important school, but his Germanic influence can be seen in a number of windows in other parts of Lorraine.

During the first part of the sixteenth century a great deal of stained glass was produced in the Paris region by both Frenchmen and foreigners, but after the middle of the century the quality, as of the glass elsewhere in France, rapidly declined. One of the few important works of the mid-century is the now greatly damaged series of knights dressed in the regalia of the Order of St Michael, in the chapel of the castle of Vincennes. Among them is Henry II; his mistress, Diane de Poitiers, makes her appearance among the Holy Martyrs.

The most interesting windows of this period in the Paris region, although not all of them are among the best, are those associated with the Montmorency family. The windows are legion, because Anne, the Duke of Montmorency, Marshal and Constable of France, had a weakness for seeing himself portrayed in stained glass, along with his wife, five sons and seven daughters. Anne (curiously self-named after the second wife of Louis XII) was a distinguished commander—although he managed to be taken prisoner three times, twice by the Spanish and once by the Huguenots. He was one of Francis I's chief councillors and a leading opponent of Francis's widow, Catherine de Medici. He can be seen kneeling in windows of the parish church of St Acceul at Ecouen, but with only five of his daughters; at St Martin's Church, Montmorency, with the full complement of daughters; at the chapel of Chantilly, in glass originally in the chapel of the château of Ecouen; and, now white-haired, in the church of Mesnil-Aubry.

The Montmorency glass is completed by forty-four scenes of the adventures of Cupid and Psyche. These were made for the family château at Ecouen, but disappeared during the Revolution and are now in the château of Chantilly. They are strongly Italian, derivative of Raphael. They foreshadow what was to happen to French stained glass in the second half of the century—the suffocation of all originality and humanity by a sterile Classicism.

Although St Augustine was speaking metaphorically when he compared Christ with a bunch of grapes crushed in a wine press, sixteenth-century French glaziers frequently showed the body of Christ itself trapped in a press and yielding blood. This window, however, in Ste Foy, Conches, depicts the theme less brutally. Christ, standing on a cruciform wine press, treads the grapes and the juice flows into the tub.

SIXTEENTH-CENTURY ITALY

Reviving a Dying Art

German glaziers took the art of stained glass to Italy in the thirteenth century. In the sixteenth century, a Frenchman, Guillaume de Marcillat, and a German, Konrad Much, each briefly breathed new life into the dying art of Italian stained glass. None the less the art was doomed in Italy, for it proved to be incompatible with the ornate interiors of High Renaissance architecture.

Guillaume de Marcillat was an artist who had become a monk to escape the penalty for having killed a man. In the first decade of the century he was summoned to work in Rome by Pope Julius II, who, whatever his spiritual inadequacies, was a generous patron of the arts. Only two windows by De Marcillat have survived in Rome and these are in the choir of Santa Maria del Popolo. De Marcillat left Rome in 1506 and worked in Cortona for a while before going on to Arezzo. Here, in the cathedral, is his best work.

In five double-light windows depicting scenes from the life of Christ, De Marcillat reached the ultimate in stained-glass pictorialism, both in the figures and in the architecture. In the backgrounds of the pair of windows which illustrate Christ driving the moneylenders from the temple and his encounter with the adulteress, the buildings are vast Classical edifices, depicted in great detail. The people, too, are painted in the most minute detail. Their faces convincingly express surprise, horror, disgust, resignation or compassion. The styles and textures of their clothes are extraordinarily realistic. Lazarus being raised from the dead and emerging naked from his tomb is greeted by haloed women dressed in sumptuous gowns on which every stitch of embroidery is delineated.

These and other windows in the cathedral, as well as De Marcillat's windows in the two Arezzo churches of San Francesco and SS Annunziata, are exquisitely executed, but they can hardly be called stained glass. They are like frescoes transferred to glass which, because of the artist's skill in the use of coloured enamels, succeeded. It was a skill that his followers did not possess. Curiously, De Marcillat's frescoes, in the vaults of Arezzo Cathedral, were not as successful as his stained glass and are completely eclipsed by those in the Church of San Francesco, which were done by the Renaissance painter Piero della Francesco.

Much of the reputation that De Marcillat has enjoyed stems from the writings of his contemporary, Giorgio Vasari, a citizen of Arezzo, an architect, a painter, a writer, an impresario and an avowed disciple of De Marcillat. He may have been somewhat biased because of his lack of interest in medieval glass and his belief that the nearer painted glass came to fresco painting the finer it was. Vasari and his followers have to their credit, however, some attractive secular glass, such as that in the Laurentian Library in Florence, which dates from the middle of the century. A whole series of windows is devoted to mythical scenes, cherubs, birds, grotesqueries and the arms of the Medici, all painted with enamel and silver stain.

The German, Konrad Much of Cologne, known to the Italians as De Mochis, was invited to Milan in 1544 to head a team of glaziers and also to design some windows for the cathedral. Although the work in which he was involved was interesting and included simple and boldly coloured designs of the Ark, Bathsheba at her bath and the grapes of Canaan, it was not long before the artistry became uninspired and the craftsmanship pedestrian—as a result of the speed with which many of the windows were executed. Valerius Diependale, a Fleming from Louvain, succeeded De Mochis, but when he left at the end of the century all work stopped.

Such was the brief life of Italian stained glass. It came from what the thirteenth-century Italians regarded as the barbaric North. In Italy it was transformed into something more to Italian taste. The new style, in its turn, travelled northwards beyond the Alps, carrying with it the seeds of its inevitable decay.

A chaotic scene in the temple where Christ is expelling the moneylenders was depicted by the French artist Guillaume de Marcillat in one of the five windows which he designed for Arezzo Cathedral. Their facial expressions very convincing, the moneylenders clutch their possessions as they pour out of the impressively drawn Classical temple.

The woman who was taken in adultery and brought into the temple at Jerusalem is the subject of a window, above, by Guillaume de Marcillat in Arezzo Cathedral. The assembled Pharisees turn away in disgust as the adulteress, in a beautiful velvet gown with the pleated decorative apron characteristic of the rich bourgeoisie of the sixteenth century, stands demurely before Christ, who is represented in a left-hand lancet.

THE SEVENTEENTH AND EIGHTEENTH CENTURIES
The Impoverished Years

Over a span of five centuries it was inevitable that in various countries there should have been good and bad periods for stained glass. But never before had the art come so close to extinction everywhere as it did in the seventeenth and eighteenth centuries. Indeed, the fates seemed to conspire to make this a barren time for stained glass. During these two hundred years, the art was undermined by its practitioners and the old masterpieces were destroyed by Puritanical hatred and Philistine indifference as Christendom, once united at least in its Catholicism, gave way to a Europe of warring Catholics and Protestants.

The destruction began in the sixteenth century. In the Netherlands the Calvinists reacted to Spanish repression by sacking churches. In England, Henry VIII's break with Rome, in 1534, inspired pious vandalism. It was not stained glass itself to which Protestants objected but the religious images it portrayed. Images of the Blessed Virgin and of Christ on the Cross were, in particular, anathema to many. There were, too, the fundamentalists, such as Henry Sherfield of Salisbury, who objected to the way in which religious images were depicted. In 1632, Sherfield, who held the official post of Recorder of Salisbury, broke a window in one of the city's churches because he regarded it as a blasphemous representation of the Creation since it had "little old men in blue and red coats, and naked in hands and feet, for the picture of God the Father". He also complained that the glazier was in error for showing God creating the sun and moon on the third day of Creation, instead of the fourth. Moreover, he claimed, Eve should not have been shown, partly naked, rising out of a naked man, when she had been made out of one of Adam's ribs while he slept. None the less, the outraged recorder was heavily fined and imprisoned.

It was, however, in the years 1642 to 1653, during the Civil War and Cromwell's Commonwealth, that destruction was most rampant in England. In 1643 and 1644 the English Parliament ordered all images of the Virgin Mary and of the Trinity to be removed and commissioners and parliamentary visitors were appointed to see that the law was enforced. This many did with relish, none more than the visitor William Dowsing, who is described as having gone through East Anglia "like a Bedlam", keeping a diary of his vengeance. Canterbury Cathedral suffered grievously, and, what is more, at the hands of a fanatically Puritan rector, Richard Culmer, referred to as Blue Dick. He left a detailed description of the way he attacked the image of Archbishop Becket, then in the large north transept window, from "the top of the citie ladder, near sixty steps high", with a whole pike in his hand, "ratling down proud Becket's glassy bones", and deeming it an honour to destroy these "fruits and occasions of idolatry".

The cathedrals of Lincoln, Lichfield, Peterborough and Chester were sacked by Roundhead soldiers and at Winchester Cathedral they broke the windows by hurling chests containing the bones of early Anglo-Saxon kings. York fared better. The glass of its minster and churches was spared as part of the terms of York's capitulation in the Civil War to Thomas Fairfax, the commander of the parliamentary forces. In gratitude the city gave Fairfax "a butt of sack", Spanish wine, and "a tun of French wine". In some churches in other places the glass was salvaged by being taken down and hidden.

The Counter-Reformation was also responsible, directly and indirectly, for the death of the art of stained glass. Many stained-glass workshops in Germany and France were destroyed during the Thirty Years' War, which, from small beginnings, developed into a confrontation between Catholic and Protestant Europe. In 1636, Cardinal Richelieu and his puppet Louis XIII, having subdued Lorraine, vindictively ordered all its palaces and castles to be razed to the ground, and with them went the glass workshops. Their loss was disastrous for much of Europe, since Lorraine had been the main centre for the manufacture of pot metal glass. By 1640 coloured glass was scarce and soon it was virtually unobtainable.

This widespread famine of coloured glass led to either of two developments—the use of clear glass in church windows or the painting of clear glass using the then new range of enamels. In England, when glass-painting was resumed after the restoration of the monarchy in 1660, glaziers turned even more to the use of enamels, sacrificing luminosity rather than abandoning colour. France and Germany, however, turned to clear glass, but this was not only because of the lack of coloured glass. The artistic style associated with the Counter-Reformation was voluptuous Baroque, followed by the even more extravagant Rococo. Baroque spread from Italy to Spain and, in the late seventeenth century, to Germany and Austria, where it was extremely popular. In France it evolved a more Classical form, and in England made little headway at all.

The interior of a Baroque building needed bright light to show off the sumptuousness of the paintings and sculpture that covered its walls. It was natural, therefore, that no stained glass would be put in the windows of the new Baroque churches. But, sadly, coloured glass began to disappear from old churches, too, particularly in Paris. This was because light had become fashionable. Indeed, according to one French critic, the art of the Counter-Reformation in its conquest of much of Europe did as much damage to stained glass as the Protestants had done and had destroyed the glass workshops of Germany and Lorraine as effectively as did the Thirty Years' War.

Stained-glass windows in Europe suffered rather less at the hands of Protestants than those in England. England, however, escaped the wide-scale destruction that followed the French Revolution. Two major European cathedrals fell victim to the revolutionaries. The still unfinished cathedral in Cologne was sacked and used for storing hay. At Strasbourg Cathedral the damage included three hundred pieces of sculpture in one week, and the building was turned into a Temple of Reason. The famous 466-foot spire had a narrow escape. A local official of the revolutionary regime argued that the great height of the spire offended the spirit of Equality. But a compromise was reached—the top of the spire was hidden under a covering of sheet iron.

Although much damage was done to European stained glass during the Revolution, much was saved. Some found its way to England, where it is now in churches and private collections. There was a large exhibition in London in 1802 of stained-glass windows which had been bought by enterprising Englishmen from churches closed by the French revolutionaries in the last decade of the eighteenth century. Many of the windows which were on sale were from Paris, but there were some from Rouen, including the Visitation window from the Church of St Nicolas, which is now in York Minster.

As though war, revolution, religious principles and changes in architectural style were not sufficiently menacing, the greatest threat during these two centuries to the stained glass of the previous five hundred years was neglect. As the skills of creating traditional stained glass declined, so the taste for it disappeared. Everywhere stained-glass windows perished through lack of attention. Some, as at Canterbury, were insensitively restored, some, as at Salisbury, were recklessly thrown away, and some, as at York, were mysteriously purloined.

The declining art of post-Renaissance glass-painting languidly interpreted Bible stories that had fired the medieval imagination. A spurious Classicism marks the style of Joshua Price's eighteenth-century window, right, in Great Witley Church, England, which shows the idolatrous Israelites with their golden calf.

THE SEVENTEENTH AND EIGHTEENTH CENTURIES

Curiosities and Pastiches

Among the considerable amount of English glass produced during the seventeenth century, and the even more prolific output during the eighteenth century, there was some that compensated a little for what had been destroyed by the iconoclasts. Between the iconoclasm of the sixteenth century and the iconoclasm of the Civil War in the middle of the seventeenth century, there was a brief re-emergence of glass-painting in England. Its leading patron was William Laud, Archbishop of Canterbury and close adviser of Charles I. Indeed, Laud's fondness for stained glass helped to bring him to the block. His enemies, convinced that stained glass was papist, took his encouragement of it as a further sign that he was trying to reconvert England to Catholicism.

Most of the glass of this short revival was done for colleges in Oxford and Cambridge. Laud, appointed Chancellor of Oxford in 1630, had an ally in his enthusiasm for stained glass at Cambridge University—Bishop Cosin, the Master of Peterhouse College. It was Cosin who commissioned the beautiful east window in the chapel at Peterhouse that was later mentioned in evidence against Laud during his trial for treason.

Oxford has much glass from this period. Many of the windows were painted by Abraham and Bernard van Linge, members of an Emden glass-painting family. Abraham's best windows are in University College Chapel, but there are others in the chapels of Balliol and Queen's colleges, and a striking window in Christ Church Cathedral, which has an unusual preponderance of blues, greens and yellows. Painted in enamel, with detail characteristic of the Flemish school, the window depicts the prophet Jonah sitting under a gourd tree and gazing across a harbour at the city of Nineveh. Bernard painted windows in the chapel of Wadham College and in Christ Church Cathedral.

There was another English revival in the third quarter of the seventeenth century, but, because of the ecclesiastical prejudice against pictorial windows in churches, glaziers sought other outlets. Henry Gyles, for example, a prolific York craftsman of the period, advertised "glass painting for the windows in Armes, Sundyals, History, Landskipt etc." For a time there was a craze for stained-glass panels

The largest private collection of Swiss stained glass in the world is in Wragby Church, Yorkshire. After the invasion of Switzerland by the French in the late 1790s, and the ensuing impoverishment of the country, many owners of antiquities were anxious to sell them, and the glass now in Wragby—489 panels— was acquired by an ardent British collector, Mr Winn of Nostell Priory, Yorkshire. Heraldry, donors' inscriptions and brightly coloured biblical and legendary scenes are depicted within the eight seventeenth- and eighteenth-century roundels, right, which are each six inches in diameter. From left to right are the Virgin and Child in a landscape, St Michael defeating Lucifer, St Martin dividing his cloak for a beggar, Jacob's dream of a ladder to heaven, the Crucifixion, the Deposition, Tobias curing Tobit's blindness and the beheading of John the Baptist.

Typical of seventeenth-century Dutch glass-painting, a crowded scene on a roundel, below, in Bishopsbourne Church, Kent, illustrates the Massacre of the Innocents.

LIGHT AND TIME

Stained-glass sundials were designed by the York craftsman Henry Gyles, above, as harmless alternatives to "idolatrous" religious windows. Despite its secular function, the sundial, right, in University College, Oxford, equates light with Christ, who is depicted below the inscription, *Sum vera lux* (I am the true light).

depicting sundials and Henry Gyles offered one free to each customer who commissioned a whole window. Gyles's designs were not remarkable, but he did have two highly talented pupils—the Price brothers, William and Joshua, who, with their pupils, were among the most active glass-painters of the eighteenth century.

Much of the work of the Price brothers was for Oxford colleges. William's son, also named William, glazed the large windows portraying saints, patriarchs and bishops on the south side of New College Chapel, constructing them from some of the original fourteenth-century glass, some glass he brought from Flanders and some new glass. He also painted glass for the west window of Westminster Abbey.

Another eighteenth-century glass-painter who was much sought after was William Peckitt, a carver and gilder who turned to glass-painting and was probably taught by William Price the Younger. Peckitt glazed windows in the cathedrals of Lincoln and Exeter, in York Minster and in Cambridge and Oxford colleges, but most of them are inferior in colour and design to Price's work. On the credit side he carried out numerous experiments in the making of coloured glass; he is even believed to have rediscovered the lost art of producing flashed glass.

Peckitt's windows in the chapel of New College, Oxford, made to designs by the Italian artist Biagio Rebecca, include the figures of Adam and Eve. They started their existence with only the fig leaves accorded to them in *Genesis*, but, to satisfy Victorian morality, Adam later acquired a leopard skin and Eve was painted wearing velvet.

The eighteenth century was not a happy time aesthetically for New College. Medieval glass in the chapel, which had escaped destruction during the Reformation and Civil War, was replaced by the Price and Peckitt windows, and in the antechapel the disastrous Virtues window was installed alongside the medieval glass. This window was designed by Sir Joshua Reynolds, portrait painter to the aristocracy, and enamelled, in now dirty browns, by a Dubliner, Thomas Jervais. The figures of its perpetrators are included—dressed as shepherds in the Nativity scene.

Another Dubliner, James Pearson, contributed rather more to the art by making improvements in the colouring of glass, as Peckitt had done. He was helped by his wife Eglington Margaret, daughter of the eighteenth-century bookseller and auctioneer Samuel Paterson, who held the first auction in London of stained glass from abroad.

For one artist, Francis Eginton, glass-painting was almost big business. Much of his best work went abroad, especially to Holland, but his Birmingham factory turned out windows for many buildings in England and Ireland, including the Solomon and Sheba window for the banqueting room at Arundel Castle in Sussex. For the windows he glazed for Fonthill Abbey in Wiltshire, which included kings and knights, he was paid twelve thousand pounds.

However unsuitable the use of enamel was for painting large pictorial windows, it was an excellent medium for small-scale intricate heraldry, and heraldic panels are among the best examples of English seventeenth- and eighteenth-century glass, even if they did not achieve the standards of the Swiss roundel painters.

By the eighteenth century the Swiss taste had changed to engraving on glass and the no longer fashionable roundels were bought in large quantities by English collectors. Many roundels were also bought from Holland, where they had been made in vast quantities during the seventeenth century.

It was perhaps as well that almost everywhere the glass-painting skills of these centuries were as small as the outlets for them were limited. The great master glaziers of the past would have been desperately frustrated by a religious climate that was antipathetic to stained glass and by the architectural styles of Baroque and Rococo, in which stained glass had no place.

Horace Walpole, above, the eighteenth-century art collector, connoisseur and man of letters, had a predilection for the Gothic style. His taste was reflected in his villa, Strawberry Hill, near Twickenham, complete with medieval stained-glass windows. His attitude to contemporary stained glass was critical. He referred, for example, to a Joshua Reynolds window in New College, Oxford, as "Sir Joshua's washy Virtues".

King Solomon, dressed in eighteenth-century regalia beneath a Baroque arch, above, was designed for a south transept window in York Minster by William Peckitt, one of the most active eighteenth-century glass-painters.

A lack of vitality, flaccid forms and pallid colours distinguish the stained glass of Sir Joshua Reynolds. Dominated by its grid of iron bars, the vapid Nativity scene, right, in New College Chapel, Oxford, was designed by Reynolds and executed in 1778 by Thomas Jervais.

THE NINETEENTH CENTURY

The Age of Revival

For the art of stained glass the seventeenth and eighteenth centuries were a period of destruction. But the nineteenth century was, on balance, a time of reconstruction. In this reconstruction process there were several strands—literary, historical, artistic and scientific. Writers, artists, architects—indeed practitioners of all the arts—were involved. And even when they were in querulous disagreement, as they often were, each contributed something to the gradual recovery of the art of stained glass.

First there were the men who improved the quality of the raw material—the glass. For centuries, the technical improvements in the manufacture of coloured glass had perversely had the effect of reducing its splendour. Now there was the problem of rediscovering, if possible, the secrets of the radiance of medieval glass. In England, the man who contributed most to this understanding was Charles Winston, a barrister by profession, but an archaeologist and connoisseur of the arts, especially of stained glass, by inclination. His theory was simple: a stained-glass window would appear dull if its light areas were not clear and bright; it would appear opaque if the shadowed areas were not transparent; and it would appear dark and heavy if there was more shadow than light. Since a coat of enamel paint was the surest way to exclude light, methods had to be found to make pot metal glass which was equal in brilliance to the glass of the Middle Ages. Winston, therefore, carried out innumerable and elaborate chemical experiments with glass and, in collaboration with the Whitefriars glassworks of James Powell and Sons, produced glass which was sometimes actually better than medieval glass. Working along similar lines, William Edward Chance, a Birmingham glass manufacturer, succeeded in 1863, after years of experiment, in producing "antique glass". His red glass in particular was considered to be superior to medieval glass. Other glass workshops followed their lead and, with increasing supplies of good glass, glass-painters no longer found it necessary to use coloured enamel paints.

In France, Eugène Viollet-le-Duc, an Inspector-General of the newly founded Service des Monuments Historiques, was also seeking to understand the reasons for the pre-eminence of medieval glass. He had great opportunity for his research, since he was responsible for the restoration of countless stained-glass windows throughout the country. Although his scientific explanations are disputed today, his basic conclusion was the same, and as simple, as Winston's—that effective stained glass depends on pure colour. This simple theorem, according to Viollet-le-Duc, had been "perfectly understood and employed by the glass-painters of the twelfth and thirteenth centuries, neglected from the fifteenth century on, and afterwards disdained in spite of the immutable laws imposed by light and optics".

In the United States, which in the middle of the nineteenth century was not only producing its own bad glass but was also importing even worse glass from Europe, the search for quality went astray. This was largely due to John La Farge and Louis Comfort Tiffany, both of whom were working in the medium of stained glass and were dissatisfied with the glass they could buy in the United States and in Europe. They experimented with making opalescent glass, in which strands of colour were introduced into the molten glass. Unfortunately, opacity, the antithesis of the vital characteristic of glass for stained-glass work, was also introduced. Other less publicized American glass workshops, however, made great advances in the production of the traditional pot metal glass.

By the end of the century the progress that had been made in manufacturing better glass was unmistakable. In the actual design, creation and restoration of stained glass the progress was less clear. In England, the stained glass made by William Morris's company dominated the second half of the century. Yet technically the early windows were poor; the enamelling was badly done and the proper use of leads was not understood. But Morris learned quickly. In *English Stained Glass*, Sir Herbert Read, the English art historian, wrote about Morris, at his peak in the 1870s and 1880s, "His selection and disposition of colours is admirable and he was not afraid of using new colours to achieve effects unknown to previous ages. In the use of leads to emphasize design he is masterly and we must again go back to the thirteenth century for an adequate comparison." That judgement is still valid, although the designs of the windows, many of which were done by Morris's partner, Edward Burne-Jones, do not stand comparison with the bold approach of the medievalists. Nevertheless, Burne-Jones's windows rose far above the morass of pious sentimentality in which so many designers of the period wallowed.

The simple fact was that in Europe and in the United States there were too many windows to be glazed and too few skilled and talented glaziers. The Gothic Revival and the craze for church restoration together produced a demand for ecclesiastical stained glass which had not been matched since the Middle Ages. There were also many workshops which were producing large quantities of secular glass and exploiting the public's reborn interest in stained glass. One English workshop's catalogue recommended "the varied resources of glass staining . . . for the decoration of mansions, affording an exquisite adornment for the windows of halls, corridors, staircases, etc., and in many cases effectually screening the objectionable sights at the back of the house".

One of the sad ironies of the nineteenth century was that while writers, painters and architects became obsessed by medieval legends and art and by Gothic architecture, many medieval windows were either replaced by mock medieval creations or were ruined by horrendous "restoration". This happened to varying degrees in England, in Germany and in France. Few people had a true understanding of the Middle Ages, for medieval thought was basically alien to the nineteenth-century mind. While outward forms could be imitated, the spirit could not be recaptured. And yet the Gothic Revival did help to release the art of stained glass from the post-Renaissance torpor into which it had sunk.

New life was also given to stained glass by the Pre-Raphaelite and the Art Nouveau movements. The influence of the Pre-Raphaelites was not only direct—through the windows they did for William Morris's company—but through the concept of naturalism which they introduced into art. Lyrical naturalism was also the basis of Art Nouveau, however artificially it might have been expressed.

Even though the Art Nouveau movement was short-lived—it lasted little more than twenty years—its influence was felt throughout Europe and in the United States. Largely inspired by Morris's ideals, the movement was essentially a reaction against the Machine Age and the intrusion of the machine into the world of art. The softly swirling, sensuous shapes that characterized the work of this period, from posters to stained-glass windows, were in themselves a defiant assertion of artistic autonomy, the antithesis of mass-produced products.

At the end of the nineteenth century, as a result of the determined if disparate efforts of many people in many countries, stained glass had regained an important place among the arts. By contrast, the opening years of the twentieth century were something of an anticlimax. But after the Second World War the ferment began working again.

The perpendicular design of the east window in Wickhambreux Church, Kent, is dominated by the vigorous, twisting rhythms and dazzling colour of Arild Rosenkrantz's Annunciation scene. Reputedly the first American stained glass to be commissioned for Europe, the window was designed in 1896 and donated by Count James Gallatin of New York in memory of his mother.

NINETEENTH-CENTURY UNITED STATES AND EUROPE

Restoration and Mass-production

Pious monarch and warrior king, Louis IX of France is depicted in two nineteenth-century painted windows in the Chapelle Royale, Dreux. Both windows were made in the stained-glass studio at the Sèvres porcelain factory, which was established, with government assistance, to encourage the revival of the art in mid-nineteenth-century France. One of the windows, designed by Ingres, famous for his portraiture, shows Louis in the cloak of the French kings, detail right. The other window, detail below, designed by Delacroix, known for his large-scale battle scenes, portrays Louis at the Battle of Taillebourg, where he defeated Henry III's English army.

St Arnold washes the feet of a pilgrim, left, in a detail from a window in the Chapelle Royale, Dreux. Executed in 1845 by Béranger, a master glazier, the window was designed by the genre painter Charles Larivière.

The Benedictine monk Dom Pérignon supervises a champagne vintage in a detail, right, from a window in the Moët et Chandon factory at Epernay. The window was made in the nineteenth century to celebrate the discovery of the champagne process by the monk when he was cellar-master at the Abbey of Hautvillers. The abbey is commemorated in the window as "the cradle of the wine of champagne".

Stained-glass windows would hardly have been uppermost in the minds of the early Puritans when they landed on American soil after a perilous Atlantic crossing. The handful of glass-workers among them were expected to produce bottles rather than expensive stained-glass images, which, in any case, the early settlers considered idolatrous. In the eighteenth century, there were a few congregations which could afford stained-glass windows and they ordered them from Europe. This was doubly unfortunate, since it discouraged the growth of an American style, and it spread the pseudo art of enamel painting on glass into which the genuine art of stained glass had declined.

Some of the early colonists started stained-glass workshops, but few survived for long. One of the first exceptions, in the mid-seventeenth century, was the workshop of the Dutchman Everett Duycking, who settled in New Amsterdam. He was paid in beaver skins for his windows, most of which were heraldic. Thomas Godfrey, an eighteenth-century glazier, was paid in real money—the considerable sum of eight hundred and fifty dollars—for glazing windows in Independence Hall in Philadelphia. One German immigrant, Caspar Wistar, having made his money in brass buttons, turned to stained glass in New Jersey, and another, Heinrich Wilhelm Steigel, started a glass workshop in Philadelphia with the proceeds of real estate speculation. Many of these glass firms failed during the depression that accompanied the American War of Independence, but the return of prosperity early in the nineteenth century brought a new crop of glaziers. Stained-glass windows were in demand for such diverse settings as steamboats and the mock-medieval homes of wealthy New York merchants.

However, an increasing number of immigrant craftsmen brought with them the worst traits of contemporary European glass-painting. A hotch-potch of architectural fashions was imported. The Gothic Revival took root beside a fashion for Oriental art. Into this cultural maelstrom were drawn wave after wave of German, Irish, Italian and Slavic Catholics and German and Scandinavian Protestants. From

these disparate elements an American identity and culture slowly emerged.

It was unfortunate that the first distinctly American contribution to stained glass was misguided. The use of opalescent glass by Tiffany and La Farge was as much a negation of stained glass as was enamel painting. Nevertheless, the foundation of a wider interest in stained glass had been laid on which the twentieth century was to build.

It was the same in Europe, although there the newly generated enthusiasm for the art was not always matched by an understanding of it. In France a stained-glass workshop supported by the government was established at the Sèvres porcelain factory. For twenty-five years the workshop produced windows which were either copies of old paintings or made from designs by such celebrated painters as Jean Ingres, Eugène Devéria and Eugène Delacroix.

The inevitable reaction came towards the middle of the century when a group of architects and medievalists rebelled against the mechanical copying of paintings in stained glass. The rebels, known as the "scientific romantics", included Eugène Viollet-le-Duc, Baptiste Antoine Lassus and Adolphe Napoléon Didron. They had the invaluable support of the versatile novelist Prosper Merimée in his role of Central Inspector of the Service des Monuments Historiques. As a result, between 1840 and 1860, extensive projects of restoration, especially of stained glass, were undertaken. The number of stained-glass workshops in France increased from three to about forty-five and the notable artists working for them included Antoine Lusson, Maréchal de Metz and Henri Gérente, who won a competition for restoring the windows of Ste Chapelle.

In Germany, encouragement for the revival of stained glass came from that eccentric patron of the arts Ludwig I of Bavaria. But in spite of all its resources much of the output of the Munich state workshop was dreary in design and poor in craftsmanship. Many Munich windows were exported, some to the United States, some to England and Scotland. Ten artists of the Munich school designed 123 Bible scenes for Glasgow Cathedral when it was decided to reglaze the windows in the middle of the century. Their sugary Raphaelism was ill-suited to Scottish taste and the deterioration of the pigments in the Scottish climate was debatably a cause for satisfaction or for commiseration.

Probably no cathedral suffered so blatantly from nineteenth-century stained-glass "restoration" as did Milan Cathedral. The Bertinis started this havoc in 1827 and continued it for seventy years, in spite of a continuous barrage of criticism. Giovanni Bertini, who presumably influenced contracts in his favour, was a compulsive restorer, restoring windows which needed no restoration and replacing others with his own windows. The work was continued by his two sons, who were even less talented.

Such barbarities apart, it is easier to forgive the sins of the glass-painters of the nineteenth century than those of the seventeenth and eighteenth centuries. Hindsight shows, in Europe as in America, that stained glass was about to come into its own again, and the usurper—painting on glass—was in the process of being dethroned.

The expatriate William Jay Bolton completed the Nativity window, left, in 1847 for Holy Trinity Church, Brooklyn, New York. An amusing feature in the top right-hand panel of this window is the inscription on the inn to which Joseph and Mary had been refused admission. With his brother John, William glazed windows for several of the city's churches before returning to England, where they both took Holy Orders.

Ludwig I of Bavaria, portrayed above, was an active patron of the arts and in 1827 founded the Munich state workshop, which became the chief centre of the stained-glass revival in nineteenth-century Germany. Influenced by the artists of the Italian cinquecento, the Munich school was prolific in the production of biblical windows, many of which were exported abroad. The typical Raphaelesque painted window, right, in St Giles' Church, Stoke Poges, Buckinghamshire, was created as a memorial to a child of the local Howard-Vyse family.

NINETEENTH-CENTURY ENGLAND

Gothic Reborn

For England the nineteenth century was the century of the Industrial Revolution, the British Empire and the Gothic Revival. The Revival began harmlessly enough. In the eighteenth century, Horace Walpole's house, Strawberry Hill, in West London, had made Gothic art and architecture fashionable again and, as a change from his Regency terraces, the eminent architect John Nash began to build "Gothic" mansions for wealthy clients. When, in 1798, the French architect Augustus Charles Pugin, fleeing from the French Revolution (or the possible consequences of a duel), arrived in London, Nash employed him to make drawings of ancient buildings. Pugin was helped in this work by his precocious son, Augustus Welby Northmore Pugin, who thereby developed a love for Gothic church architecture that before long became an obsession. Another of young Pugin's obsessions was sailing, and he is said to have stated, "There is nothing worth living for but Christian architecture and a boat."

The younger Pugin was shipwrecked at eighteen, married at nineteen, widowed at twenty and remarried and converted to Roman Catholicism at twenty-one. Three years later he wrote his famous *Contrasts*, which damned Classicism as pagan and lauded Gothic as Christian. It was his artistic inclinations that first led him towards Catholicism and he came to believe that it was the religious duty of all Catholics also to be devotees of Gothic architecture. He built and restored innumerable churches throughout the country and designed stained-glass windows for some of them. For more than six years he worked with Sir Charles

Angelic faces in the window, left, in Amersham Church represent the thirty-three children of William and Catherine Tothill who, in the sixteenth century, lived at Shardeloes Manor in Amersham. The stained glass, installed in 1889, commemorates Thomas Tyrwhitt Drake, a nineteenth-century descendant of the eldest Tothill child.

Stained-glass panels were popular additions to the nineteenth-century home and were advertised in many publications, including *The Furnishing Hardware Guide*, left. Considered attractive as decoration, the panels were also useful as screens against unwelcome sights. The use of a flower motif, as exemplified by the bunch of lilies, above, in a window in Lilford Lodge, Oxford, was inevitable.

Barry on the new Houses of Parliament, one of the more credible manifestations of Neo-Gothic. Soon after his appointment as Fine Arts Commissioner for the Great Exhibition of 1851, Pugin went mad and died within a year.

Pugin's understanding of the medieval spirit, and not just its outward forms, was remarkable. This was not so of some of his followers, such as the architect Sir George Gilbert Scott, who came under the spell not only of the writings of the Catholic Pugin but also of the High Church Cambridge Camden Society, the group which started the Victorian craze for "restoring" churches in order to rid them of any mixture of styles. Scott was appointed restoring architect to Ely Cathedral in 1847, and from then until his death in 1878 he built or restored 732 buildings, including the Albert Memorial in London, thirty-nine cathedrals in Britain and the Empire and 476 churches.

With the building and rebuilding of so many churches by Scott and his followers there were thousands of windows to be glazed; there had not been so many since the fifteenth century. Unfortunately, the old skills of glazing had been lost and they were only slowly and hesitantly relearned during the nineteenth century. Consequently, there were many bad windows, even more that were dull and only a few which were truly inspired. Even those windows which are to be praised for a vast improvement in craftsmanship over those of the eighteenth century are often marred by Victorian sentimentality.

The William Morris workshop heads any list of nineteenth-century glaziers, but the work and names of many others are frequently encountered all over the country. John Richard Clayton and Alfred Bell, for example, worked together for forty years producing windows, which, although frequently uninspiring, were of a high standard of craftsmanship. The west window of King's College Chapel, Cambridge, is theirs. William Raphael Eginton, son of the eighteenth-century glass-painter Francis Eginton, was glass-stainer to Princess Charlotte and made windows for King George IV and for many members of the aristocracy. Thomas Willement, "heraldic artist" to King George IV and "artist in stained glass" to Queen Victoria, was especially prolific and skilled in heraldic stained glass. His major work was the memorial window for the Great Hall at Hampton Court. Charles Eamer Kempe had a considerable reputation in his lifetime, but it tarnished quickly. Among his most successful windows are those in the choir of the cathedral of Bury St Edmunds and the John Milton window in Horton Church, Buckinghamshire. Henry Holiday, who died in 1927 at the age of eighty-eight, designed all the earthy and colourful windows in the chapel of Worcester College, Oxford. Better work by him is in the United States, however, notably in Holy Trinity Church, New York.

London's Great Exhibition of 1851 both reflected and increased public interest in stained glass. Twenty-four firms or individuals exhibited their work and the setting was appropriate—Sir Joseph Paxton's vast Crystal Palace of glass, which covered nineteen acres of Hyde Park. "It has been a popular notion that this art was lost to us; such is not the case," confidently stated the catalogue. "It has indeed been dormant, but never extinct. The fine work exhibited this year—the production of living artists—announces its revival." Although the artists may have been living, most of their exhibits were living in the past. There were windows "treated in strict accordance with glass of the Norman period", or in transitional style from Norman to Early English, or in any one of many other styles, including Decorated, Perpendicular and Elizabethan. The exhibitors were nothing if not versatile. One Hampstead glazier offered glass-painting in the style of Sir Joshua Reynolds, Rubens, Correggio and Carlo Dolci.

William Morris was seventeen at the time of the Great Exhibition. His family took him to see it, but when they arrived at Hyde Park he would not go in. His refusal may just have been through boredom, but it seems prophetically significant today.

The sturdy figure of Cleopatra, left, premeditates suicide and reveals the breast which the asp will strike. By Henry Holiday, the window is now in Chapel Studio, King's Langley.

The languid sentimentality of sickly faces, above, in a richly coloured medallion in Lincoln Cathedral, is characteristic of nineteenth-century glass.

A real garden, seen through the window in Horton Church, Buckinghamshire, is the background for the painted figure of the blind poet Milton.

THE NINETEENTH CENTURY

An Inspired Partnership

THE ROMANTIC CRAFTSMEN

William Morris, above left, and Edward Burne-Jones, above right, painted by G. F. Watts, were caricatured as stained-glass figures by Burne-Jones. Their life-long partnership began at Oxford, where they shared a taste for the romantic, religious and legendary. Although influenced by the medieval dreamlands painted by the Pre-Raphaelites, Morris and Burne-Jones applied their love of exoticism to interior design as well as to fine art. In 1861 The Firm of Morris, Marshall, Faulkner and Co. was established. Based on such wholesome principles as equality of members, a high standard of craftsmanship and a respect for natural forms, The Firm, later re-formed into Morris and Co., produced tapestry, wallpaper, furniture and stained glass of which Burne-Jones became the exclusive designer, reproducing the unearthly atmosphere and languid beauty of his paintings.

First shown at the International Exhibition in 1862, the cabinet, above, was designed by the architect Philip Webb and painted by William Morris with scenes from the legend of St George. It now stands against a background of Morris wallpaper in the Victoria and Albert Museum, London.

Literary scenes, as sources of moral instruction or romantic drama, were illustrated in detail by the painstaking Pre-Raphaelite painters. Mariana, deserted by her lover, Angelo, in Shakespeare's *Measure for Measure*, inspired a gloomy poem by Tennyson which, in turn, inspired the painting, right, by John Everett Millais. Slack with boredom, the dejected woman stares vacantly at her stained-glass windows, which Millais copied from those in Merton College Chapel, Oxford.

When he was eight years old William Morris was taken by his father to Canterbury Cathedral, and it was, he recalled, as if the gate of heaven had been opened to him. From the age of fourteen he spent long hours in the library of his public school, Marlborough, absorbed in books on medieval architecture. In 1854, when he was twenty and a theology student at Oxford, he read a lecture by the famous art critic John Ruskin on the Pre-Raphaelites which filled him with such excitement that he ran to tell his bosom friend, Edward Burne-Jones, the glad tidings of this revolutionary approach to painting. These were important influences in shaping the life of William Morris, who himself was to affect so many aspects of English art.

"Pre-Raphaelitism", declared Ruskin in that heady lecture, "has but one principle, that of uncompromising truth in all that it does, obtained by working everything down to the most minute detail, from nature only." This was the concept behind the Pre-Raphaelite Brotherhood, founded in 1848 by two close friends, William Holman Hunt and John Everett Millais, with Dante Gabriel Rossetti. Other painters joined them, but in fewer than ten years the Brotherhood had disintegrated.

Morris was never a member of the Brotherhood, nor, indeed, truly a Pre-Raphaelite. But he was anti-Renaissance. He acknowledged the "outburst of genius" behind the Renaissance, but damned it for making art academic and "inorganic". Artists, he believed, should go back to the finest days of the Middle Ages for inspiration.

Rossetti drifted away from the Brotherhood as he became more and more involved with Morris and Burne-Jones, who had both given up their intention of taking Holy Orders and instead vowed to dedicate their lives to art. Their entry into what was to become a major business had an undergraduate, casual air. According to Rossetti, "... someone suggested—as a joke more than anything else—that we should each put down five pounds and form a company."

Thus, in 1861, The Firm was born. Its activities were to embrace mural decoration, architectural carving, stained glass, metalwork, jewellery, furniture, embroidery, "besides every article necessary for domestic use". The Firm's members were Morris, who turned his hand to everything, Ford Madox Brown and his sanitary-engineer friend P. P. Marshall, Burne-Jones, Rossetti and the architect Philip Webb, all of whom did glass-painting, and C. J. Faulkner, who looked after the accounts and helped to fire the glass.

All the partners were equal, but some were more equal than others because of the beauty of their work or their industry. They all adored beauty, which they saw in each other, and which many of them were inclined to see in each others' wives. This gave rise to some tension, and Rossetti's passion for Morris's wife contributed to Rossetti's death. They also left portraits of each other in some of their windows. Morris's wife Jane, for example, appears in windows designed by her husband and by the lovesick Rossetti, and Rossetti portrayed Morris as Christ and also as a man dropping a stone on the head of a bailiff.

Although today many of the group's enthusiasms, passions and tragedies may seem to have a comic side, in its art the group was serious and industrious. For stained glass alone, Morris and Ford Madox Brown each produced a hundred and fifty cartoons, Rossetti did thirty-six, and Burne-Jones did hundreds. When the original partnership was dissolved in 1875 and re-formed, Burne-Jones and Morris remained together. Burne-Jones became responsible for stained-glass designs, while the glazing was either executed by or under the supervision of Morris.

Burne-Jones's earliest windows, done between 1857 and 1861, were glazed not by Morris but by James Powell and Sons. Their style is bolder and their colours more vivid than in the Burne-Jones–Morris windows. Burne-Jones's first

The Vyner Memorial window, left, by Burne-Jones in Christ Church Cathedral, Oxford, commemorates an undergraduate who was murdered by bandits in Greece. Against backgrounds of foliage stand four golden-haired youths—the prophet Samuel, King David, John the Evangelist and Timothy. (Burne-Jones's cartoon for Timothy is shown above.) Below the figures four biographical scenes depict Samuel talking to Eli, David slaying Goliath, John at the Last Supper and Timothy as a child.

window, of the Good Shepherd in the United Reform Church at Maidstone in Kent, drove Ruskin "wild with joy", because Christ was shown as a real shepherd, suitably dressed for walking over the "Gothic" hills.

The contrast between early and late Burne-Jones windows is obvious in Christ Church Cathedral, Oxford. In the Latin Chapel is the St Frideswide window of 1859, crowded with people and executed in Powell's most resplendent colours. In the Lady Chapel is the four-lancet Vyner Memorial window dating from 1872–3, when Burne-Jones had been designing for The Firm for more than ten years. The window was a memorial to a young undergraduate who had been murdered. Its colours are pale and the figures of Samuel, King David, John the Evangelist and Timothy could be those, appropriately, of undergraduate aesthetes. The window also shows how confident and skilful Morris had become in his use of lead-lines. After centuries of misuse they were once again a vital part of the design.

Morris had a rule, seldom broken, that The Firm would not make windows for churches and other buildings which were "monuments of Ancient Art, the glazing of which we cannot conscientiously undertake, as our doing so would seem to sanction the disastrous practice of so-called Restoration". He was not a Gothic Revivalist, but an innovator steeped in medievalism, with an unwavering belief in the satisfaction to be obtained from skilled craftsmanship.

The Old Testament patriarch Abraham, dressed as a warrior, left, is given bread and wine after a battle by the high priest Melchizedek. Considered during the Middle Ages a prefiguration of the Last Supper, this subject was chosen by the nineteenth-century painter Ford Madox Brown for his window in All Saints' Church, Middleton Cheney, Buckinghamshire. Ford Madox Brown was less of a romantic idealist than the Pre-Raphaelites and although he came under their influence he never joined the Brotherhood. He was a member of William Morris's firm between 1861 and 1874 and, as one of its most talented painters, was responsible for designing much of its early stained glass.

THE TURN OF THE CENTURY

Style of Sensuous Elegance

Art Nouveau flashed like a meteor through Europe and America at the turn of the century and burned itself out within twenty years. Its greatest impact was on architecture and the applied arts in domestic settings, where the ideal was a total Art Nouveau look.

Although easily recognizable, Art Nouveau is hard to define; it grew out of so many influences, embraced so many styles and contained so many contradictions. The essence of the style was an exotic use of line, and the main inspiration came from the curving lines of plants and women. However (and here is one contradiction), the plants became stylized and the women asexual.

Art Nouveau had no single founder; it evolved in a variety of ways in different countries, occasionally under

Designed in 1884 by Eugène Grasset, a leading French architect and painter, the stained-glass window *Spring*, right, is a fine example of the decorative style of Art Nouveau. In a landscape heavy with vernal imagery, the overall sense of movement, most obvious in the flowing robes of the maiden in the foreground, is enhanced by the irises and by the swifts, harbingers of spring, which swoop and dive against a background of scudding clouds and blossom-laden trees. The window is now in the Musée des Arts Décoratifs, Paris.

Milky white blooms of opalescent glass contrast with the ruby red flowers of translucent glass in the detail above from *Red and White Peonies*, a window by Tiffany's contemporary John La Farge. The window was made, in about 1885, for the London home of Sir Laurence Alma-Taddema, the Victorian artist. It is now in the Museum of Fine Arts, Boston, Massachusetts.

In the Colonia Güell, Barcelona, extraordinary tilted columns and fantastic twisted surfaces characterize the interior of the unfinished chapel, above, designed by Antoni Gaudí. The detail, left, is one of the flower-inspired abstract windows which are set seemingly at random in the curved walls of the little chapel.

a different name. The movement's philosophical base—of inculcating good taste in art in the masses through the applied arts—was largely that of the Pre-Raphaelites and the Morris circle. There was, however, another contradiction here. Art Nouveau was generally so esoteric and expensive that it could be appreciated and afforded only by the sophisticated rich.

In England in 1883 the architect Arthur Mackmurdo heralded the new style in a book on Wren's churches with a title page full of curvaceous plants and peacocks. Japanese influence was contributed by the newly opened Oriental department of Liberty's in Regent Street and by the American painter James McNeill Whistler, then living in London.

A Scottish architect, Charles Rennie Mackintosh, who designed not only buildings but almost everything in them, was regarded on the Continent, particularly in Vienna, as one of the most important exponents of the movement. He in his turn adapted ideas from Austrian artists, including Gustav Klimt, who gave back to Art Nouveau women their sensuality. Three of the Mackintosh buildings in Glasgow became famous—the Art School, Miss Cranston's Buchanan Street Tearooms and the Willow Tearooms in Sauchiehall Street. Mackintosh designed everything for the Willow Tearooms, including the remarkable stained-glass doors.

The first important house on the Continent in Art Nouveau style was the Maison Tassel in Brussels, which was designed by the Belgian architect Victor Horta and completed in 1893. Stained glass was an integral part of its interior decoration. A fellow countryman, Henri van de Velde, who had started as a Pointilliste painter, turned to architecture, and also designed an impressive range of works of art, including stained glass.

In Spain Art Nouveau received its ultimate architectural expression in the buildings of Antoni Gaudí. His work in Barcelona included a bizarre palace for his patron, the rich Spanish intellectual industrialist Count Don Eusebio Güell, the extravagant Church of the Holy Family, which is still incomplete, and the small Güell church with its oval, flower-shaped windows.

Stained glass played an especially prominent part in the Art Nouveau movement in France. The "new style" was late arriving there, but for a decade it dominated the scene in the applied arts (although not in painting). The influence was strongly Japanese. Japanese *objets d'art* had been popular with French collectors since mid-century and the most celebrated dealer in them was Samuel Bing. He encouraged the new-style artists and, when supplies of good Japanese works of art ran low, opened a shop in 1896 called "L'Art Nouveau", and thus established the movement's name. A rival shop, "La Maison Moderne", designed by Van de Velde, opened two years later. Both dealt in stained glass, and among those who worked for them were the then unknown English painter Frank Brangwyn and the Americans John La Farge and Louis Comfort Tiffany.

In Europe the application of Art Nouveau was mainly domestic, but in the United States Tiffany made the style, particularly in stained glass, acceptable for churches. In England genuine Art Nouveau church windows are rare. One of the few, the Annunciation in Wickhambreux Church, Kent, has the reputed distinction of being the first window to be made in America for Europe.

"Splendour, London" was the highly appropriate telegraph address of Cakebread, Robey and Company, who made the stained glass for several of London's Victorian public houses. An example of the firm's best glass, dating from about 1901, is in the Queen's Hotel, Crouch End, where the large arched windows, detail above, are decorated with graceful floral patterns.

Created by Charles Rennie Mackintosh between 1903 and 1904, the leaded-glass door panels, detail above, of the Willow Tearooms, Glasgow, exemplify the decorative skill of the Scottish school. Mackintosh's style was all-pervasive in this famous suite of rooms—part of which is in use today in Daly's, a Glasgow department store—for he designed all the fittings, including the tableware. The result was a complete unity of colour, form and design.

Gently spiralling shapes ornament a dome-shaped skylight designed by Victor Horta, Belgium's pioneer of Art Nouveau. The regular, almost geometric leading, detail right, creates an effect resembling a Japanese screen. The window was probably made for one of the Brussels houses that Horta designed in the 1890s.

Elegant swirling curves of gilt bronze, in natural, plant-like forms, ornament the mahogany banisters of the main staircase in the Hôtel Solvay, Brussels. Designed and decorated by Belgian architect Victor Horta between 1895 and 1900, this house was built for the industrial magnate Armand Solvay.

THE TURN OF THE CENTURY

Tiffany – Creator of Opulence

Louis Comfort Tiffany, above, was internationally acclaimed for his invention of Favrile glass, which he used to create a wealth of vases and lamps and other *objets d'art*.
He described his secret formula as "a composition of various colored glasses worked together while hot". The resultant metallic iridescence became the hallmark of Tiffany glass.

Heavy trellis-work emphasizes the delicacy of the wisteria vines and the soft, muted pastels in the famous Oyster Bay window, right. A major technical innovation was the use of a single piece of glass to create the mottled bluish effect of the blooms in the upper centre section. Made from the same glass as the equally well-known dome-shaped wisteria lamp the window, commissioned for the William Skinner House in New York, was completed at the Tiffany Studios in about 1905. It is now in the Morse Gallery of Art, Florida.

Louis Comfort Tiffany was a man of immensely varied talents who frequently talked and created meretricious rubbish. He insisted that his stained-glass windows were a purer expression of stained glass because he could dispense with any pigment—all the colour was in the glass. What he overlooked was that by using opalescent glass he was destroying, as effectively as the seventeenth- and eighteenth-century glass enamellers had done, the translucency of glass, which is the very soul of a medieval window. He proclaimed his faith in creating beauty for the masses and became the darling of the wealthy followers of fashion. His influence on art died long before he did, and his reputation since his death has varied so much that his artifacts could at times be bought for pennies while at other times they have been fought for at auctions.

Tiffany was the son of the jeweller Tiffany, but he chose to study art rather than enter the family firm and be tainted by commercialism; beauty was to be all. He started painting, was introduced to Oscar Wilde and travelled in North Africa and in Spain, where he discovered that the deep reds and blues of medieval stained glass were too sombre for his taste. Although he continued painting for several years, his first business venture was in interior decoration, and to the end of his life he argued that the "decorative" arts were more important to a nation than the "fine" arts. "Artists who devote their talent to making things of use beautiful", he said, "are educators of the people in the truest sense."

Early in the 1880s Tiffany's firm was the most fashionable firm of interior decorators in New York. In 1882 Tiffany was even invited to decorate the White House. Unfortunately, the great opalescent glass screen which was the showpiece of his alterations was broken into small pieces about twenty years later on the orders of President Theodore Roosevelt.

While Tiffany was working as an interior decorator his interest increasingly turned to glass. In 1878 he established a glass workshop where he also made glass, because glass manufacturers were not making the kind of glass which could create the effects he wanted. In the same year the

Piqued by the success of a John La Farge window, which had been hailed as a masterpiece when it was displayed in Paris in 1889, Tiffany designed the massive Four Seasons window to outshine his rival. Each season is illustrated in a symbolic landscape within a *cartouche*, left. Tulips represent spring, poppies summer, grapes and corn autumn and a snow-laden bough embodies winter. Although definitely Art Nouveau in character, Tiffany's window reflects the influence of the contemporary Symbolist painters, with the economical use of leading creating clean, sharp lines and the use of bright, clear colours. The window, made of opalescent glass, caused a sensation in Paris, in 1890. It was later divided and installed at Laurelton Hall, Tiffany's vast mansion. Four panels were later acquired by the Morse Gallery of Art, Florida.

Combining iridescent Favrile glass and clean, sculptural shapes, Tiffany's handmade lamps are outstanding for high-quality craftsmanship and inventiveness of design. The dome-like shade of the peacock lamp, below, is leaded with copper foil in an overall pattern of peacock feathers. A webbing of opalescent aquamarine glass decorates the conical shade of the lily pad lamp, bottom, which is set on a bronze rod standard, ornamented with trailing tendrils.

results were seen in his first window to combine opalescent and antique glass, which he made for the Episcopal Church in Islip, Long Island.

Although Tiffany's reputation continued to grow, he was not content, and he embarked on a Wilde-inspired diversion of decorating the new Lyceum Theatre in New York in a style which was described by the New York *Morning Journal* as "ultra-aesthetic". The project was a financial disaster, and crippling losses suffered by Tiffany forced him to reorganize his business and what his father regarded as his too fast life.

During the next few years Tiffany's reputation for stained glass reached its peak and after he began an association with the Parisian art dealer Samuel Bing in 1889 his name became established in Europe. He was always making news—from the opulent chapel with its million pieces of glass built for the Chicago World Fair of 1892 to the fantastic twenty-ton glass curtain made for the National Theatre in Mexico City in 1911.

These were mammoth projects, but Tiffany's name was just as famous for the domestic objects he produced, particularly for the Tiffany lamp, one of the most popular offshoots of this period. After 1900 Tiffany became more involved in art glass and his iridescent Favrile glass soon eclipsed his previous achievements. Bing described it as "like skin to the touch, silky and delicate".

Early in the twentieth century, Tiffany bought a 580-acre estate at Oyster Bay, Long Island, and to his own designs built Laurelton Hall, a vast Art Nouveau house which, for a decade, received controversial attention from newspapers and magazines all over America. The house had eighty-four rooms, including twenty-five bathrooms, a yacht basin and a bell tower which pealed the Westminster chimes. Tiffany, however, was becoming increasingly eccentric and increasingly out of favour with public taste. He died in 1933 almost forgotten, and when he was remembered during the next two decades it was only to be derided. But after 1950 opinion turned in his favour, and although the craze to imitate him passed towards the end of the sixties, his work is firmly established again.

THE TWENTIETH CENTURY

The Age of Expanding Horizons

The stained glass of even the early years of the twentieth century is too recent to be seen in true historical perspective. But it is clear that the middle of the century saw the start of an unusually creative period in parts of Europe and in the United States, when exciting, unusual and often beautiful stained glass began to be produced.

Stained glass is an art which is basically dependent on architecture. It flourished when Romanesque architecture gave way to Gothic; it had no place amid the florid ornamentation of Baroque or Rococo. The clean lines and structural innovations of twentieth-century architecture, based on steel and concrete, have given stained-glass artists potential opportunities such as they have never had before. Whether they are allowed to make full use of these opportunities depends on the imagination of the architects, for it is they who decide what type of skin is to cover the framework of a modern building. German architects have responded more than most by giving stained-glass artists whole walls to glaze, and the results have been striking.

In France and the United States innovatory building methods have been excitingly exploited through the use of a technique, which is fundamentally that used in the Byzantine world, of setting thick glass direct into stonework to create a window. Known today as *dalles de verre*, pieces of slab glass, each about one inch thick, are held in place in concrete or with epoxy resin. The resulting windows are integral parts of the structure and not just a means of filling apertures.

There were other twentieth-century innovations as well as developments of old techniques. One is fused glass; the pieces of coloured glass which form the design are all fused to a sheet of clear glass, thus dispensing with the need for leads. Modern stained-glass artists have also painted glass on both sides, have painted glass with gold leaf designs and have combined glass with plastics, mosaic and mirrors.

But something more than technique and innovation is needed to produce great works of art. In the nineteenth century, stained-glass artists had striven to relearn and to develop the honest technical skills of the Middle Ages, but the medieval nostalgia that motivated many of them was bogus. Where was the twentieth-century glass-painter to find the inspiration that his medieval counterpart had drawn from a religion dominated by a concept of heaven and hell that is alien to modern thinking? There were, of course, some aspects of the twentieth century which would not have been out of place in the murkier periods of the Middle Ages. Certainly dread of a nuclear holocaust replaced the medieval terror of hell. But the twentieth-century stained-glass artist is a different man from the medieval glazier. He is not an anonymous member of a team working within the confines of accepted doctrine and acceptable themes: he is an individualist expressing himself through his art.

The modern glazier has, however, often been dependent upon the Church for the chance to exercise his art, for the twentieth-century Church needed stained-glass artists to replace the hundreds of thousands of windows which had been destroyed in two world wars. After the First World War much of the new glass in rebuilt churches was conventional, imitative and mediocre, not least in war memorial windows. But after the Second World War the new architecture and the Church's new readiness to use famous artists, whatever their religious beliefs, combined to initiate bold experiments. France led the way; Matisse, Braque and Léger were among those who created church windows which were not ecclesiastical art in the traditional sense. Abstract and semi-abstract designs with a smattering of symbolism replaced the figurative approach; the day of what Horace Walpole called "lean windows fattened with rich saints" had gone. What replaced them were works of art in their own right. And gradually an initially outraged public came to accept that great works of art have in themselves a spiritual content. The horizons of church art were extended not only by the modern concepts of profane art but by the eagerness of architects and artists to use glass in new ways.

The revival of stained glass in France and Germany did not get under way until the middle of the century, but Ireland had a rich period during the first fifty years. It was presided over by Sarah Purser, the grand old lady of Irish stained glass, who ran her studio until she died at the age of ninety-three. The outstanding members of the Irish school were Harry Clarke, Michael Healy and Evie Hone. Clarke combined tradition with a rare originality; his work in Ireland and in many parts of the world is distinguished by the warm brilliance of its colour. Evie Hone, deeply involved in abstract art in Paris, turned to stained glass in the 1930s, and the representational style she developed owes much to Georges Rouault. But her late, great works (the best known is the window in the chapel of Eton College) are distinctively her own. Both Harry Clarke, who died in 1931, and Evie Hone, who died in 1955, strongly influenced younger Irish and English stained-glass artists.

By comparison with French, German and American glass-painters those in England were timorous. Fewer churches were destroyed in England than in France or Germany and there was, therefore, less rebuilding. But even in new churches most architects and church authorities shied away from unorthodoxy. Two cathedrals are notable exceptions—Coventry, which replaced the cathedral destroyed in a German air raid, and the Roman Catholic cathedral at Liverpool. Glass is a dominant element in both cathedrals. The whole of Liverpool's immense lantern tower is filled with glass (designed by John Piper and made by Patrick Reyntiens) which in abstract form depicts the Holy Trinity in a progression of colour from yellow to red to blue. By night it is illuminated, a brilliant beacon shining over the city.

Among the established British artists—as well as those who worked at Liverpool and Coventry—are Brian Thomas and Moira Forsyth, and, for their interesting heraldic work, Francis Skeat, Rupert Moore and Harcourt Doyle. A later generation includes Alan Younger, Antony Hollaway, Peter Tysoe (for his slab glass) and Ray Bradley. Many windows of distinction have also been created by firms, which are a feature of the English stained-glass scene.

Today, however, there is a growing number of young British artists eager to work in stained glass but frustrated through lack of outlets. Some critics have predicted that since in France and Germany there are few young glass-painters of genius to follow the older generation, the lead in stained glass might pass to Britain and the United States. Many European artists might well wish that stained glass was not so firmly linked with the Church. If, as in Japan, it had no such association, it might be easier to persuade architects, their clients and the public to accept stained glass as an essential part of public buildings and homes—as, indeed, many American stained-glass artists have already done. Where once more the Church has led, public authorities and multinational companies could safely follow.

Influenced by Joan Miró's surrealist paintings of microscopic life, the German artist Georg Meistermann designed a wall of stained glass, detail right, for the five-storey West German Radio Station in Cologne. The huge expanse of glass, called *Colour Tones of Music*, incorporates brightly coloured embryonic forms within its network of sinuous black lines.

TWENTIETH-CENTURY GERMANY

Resurgence of an Architectural Art

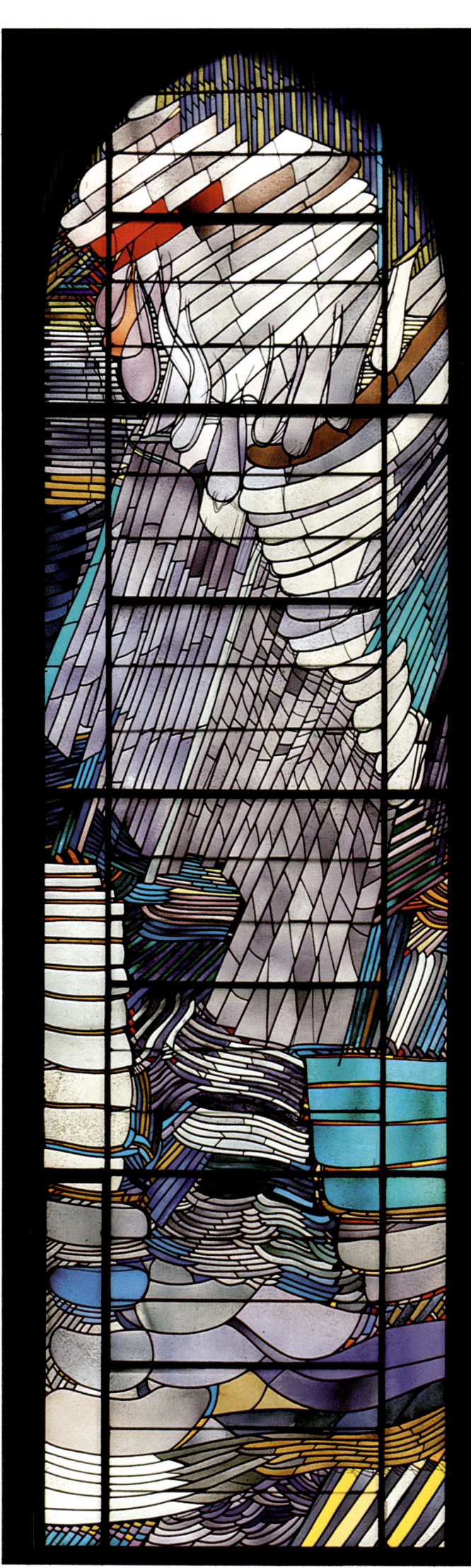

Since the Second World War, German architects have been outstanding in their imaginative use of walls of stained glass, not only in the churches which have been built to replace the thousands destroyed in the war but in secular buildings as well. Happily, the imagination of these modern architects has been matched by the brilliance of a generation of stained-glass artists such as has not been seen since the Middle Ages. Despising the enamel-painting methods of the Munich school of the nineteenth century, they returned to the fundamental technique of creating designs with coloured glass and lead-lines. The leads became particularly important because of greater reliance on line and form than on bright colours.

The harbinger of the modern movement was Jan Thorn Prikker, who designed Cubist windows before and after the First World War. His pupil, Anton Wendling, linked the years between the wars and the 1950s, when he designed his most notable work—the towering side windows in the choir of Aachen Cathedral, which have varied geometrical patterns in differing intensities of red and blue. Georg Meistermann created another bridge between the 1930s and the 1950s, and the vast scale of German rebuilding after the Second World War gave him the opportunity in his old age to design exciting walls of glass—among them the five-storey window in the staircase of the West German Radio Station, Cologne, and the immense curved east window at St Kilian's, Schweinfurt.

After the war, a new generation of outstanding designers created a distinctively modern German style. Among the leaders were Ludwig Schaffrath, Wilhelm Buschulte and Johannes Schreiter. Schaffrath moved from his early basically architectural approach to a greater variety of line, particularly circles and arcs. He also became more sparing with colour, using predominantly black and grey as a contrast to white. Buschulte's designs are organic. Many of them, such as the windows in St Ursula's, Cologne, look like large-scale, freehand representations of the structure of a living cell. Through much of Schreiter's glass runs a Japanese-like "wandering line". Schreiter also has the ability to design atmospheric windows which do not dominate the buildings they are in, even when they have a major architectural role, such as his window walls in the Johannesbund Chapel in Leutesdorf.

In the Church of St Maria Königin, Cologne, Dominikus Böhm, another leading stained-glass designer, has shown how effectively cheaper rolled glass can be used in window walls. The design is restrained, in delicate shades of grey and brown.

Although walls of stained glass are certainly the greatest achievement of this generation of German glass-painters, some artists have experimented with *dalle de verre*, the slab glass and concrete technique in which the French and Americans were so successful. Jochem Poensgen is particularly worthy of note for his ambitious use of glass and concrete at Christ Church, Dinslaken.

How long German pre-eminence in stained glass could be sustained became a subject of debate early in the 1970s, when some critics complained that the established glass artists had failed to train a younger generation worthy of following them. But at least they had inspired young artists abroad, and their influence had been wholly good.

A painter, printmaker and stained-glass artist of outstanding importance, Johannes Schreiter developed the post-war style of German stained glass, which is distinguished by its linear restraint. Influenced by the delicate edge of burned paper, which also inspired Schreiter's "burned collages", lines of infinite variety cross and recross his windows. Schreiter is acutely conscious of the architectural surroundings of his stained glass, which he designs as an extension of a specific environment. His planes of opalescent blue glass, enclosing the chapel of the Johannesbund Convent, Leutesdorf, below, harmonize with the geometric purity of the architecture without echoing it. Influenced by the paradoxes of Eastern philosophy, this glass is a perfect example of what has been called Schreiter's "grandiose reticence".

The stained glass of Georg Meistermann is a bridge between the work of Thorn Prikker and that of artists such as Schaffrath, Poensgen, Buschulte and Schreiter. More obviously dramatic than the glass of this later generation, Meistermann's designs hover between abstractionism and realism by finally eluding the interpretations which they seem to encourage. Storms, rainbows or shafts of light are deliberately suggested but never defined; that which is nearly decipherable as a boat or a cloud dissolves into currents of line and colour. The spectacular window, left, in the south aisle of St Mary's Church, Cologne-Kalk, is characteristic of his work.

The controlled, mysterious work of Ludwig Schaffrath, such as the window, left, in Aachen Cathedral, destroys preconceptions of stained glass as a naïvely expressionistic craft. Its unique language, based on a curling, deliberative line, resists interpretation, transcends pattern-making and is the antithesis of the colourful obviousness often associated with modern stained glass. Of equal importance to his window designs, Schaffrath's slab-glass compositions incorporate areas of concrete pierced by coloured glass rods, as in the detail above from St Michael's Church, Schweinfurt.

Recalling a monumental organic structure, Wilhelm Buschulte's window, above, in Essen Minster combines a mesh of crinkled lines and overlapping tonal colour. Buschulte's stained glass is less consistent in style than that of his contemporaries, but its economical use of colour and dependence upon line unites it with the style of modern German glass.

TWENTIETH-CENTURY UNITED STATES

An Experimental Approach

The inward-tilting walls of the monolithic fish-shaped First Presbyterian Church, Stamford, Connecticut, are constructed of precast concrete. Twenty thousand pieces of multicoloured pot glass were imbedded in the concrete "branches" by French glazier Gabriel Loire, creating a forest of filtered light. The glowing, fragmented images of the Resurrection, and of the Crucifixion, detail below, in nave windows which reach up to the roof ridge, give one the feeling of standing inside a vast, glittering jewel.

There was an inevitable feeling of anticlimax in the United States early in the twentieth century as the excitement engendered by Tiffany waned. Painstakingly, the purists among stained-glass painters directed the art back to older traditions.

The style of the first half of the century is reflected in the windows of two, still unfinished, American cathedrals—the Cathedral Church of St John the Divine in New York City, begun in 1892, and the Cathedral of St Peter and St Paul in Washington, D.C., begun in 1907—both built on the vast scale of medieval Gothic churches. The windows of the two cathedrals were glazed by many of the century's most notable traditionalists.

One of the best known, both for his prolific output of stained glass and for his enthusiastic book *Adventures in Light and Colour*, was Charles J. Connick. His work was in the tradition of Otto Heinigke, the leader of the movement away from opalescent glass to translucent glass and old techniques in the use of leads. Connick, working from his Boston studio, which still continues, designed windows—usually with a blue background, as at Chartres—for churches throughout the United States. Princeton University Chapel in particular has some sparkling windows which he designed. But his greatest work is the west rose window in St John the Divine. It is forty feet in diameter and contains ten thousand pieces of glass. Other glaziers whose work appears in one or both of the cathedrals include Henry Wynd Young, Ernest Lakeman, Nicola D'Ascenzo and Henry Lee Willet, son of the great William Willet, who founded the stained-glass firm that is today the largest in the United States.

Washington Cathedral has a fascinating variety of subjects in its windows. Among the traditional biblical scenes are two showing the conversion of Paul on the road to

Damascus and God speaking to the missionary who made a Chinese translation of the Bible. Labour unions donated several windows, and their seals appear in the borders.

In the south nave aisle, among the windows depicting artists, architects, writers, musicians and craftsmen, the so-called Space window represents a startling break with ecclesiastical tradition. Commemorating man's landing on the moon in 1969, it was donated by Dr Thomas Paine, the former director of the National Aeronautics Space Administration, and was designed by Rodney Winfield of St Louis. In the vastness of space, containing solar spheres and countless stars, is a thin white line—the trajectory of a manned spaceship that shows man's puniness in God's universe. High in the window, a small piece of brilliantly clear glass is designed to hold the fixed fragment of a rock which astronauts Neil Armstrong and Edwin Aldrin brought back from the moon. The rock is estimated to be 3.6 thousand

Pulsating with light, an electric mosaic decorates a wall of the New York ticket office of KLM Royal Dutch Airlines. Designed by Gyorgy Kepes to evoke night flights over cities, this *Light Mural*, detail above, is composed of coloured slab glass backed by a perforated aluminium screen. A barrage of flashing bulbs set up at the rear of the mural provides artificial light for the stained glass at the front and creates a shimmering effect, reminiscent of space seen from an aeroplane.

A window on infinity—this dramatic, semi-abstract window, left, was installed in 1974 in the nave of Washington Episcopal Cathedral to commemorate the exploration of space and man's first lunar landing. This essentially twentieth-century design is set within elaborate stonework which echoes Gothic tracery. A small piece of clear glass in the upper part of the central lancet is designed to hold a chip of basaltic moon rock, brought back to earth by the crew of *Apollo 11*.

An Experimental Approach

million years old and contains pyroxferroite, a mineral unknown on earth. Tiffany would have loved that.

It is questionable, however, whether he would have approved of the bold experiments with glass in architecture which have excited a new generation of American glass-painters. There have been dramatic successes in the use of faceted glass and concrete which have put the United States far ahead of Europe, where *dalle de verre* originated. This technique arrived in the United States just before the Second World War, but it was almost twenty years later before it was employed on any scale. The earliest and most remarkable church constructed in this way was the First Presbyterian Church at Stamford, Connecticut. Built in 1958, the solid walls are made from precast concrete panels, but most of the nave walls are of glass, designed by the French stained-glass artist Gabriel Loire. The glass stretches from floor to roof, and the multicoloured, faceted, triangular panels are built up into a pattern that from the outside suggests huge paper darts.

Since the building of this church, many hundreds of windows of slab glass set in concrete or epoxy resin have been made for buildings throughout the United States. The Willet Studios alone have carried out more than four hundred commissions in slab glass since they adopted the technique in 1954. Emil Frei in St Louis, Bernard Gruenke of the Conrad Schmitt Studios, Milwaukee, Harold Cummings of San Raphael and Roger Darricarrere of Los Angeles were among other pioneers. One notable example, high in the mountains near Colorado Springs, is the Air Force Academy Chapel—a gleaming tent-like church constructed of metal. Almost twenty-five thousand pieces of slab glass, set directly into the metal, were designed and made by Judson Studios, Los Angeles.

Other successful experiments beyond the conventional boundaries of stained glass are the illuminated mural of aluminium and slab glass in the KLM Royal Dutch Airlines ticket office in New York and endomosaic, a combination of stained glass and mosaic. According to long-accepted doctrine, artificial light is fatal to stained glass, but it is an integral part of the KLM mural, designed by Gyorgy Kepes, Professor of Visual Design at Massachusetts Institute of Technology. The concept, space in the air age, is inspired by the excitement of night-flying with the stars above and the city lights below. The effect is achieved by six hundred thousand small perforations and larger openings in the wall, fifty-one feet wide by eighteen feet high, with a battery of blinking lights behind.

The idea of combining stained glass and mosaic attracted a number of American artists. One such wall on a grand scale is that designed by the Californian artist Emile Norman for the Masonic Memorial Temple, Nob Hill, San Francisco, depicting the arrival of masonry in California. Conversely, leaded glass has been used to create a mosaic-like effect. For the American Airlines terminal at Kennedy Airport, New York, Robert Sowers used densely coloured opal glass, joined by broad leads, to create a vast mural which looks very much like a glittering mosaic. Sowers's other work, on a smaller scale, includes some interesting stained-glass doors for houses and offices.

There is a lively younger generation of American stained-glass artists very much at home with contemporary subjects in secular glass. Paul Marioni is one of the most adventurous in exploring the possibilities of glass: some of his windows include two-way mirrors, plastic and photo-silkscreen. One much publicized panel is of a wash-basin with a real waste pipe of clear plastic filled with water.

Not all attempts by American stained-glass artists to exploit to the full the qualities of glass have been successful, either artistically or technically, but that such imaginative experiments have been made is vital for the future of stained glass—and not only in the United States.

Myriad tiny flowers in stained glass, designed in the style of Tiffany, form part of the ceiling of Maxwell's Plum, the well-known Manhattan restaurant and gathering place. The panel, measuring sixteen feet by twenty-eight feet, was installed in the late 1960s.

Jimmy Brown, the world-famous American fullback with the Cleveland Browns, is portrayed in a window in the Blue Grass Restaurant, Maple Heights, Cleveland, Ohio. This football window, detail below, one of a series illustrating American sports, was designed and executed by the Winterich Studios in Cleveland.

Eight windows, symbolizing eight stages of spiritual evolution, were designed by Robert Frei of the Emil Frei Studios for the Trinity Lutheran Church, Decatour, Illinois. Pentecost, the last stage in the series, is represented, below, by a translucent wheel whose fiery centre is surrounded by splintery red triangles.

Bold areas of translucent coloured glass contrast with heavy leading in a window designed by Robert Sowers, detail below. This is one of a series of twelve windows made in 1957 by Sowers for the chapel of Stephen's College, Columbia, Missouri.

Kathie Bunnell, who started working in stained glass in the 1970s, created the *Young Buckeye Tree* window, left, in 1973 for a nunnery in northern California. The variegated effect of the surface has been achieved by the use of three types of glass—English "seedy" and reamy antique glass and the commercial American Cathedral glass. The close detail of the leaves has been etched.

Old Glory in the stocks—this small glass panel, right, entitled *Monetary Gain*, symbolizes the exploitation of things American. It was made in 1973 by Paul Marioni, one of the most innovative American glaziers. To depict the American flag, opaque glass has been flashed and carved.

Composition IX, created in 1974 by Robert Kehlmann, is made of opaque, translucent and mirror glass. A sculptural dimension has been added to the panel, left, by the extension of wires and glass to its surface so that from different angles the relationship varies between the disparate forms and textures.

TWENTIETH-CENTURY SYNAGOGUES—ISRAEL, UNITED STATES AND EUROPE

The Quintessential Light

The six-pointed star, or *Magen David*, appeared for the first time in an American synagogue in a stained-glass window. Made at the turn of the century in the Tiffany Studios, the window, right, was installed in the late 1920s in Congregation Emanu-El of the City of New York. The centre vertical panels depict the Law, and the side panels Mount Sinai, where Moses received the Law from God.

"A crown offered to the Jewish Queen" was how Marc Chagall envisioned the synagogue of the Hadassah-Hebrew University Medical Center, Israel, for which he designed the twelve Jerusalem windows, each representing one of the tribes of Israel. Installed in 1962, the windows are outstanding for the modulations of dazzling colour, accentuated by areas of snowy-white. Irregular glass shapes are held by curvilinear leading remarkable for its suppleness. The proscription of graven images by Mosaic law led Chagall to create a magical world where the wildlife, which has long been part of his iconography, takes on new symbolic significance. The Tribe of Joseph window is below left, that of Benjamin below centre, and that of Reuben below right.

There is a deep feeling for the spirituality of light in both the Christian and the Jewish religions, but it has been interpreted differently. The most notable Christian exponent was the twelfth-century Abbé Suger, who filled the windows of his Abbey Church of St Denis, near Paris, with stained glass "to illumine men's minds with God's light". On the other hand, the eleventh-century French Jewish scholar Rashi argued that a man at prayer should be able to see the sky through the synagogue's windows so that he would be inspired with reverence and devotion.

Historically, the Jews have had other objections to stained glass. The use of imagery was held to be against the Second Commandment condemning graven images. It was also felt that such windows were likely to distract the worshipper from his devotions. Furthermore, stained glass was considered a Christian art, and Gentile practices were generally avoided.

Synagogue stained glass has, nevertheless, a long if scanty history. There are records of stained-glass windows in a twelfth-century synagogue in Cologne. Also recorded is the rabbi's insistence on the removal of the snakes and lions which were depicted in it. Today, stained glass is commonplace in Reform and Conservative synagogues, particularly in the United States. In England and in France it is also to be found in Orthodox synagogues.

There is no specifically Jewish style of stained glass. The windows reflect varying degrees of rejection of or adherence to the old traditions of glass-painting. There are many abstract windows, which avoid the offence which might be given by the depiction of images—humans, animals or plants—and at the same time complement modern functional architecture. The inclusion of figures, and sometimes of faces, is increasing in the decorative art of Reform synagogues, and even in the Orthodox Central Synagogue, London, a figure appears in the Creation and Day of

Judgement window, but he is seen from the rear so that his face remains concealed. In his well-known windows for the synagogue in the Hadassah-Hebrew University Medical Center in Jerusalem, Marc Chagall, proscribed by Mosaic law from the portrayal of human figures, depicted birds, animals and fish embodying human characteristics.

American stained-glass artists are especially adventurous in creating new themes for synagogue glass while incorporating in them ancient Jewish motifs. In the Temple B'nai Aaron, St Paul, Minnesota, for example, ten windows were executed by William Saltzman on the life cycle of a Jew, including birth, education, Bar and Bat Mitzvah—the ceremonies at which the boy or girl enters the adult community—marriage, old age and immortality. These were done wholly in abstract design. Jewish contributions to American civilization are illustrated in four windows designed by Helen Carew Hickman for the Tree of Life Synagogue, Pittsburgh, Pennsylvania. The windows contain figures ranging from Elijah and Jeremiah to Justice Felix Frankfurter, a Supreme Court Judge, and an anonymous garment worker, musician, farm worker and dramatist. Rather less successful artistically is an overambitious attempt to crowd four thousand years of the spiritual history of the Jewish people into twelve windows in the Har Zion Temple, Philadelphia.

Many windows in contemporary American synagogues and Jewish community centres are being conceived on a grand scale—from the vast stained-glass façade of Milton Steinberg House, New York, to Abraham Rattner's window for the Loop Synagogue, Chicago, which measures forty feet by thirty feet. The scale of such works is indeed striking in view of past antipathy to stained glass and it testifies to the recognition of stained glass as an acceptable and adaptable art form, which can embellish without obscuring the quintessential light.

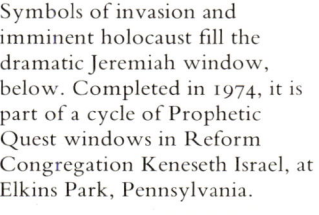

Symbols of invasion and imminent holocaust fill the dramatic Jeremiah window, below. Completed in 1974, it is part of a cycle of Prophetic Quest windows in Reform Congregation Keneseth Israel, at Elkins Park, Pennsylvania.

In the arch of the Creation and Day of Judgement window, above, a cantor blows the *shofar*, the ram's horn sounded at Jewish New Year, or the Day of Judgement, an autumn festival also celebrating the Creation. The central Creation panels are bordered by depictions of the *Torah*, the Scrolls of the Law, musical instruments and biblical commentaries. The window was installed in 1964 in the Central Synagogue, London.

Ben Shahn included verses from *Psalm 150*, part of the Morning Service, in his design for the curved window in the Temple Beth Zion, Buffalo, New York.

SYMBOLS IN JUDAISM

The wealth of symbolism in Jewish ritual is frequently reflected in stained glass. The window, right, installed in 1963 in the chapel of Temple Beth Tikvah, New Milford, New Jersey, is dense with such imagery. Among the major symbols are the seven-branch candlestick of the Temple (1) and the *shofar* (2), the ram's horn blown at New Year and on Yom Kippur, the Day of Atonement. Scales (3) may stand for justice on the Day of Judgement or may represent one of the signs of the zodiac—a favourite theme in synagogue art. Part of an important Jewish prayer, the *shema* is written on the Scroll of the Law (4). The latticework (5) indicates the *sukkah*, an arbour erected during Sukkot, the eight-day Festival of Tabernacles, during which the festival candles, the *etrog*—a citrus fruit—and a palm branch are all used (6). The *menorah* (7) is lit throughout Hannukah, the Festival of Lights. Hebrew letters (8), from right to left, spell out a name of God. The *Book of Esther*, the *Megillah* (9), is read at Purim, a festival commemorating the deliverance of the Jews from the Persians, while the exodus from Egypt is commemorated at Passover with unleavened bread, known as *matzot*, a roasted egg and bitter herbs (10). The Sabbath table is laid with candles, wine and two plaited loaves (11), and near it is the spice box which is used at the ceremony marking the end of the Sabbath at sunset on Saturday. The Ten Commandments are listed on the Tablets of the Law (12).

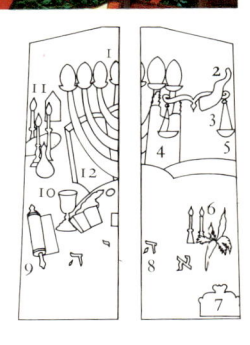

TWENTIETH-CENTURY ENGLAND

Coventry – Symbol of Rebirth

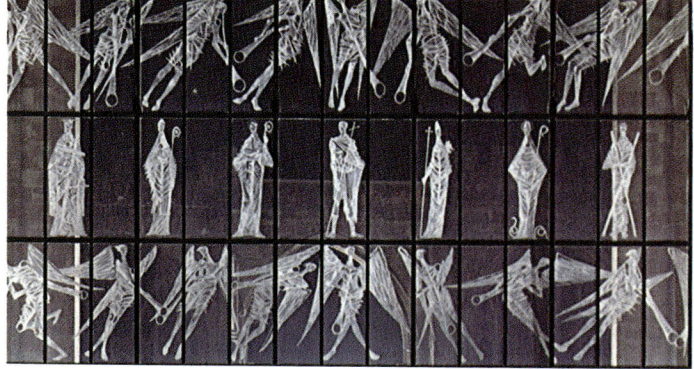

The west screen of clear glass, seventy feet high, is engraved by John Hutton with spectral figures of angels, saints and prophets. It looks out on to the ruins of the old cathedral.

The medieval cathedral in Coventry was largely destroyed by German bombs in November 1940. The architect, Sir Basil Spence, linked the new cathedral to the remains of the old, the juxtaposition symbolizing the indestructibility of faith as well as death and resurrection. Although the design seemed to represent a break with the past, the plan is in fact conventional.

When the new cathedral was consecrated in 1962, the stained-glass windows were as much a subject of controversy as everything else in the building. The design of the windows and the way in which they are integrated into the cathedral structure do indeed represent a radical break with tradition. The ten nave windows, angled to catch the southern light —Spence's solution to the problem posed by an "east" end that faces north—are recessed so that they are fully visible as an ensemble only from the altar end. Towering to a height of seventy feet, the windows have as their overall theme the relationship between God and man at different stages of man's life. The windows along the "north" aisle represent the divine order (God) and those along the "south" aisle the natural order (man). The various stages are expressed through the symbolic use of colour.

The dominant window in the cathedral is, however, the huge and dramatic curved window of the baptistery, which reaches from floor to ceiling. Designed by the artist John Piper and made by Patrick Reyntiens, it symbolizes the light of the Holy Spirit breaking through into the world. The centre is a sun-like blaze of yellow and white, and around it are areas of blues, reds, purples, browns, ochres, greens and greys. Even on the dullest day the rays of the sun appear to come streaming through on to the stonework.

When the controversy about the break with tradition had subsided, the intrinsic worth of the Coventry windows and their importance as a landmark in British church glass were recognized. The bold use of concrete and glass by the architect and glazier at Coventry served as a prototype, establishing a new tradition in British stained glass.

John Piper, famous for evocative watercolours of landscapes and architecture, designed spectacular windows for Coventry and for the Roman Catholic Cathedral, Liverpool.

Patrick Reyntiens has designed and executed stained glass for buildings in England and abroad and has been the exclusive creator of windows designed by John Piper.

The five pairs of nave windows, detail left, are slanted to catch the southern light in the north-facing cathedral. Although from the entrance the windows themselves are hidden, their five distinctive colours are reflected on the white walls and on the black marble floor of the aisles. Designed by Lawrence Lee, Geoffrey Clarke and Keith New, the windows represent five stages of existence. Each stage is expressed through the symbolic use of colour—birth is green, youth red, maturity multicoloured, death blue and purple and resurrection golden.

A giant chessboard of stone and glass, the baptistery window, far right, symbolizes the light of the Holy Spirit bursting through the complexities and confusions of the world. John Piper's cartoons for the window, detail right, were interpreted into rectangular, abstract patterns of glass by Patrick Reyntiens. Dwarfed by the blaze of chequered light, the font is made from a boulder brought from a hillside near Bethlehem.

TWENTIETH-CENTURY FRANCE

Mirror of Modern Painting

Painters in the seventeenth century gave the kiss of death to the art of stained glass by imposing on it the art of painting. In the twentieth century, some of the most famous painters in France gave stained glass the kiss of life by releasing it from the incompatible conventions of painting.

The initiative came from within the Church, and the Church of Notre Dame de Toute Grace at Assy, in the Haute Savoie, led the way. In 1937 the influential Dominican priest Le Père Couturier, convinced that the art of ecclesiastical stained glass would benefit from the influence of profane art, invited a number of artists to submit cartoons for the windows at Assy. They included Fernand Léger, Marc Chagall and Georges Rouault, who, as a young man, had been apprenticed in a stained-glass workshop, where he had absorbed the technique of the heavy black outlines which marked his paintings, whether of biblical scenes or of prostitutes.

The Assy experiment was not an unqualified success, because of the multiplicity of styles, but no such criticism can be made about the Dominican Chapel of the Rosary at Vence, near Nice, where Henri Matisse worked from 1947 to 1950, the last four years of his life. The windows, murals, marble floors and vestments were all designed by him. His aim was to create an atmosphere in which those who entered the chapel would feel purified and relieved of their burdens, most likely to be achieved, he thought, by seeing his windows at eleven o'clock on a winter's morning.

Léger, a non-believer, had a similar aim—to fill the

Light, the intensity carefully controlled by small, deep-set apertures, is the atmospheric agent of Le Corbusier's austere, inspiring masterpiece, the Church of Notre Dame du Haut, Ronchamp. Windows of clear and stained glass, arranged at irregular intervals in the thick white walls, admit points of light and colour, above, without excluding the external world. Sky and trees, visible through the areas of transparent glass, counterpoint the vibrant squares of primary colour, the simple images and the messages to the Virgin, which Le Corbusier painted with contrived artlessness on some of the windows. His comparatively complex design, above right, in brilliant enamel, is on the exterior of Ronchamp's east door.

Georges Braque, who lived and worked for a time at Varangeville, near Dieppe, designed stained-glass windows for the Chapel of St Dominique in 1953 and 1954. Unrelated to his contemporary still lifes and seascapes, one of the windows shows St Dominique, surprisingly wearing a red fez and standing between two decorative serpentine forms.

hearts of believers and unbelievers with joy and light—when, between 1950 and 1952, he created his stunning masterpiece in the Church of the Sacred Heart at Audincourt. Running around three sides of the church, his brilliant abstract frieze, made of one-inch-thick slab glass set in concrete, established the popularity of *dalle de verre*.

Alfred Manessier, a deeply religious artist, also handles slab glass and concrete with skill and imagination. An excellent example is in the chapel of Hem, Nord. His conventionally leaded abstract windows, for instance at Les Bréseux and Le Pouldu, are equally effective.

At the Church of Notre Dame du Haut at Ronchamp in the Vosges, the architect Le Corbusier was responsible for both the architectural design and the stained glass. The church is small, but looks monumental with its thick concrete walls. Their whiteness is softened by the light from the stained-glass windows which perforate the south wall. Some of the windows are only a few inches square and none is more than three feet square. Le Corbusier's sketchy designs, which incorporate child-like writing, are perfect for the setting, a consummate fusion of art and architecture.

Inevitably, not all the thousands of churches and windows that replaced those destroyed in the war have been masterpieces, and the worst disasters have arisen through slavish imitation. For example, while Le Corbusier's marvel at Ronchamp looks as though it has grown out of the ground, an attempted copy at Colombes, near Paris, appears to have been dropped from outer space.

Alfred Manessier, who was called the greatest religious painter within abstractionism, designed stained glass for many French and German churches and promoted the modern concept of stained-glass architecture, rather than isolated stained-glass windows. The religious themes of his paintings, expressed more explicitly in the titles than on the canvases, are conveyed by darting black lines or a black network of forms which, vibrating against deep colour, recall abstract stained-glass windows. One of Manessier's eight *dalle de verre* windows, left, in the crypt of Essen Minster achieves a deep translucence with thick slabs of glass held in a pattern of concrete.

Although an atheist, Fernand Léger exploited the formal elements of Christian symbolism in his monumental *dalle de verre* frieze, detail below, for the Church of the Sacred Heart, Audincourt. Its assertive colours, tubular forms and thick black outlines are reminiscent of Léger's Cubist paintings of machinery and of city life. Subdued in comparison, but uniting rigid and sinuous forms in a similar way, his *Animated Landscape*, above, contrasts mechanized men with a curvaceous cow and soft green trees.

171

TWENTIETH-CENTURY JAPAN

Fusion of East and West

Japan does not have a long and rich tradition of stained glass, for the art form was not introduced there until the middle of the nineteenth century. But Japan does possess a modern work of stained glass that must be unique in the world—a glass tower created for the sole purpose of making people happy by recalling for them the marvellous world of childhood. The tower was designed and executed by Gabriel Loire, one of the best-known modern stained-glass designers. Loire once said that it is not the task of the glass-painter "to come in at the last moment and fill in the holes" left by the architect, and that was certainly not his role in designing the stained glass for the sixty-nine-foot-high tower at Hakone in Japan; the glass exists in its own right and the building is there only to support it.

The Rainbow Tower, or the Symphony Tower of Joy for Children, two of the names by which the structure is called, lies at the foot of the mountains around Hakone, sixty miles south of Tokyo, and is part of the open-air Museum of Modern Art founded by Nobutaka Shikanai, a generous patron of the arts. The tower is composed of faceted *dalle de verre*—a technique hitherto unknown in Japan. The 480 panels of glass cover some 3,500 square feet, and as you climb the spiral staircase within it the medley of images from the seasons of the year is revealed—from flowers, snowflakes, stars, clowns and games, to lovers nestling in a crescent moon. Such profusion, according to its creator, is meant "to lead to a kind of apotheosis of joy, purity and vitality".

Loire has many achievements in stained glass on a grand scale—among them the First Presbyterian "Fish" Church at Stamford, Connecticut, and the Kaiser Wilhelm Memorial Church in West Berlin with its 22,000 glass blocks, each one foot square, in abstract designs—but there is nothing to compare with the Hakone tower.

In Japan, stained glass has none of the religious associations that it has in the West. But one most promising young Japanese stained-glass artist, Yoshiro Ohyama, gained his first practical experience working on church windows in Montpellier while studying architecture at Montpellier University. He also worked as assistant to Patrick Reyntiens on windows for Washington Cathedral, including the Winston Churchill memorial window, designed by John Piper. Japanese art greatly influenced Art Nouveau stained glass, but then it was interpreted through Western eyes. Now the process is admirably reversed.

The Symphony Tower of Joy for Children, a tower of stained glass, was created by the French artist Gabriel Loire for the open-air Museum of Modern Art in Hakone near Tokyo. Its 480 glittering panels of faceted slab glass enclose a spiral staircase by which the images of birds, flowers, stars, moons, lovers and clowns are explored as an evolving frieze of childhood fantasy.

The influence of France and of French Post-Impressionist painting is discernible in the stained-glass panel, right, by the Japanese artist Yoshiro Ohyama, who was trained as a stained-glass artist in Montpellier, France. A packet of French cigarettes is shown on the table in a rustic room, whose stylistic simplicity is reminiscent of Van Gogh's painting of his bedroom.

Unmistakably Oriental in style and content, a procession of Japanese figures is depicted in a stained-glass panel in the Fujiya Hotel, Hakone, near Tokyo.

TWENTIETH-CENTURY AUSTRALIA

Adapting an Ancient Art

The work of the Australian artist Leonard French, influenced by romantic, ritualistic and universal themes, aspires to the monumental grandeur of Romanesque art. Twenty-four feet in diameter, his slab-glass ceiling, left, in Blackwood Hall, Monash University, near Melbourne, is considered by French to be his "most important work to date". It recalls a symmetrical pattern of a vast kaleidoscope in which geometric shapes, detail above, are divided and sub-divided into symbols.

Inspired by teeming, organic life, stained-glass panels by the Australian artist David Wright depict graceful, stylized patterns of coiling tendrils, aquatic plants, spores and fungi. The composition of swaying leaves entitled *Forest*, detail below, is reminiscent of the foliar patterns of Matisse's windows in the Chapel of the Rosary at Vence in southern France.

The art of Australia is still young by comparison with the art of Europe, and the art of stained glass is younger still. England was the native source of Australian art, but the art has had to develop in a new land influenced by a totally different environment.

The culmination of many influences, an "Australian style" of stained glass has emerged and can be seen in the work of the artist Leonard French. Born in Melbourne in 1928, French spent his early twenties in Europe and his canvases, murals and stained glass show the influence of Léger, Manessier, Delaunay and of Celtic art. They are also, in the Melbourne artistic tradition, rich in symbolic forms.

French's work has become increasingly religious in its themes; creation is one of the most recurrent and fish and birds are favourite symbols. In his vast dazzling ceiling for the National Gallery of Victoria in Melbourne, the centre-piece, a sun forty-eight feet in diameter, is flanked by thirty-foot turtles, "the containers of life", as French describes them, which in turn are surrounded by twelve-foot-high birds. With its 224 triangles of glass covering an area of 164 feet by 48 feet and ranging through a spectrum of fifty colours, the ceiling shines resplendently in the sun and colours the floor below. In a building which houses art, it is a significant work of art itself.

Bold Statements in Glass

Almost all the stained-glass windows of Scandinavia's medieval churches have disappeared. They were a casualty of Lutheranism, the area's dominant form of Christianity, which has been described as "a low-temperature religion adapted to the long winters of the rigorous north". Only in the churches of the Baltic island of Gotland has any appreciable amount of medieval glass survived.

Stained glass began to come back into favour only in the nineteenth century and since then a recognizably Scandinavian style has emerged, which has much in common with the "Scandinavian look" in other applied arts. This is epitomized by cleanness of line and boldness of colour.

A Norwegian artist, Emanuel Vigeland, who died in 1948, greatly influenced modern stained glass in his own country and in Sweden. Rejecting the technique of painting on glass, he produced windows in warm, rich colours. Early examples of his work are the Prodigal Son windows in Vålerengen Church in Oslo. In the first window the father gives his son his inheritance; in the second the son is wasting it on high living and on harlots. At this point not only did the Prodigal's money run out but the church apparently found itself short of funds for two further windows which would have completed the series. Vigeland's major work was done in the 1920s, when he designed and executed thirty-three windows in the Oscarskyrkan in Stockholm.

Vigeland influenced Einar Forseth, one of Sweden's leading glass-painters, who is also a designer of mosaics and an oil painter. Forseth's windows are richly coloured, usually with one colour dominant, and most of them include a topical or local allusion. His 1939 choir window in St Mary's Church at Hälsingborg, for example, shows the fraternization of soldiers from opposing sides during the Italian–Ethiopian War, and a window in Lapland depicts Lapp working scenes—mining, lumbering and looking after reindeer. Forseth also designed five small but splendid windows for Coventry Cathedral.

The major work of Bo Viktor Beskow, another prominent Swedish stained-glass artist, is the ensemble of windows in the medieval Gothic cathedral of Skara. Among them is the window to the Virgin, a bold, richly coloured pattern containing five thousand pieces of glass—the result of Beskow's experiments to recapture the brilliance of medieval stained glass. The stylized elongated figures with blank faces are reminiscent of wooden dolls.

Only in the twentieth century has stained glass established itself in Iceland, through the work of such artists as the mid-century pioneer Nina Tryggvadottir, who designed windows for the National Art Gallery in Reykjavik, and Leifur Breidfjord. As Breidfjord's style evolved, his designs and colours became bolder and his use of various techniques more adventurous. His commissions include a stained-glass wall in deep reds and blues for the restaurant of the National Theatre in Reykjavik.

Unlike Scandinavia, Holland and Belgium still have a rich tradition of stained glass, and modern work there has consequently been on a more limited scale. In Holland, Jan Thorn Prikker began to put new life into the art of stained glass at the beginning of the twentieth century, and in the 1920s Theo van Doesburg introduced abstract art into windows. After the Second World War, contemporary art

Translucent hands, wearing rings, below, or grasping fruit, pens or glasses of lemonade, were designed by the Dutch artist Marte Röling for windows of a school in Amsterdam. A versatile and prolific artist, Röling has created murals, sculpture and stained glass for many other buildings in Amsterdam and has designed theatre sets, clothes, record sleeves and posters. She has exhibited drawings, silkscreen prints and lithographs in Europe and America.

Bright, interlocking areas of colour entitled *Mouths 25*, detail above, were designed by Marte Röling for the Sociaal Fonds Bouwnijverheid, Amsterdam.

A garden is the background for the leafy shapes and straight lines of *Spring Buds*, below, a window designed by the Icelandic artist Leifur Breidfjord.

influenced many Dutch stained-glass artists, including Charles Eyck, A. J. Der Kinderen and H. Jonas. The 1960s and 1970s have been marked by the emergence of highly original experimental work such as that by Marte Röling.

In Belgium there was some revival of the art in contemporary abstract style in the middle of the century with the work of Louis Marie Londot in Namur and Michel Martens in Flanders. As well as abstract windows, however, figurative windows continued to be made in Belgium, and some windows combine figurative and abstract elements.

The modern stained glass of Holland and Belgium has, however, a long way to go before it can be compared with the achievements in these countries in the sixteenth century. In part, this is simply the result of lack of opportunity—there are not enough churches. But there is also the inexplicable ebb and flow over the centuries that determines whether a nation at a given time is to excel in one particular branch of art. It is a mystery that has defied analysis during ten centuries of stained glass.

Dalles de verre, moulded with primitive masks and animals by the Swedish artist Eric Hoglund and set in concrete, in the Boda glassworks, Sweden.

The Swedish artist Lennart Rohde is inspired by the movement and structure of trees. Currents and counter-currents of lines suggest the patterns of light and shade among leaves in *The Orchard*, detail above, which he designed for the Swedish Trading Bank in Stockholm.

Irradiant stonework surrounds the vivid mosaic of stained glass, above, designed by the Danish artist Sven Havsteen-Mikkelsen for Klarup Church, North Jutland.

Gluttonous prostitutes entertain a dispirited-looking Prodigal Son, right, in a window by Norwegian artist Emanuel Vigeland in Vålerengen Church, Norway.

5

ANCIEN TESTAMENT

DAVID
E

MOÏSE
D

ADAM
A

J. BAPTISTE
F.

ABRAHAM
C

NOE
B

Gabriel Loire
nov 74
Xᵇʳᵉ 74

Making a Stained-Glass Window

Almost every cathedral, abbey or parish church has at least one stained-glass window. It may be ancient and aglow with rich colours, or a vivid contemporary window, angular and modern in style. Stand near the window and the way in which it is made will be revealed.

Immediately obvious is the overall design, the picture, which is composed of pieces of coloured glass, generally with one colour to each element—a red hat, for example, a blue cloak, green grass. Painted on the pieces of glass, in a thick black-brown paint, are such details as the folds of the garments, the features of the faces, the leaves of a tree. All the pieces of coloured glass are held together in a lattice of lead strips, and the whole window is made up of a series of panels, cemented into the stonework and supported at intervals by horizontal metal bars.

The creation of a traditional stained-glass window follows the same scheme. First, the design is conceived, sketched and then drawn to the full size of the window. Then the glass is chosen and cut. Next the painting is done and the glass is fired in a kiln. After that it is leaded and, finally, the panels are fixed into position in the building.

The processes of making a stained-glass window have changed little from medieval times. A description of the way a window was made in the twelfth century is included in an exhaustive Latin work, *De Diversis Artibus*, A Treatise Upon Various Arts, which describes many crafts. The author, a monk named Theophilus, is believed to have been a skilled metalworker in northwest Germany. Essentially the method of "composing windows" described by Theophilus differs only slightly from today's practice. The main differences stem from such technical innovations and improvements as steel-wheel glass cutters—instead of the old dividing iron—and gas and electric soldering irons.

While the old traditions still obtain today, the horizons of stained glass have expanded enormously since the beginning of the twentieth century, for the discovery and use of new materials have coincided with an infusion of new life from contemporary painting. Stained glass has become part of secular as well as ecclesiastical decoration and the established form of leaded glass vies with new forms. These include *dalle de verre*, thick glass set into concrete or epoxy resin, glass appliqué, a collage of pieces of coloured glass glued to plate glass, and fused glass, different glasses bonded together by heat. Although many of the materials are new, the processes involved in the making of these modern windows nevertheless follow most of the traditional steps, from the sketch to the cutting of the glass, its assembly into panels and, finally, its installation in the building.

Whatever the type of window, it is made in a workshop known as a studio. A studio can vary in size from a factory-like building with many workshops to a single room or a corner of the artist's home. Large studios sometimes provide facilities for outside artists, particularly for cutting and glazing, and are usually headed by a well-established artist who, rather like the great painters of the Renaissance, has a team of assistants and craftsmen working under his direction.

It is the artist who sets the style for, and the approach to, every project. He may insist on an exact transcription of his detailed designs as, for example, the French artist Marc Chagall, for whom every brush-stroke of the cartoon is laboriously translated by aciding, or etching, and plating. Alternatively he may give his craftsmen freedom to adapt his design into glass. Or, like the influential English artist James Hogan, the artist may himself be a capable craftsman and take part at every stage. Indeed, the making of a stained-glass window is and has always been an inextricable blend of art and craft. Lines between artist and craftsmen are blurred, and only when artistry and craftsmanship unite can truly satisfying stained-glass work be produced.

The artist's particular areas of work are the drawing office, where the designs are prepared, and the main workshop, where on one side are the great drawing-boards and on the other are tall windows against which the coloured glass is hauled up to be viewed and painted. The artist probably spends as much time, however, in other areas of the studio—in the cutting shop, for example, or in the glazing shop, where strips of lead are trimmed and soldered around the glass to make up the panels which form the window. He also anxiously shares with the kiln man the tense moments when the glass goes through the critical process of firing. He may supervise the initial measurement of the window and, later, its installation.

In much the same way, the early stained-glass artists and craftsmen worked together in small, tightly knit bands. International in outlook, they moved to where there was work, through France, Germany and England, enriching the newly built cathedrals and churches with their art. In the later Middle Ages, however, they settled in such cities as Paris, Ulm and York and established permanent workshops where they perfected their art and their techniques.

The first stage in the making of a stained-glass window is usually a commission from an architect or a donor. Increasingly today, as stained glass becomes widely accepted as a secular art form, the identity of the donor is changing. Whereas the most notable donors of the past were the monarchy, nobility and clergy, today householders, business organizations, hospital and airport authorities are among the many branches of society which are increasingly commissioning stained glass. The major patrons, however, are still the churches.

The artist always consults the donor about the theme and, if the window is designed for a modern building, he consults the architect about the form it should take. Often the patron has a definite subject in mind—a biblical scene, for example, or emblems, heraldry, references to contemporary events or a memorial. Today, the preference is frequently for an abstract modern window.

If possible, the artist visits the building for which the window is to be designed. He soaks up the atmosphere and the style and aims of the overall architectural conception, noting particularly the design of any other windows. He observes the building at different times of day and in varying lights—his glass must take advantage of strong sunshine and cool shadows, half-lights and high noon. The artist also takes careful note of the dimensions of the aperture and particularly of the arrangement of the tracery. In an old window he checks the existing bars, as he may decide they are worth keeping; otherwise, as in new buildings, he makes his own design for the ironwork.

The sketch

The next stage is the preparation of a small coloured drawing, usually to a scale of about half an inch to one foot. This drawing, the sketch, or design, is done in watercolours and inks and gives an accurate impression of how the artist visualizes the finished window. The extent to which the sketch is perfected depends upon the artist's method of working and upon the preferences of the person to whom it will be submitted for approval.

Although Theophilus did not mention any design or coloured sketch, something of this kind must have been prepared in the Middle Ages for submission to the donor. No doubt small designs were drawn up on vellum, rather like the illuminations in manuscripts of the time. Often, however, the medieval artist had no need to originate a design, for many contracts specified that the newly commissioned work should imitate an existing artifact. A rood screen, for example, was to be made "as in St Katherine's Church in the hundred of Eastley"; a spire was to be built "in all respects like" one in a town twenty miles away. So it must often have been with stained glass. When the design was agreed, the main work then began.

The detailed sketch, usually done in watercolours and inks, is the first stage in making a stained-glass window. This sketch was done by the French stained-glass artist Gabriel Loire for a traditional leaded window at the church at Coignières in northern France. Designed in November 1974, and completed and installed in July 1975, the window depicts scenes from the Old Testament.

Making a Stained-Glass Window

The cartoon

After the sketch, the cartoon is the next stage in the making of the window. The cartoon is the full-size working drawing for the stained-glass window and is done by the artist. All the dimensions and details must be exactly right, so careful measurements are taken on the site. Templates—thin pieces of card pressed into each aperture and then cut to shape—are made to establish the precise size and shape of such details as the heads of Gothic windows and curvilinear tracery.

The original sketch is then enlarged to the actual size of the window. Traditionally, the cartoon is drawn by hand in the studio and, to position the main lines and masses correctly, the process known as "squaring-up" is used. This is done by placing a grid on the sketch and an equivalent scaled-up grid on the cartoon. Some artists, however, simply have the sketch enlarged photographically. Adjustments are then made to the enlargement so that it matches the window shape perfectly and the design is elaborated or clarified as necessary. Those who use this method believe that it retains the freshness of the original sketch.

Next, the fine details are added—the folds of the garments, features, lettering and heraldry. The degree to which the cartoon is completed depends upon the artist. If he is going to do the painting on the glass himself, he will probably require only the minimum of guidelines. If a colleague in his studio is going to do the painting, then the artist will want to make his own intentions as clear as possible.

The early stained-glass artists drew their cartoons on whitewashed boards, which were easily transportable, like the rest of their equipment. Theophilus, writing in the twelfth century about making stained glass, began his treatise with instructions for the preparation of the board for the cartoon. First, the board was to be whitened all over with chalk, then the correct dimensions of at least two panels were to be marked out. "Which done," he continued, "draw out whatever figures you will, first with the lead or tin, then with a red or black colour, making all outlines with care. . . ."

In later medieval times, cartoons must have been drawn in much the same way as they are today. In the fifteenth century "instruments and drawings" and "all my scrowles" (the rolled-up cartoons) were bequeathed by glass-men to their successors. Indeed, there are many windows where clearly the same cartoons have been used for different figures. The artist merely varied the colours or reversed the drawing. In one window in York Minster, for example, the same cartoon with slight variations does duty for no fewer than six different figures of kings and ecclesiastics.

The cutline

When the cartoon has been completed, the next step is to make the cutline. This is a tracing of the lead-lines of the cartoon, which forms the pattern from which the pieces of glass will later be cut. A sheet of tracing paper or tracing linen is placed over the cartoon and a pencil line is drawn down the centre of each lead-line.

Early craftsmen did not use a cutline. Their glass was marked with the cutting pattern directly from the boards, or cartoon. For the modern artist, however, the cutline is an important stage. By looking at the tracing, he can see whether the window is artistically and structurally viable. The overall abstract pattern of the lead-lines should convey an impression of strength or delicacy, of rhythm or movement. If this basic foundation of the design is not right, no amount of colour or paint will compensate.

It is at this stage, too, that possible technical problems become obvious. These might include awkward "necks", which can break easily, difficult curves, sharp angles and thin sections, which may disappear under the lead, or poorly designed areas, where several lead-lines join or where the lead forms an ugly pattern. Such failings are corrected.

When the pattern of the leads is finally established, the pencil lines are painted over in black ink or paint, with a special thin, long-haired brush. Ideally, the ink lines are exactly one-sixteenth of an inch thick—the width of the core of the lead and the distance the pieces of glass will be held apart by the leading in the window. Later, one side of the line is used for cutting one piece of glass and the other

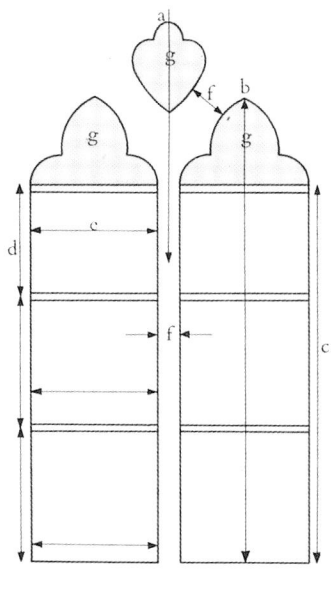

The aperture is measured to ascertain the window's precise size and shape. A plumb-line (a) determines the window's perpendicularity. Measurements are then made of the overall height (b), the height from springing line to base (c), the position of the glazing bars (d), the width (e), the mullions (f) and, with templates, the tracery (g). This information is used to draw a full-size outline of the window for the cartoon.

To make the cartoon, which is exactly the size of the window, the sketch is enlarged panel by panel. Bold black lines represent the leads and shading suggests later painting on the glass. Gabriel Loire, above, is finishing a detailed cartoon of the Noah panel for the window at Coignières Church. The full cartoon, right, with all the black-and-white drawings of the panels joined together, is a working blueprint for the stained glass of the whole window.

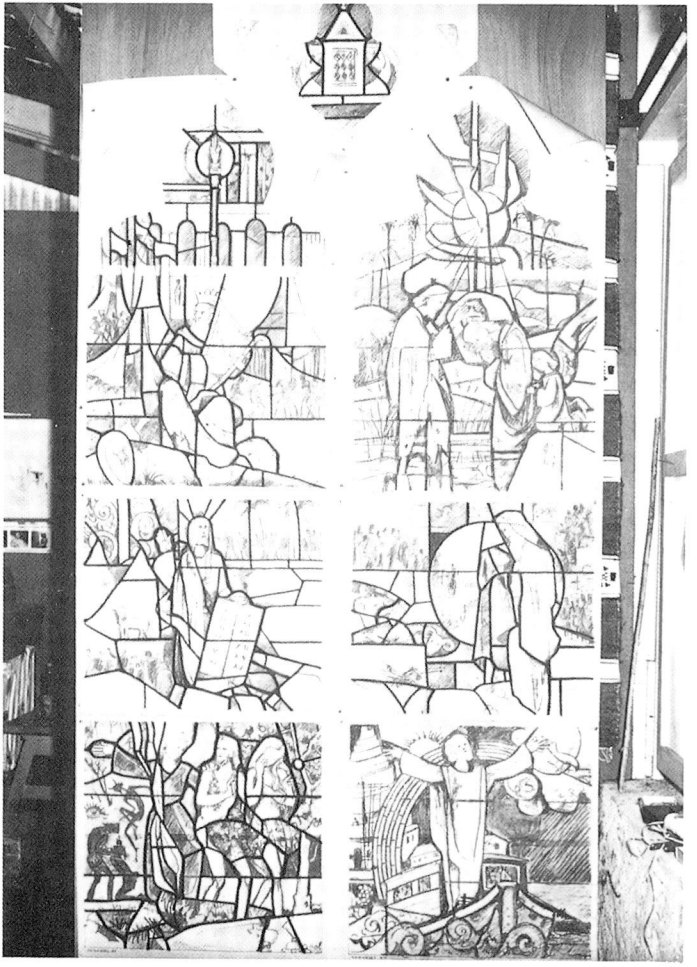

178

DALLE DE VERRE—A NEW FORM OF STAINED GLASS

One of the most modern forms of stained glass becoming increasingly popular, *dalle de verre*, or slab glass, is a cast glass, usually about one inch thick, which is set either in concrete or in epoxy resin. It creates windows which are monumental in appearance and are, in fact, frequently load-bearing structures. While the glass and techniques used differ, the stages in making a *dalle* window follow most of those of the traditional leaded window— sketch and cartoon, cutting and modifying the glass and, finally, assembly into panels. Structurally, the divisions between the glass must be wide and so the dark framework is a dominating feature of the overall design

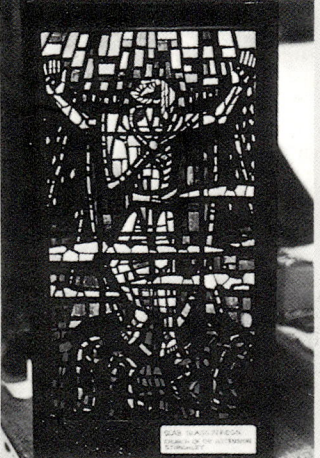

The sketch of the central light of an Ascension window, made in *dalle* and epoxy resin for an English church.

The window's designer, John Lawson, compares the sketch with the cartoon of the middle panel of the centre light.

The *dalle* glass is chosen and marked, prior to cutting.

for the adjoining piece, thus leaving the correct one-sixteenth of an inch for the lead.

If the ink lines are not accurate, the glass will be cut either slack, a little too small, or full, a little too large. Later, as piece after piece is leaded up, the effect increases and the final panel will be noticeably either too large or too small. Although these mistakes can be overcome, they can be avoided if the ink line is precise.

The artist usually numbers each segment of the cutline and indicates the colours—R for ruby, for example, and G for green. He also notes the position of unusual leads, such as those that will have particularly thick or thin flanges. The extent of the detail written on the cutline largely depends on the artist's subsequent method of working.

In the template method, the method most widely used in France and Germany, the cutline is not retained intact. Instead, it is drawn on thick tracing paper—or is transferred from thin tracing paper to stout card—marked and then divided into its component pieces with either a two-bladed knife or special three-bladed scissors. The thin strips, corresponding to the lead cores, are discarded and the cut shapes of card, each marked with colour and panel reference, are used as templates around which the glass is then cut.

The alternative method is commonly used in Britain and occasionally in the United States. The artist does not make individual templates but instead cuts the glass directly on the cutline. This cutline, which is retained as a working drawing for constant use as the window is made, has to withstand considerable wear and tear and, therefore, tracing linen rather than paper is used.

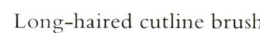
Long-haired cutline brush

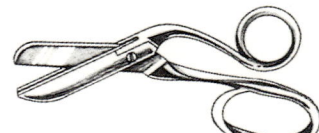
Three-bladed scissors

Two-bladed knife

The cutline is a tracing of the lead-lines from the cartoon. Here, at the first stage in its preparation, Gabriel Loire's chief craftsman carefully pencils the centre of each lead on to a sheet of tracing paper. In many studios the cutline becomes the pattern over which glass is cut and leaded, but in the Loire studio, and in most others in France and Germany, the tracing is transferred to thin card and then separated into templates around which the glass is cut.

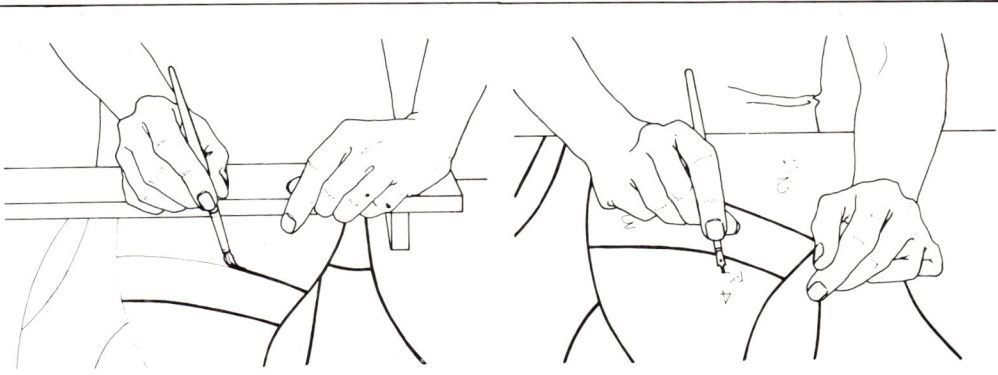

The pencil lines on the cutline are painted over to represent the width of the lead core— usually one-sixteenth of an inch.

Each segment of the cutline is numbered and a note made about colour and any special treatment which the glass will require.

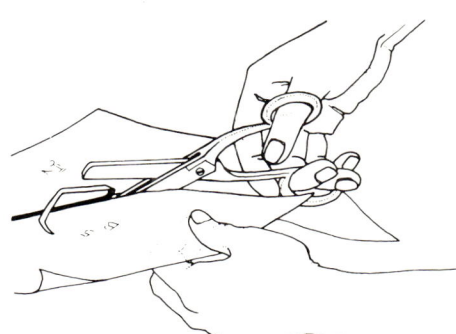

Three-bladed scissors, which leave a central strip one-sixteenth of an inch wide, are used to cut templates from the cutline.

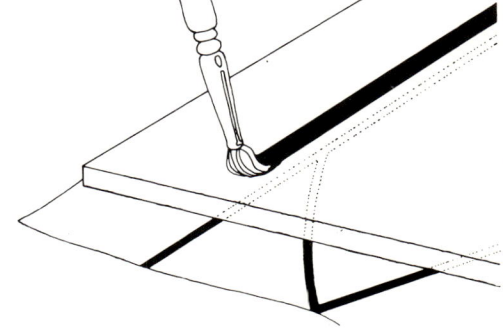

In some studios the lead-lines are transferred from the cutline to plate glass, to check their pattern against the light.

Making a Stained-Glass Window

The choice of glass

No matter how carefully the cartoon and cutline are prepared, good design and drawing will count for little if the colour is poor. The next stage, therefore, the choice of glass, is critical and the artist devotes much time and care to it.

At the beginning of the Middle Ages, glass was probably made on the site where the glass craftsmen were working. Today, however, most artists buy their glass from a specialist glass manufacturer in sheets, approximately two feet by one foot six inches, and store them in racks in the studio.

As the artist chooses the glass, he refers to his original small coloured sketch and to the cartoon, pinned conveniently on the wall. He continually holds pieces of glass against the sky, to see the effect of two or three colours together and to look for interesting variations, streaks and textures. Lifting the large sheets of glass is not easy—thick gloves are essential—and sliding them in and out of the racks is a chore. But the selection of glass is so important that a great deal of time and effort is unstintingly spent amid the dust and chips and splinters.

Often the artist marks particular sheets of glass, chalking out on them the exact area to be used. He will not merely want a colour, but a particular area of a particular sheet, as the glass in other areas is too dark, too light or too streaky, and he feels that only in the one precise spot are the colour and texture exactly as he desires.

He also rummages about in the cullet, or waste glass, and in the boxes and racks of bits and pieces that accumulate, looking for something special. Perhaps he will find a cast glass "jewel" that might light up a robe, or some piece of curious, as the manufacturer's mistakes and oddments are called, for an unusual cloud effect, for example.

Almost any kind of glass can be used in stained-glass windows. Even ordinary commercial glass of various types—frosted, ribbed and embossed, reeded, or ridged, and sanded glass—may be combined to produce a surprisingly varied range of tints and textures. Traditionally, however, the glass used is hand-made antique glass. The great difference between antique glass and ordinary window glass, which is machine-rolled, is in its feel—its variations of thickness and texture. Antique glass is pleasant to handle, the different thicknesses give it a living quality and its texture is crumbly, soft and almost toffee-like in comparison with the sharp, brittle, splintery sheets of machine-made glass.

Different types of glass are classed as antique. The one

The selection of glass for the Noah panel is begun by an apprentice at the Loire studio. Behind him is the black-and-white cartoon, and on the bench in front the templates are laid out beside the coloured sketch. Holding a template for reference, he lifts a piece of muff glass to the light to gauge its colour—a process repeated many times before all the pieces of glass are finally chosen. In the studio, glass is stored upright in racks, left, which have deep shelves for whole sheets and smaller sections for fragments.

HOW STAINED GLASS IS MADE

Most stained glass is hand-made. A blob of molten glass is picked up on the end of a blowpipe. It is blown into a bubble and shaped by rolling. For crown glass, the bubble is rounded and a thickened nub is made. For muff and Norman slab, the bubble is elongated by swinging. The glass is then ready for the next process of manufacture.

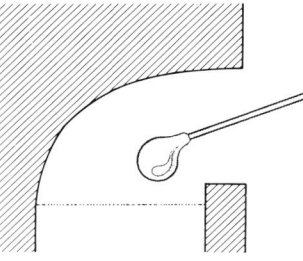
Gathering molten glass

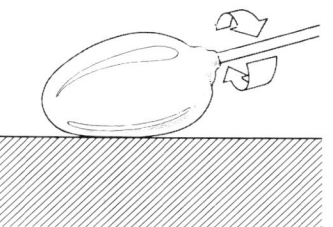
Blowing and rolling

Crown, or spun, glass is rare today, but was widely used in early windows. The round twirling bubble of blown glass is attached at the nub to an iron rod. The blowpipe is cut off, leaving a hole. The rod is spun rapidly and the hole is widened with a stick. The glass flares out to form a disc with a central knob, or bull's-eye.

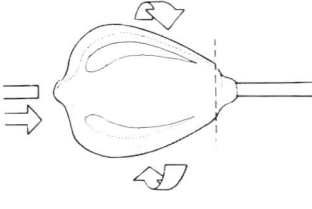
Transferring from pipe to rod

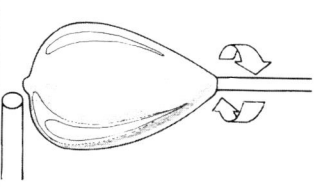
Shaping for crown glass

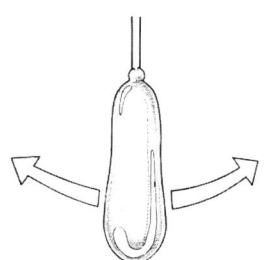
Swinging for muff glass

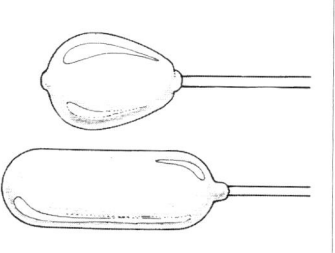
Two shapes of the blown glass

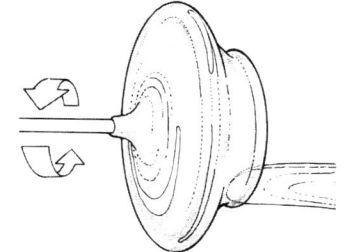
Widening the hole

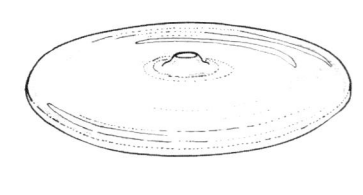
The final disc

The glass is cut to shape either on top of the cutline or around templates. Glass is a material that has to be cut in two stages. First a line is incised, which starts a fracture. This line, or trail, is then deepened either by hand pressure or by tapping, and the glass divides. As glass cannot easily be cut into sharp angles or curves, these are cut in tiny sections, or grozed, that is the edges are slowly nibbled away to produce the required shape, which must be accurate. The final piece of glass must match the pattern exactly.

Medieval cutting tools

The dividing iron cracked the glass with its heated tip.

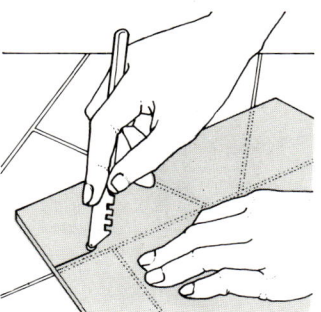
In the cutline method, a steel-wheel cutter is run over the glass on top of the cutline, leaving a thin incised trail.

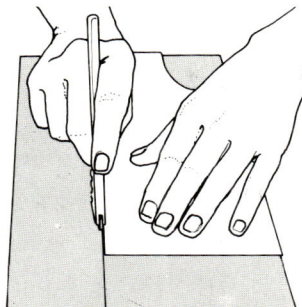
In the template method, the template is placed on the glass and the steel-wheel cutter is run along one side of the pattern.

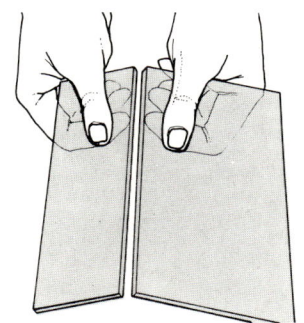
To divide the glass, the thumbs are placed parallel to the trail and pressure is applied. Usually the glass splits.

Grozing irons were used to nibble the glass to shape.

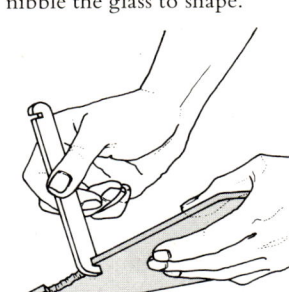
The iron, levered gently on the glass, broke off tiny pieces.

Modern tools

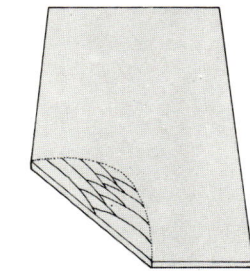
If the glass does not come apart under hand pressure, it is tapped with the glass-cutter and then separates easily.

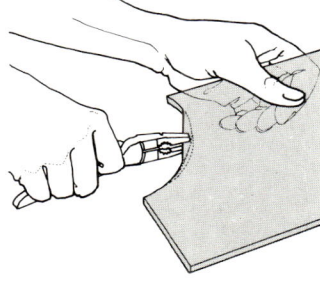
To cut deep curves, first the full curve is outlined with the cutter, and then a series of small incisions is made.

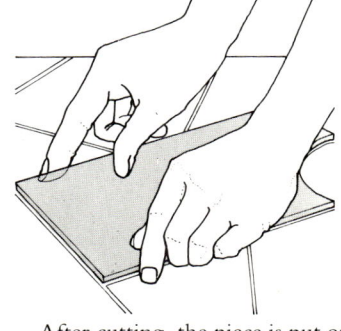
The segments within the curve are either tapped out or are grozed away little by little with special grozing pliers.

After cutting, the piece is put on the cutline or template. If it is too large, it is grozed; if it is too small, it is re-cut.

The diamond cutter, used rarely, cuts straight lines.

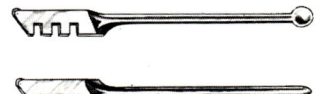
Steel-wheel cutters are the most widely used cutting tools today. Some types have weighted ends for tapping the glass.

Square-ended pliers have replaced the old grozing iron.

most commonly used in stained-glass windows is muff glass, a cylinder of blown glass which is split along its length to form a rectangular sheet. Crown glass, made by an even simpler and possibly earlier method, which results in a disc of glass, is fairly flat, though somewhat variable, and has a bull's-eye, or knob, in the centre. Norman slab, or bottle glass, made by blowing glass into a square-shaped mould, is very irregular in thickness. It can give vivid results, but is extremely difficult to handle. Most manufacturers now make only muff glass and rare pieces of crown or Norman slab are jealously saved for special effects.

Cutting the glass

After the glass has been chosen, it is usually cut to shape by a craftsman. Great skill and experience are required to cut glass correctly and economically. The medieval artist used a hot iron. "Heat in the fire the dividing iron," wrote Theophilus, "which should be thicker at the end. When it glows, apply it to the glass which you wish to divide, and presently the commencement of a small fissure will appear. . . . Being cracked, draw the iron along where you wish to divide the glass and the fissure will follow."

For shaping the cut pieces more precisely, a grozing iron was used. This was a bar of iron, with a slot or hook at either end, which was used to nibble away at the glass until the required outline was made. Consequently, the edges of old glass are usually very uneven.

Today, the main tool for glass cutting is the steel-wheel cutter, an American invention. Diamond cutters are used to cut commercial glass, but are rarely used for stained glass,

Muff, or cylinder, glass, the most commonly used form of stained glass, is made from a long bubble of blown glass. In the United States a removable mould is used to shape the bubble. The top and bottom of the sausage shape are cut off, and the resulting cylinder is split along its sides. In a hot kiln it opens to a flat sheet.

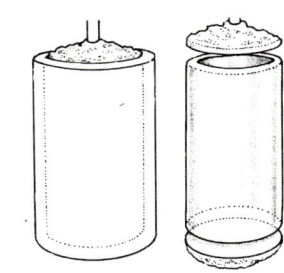
Moulding the glass cylinder

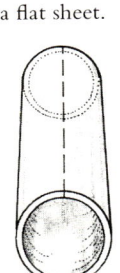
Cutting the cylinder

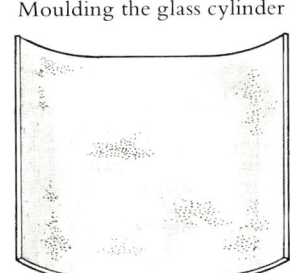
Flattening the cylinder

Norman slab, or bottle glass, a nineteenth-century invention, was made by blowing a long bubble of glass into a rectangular mould. A hollow box shape was left when the mould was removed. The blowpipe end was cracked off and the box divided into five pieces. The glass is uneven, but has a brilliant effect.

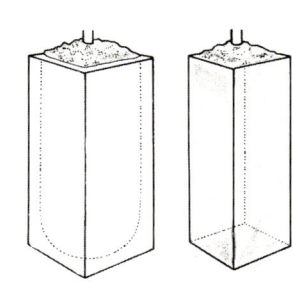
Moulding

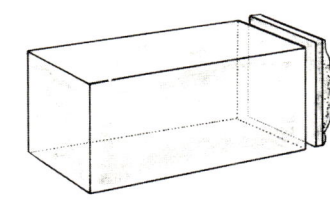
Removing the end

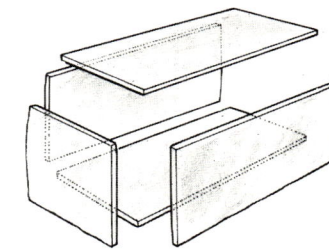
Dividing the sides

DALLE DE VERRE

The thick glass known as slab or *dalle de verre*, which is set in concrete or epoxy resin and used in modern windows, is made by scooping molten glass from the furnace and casting it in moulds. The bottom of the slab always bears the mark of the mould. The slabs are usually an inch deep and a foot long.

Casting the molten glass

Making a Stained-Glass Window

since they are difficult to manoeuvre and are of little use for curves or intricate cutting.

When the continental method of using a template is employed, the glass is put down on a flat surface with the template on top. The glass is then cut around it. This method is advantageous for large windows, since several cutters, each with his own templates, can cut the glass.

In the alternative method, the cutline is placed on the bench, with the glass on top. The glass is then cut directly on the cutline. Sometimes, however, the glass is too dark a colour for the lines of the cutline to be seen clearly. The cutline is then usually transferred to a plate-glass frame or table, with a mirror or a light bulb beneath. The additional light enables the glass to be cut easily. Sometimes a template is made or chalked paper is used to transfer the required shape from cutline to glass sheet.

The medieval method, according to Theophilus, was to place the glass for each piece over the cartoon and trace out the cutting line in wet chalk. "And if", he wrote, "the glass should be so thick that you cannot perceive the lines which are upon the table, taking white glass, draw upon it and when it is dry, place the thick glass upon the white, raising it against the light, and as you look through it, so portray it."

To cut the glass today, the cutter, held almost vertically, is moved over the glass on the required line. It makes a distinctive little purring noise, which indicates that the wheel is biting, and a thin, sparkling line, or trail, appears on the surface of the glass. The surface has been broken through and a vertical fracture begun. If the underside is tapped smartly, a silvery line runs along the trail and the glass comes apart. For a simple straight line, finger pressure is usually sufficient to separate the pieces.

Curves need special consideration. Gentle sweeps can be tapped, but a bite, or deep curve, is nibbled out little by little with steel pliers, although the trail of the main curve of the line is incised first. Sometimes a series of little cuts is made, rather like dividing an orange into segments.

Usually the white, the flesh and other light colours are cut first. As each piece of glass is cut, it is wiped with another piece of glass to blunt the razor-sharp edges.

Aciding

When all the glass has been cut, the artist refers to his drawing and then separates out those pieces which require aciding. Aciding, or etching, is the process of removing the coloured layer, the "flash", from flashed glass, which consists of a layer of white or light-coloured glass with a thinner top layer of a darker colour. An area of this thin upper layer can be removed by aciding to produce a white lion, for example, on a red background. This is particularly useful in heraldry for small or complicated coats of arms. Today, aciding is also used on a larger scale to interpret designs which require subtle variations in colour. Outstanding examples of extensive aciding include windows by the Irish stained-glass artist Harry Clarke and by Marc Chagall.

The medieval artist ground the coloured layer away using powdered stone as an abrasive, a difficult and slow process. Today, hydrofluoric acid is used. Although it is dangerous and must be used carefully, it produces the same effect much more easily.

The process consists of coating the areas of the glass which are not to be acided, including the back and the edges, with a protective layer of beeswax or bitumen paint and then immersing the glass in a bath of dilute acid. For quick results, the glass is placed face upwards in strong acid and the whitish sludge, which forms as the acid eats away the unprotected glass, is carefully scrubbed away. If there is no hurry, the glass is supported, face downwards, on pieces of lead or plastic and left for as long as is necessary in dilute acid.

There is considerable variation in the effect of aciding and the time required to obtain different effects. Some flashes, notably thin red and thin blue, are eaten away in a few minutes, while greens and purples generally need hours. In the final stage of aciding, the glass is washed thoroughly in running water and the wax or bitumen is removed.

As hydrofluoric acid is dangerous, aciding is preferably done well away from the studio in a small open shed with its own water supply and drain. Deep and extensive burns can be caused by careless handling of the acid, but probably the safest method is to use bare hands, continually rinsed and immersed in water, finishing with a careful washing under

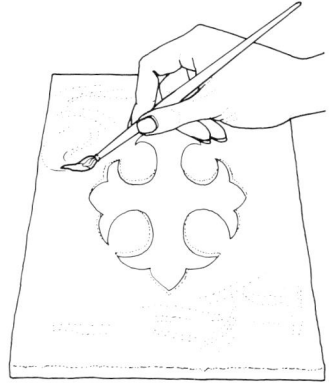

Aciding, the modern way to obtain two colours on one piece of glass, entails using flashed, or double-layered, glass and finely etching away part of the thin flash layer with acid.

To prepare the glass, the area to be removed is first outlined

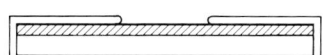

then all other parts of the glass, including back and sides, are coated with bitumen or wax for protection from the acid.

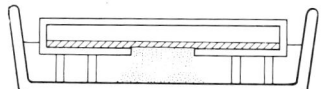

The piece of glass is then immersed in hydrofluoric acid and supported on pieces of lead. The flash side is downwards if the glass is of a type which dissolves slowly.

An alternative method, which is used for glass which reacts quickly, is to put the flash side upwards and to swab the unprotected area with the acid.

When the unprotected flash has been eaten away, the glass is rinsed. The acided area now appears inset and differs in colour from the rest of the glass. Subtle variations in tone and colour can be achieved if the flash layer is only partially removed.

DALLE DE VERRE—CUTTING AND FACETING

Thick *dalle* glass is usually cut around templates which are traced from the cartoon. Steel-wheel cutters mark a line of fracture, and the glass is then broken on an anvil—a steel chisel set in lead or wood—either by hand or by tapping. Although *dalle* is rarely painted, decorative lustre and sparkle may be added by faceting the inside edges. The surface which is dull from the mould usually goes inside the window.

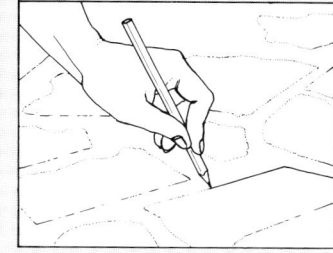

The cutline is traced from the cartoon and then cut out to make templates, or patterns, for cutting the glass.

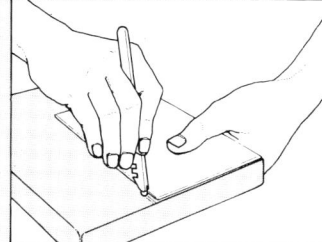

A template is placed on the glass and a steel-wheel cutter is used to incise a line along one side of the template.

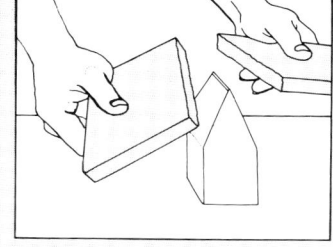

If the glass is lifted and brought down smartly on an anvil at the line of incision, the glass usually splits neatly along the line.

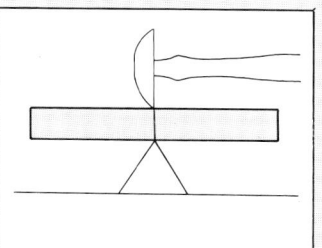

To split the glass, the incision is sometimes placed on the anvil and tapped with one of the many kinds of *dalle* hammer.

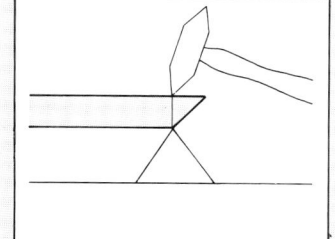

Sometimes a vertical edge is required, and to achieve this the *dalle* is struck lightly, with the hammer held at an angle.

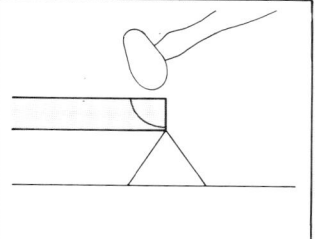

For a faceted effect, the edges of the inside surface of the glass are chipped away with light blows from a *dalle* hammer.

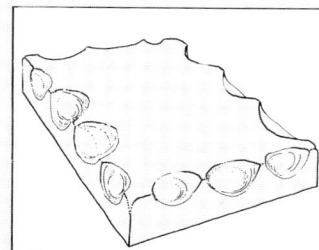

The chips on a faceted slab always enliven and highlight the *dalle* and may be large or small, deep or shallow.

In preparation for painting, after cutting and aciding, the glass is thoroughly cleaned and the pieces for a panel are placed together. Each piece has to be correctly positioned so that paint lines will match across the panel. The pieces are usually laid out and fixed on to a sheet of plate glass in a frame, which is then raised on the easel. Often the pattern of the leads is painted in black on to the back of the plate glass. The lead-lines facilitate painting with the glass against the light, because they cut out unwanted light and indicate the width that the leads will be in the window.

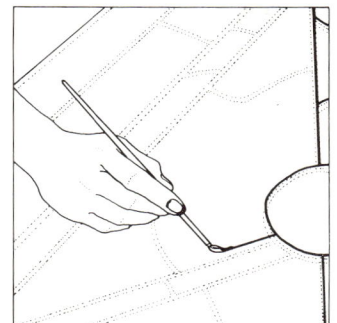
The lead-lines are traced from the reverse of the cutline on to plate glass. They are painted to the same width as the flanges of the final leads.

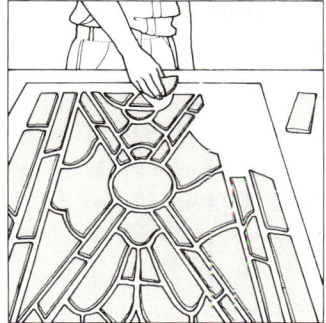
The plate glass is turned over, and the pieces of glass for the panel are cleaned and placed meticulously in position, with their inside surface upwards.

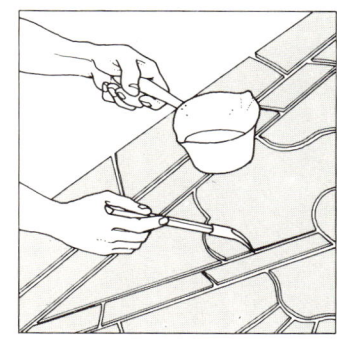
Hot, melted beeswax is dripped between the pieces of glass. As the wax cools, it solidifies and attaches, or "waxes", the pieces firmly to the plate glass.

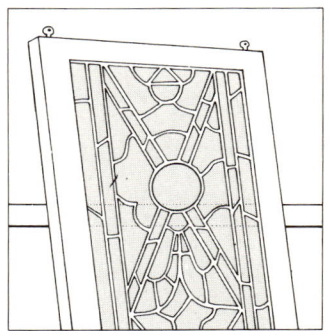
The plate glass and stained glass are hoisted on to the easel. The colour effect against the light can now be judged, and any discordant pieces are changed.

running water. Since the fumes, too, are harmful, an extractor fan is essential if aciding is done indoors.

Lead-lining

The next step is to attach the newly cut and acided pieces of glass to the easel, ready for painting. The easel has a plate-glass frame, on the back of which lead-lines are painted. They are usually traced from the cutline, or from the cartoon, using black powder colouring mixed with gum arabic and water. The object of painting these lines is to get as correct an impression as possible of the final window for, without lead-lines, so much white light comes through between the coloured pieces that it is often impossible to judge tonal qualities and overall effect.

Beside the lead-lines, an edging of black, at least two inches wide, is made all round the panel. The cusping of the head—the tracery—is also painted in.

In lead-lining, as with all the stages of making a window, different artists follow different procedures. Some artists paint the lead-lines on the plate glass at the cutline stage. Other artists, especially when working on small panels, do not use lead-lines at all. Others follow an earlier tradition and lead up the glass immediately it is cut, using light lead,

soldered only on one side. When painting is finished, they dismantle the glass and melt the lead for reuse.

After the lead-lines have been painted, the plate glass is turned over and the pieces of stained glass are laid out flat on the unpainted side. Before each piece is put down, it is cleaned to remove any grease, dirt or chalk marks.

The best and most accurate way of fixing the pieces of glass to the easel is with melted beeswax. The wax must be very hot or the glass will not stick. The hot wax is spooned or dribbled between the pieces of stained glass and the plate glass. It solidifies quickly and is an excellent adhesive. Some artists, however, prefer Plasticine, or modelling clay, to beeswax, although it is liable to soften in hot weather. Small blobs are fixed to the corners of the pieces of glass and each piece is then pressed firmly into place. Modelling clay is also useful when a few pieces of glass have to be changed.

After a panel has been waxed in pieces to the plate-glass, it is set up on the easel against the sky so that the artist can see the effects of changing daylight on the glass. He studies the colour effects, checking if necessary against his sketch, to see if the window in embryo has substance as a scheme of colour and tone. Any discordant pieces are taken out and new pieces cut and inserted. Then painting begins.

Glass-painting techniques are many and various, but the main aim is almost always to control and modify the light coming through the window. Unpainted, the glass often presents a confusing glare of light and colour. The paint used is brown vitreous enamel and, for many painting effects, it is applied with a flat brush as an initial, even wash of paint. This wash can then be varied or broken up. While still wet, it can be gently brushed or whipped with the long-haired badger to make a dull matt. It can be stabbed with a badger or with a stippling brush to make a stippled matt. The dry shaded wash can be further lightened with short-bristled scrubs. Delicate details are often traced from a cartoon with a fine liner brush. For broader lines and spatter effects, soft and Chinese brushes are used. Most important, among numerous other techniques, is removing or "picking out" the paint, usually with needles or sticks, to allow the light to penetrate as white areas, which stand out against the background of dark paint.

Badgered matt / Stippled matt

Scrub shading / Traced line

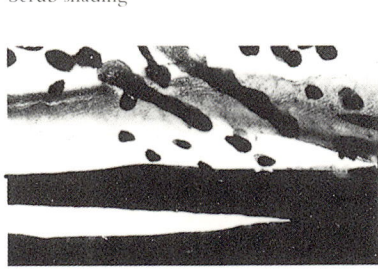
Soft lines and spattering

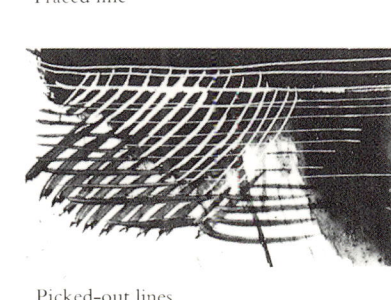
Picked-out lines

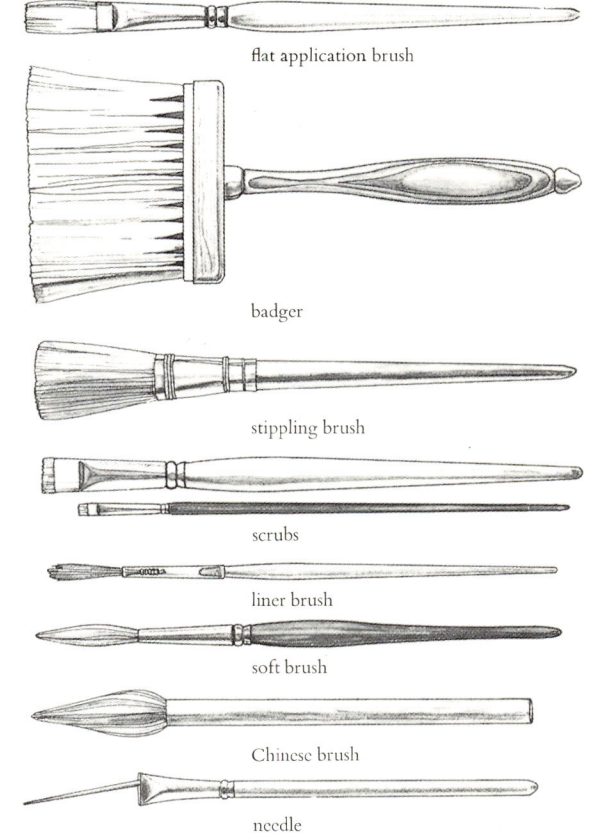
flat application brush / badger / stippling brush / scrubs / liner brush / soft brush / Chinese brush / needle

183

Making a Stained-Glass Window

The first stage in painting is to trace the main outlines with the glass laid flat. To avoid smudging, the painter rests his hand on a wooden bridge. At the end of this stage, the final form of the Noah panel, right, has been defined. Most of the areas and lines that appear black in the photograph have been painted. In the Loire studio, no lead-lining is done and light penetrates between the pieces of stained glass.

Painting against the light is the next stage. The glass is set vertically on the easel and a wash of paint is applied. This is badgered or stippled, details are picked out with sticks or scrubs and more paint is added. The ox and the ass, which were at first just outlined by a heavy wash, exemplify the fine changes achieved in the painting. They are, however, only a tiny part of the completely painted Noah panel, right.

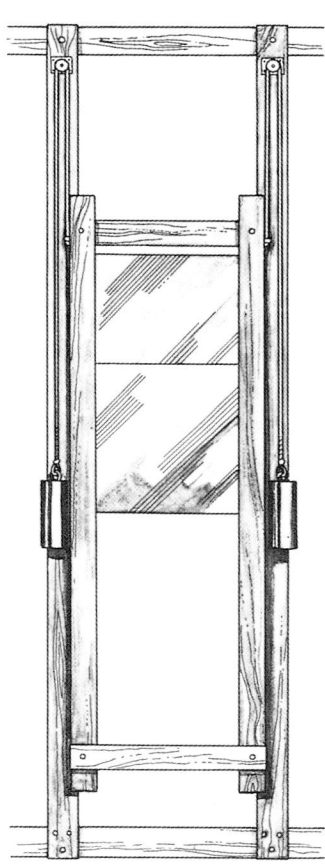

The traditional easel extends from floor to ceiling. The frame holding the plate glass, on to which the stained glass is fixed, is suspended on ropes over pulleys. Counterweights make it easy to raise and lower. Often the uprights are on rails and are held there by removable screws so the easel can be slid sideways.

Painting

In stained glass, all the colours are in the glass itself and no colour, with the exception of silver stain, is actually applied in the painting. The only paint used is a dark-brown vitreous enamel, and it is used for shading and for linework—folds of garments, for example, details of heads and hands and lettering—and in washes, or thin coats of paint, which tone the colour of the glass. The effects possible with the glass paint range from a heavy line, such as was used in the twelfth century, to the subtle modelling typical of fifteenth-century faces and details, to today's free brushwork and textures, which have been adapted from modern painting.

The paint is basically finely ground iron oxide and powdered glass, mixed with borax as a flux. When heated in the kiln, it fuses with the surface of the glass. Although the paint is supplied in a powdered form, it is ground further to suit the artist and is then mixed with water and a little gum arabic to make it adhere to the glass. A muller, a kind of pestle, or a palette-knife is used for grinding the paint and a piece of plate glass is used as a palette.

To paint the glass, a variety of brushes is used—long, fine brushes for traced linework, shorter, flat brushes for washes and Chinese or watercolour brushes for soft, variable lines. But the most important brush of all is the badger. A wide, soft brush with hairs three or four inches long, it is used to smooth a wash of paint to a matt—a muted, even finish. Only the lightest and gentlest of movements is used, so the badger never gets wet, except at the very tip. The badger is also used for stippling, when it is handled with a stabbing motion to create minute dots on a drying wash. In the technique known as whipping, the badger is fanned lightly over a drying matt, barely touching, so that the paint is dragged into small black spots on a clear ground.

In stained glass, the artist is concerned primarily with the light coming through the window and the application of paint is not in itself an end, since it is the light, not the paint, that creates the major effect. Removing paint to allow light to penetrate is, therefore, an important aspect of painting and for this every artist has his own collection of needles and sticks—sharpened brush handles, for example, and pieces of bone or horn—and scrubs, which are usually old oil-paint brushes.

The paint can be modified by many other devices in addition to brushes, sticks and scrubs. Rolled-up paper, cloths of various weaves and corrugated card produce interesting textures. Wax or grease can be spread on areas of the glass before painting so that the water-based paint rolls off. Tape or adhesive paper can be used as a mask. Paint can be splattered or dripped or flicked at the glass to create particular effects. And the finger can produce subtle results. Lightly rubbed over a general matt, it enhances the natural surface textures and brings the glass to life.

Many artists prefer to begin painting with the glass laid flat on top of the cartoon. The artist rests his arm on a wooden rest, or bridge. When the glass is in a vertical position, a soft-tipped mahl-stick, from the German for painter's stick, is used. Both these simple devices keep the artist's hand away from the glass surface and also give his hand firm support.

The main linework is usually traced from the drawing beneath. Instead of water, a dilute solution of acetic acid is used as the medium, the advantage being that, when dry, the acid line is resistant to water. The next stage of painting, the shading and toning, can then be done on top of the acid paint and the two paints fired simultaneously.

Early glass was painted flat. There were no plate-glass easels to enable the artist to judge his work in its entirety while he was painting it. At most he would have been able to hold up only two or three pieces together against the sky. Today, however, once the main lines are traced, the glass is usually raised on a plate-glass easel, and then the most skilled work is done—toning, shading and subtle effects.

Silver stain

The next stage, after most of the painting has been done, is usually the application of silver, or yellow, stain. In this process, a silver compound—generally silver nitrate—is painted on to the outer surface of white glass. When it is fired, the silver reacts with the substance of the glass to give a transparent yellow colour, varying from pale lemon to deep orange, depending on the glass, the amount of stain and the firing. Introduced about 1300, silver stain enabled the medieval artist to paint heads with crowns, mitres and haloes all on one piece of glass, to paint gold charges on coats of arms, and to add touches of yellow to canopies, vestments and ornaments. On coloured glass, silver stain gives interesting results. Often the little landscapes in the backgrounds were painted on pale blue glass, stain being used for the grass and trees. Today stain, like aciding, is widely and freely used in contemporary abstract designs.

Stain is mixed with gum and water in the same way as brown glass paint. A glass muller is used to grind it, how-

ever, since its chemicals corrode metal. For the same reason, most artists keep special brushes for stain. Generally, silver stain is painted on the outside surface of the glass because, unlike paint, it is not affected by weather.

Firing

After the glass has been painted, it is fired in a kiln. Firing is the process of heating the painted glass so that the paint and glass are smoothly and securely fused together. Properly fired, today's painting will last, like the work of the medieval masters, for hundreds of years, but much depends on the skill and experience of the craftsman who operates the kiln.

For proper firing, the glass must be gradually heated to about 1250 degrees Fahrenheit and kept at this temperature for up to fifteen minutes, depending upon the type and thickness of the glass. It is then slowly annealed, or cooled.

At firing temperature, the glass, viewed through the spy-hole in the kiln door, looks dull red and has a slight surface gloss against which the paint appears a little less shiny. Establishing the exact moment when the glass and the paint have united is of prime importance. If the temperature in the kiln is raised too high or if the tray is heated for too long, the glass will begin to distort and then to melt—a disaster. The skilled kiln man, however, usually judges the moment by eye rather than by using a pyrometer.

Early kilns were made of clay built up on a frame of iron rods. They were fired with wood, preferably beech, which gives a clear, hot flame. Modern kilns use gas or electricity. There are two methods of firing. In one method, similar to that used in medieval days, the kiln is loaded while cold, the heat is increased to firing temperature, then gradually the kiln and glass are allowed to cool. A more economical method is continuous firing. The glass is preheated in a chamber in one part of the kiln, fired in the main kiln and then annealed in a cooling chamber. With this method more firing can be done at one session, but constant attention is necessary. In particular, great care must be taken to avoid cold draughts of air reaching the hot glass. Any sudden change of temperature may cause the glass to fly, that is, to crack, or even shatter.

For firing, the glass is laid out in iron trays, each with a layer of powdered plaster of Paris carefully smoothed to provide a level surface for the glass. Moisture or air beneath the glass can have damaging effects, so the plaster is thoroughly dried and tamped down solidly.

Ideally, different kinds of glass are fired separately. All hard glass—greens, blues and tints—are put in one tray and all soft glass—whites and yellows—in another, so that the firing can be suitably adjusted. Similarly, a strong fire is used for dark linework, while a shorter and less hot fire is better for matt or shading.

Glass paint loses some of its body when fired and, consequently, most glass needs some repainting and a subsequent refiring to achieve the full effect which the artist visualized. The more often glass is fired, however, the more brittle and liable to fly it becomes. Heads, hands and inscriptions, where there is much delicate work, often require several firings and become particularly fragile.

The heat of the kiln can also alter the colour of some glasses. Rubies, for example, may darken to almost black, although another firing will usually restore the original red. Repeated or strong firings can intensify silver stain. As stain is usually put on the outside of the glass, it can be fired simultaneously with the last application of paint. Preferably, however, it is fired alone. It requires the shortest firing of all.

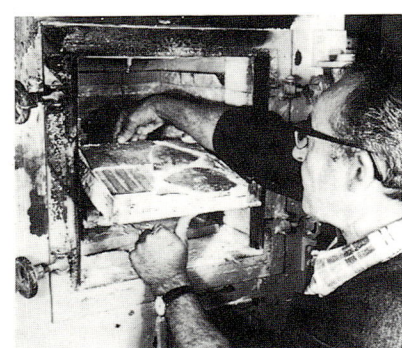

In readiness for firing, the pieces of glass are dismantled from the easel after painting and laid on powdered plaster of Paris in iron trays. Types of glass which need the same firing go together. At the Loire studio a one-chamber kiln is used. It is loaded with trays of glass, slowly heated to firing point, about 1250°F, and then cooled. As the paint lightens unpredictably in the heat, a piece of glass frequently needs to be repainted and then refired. Sometimes several repaintings and refirings are required.

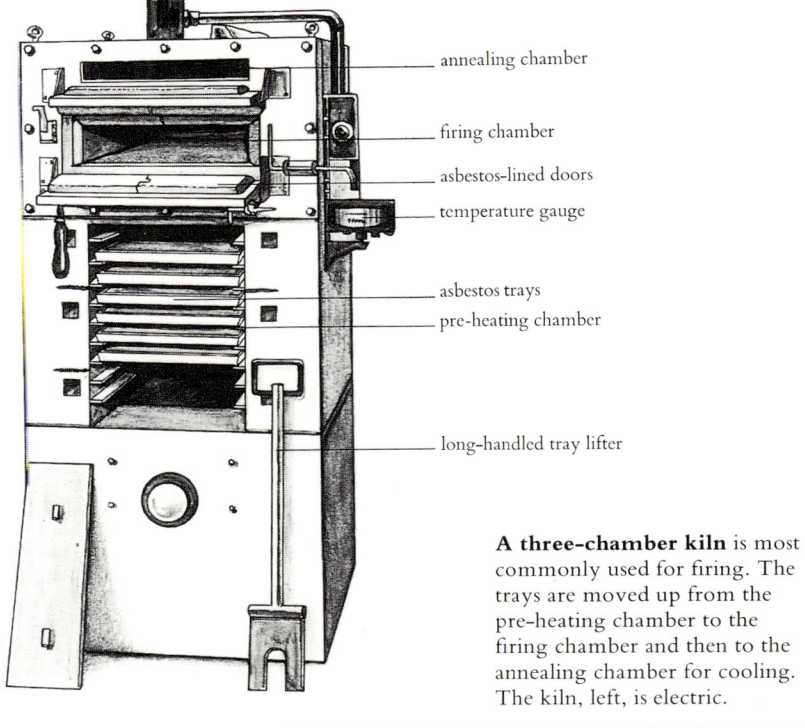

A three-chamber kiln is most commonly used for firing. The trays are moved up from the pre-heating chamber to the firing chamber and then to the annealing chamber for cooling. The kiln, left, is electric.

Making a Stained-Glass Window

Leading-up is the assembly of the glass into leads and is done on a wooden bench with the cutline or templates for guidance. Great skill is needed to lead an intricate area, such as the rainbow of the Noah panel, shown here. First a wooden right-angled frame is fixed to the bench to hold firm the side leads of the panel. A lead is then stretched, cut and put in place. Glass is inserted and more leads added. Nails hold everything tightly in position.

Once in place, the soft strips of lead are cut to the exact length with a special knife.

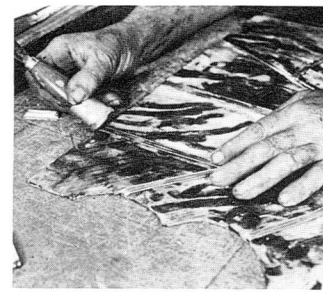

The lead is tapped with the handle of a stopping knife to fit it to the glass.

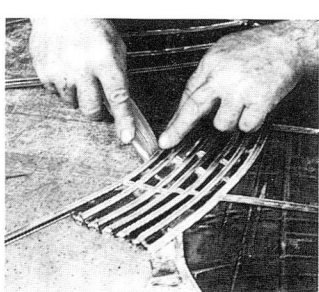

To open and smooth the lead, a lathekin is run along the sides of the flanges.

The piece of glass is pushed into the flanges until it touches the core of the lead.

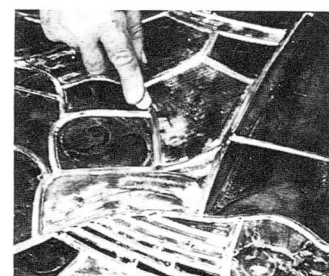

Before soldering, the joints between the leads are pressed together, cleaned and tallowed.

Leads vary in shape and depth, but their core is almost always one-sixteenth of an inch wide. The tops can be round, flat or filleted. Panel leads have wide flanges. Deep and eccentric leads (leads with one wide side) are only two of many other types. Round leads are most common.

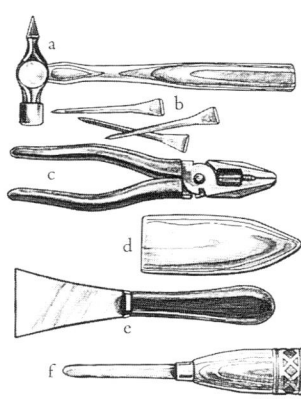

Leading tools include a light hammer (a), which nails the frame into place. Farriers' nails (b) hold the lead and glass in position and are easily moved as new pieces are inserted. Pliers (c) stretch the lead. The lathekin (d), a bone or wood tool made by each craftsman for himself, opens and shapes the lead. The cutting knife (e) is a shortened putty knife. The stopping knife (f) is an oyster knife with a weighted handle which taps the glass into the lead and hammers the farriers' nails into the bench.

Leading-up

Each panel of a stained-glass window is a construction of pieces of glass held together by lead strips and cement. The assembly work, which is done after the glass has been fired, is carried out by the artist himself or, more usually, by craftsmen who retain the traditional title of glaziers.

First, the pieces of glass are laid out in their order. They are then fitted systematically into malleable lead strips, which are worked and pressed around every piece. Viewed in cross-section, a lead strip looks like a sideways H and the glazier inserts a piece of glass into both sides of the lead so that each piece just touches the centre. This central core is the width of the line allowed on the cutline—almost always one-sixteenth of an inch. The flanges of the lead vary, however, from flat to round, from an eighth of an inch to one inch in width.

Lead is used because it is a relatively cheap material which is easily worked and is resistant to weather and temperature. The combination of leading and iron bars provides the adaptability needed for the intricate shapes of glass, plus the strength to withstand considerable pressures of wind and rain. Occasionally, for extra strength, the leads are made with centre cores of steel.

In medieval days the leads were cast on the spot. The craftsmen poured hot metal into boxes lined with reeds, called calmes, and that name is still used for a length of lead. Today some studios still make their own leads, but most buy them from metal-founders. Modern leads are cast in iron moulds and shaped by a lead mill.

According to Theophilus, the medieval glaziers began leading in the centre of the panel, perhaps with the head of the main figure, then progressed outwards. Today, however, the usual practice is to begin with one of the lower corners. First, two lengths of wood are nailed down to a wooden bench to form a right angle. Then the first long strips of lead are stretched to remove twists. Now straight and taut, they are cut to size with a sharp, chisel-like knife and laid in place to form the outer frame of the base and the side of the panel.

With the cutline or templates for guidance, the first

The leads are soldered to make a permanent join at the places where two strips of lead meet. The joints are first tapped down, cleaned and rubbed with tallow, which acts as a flux. A stick of blowpipe solder is then applied to the joint and a blob is melted into place with a hot, copper-tipped soldering iron. When all the joints have been soldered on one side, the panel is turned very carefully, right, and the process repeated for the other side.

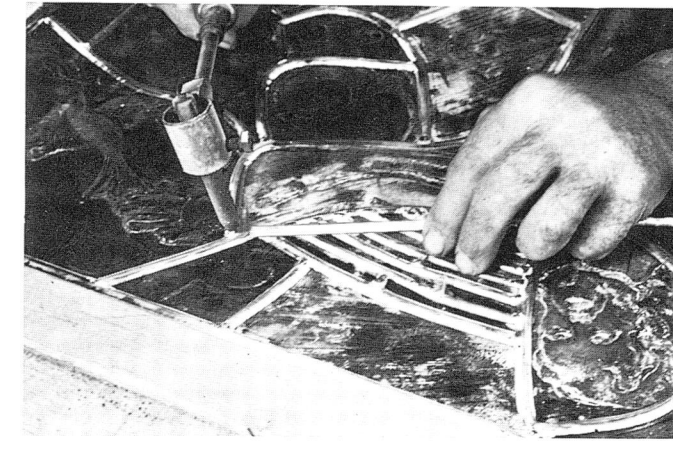

piece of glass is put into the corner and tapped into place with a stopping knife, the handle of which is weighted with lead. A strip of lead is cut to fit around the glass. This strip is bent into place and held with a few nails—usually square-section, thick-headed farriers' nails, which are easy to handle and do not mark the lead. Adjacent pieces of glass are set into their positions and more leads are cut and pressed into place. The process continues until the panel is completed.

Each joint is then cleaned, rubbed with tallow or resin as a flux, and soldered, usually with the traditional, clumsy-seeming but actually highly efficient gas soldering iron. Both sides of the joints must be soldered and the panel is turned over carefully, with a board as support, so that no glass cracks.

Other tools for leading include pliers, pincers, rule and square and the traditional lathekin—a sharpened piece of wood or bone which each craftsman makes for himself, shaped to his own hand. The lathekin is used to smooth and open out the flange of the lead before the glass is inserted.

If, by careless cutting, all the glass has been made just a little too wide, the panel risks being full, or overlarge, when finished. In leading-up, the glazier can adjust this by grozing each piece so that the cutline is matched exactly—a delicate task since the glass is fired and fragile. If, on the other hand, the glass has been cut allowing too much for the heart of the lead, the panel will be slack, or slightly too small. To correct this, slips and strips of lead are packed in to take up the extra space—an exercise in patience and measurement.

Occasionally, to modify the colour, a piece of glass is doubled, or plated, with another piece cut to the same size and shape. In this case a double-thickness lead is used to accommodate the two layers, or the top piece is separately leaded and then soldered all around into position.

Cementing

After all the soldering is completed, the next step is cementing. The cementing process and its materials are messy and most studios carry out the job in a separate room or in a shed where good ventilation helps drying.

The dark grey cement fills the spaces between lead and glass, prevents the glass from rattling and makes the whole panel waterproof. It also adds strength and rigidity. Cementing has an artistic value, too: It seems to solidify the lead-lines, merging them with the blacks of the paint lines and uniting them with the rest of the window. The type of finish given to the cementing can also affect the window's final artistic statement.

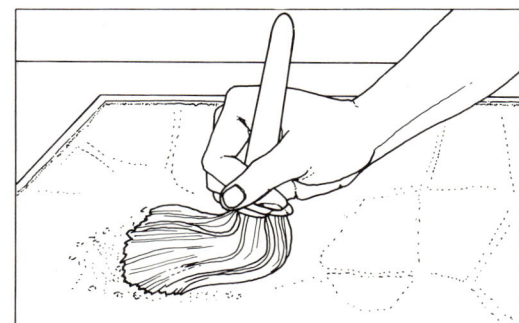

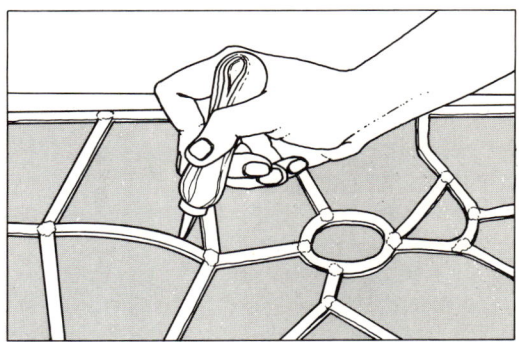

Cement is used to fill the space between the glass and the leads. After being coloured a dark grey and mixed to a porridge-like consistency, it is poured on to the panel, top left. It is then worked into every crack with a stiff brush, top right. The surplus cement on the panel is soaked up with sawdust and easily brushes off, bottom left. Finally, while the cement is still soft, the leads are cleaned.

The cement is a mixture of powdered whitening and plaster of Paris to which is added a little red lead, some lampblack, white spirit and boiled linseed oil. It is like porridge in consistency. A scrubbing-brush is used to push the mixture into the crevices between the lead and the glass so that every corner and crack is filled, first on one side of the panel and then on the other. Finally, sawdust is spread over the panel to soak up the excess cement, which is then easily brushed off, and the glass is cleaned. If a sharp edge is required, the leads are scraped with a stick when the cement is almost dry. Sometimes, however, the slightly uneven brushed finish is left, giving a softer quality to the lines.

The ordinary cementing method will not do for pieces of glass which have been plated, since the semi-liquid cement will run in between the two layers of glass and ruin the effect. In such cases, putty, coloured with lampblack, is carefully forced by hand in around the leads so that all gaps are well filled. After several hours, when the puttied areas have set, cement is used in the usual way on the rest of the panel, which is then ready for banding.

DALLE DE VERRE—CASTING THE PANEL

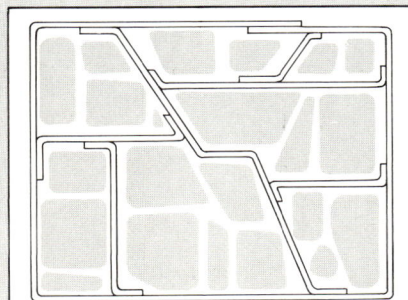

Thoroughly cleaned, the *dalle* is laid out on a specially prepared base, left. A detachable frame is put round the panel to form a mould for the concrete or epoxy resin. Concrete needs to be reinforced and metal braces are embedded between the pieces of *dalle*, above. To ensure that every space is filled and that the concrete beds down, the panel is usually vibrated.

Epoxy resin, stronger and lighter than concrete, requires no braces, nor is the panel vibrated. Poured between the glass, it levels itself out. Both concrete and resin can be coloured.

Concrete and epoxy resin both take three or four days to cure thoroughly. While the epoxy resin is still tacky, it is usually dusted with sand or metallic powder to achieve a textured finish.

Making a Stained-Glass Window

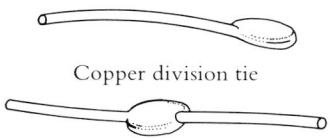

Copper division tie

Tie for the middle of a panel

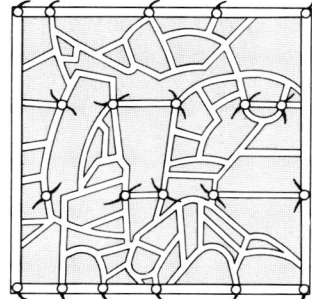

Division ties are soldered to the panel at the edges. Other copper ties go on lead joints at places where bars will cross.

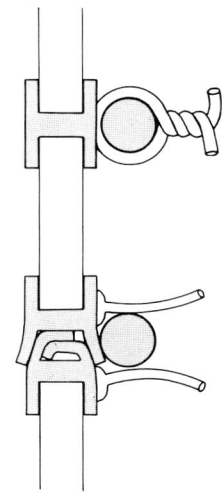

In the window, the ties are twisted around the bars. Where panels meet, the lower lead may be folded and overlapped.

In France, T-bar armatures are used between panels. On the outside of the Loire window, they appear as metal frames between the panels.

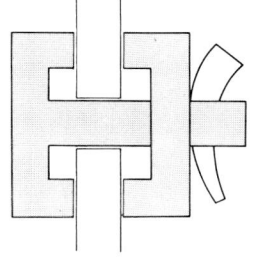

In the French T-bar armature, panels rest on the centre of the sideways T and are held firm by another frame and a key.

The first panel is eased into place once the aperture and the grooves have been cleared of old glass and cement. As the lowest of the main panels of the Loire window, the Noah panel is inserted first. Viewed from above, a panel is pushed deep into the groove on one side of the aperture, right (a). Then the other side is fitted in (b). The panel is then centred so that both sides are held by the stonework (c). If necessary, the grooves are gouged deeper to accommodate the panels and, to ease in the intricate tracery at the head of a window, for example, the flanges of the edge leads can be folded back.

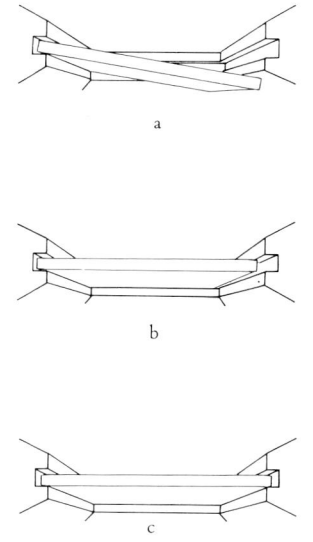

Banding

In a large building, stained-glass windows have many similarities to the rigging and sails of a schooner. Like rigging, the windows in a cathedral hum and vibrate under pressure from the wind, and they are held in place by ties against the iron glazing bars that cross the window in much the same way as ropes fixed the sails to the spars of a ship.

Soldering the ties to the leads, or banding, is the last process in the studio. The ties are made of copper wire and each panel has two types. On the edge of the panel, the so-called division ties are soldered at one end and paired with ties on another panel. Later, when the window is installed, both ties are twisted together around the division bar, the glazing bar which crosses the aperture where two panels meet. In the middle of the panel, ties are soldered at their centre and their ends are wrapped around another supportive bar. For each bar of about one and a half feet in length there are probably three or four ties.

Before the cartoon was drawn, note was made of the position of the bars and exactly where on the leading the ties were to be soldered. Now these places are carefully cleaned of cement and rubbed with tallow. The thin strips of copper wire are cut to suitable lengths, usually about four or five inches, and their centres or ends are cleaned and encased in solder. They are then soldered to junctions in the leading. After ties have been attached to all the panels, the window is ready for installation. In its component panels it will be carefully transported to the building.

Fixing

When the aperture was first measured, notes were made about the stonework, the bars and the position of the window, to aid installation. Although the artist may install the window himself, there are specialized firms which undertake the work and most large studios have their own fixers. It is often necessary to erect scaffolding and to clear away old or temporary glazing from the aperture.

If there are glazing bars in the aperture which can be reused, they are cleaned and repainted. If new bars are to be inserted, their positions are first carefully measured and holes chiselled for them. The bars are usually on the inside so that they will not corrode and will adequately support the window against the wind. New inside bars are substituted for outside bars if it is at all possible.

The stonework into which the window fits has either

DALLE DE VERRE—THE FINISHED WINDOW

The *dalle* window set in epoxy resin, designed by John Lawson of Goddard and Gibbs, was installed in the Church of the Ascension, Birmingham, England, in 1973. Its thirty-six panels are set into the masonry in steel frames, but usually *dalle* windows are supported on bronze or copper rods. As in all *dalle* windows, the glass is flush on the outside for weather resistance, and inside it projects slightly from its setting, thus intensifying the effect of the faceting. In character, resin-set *dalle* is very different from that set in concrete. Divisions between the glass, for example, can be narrower—as thin as one-eighth of an inch—making for a freer, lighter style. Increasingly, epoxy is replacing concrete and *dalle* is being used in screens and for other features of modern interior decoration.

grooves or rebates, L-shaped channels. They must be carefully cleaned out and measured to ensure that the panels can be slid into place, one by one. For windows with grooves, one side of a panel is inserted deeply, the panel is then straightened and the other side is eased into position. If the panel is slightly too wide, it is possible to spring it into place by gentle and slight bending. This is difficult, however, and can result in breaking the glass, so it is preferable to deepen one side of the groove. There are fewer problems with rebates, as the panel can be pushed in straight, like placing a picture in a frame.

Although procedure varies in installing new glass, often the most difficult portion, the tracery, is inserted first, then the rest of the panels, starting at the base of the aperture. The edge leads of upper panels have to be fitted over the lower panels so that rain-water and condensation can run down and away. The ties are wrapped loosely around their bar, and when all the panels are finally in position, they are securely tightened.

An alternative system of fixing is commonly used in France. The edges of the panels do not overlap, but instead, iron T-bar frames are used and the panels rest on the centre stroke of the sideways T. They are then held firmly vertical either with putty or mastic or by another frame fitting over the bottom of the T. To give extra rigidity, free-floating bars are tied across the panels. Similar iron or bronze T-bar frames with bars embedded in the stonework are used throughout the world for very large windows.

The final step is always cementing the window into place so that it is firm and weatherproof. Ordinary cement or mastic is used. Finally, the window is carefully cleaned. Barring war, accidents or acts of God, the window will remain intact for at least the next one hundred years.

When the window is installed, the artist will certainly want to look at his work in place. Only from the interior of the actual building can he judge whether the idea which he conceived when he first viewed the aperture has been successfully realized in the glass, stain, paint, iron and leadwork of the finished window. It is only as daylight streams through the panels and plays on the infinite variety of texture and tone, the streaks and striations, the facets, bubbles and layers, the full strength of rich colour or the delicacy of tint and pastel, that the window comes to life. Glowing and iridescent, it then makes its statement as a finished work of art.

Gabriel Loire's complete Old Testament window in place at Coignières Church, near Versailles, France.

COLLAGES OF GLASS

Glass appliqué and fused glass are becoming increasingly popular both for ecclesiastical and secular use. In glass appliqué, designs are prepared, glass is shaped, cleaned meticulously and then bonded as a collage on a plate-glass backing. All kinds of glass can be included, layered one on top of another. Epoxy resin is the bonding material. Most effective when it is lighted from behind, glass appliqué is often used for screens or room dividers. It is, of course, also used for windows. For fused glass, a collage is also made with shaped pieces of glass, but instead of being bonded with resin, the glass is fused by intense heat. Only certain kinds of glass are suitable. Although the effects can be rich, the panels are usually small scale. They are often hung, back-lit, as pictures.

The glass appliqué screen, right, made in 1975 for a London home by Goddard and Gibbs, has unusual rounded outlines. This effect was achieved by using coloured glues and by encircling some shapes, above, with a dark, epoxy-resin mixture.

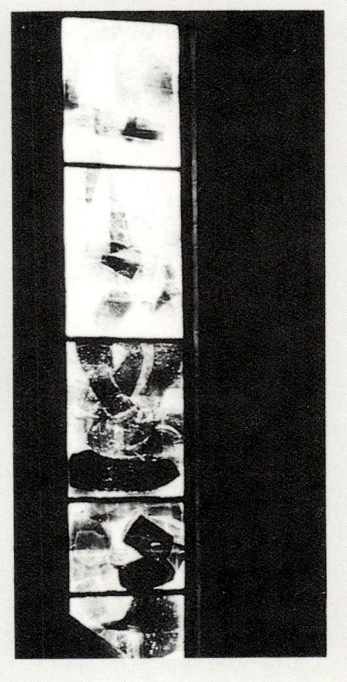

Fused glass is jewel-like when seen close up, above. An interesting innovation in the modern Church of St Andrew at Cuffley, Hertfordshire, is a series of slit windows set with fused glass, designed by Alfred Fisher of Chapel Studio, another British firm.

Restoring a Stained-Glass Window

Old stained glass shows its age. Centuries of storms, frosts and sun, as well as ancient religious conflicts and recent wars, have left their scars. The extent of the decay, however, depends primarily on the composition of the glass and on the humidity both inside and outside the building.

Glass acquires a protective skin in its manufacture and annealing, but once this skin is penetrated, disintegration begins. Moisture makes the primary assault, dissolving constituents of glass, such as soda and potash, eventually forming an alkaline solution which attacks the structure of the glass. If this alkaline liquid is washed away, by rain, for example, there is little effect, but a permanent thin film of water-condensation is deadly, for the alkalinity builds up and eats into the glass.

The decomposition shows as tiny pits in which the separated chemical components of the glass collect as an opaque white deposit. On some windows the deposit is hard, on others it is soft and powdery. In time the pits deepen and may eventually merge together to make actual holes. Certain gases in the air also react with the solution to cause further disintegration on the surface of the glass. Accumulated layers of soot and dust obscure the light. On painted glass, the paint lines may form ridges as the surrounding glass is eaten away; or the reverse may happen and the paint may prove less durable and form furrows in the glass.

Violent gusts of wind may bend or break whole panels, and fires, accidental blows, a bird that flies against a pane, as well as stones deliberately aimed, also take their toll.

The interior surface of glass is at risk, too. Dust from walls and floor, and, in a church, carbon from candles and stoves, build up into a deposit—thicker in the higher parts of the building—which dims the glass and attacks the paint.

Stained glass has suffered particularly at times of religious change. In England during the Reformation an edict of 1547 commanded, "Take away, utterly extinct and destroy all . . . paintings, and all other monuments of feigned miracles . . . and superstition . . . in walls, glass windows. . . ." Later, in the seventeenth century, the official Parliamentary iconoclast, William Dowsing, went about East Anglia "like a Bedlam, beating down all the painted glass, not only in the chapels, but, contrary to order, in the public schools, college halls, libraries and chambers". According to his diary, on one day alone, he "brake down ten mighty great Angels in glass, in all eighty".

It would be wrong, however, to blame such men for the destruction of all the medieval windows that have been lost. The idea of preservation for aesthetic reasons is quite modern. Until relatively recently, the rich donor, prelate or merchant preferred the latest and most fashionable style, and no precepts of conservation urged against destroying

The oldest windows in the world, the eleventh-century prophet windows in Augsburg Cathedral, have deteriorated very rapidly in modern times. This is evident when comparing the left-hand photograph of the Daniel window, taken in 1943, with the one to its right taken in 1973. Similarly, many other ancient European windows have decayed more in this century than in all previous centuries together. The exact chemical reasons for this are still a mystery. Damp storage conditions when windows were removed during the Second World War, the polluted modern atmosphere and injudicious restorations with untested new materials have all been blamed.

ancient stained glass. Old work was retained only for its dynastic or religious significance or for economic reasons. The tomb of an ancestor, a window in which a forebear was represented, or a statue, venerated for miraculous powers, would be spared; otherwise contemporary work would often be substituted.

At York, for example, when the great Norman church was pulled down and rebuilt between 1220 and 1472, only part of the superb twelfth-century glass was kept. Similarly, much ancient glass at New College, Oxford, was cleared out in the eighteenth century to make room for the glazing of Sir Joshua Reynolds. The architect James Wyatt, who restored Salisbury Cathedral in 1789, threw out the greater part of the old glass "by the cartload" and it was shovelled into the city ditch after being beaten to pieces to obtain the valuable lead.

The Romantic literature of the nineteenth century and the writings of Ruskin and Morris influenced attitudes to the art of the past. The "monuments of superstition" gradually became "treasures of our artistic heritage". But the first attempts at restoration were almost as bad as destruction. Much of Canterbury's old glass, for example, was just copied and the original pieces were discarded.

Modern restoration
A great advance, however, took place with the appreciation of the original glass. Treated at last with care and consideration, it was releaded, cracks were mended with thin strips of lead, known as string-leads, holes were patched, heads and fragile areas were plated, or covered with pieces of protective glass. Rearrangement made sense of some of the iconography in windows that had been inaccurately restored. At last it was realized that here were irreplaceable treasures that should be cared for.

In its original state, however, it is likely that most early glass would now seem garish and unpleasing. Although frequently destructive, the effects of time and weather have often contributed charm and beauty to ancient glass. A jumbled window of old glass glows with colour and life which can be lost in meticulous restoration. A conflict arises, therefore, between the aim of restoring glass to its original clarity and the desire to preserve it as it is with its acquired qualities of age. The solution to this problem obviously varies depending on the needs of individual windows. In many cases, however, aesthetics are unimportant compared with the urgency of saving these fragile tissues of colour before they completely disintegrate and are lost for ever.

The financing of stained glass restoration can, however, be a problem. It was estimated in 1973, for example, that the cleaning and stabilization of the five Augsburg prophet windows, the world's oldest windows, would take four years and would cost more than one hundred thousand dollars. While in some countries finance comes from government departments, in others it is dependent upon voluntary contributions from the public. Another problem which arises when the window is restored is whether the valuable window should be kept in its original architectural setting or moved to a museum for greater safety.

These and other problems of ancient glass are being considered by experts and restorers of all nations who have a common forum in the Corpus Vitrearum Medii Aevi. This project, launched in 1951 by the International Committee of the History of Art to record the world's medieval windows, enables historians, scientists, technicians, artists and conservators to meet and exchange information on the composition and restoration of stained glass and the various problems and techniques involved in its preservation. Although the differences between the windows are great, each one demands extensive care, knowledge and a spirit of dedication from its restorers.

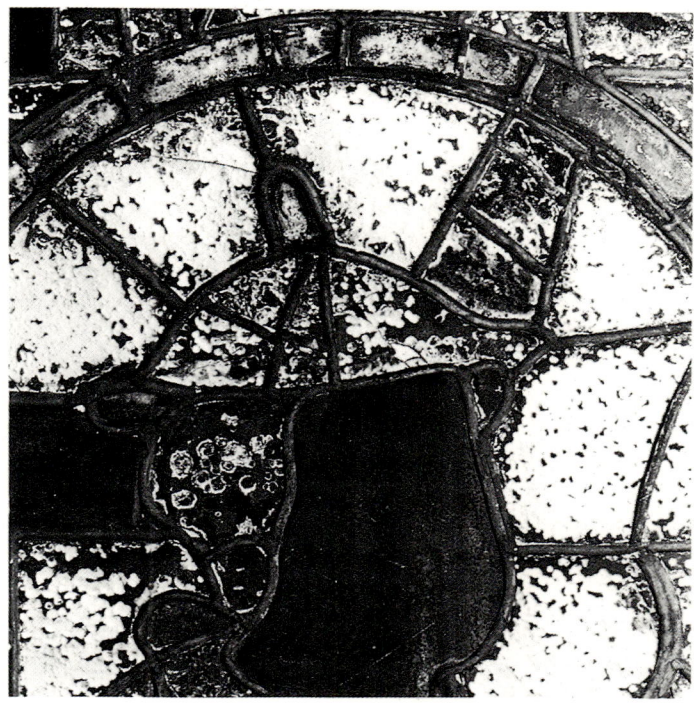

At Canterbury, a twenty-year programme is under way to save the cathedral's many twelfth- and thirteenth-century windows. The panel depicting Rhesa, one of the ancestors of Christ named in Luke's Gospel, has now been restored, but before restoration, left, its exterior was pitted and obscured. Only the face and other glass of the nineteenth century or later are unmarked. Although all glass becomes unstable with age, even pieces of glass which are of the same age and have been exposed to the same weather conditions, like those of the Rhesa panel, vary considerably in their resistance to corrosion and decay. The quality of the original annealing and tiny differences in the chemical make-up of the glass appear to be major factors. At Canterbury, certain colours of glass seem most vulnerable.

Exposed to weather, the outside of the glass suffers the worst corrosion. At Canterbury, right, it decays into numerous small pits and forms an opaque white crust—layers of carbonates and sulphates—the glass returning to its components. Corrosion is cumulative once the glass's shiny outer skin is penetrated. Moisture on the glass forms acid with sulphur and carbon dioxides in the air and attacks the surface. Eventually an alkaline solution results, which eats even deeper. Some glass at Canterbury is a quarter of its original thickness.

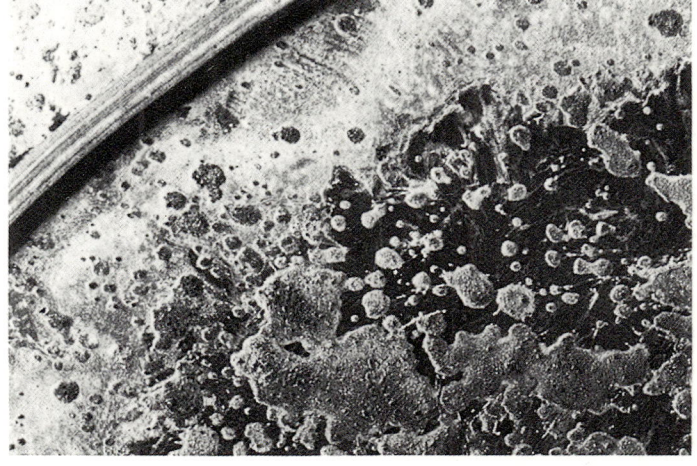

Glass corrodes less in the building's dry interior than it does outside. The inner surface, left, does, however, gradually become caked with a fine murky powder, which collects in the warm temperatures high up in the cathedral. The deposit, mainly calcium sulphate, is composed of lime dust from the stonework and soot from stoves and candles. Cement from between the leads, which crumbles with age, is another component. Although the deposit obscures the light, it seems to do little damage to unpainted glass.

The powdery sulphate on the inside of the glass is very harmful to paintwork because, in time, it attacks the pigment. Paint also tends to flake with age. Although relatively little affected, the paint outlining Rhesa's hair, right, is blurred by the deposit and in parts has lightened. Exterior pitting can be seen through the glass. Paint, like glass, varies in its resistance to decay. Some paint lines form raised ridges; others disappear, leaving deep lines of corrosion. Some old glass has paint on the outside, and this is, of course, particularly vulnerable.

Restoring a Stained-Glass Window

Preservation and repair

In France, Germany, England and most other European countries a great deal of ancient stained glass is being restored. A typical example of restoration work is that at Canterbury Cathedral, where an extensive programme was initiated in 1971 to save some of the oldest stained glass in the world. The work will take a staff of eight some twenty years to complete.

At Canterbury, as in all restoration programmes, it is important that accurate records are kept as work progresses. The glass is, therefore, photographed before it is removed from its window and after every stage in the restoration, so that the results and changes can be evaluated.

To remove an ancient window from its stonework, the surrounding cement and plaster are carefully chipped away. The old glass is then eased out. At Canterbury, this process is simplified by the system of iron and wooden frames holding some of the earliest glass, but where the window is wedged in grooves, it has to be manoeuvred very gently to avoid the slightest strain on the glass.

The window is removed in its component panels, many of which measure about one and a half feet by two and a half feet, and taken to the workshop. A rubbing is made of each panel with thin paper and heel-ball, the black wax composition used in brass rubbing.

The panels are then soaked in deionized water, which is even purer than distilled water. They are given a light brushing to remove surface dirt and dust and the condition of the painting is then appraised. Any loose paintwork is fixed with a dilute epoxy acetone solution.

Each panel is then dismantled, a process which takes the average skilled restorer three days, and the pieces of glass are put in correct position on a glass-bottomed tray. The lead-line pattern of each panel has been first traced from the rubbing and then painted on the underside of its tray. The old leads are melted down for reuse. Glass that presents any unusual problem is examined microscopically, and before its restoration proceeds, may be sent to a laboratory for analysis, thus adding to modern knowledge of medieval chemistry.

Further cleaning of the individual pieces follows. Ultrasonic vibrations in a tank of water, to which a small amount of ammonia has been added, help to dislodge greasy film, and sometimes the outer surface of the glass is cleaned in an airbrasive unit in which it is bombarded by a stream of very fine glass beads which have the texture of talcum powder. The removal of dirt exposes the weathered roughness of the glass. The inner surface of the glass is cleaned with glass-fibre brushes. One small brush cleans only two and a half square inches before it is worn out and must be replaced. The process is partly manual and partly mechanical, using high-speed rotating brush-holders with an electric motor, like dentists' equipment. The operator checks his work through a microscope, especially where

Careful record is kept of the ancient panel when it is removed from its window. Its pattern and condition are recorded in photographs but, more importantly, a full-size rubbing is made. Thin paper, laid on the panel, is rubbed with heel-ball. An exact copy of the leads, it becomes a working reference sheet.

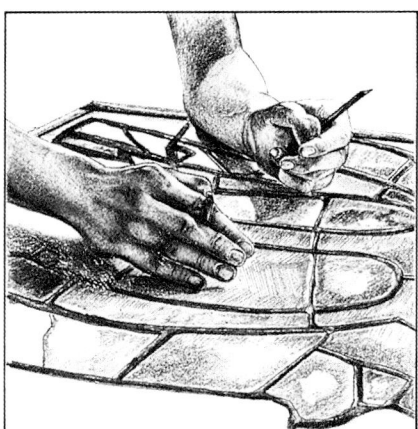

The panel is dismantled from the old leads with great care. The glass, some of it eight hundred years old, is often so thin, however, that it crumbles in the restorer's hands. The pieces and fragments are laid in order on a glass tray, on which, traced from the rubbing, the panel's lead pattern has been painted.

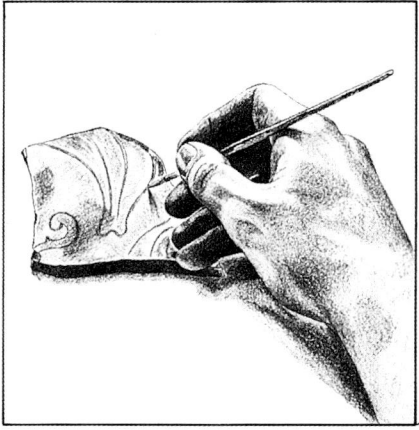

The paintwork has to be protected, even though it is usually in comparatively good condition. It is coated with a plastic solution, ten per cent dilute epoxy resin in acetone. This fixes the paint, prevents flaking and preserves the paint both from damage during the processes of restoration and against corrosion in the future.

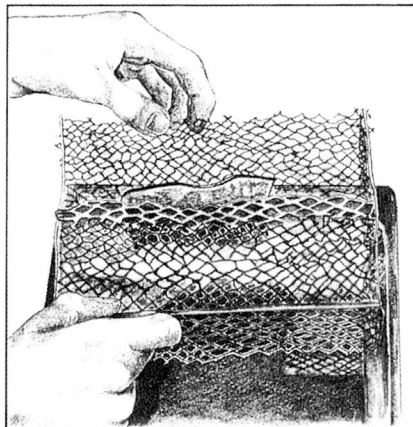

Ultrasonic cleaning dislodges loose dirt. The glass is suspended in a wire basket in a small tank containing a dilute solution of ten per cent ammonia and water. An electrical discharge sends intense vibrations, about six hundred a second, through the solution. After three minutes all loose dirt falls away.

Repairing holes in the glass is another modern process. Because the fragments must be held firm while the resin bonds, they are placed in rubber moulds, made to the full shape of the glass. In the moulds, the spaces can be filled with coloured epoxy resin. Resin takes many hours to set, at a temperature above 60°F.

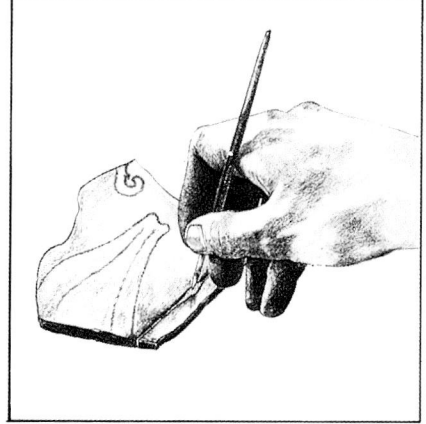

To reinforce and strengthen the joints where two fragments meet, a splint of resin is built up. Although the pieces are now whole and fairly strong, they need further protection. The next steps involve giving each piece of ancient glass its own plating, or backing, of thin, snugly fitting plain glass.

Forming a mould is the first step in preparing the backing plate. The ancient glass is covered with fine nylon mesh and, outer surface downwards, is pressed gently and firmly into wet plaster of Paris. An alternative method is to press the glass into modelling clay and to make a plaster cast from the clay.

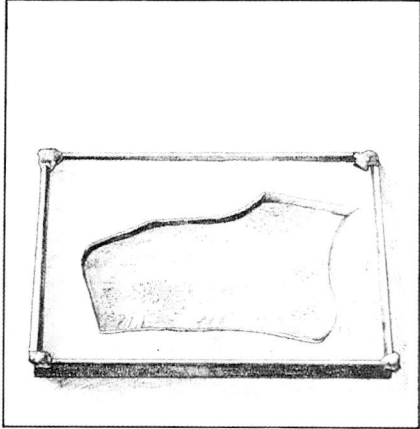

The mould is complete once the plaster of Paris has hardened. The bottom has mirrored all the pitting from the outside surface and, what is more important, has also reproduced the exact contours of the undulating ancient glass. This final mould is now put aside to be used to shape a backing plate of plain glass.

fine painted lines may be very easily confused with dirt.

The cleaned pieces are assembled and broken fragments are edge-jointed with epoxy or silicone resin whose colour is matched to the glass. Extra strength at the joints is given, where needed, by reinforcements built up in resin, and the coloured resin is also used to fill holes.

A plaster cast is made of each piece of glass and a piece of clear, thin glass—as thin as for microscope slides—is cut to the exact shape of each ancient piece. In special cases, paintwork that has deteriorated or been lost can be copied on to the new piece so that the effect of the original is restored, although the medieval glass has not been faked or repainted. Throughout, the aim at Canterbury is to return to the original image without making irreversible additions.

The glass in its plaster mould is then fired in the kiln at about 1450 degrees Fahrenheit. The clear glass takes the exact contours of the ancient glass. After firing, the old and new pieces fit together exactly, and are bound with a mastic edging ready to be releaded in the panel.

In some ancient windows the flashed, or coloured, side of the glass has faced outwards and been eroded by weather, and the restorer must replace the colour with plating. The tint of new flashed glass is chosen by checking the tiny remaining areas of the original, or by comparison with adjoining pieces. The new glass is cut to the exact shape and, if necessary, treated with hydrofluoric acid to achieve the variations and streaks so typical of much medieval flashed glass. Then the two pieces of glass are leaded together and carefully puttied by hand.

Each piece of the window's glass has now been examined and cleaned. Broken pieces have been repaired and thin, plain, modern glass has been carefully cut, shaped and applied to the face which was exposed to the outer air.

Reconstruction

Before the window can be reassembled, however, careful consideration must be given to the design, and decisions must be taken about any anomalous pieces. The iconographic expert compares windows of the same subject and studies manuscripts and miniatures which often help to resolve conflicting or difficult passages. Sometimes holes have been patched up with heads, bodies or whole sections from other windows. Indeed, at York, a complete window was recovered from patches.

Glass which has been wrongly added from a later period is often removed and replaced by plain glass. This prevents a confusion between old and new work, but it risks ruining the visual effect with glaring gaps. Although some restorers believe that there should be a contrast between any new glass and the original, others insert toned or even painted pieces of glass which tactfully merge with the old surroundings. No firm rule, however, is possible. Each window must be considered on its own merits and in relation to the position it holds in a particular building.

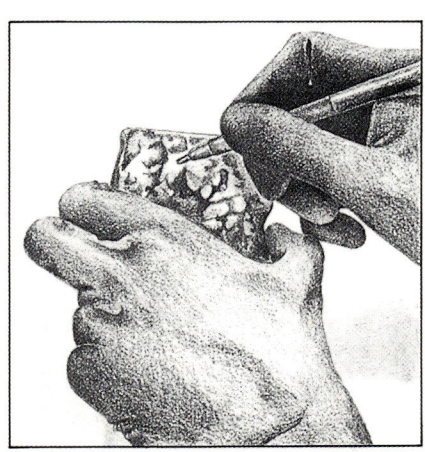

The outside of the glass usually bears an opaque crust of gypsum and other sulphates. An airbrasive gun, bombarding the surface with fine powdered glass beads at a pressure of eighty pounds per square inch, removes this encrustation without damage to the glass. Hands have to be gloved to protect the skin.

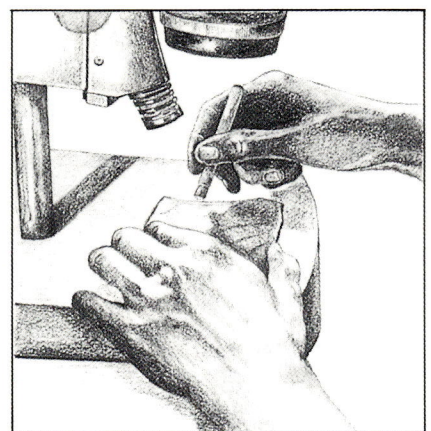

Cleaning the inside surface of the glass requires special care because there is usually ancient paintwork on it. To distinguish paint from dirt, the cleaning is generally done under a microscope. In the first stage of this process, the surface is painstakingly rubbed by hand with special glass-fibre brushes.

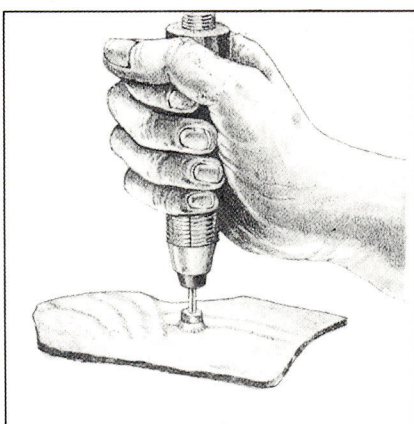

A high-speed rotary brush is now used to clean the inner surface. It is attached, like a dentist's cleaning brush, to an electric motor. Again, extreme care is taken and the restorer uses a microscope. At all stages of the restoration unusual pieces of glass are put aside for expert analysis and consultation.

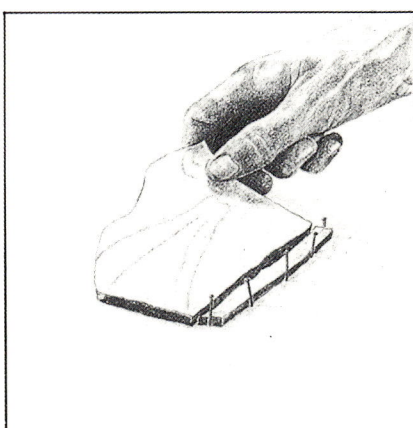

Fragmented pieces of glass need special attention. In previous centuries, extra leads were inserted between broken pieces. Today, these leads are dispensed with and the pieces are joined almost invisibly together. The fragments are assembled into the right shape and then glued with epoxy or silicone resin.

A template is next made for the plain glass. The ancient glass is laid on thin card, traced around and the outline cut out. This piece of card, the shape of the ancient glass, is used as a pattern, around which a piece of very thin, new plain glass—the kind of glass used for microscope slides—is carefully cut out.

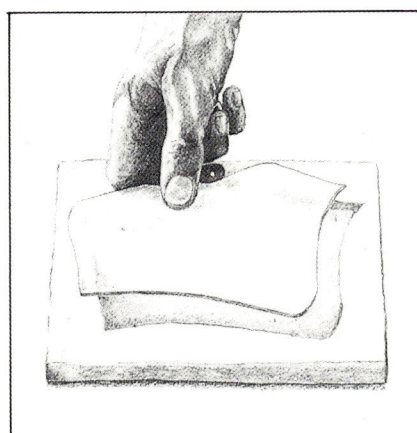

To contour the plain-glass plate, the piece of thin glass, which now has the same outline as the ancient glass, is laid in the mould. It is then fired in the kiln to about 1450°F. The glass becomes viscous, softens into the mould and emerges from the kiln, after annealing, with the exact contours of the ancient glass.

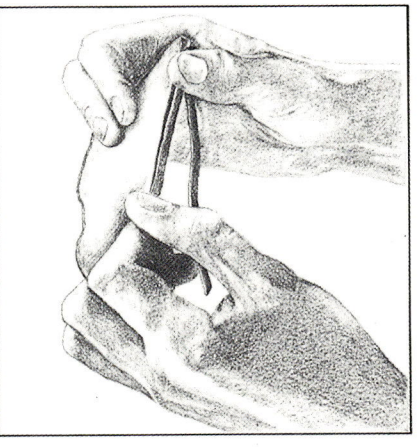

Placed together, the ancient glass and the plain-glass plate have exactly matching outlines and perfectly fitting contours. The two pieces are bound tightly together along the outside edges with a strip of rubbery mastic. Then the piece of double, or plated, glass is replaced in the tray ready for releading.

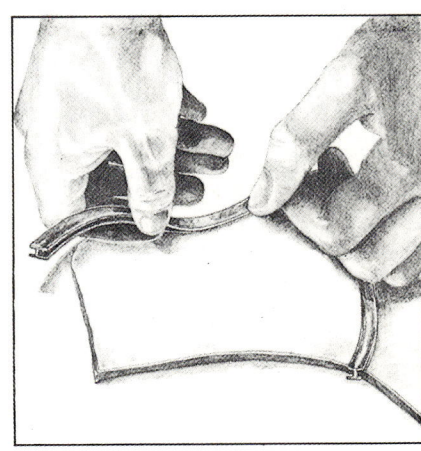

Releading, which takes place when all the old pieces of glass in the panel have been cleaned, restored and plated, is like glazing a new window, except that putty is used instead of cement and usually the leads are old leads, melted and re-milled. Once leaded up, the panel awaits the reinstallation of the window.

Restoring a Stained-Glass Window

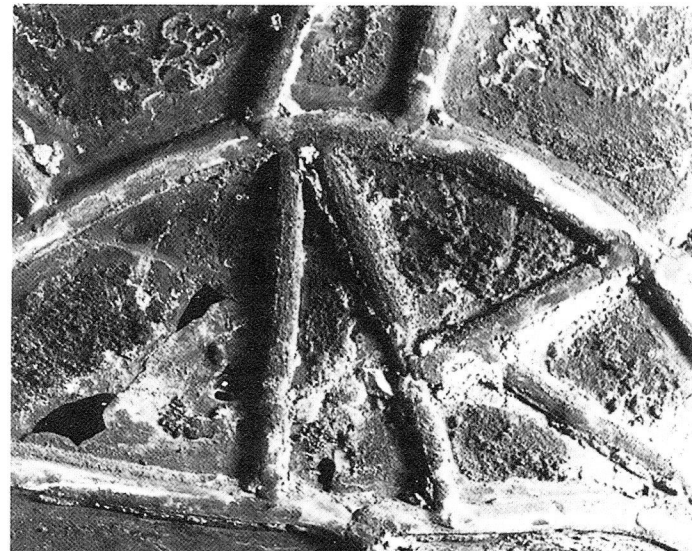

Isothermal glazing, shown here in cross-section from above, maintains the glass at the temperature of the building. It is one of the most effective systems of external glazing and affords protection from vandals, weather and condensation. A sheet of plate glass is inserted in the old grooves. The ancient glass is remounted farther forward and set into a widened metal frame. As the frame is not sealed, dry, warm air from the inside of the building circulates on both sides of the glass.

Protection

The protection of the restored windows poses some problems, but today the window is usually kept in the original building. Experts recommend that for important windows protective plain glass should be inserted into the window openings with the precious ancient glass remounted a little way inside it. Air can thus circulate around the old glass so that condensation, the chief cause of decay, occurs only on the modern glass. This type of glazing, one of many modern methods, is known as the isothermal system.

Protective outer glazing dates back to the eighteenth century. One of the earliest examples is at Byram Hall in Yorkshire, where the glazier William Peckitt protected his new window by "nine panes of strong glass fixed behind the painted glass". The Five Sisters window at York Minster seems to have been given external protective glazing in about 1860. In rare cases, because the outer glazing and the ancient glass were in close contact, the leads of the protective glass caused patterned corrosion on the medieval window and condensation effects were increased through lack of ventilation. However, such glazing certainly offered protection from the direct effects of wind, rain and storm, saving much ancient glass from destruction.

Unfortunately, the aesthetic effect of double-glazing was often unpleasant. The early, thick, greenish glass distorted the colour values, and geometric-patterned quarry-work and heavy ironwork obscured and disfigured the delicacy of medieval glazing and painting.

Today's isothermal glazing—so-called because the old glass is at the same temperature as the air in the building—uses large sheets of plate glass and very little new ironwork. In addition, it is possible to put diffuser sheets of opaque glass between the double glazing to reduce any patterns cast by the outer sheet of glass. The deterioration of medieval glass in these conditions will probably be slight. It has been estimated that one hundred years will elapse before any noticeable change will occur.

Such new techniques of restoration and conservation, dictated by the greatest respect for the original stained glass, have significantly reduced the danger of irreversible damage. It is now technically possible for the world's heritage of stained-glass windows to be preserved in museum-like conditions in the buildings for which they were intended, so that generations to come can appreciate both the genius of the artists and craftsmen who made them and the time-transcending beauty of the glass.

The interior of the Rhesa panel before restoration, top, was encrusted with powdery dirt. There were holes and cracks where the much eroded twelfth-century glass had worn through, and extra leads where, in the past, broken glass had been unaesthetically repaired. Newly restored, below, it has been cleaned of light-inhibiting deposits and the broken and disintegrating glass made whole. Clumsy extra leads are no longer needed. In the full panel, right, the painted details stand out clearly again. The panel's life has been prolonged by cleaning, repair and plating. It is ready to return to the cathedral, restored to display much of the original brilliance and clarity intended by its medieval creators.

Gazetteer

The gazetteer is a guide to the experience of seeing stained glass in its own environment, be it a cathedral, a parish church, a bank or an airlines terminal. The countries listed and the buildings within the countries are essentially selective as the gazetteer aims to include the highlights of European and American stained glass, from the Middle Ages to the present day. Besides the major stained-glass countries of Europe, Switzerland, Austria, Poland and Czechoslovakia are represented. As the victim of such diverse destructive forces as wars, religious uprisings and Baroque architecture, their stained-glass heritage is by no means as extensive as that of, for example, France and Germany. Much of the glass that remains is fragmentary, but it testifies none the less to a tradition of great artistic merit.

Inevitably readers will find their own favourite glass which is not listed here, but it is hoped that the gazetteer will serve as a preliminary basis for exploring—preferably with binoculars—the wealth of stained glass in Europe and the United States.

The entries state, in the following order, the name of the city, town or village, the name of the building in which the glass is to be found, the century or centuries of the most noteworthy glass, the names of its major artists (where known) and, in parentheses, its country of origin if different from the country in which it is now located. The illustrations relate to the buildings below them.

AUSTRIA

Burg Kreuzenstein, near Vienna, *Museum*: 13c, 14c, 15c, 16c.

Friesach, *St Bartholomew's*: 13c.

Graz, *St Maria am Leech*: 14c. *Landesmuseum Joanneum*: 13c, 14c, 15c.

Heiligenkreuz, *Abbey Church*: 12c, 13c, 14c.

Innsbruck, *Landesmuseum*: 16c.

Judenburg, *St Magdalena*: 14c, 15c.

Klagenfurt, *Diocesan Museum*: 12c.

Laxenburg, *Castle, Knight's Hall and Chapel*: 15c, 19c.

Leoben, *St Maria am Wasen*: 15c.

Mariazell, *St Lambrecht*: 15c.

Murau, *Chapel of St Leonhard*: 15c.

Pasching, near Linz, *St John's*: 15c.

St Erhard in der Breitenau, *Parish Church*: 14c.

St Leonhard im Lavanttal, *St Leonhard*: 14c, 15c.

St Michael bei Leoben, *Walpurgis Chapel*: 14c.

Salzburg, *St Peter's cemetery*: 15c Hemmel von Andlau. *Stift Nonnberg, Abbey Church*: 15c Hemmel von Andlau. *City Museum*: 16c.

Steyr, *Parish Church*: 14c, 16c.

Stift Ardagger, *Abbey Church*: 13c.

Stift Klosterneuburg, *Cloisters*: 14c, 15c.

Stift St Florian, near Enns, *Abbey Church*: 14c, 15c, 16c.

Stift Seitenstetten, *Abbey Church*: 15c.

Stift Zwettl, *Abbey Church*: 15c.

Strassengel, near Graz, *Wallfahrtskirche*: 14c, 15c.

Tamsweg, *St Leonhard*: 15c.

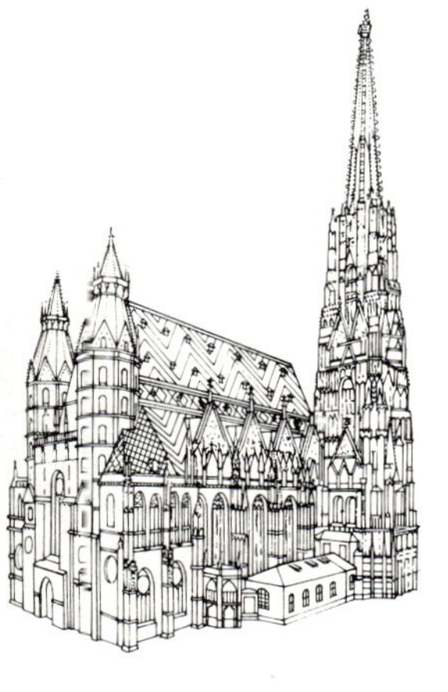

Vienna, *St Stephen's Cathedral*: 14c, 15c, 16c. *St Maria am Gestade*: 14c, 15c. *Ruprechtskirche*: 14c. *Austrian Museum of Applied Art*: 14c, 15c, extensive 16c collection. *Historical Museum of the City of Vienna*: 14c.

Viktring, *(former) Monastery Church*: 14c, 15c.

Wiener Neustadt, *Castle*: 15c, 16c, 17c.

BELGIUM

Anderlecht, *St Pierre and St Guidon*: 15c, 16c.

Antwerp, *Notre Dame Cathedral*: 16c Nicolas Rombouts, 17c. *Christ the King*: 20c Yoors, Colpaert, Vosch. *St Jacques*: 16c, 17c. *31 Longue Rue Neuve* (formerly Chapelle de Bourgogne, St Lierre): 15c, 16c. *Musée Mayer van den Bergh*: 13c. *Vleeshuis*: 15c.

Beauraing, *Parish Church*: 20c Londot.

Bruges, *Notre Dame*: 16c. *Jerusalem Church*: 16c. *Chapel of the Holy Blood (St Sang)*: 20c. *Musée Gruthuuse*: 15c, 16c.

Brussels, *Cathedral of St Gudule*: 16c Nicolas Rombouts, Bernard van Orley, 17c, 19c. *La Madeleine*: 20c Steger. *Hôtel Solvay*: 19c Horta. *Maison Tassel*: 19c. *Musées Royaux d'Art et d'Histoire*: 13c, 14c, 16c, 17c.

Courtrai, *Burggraeve Collection*: 14c.

Diest, *St Sulpice and St Denis*: 16c, 17c.

Ecaussines d'Enghien, *Château*: 16c.

Enghien, *Chapelle Castrale*: 16c.

Halle, *St Martin's*: 15c.

Herenthals, *St Waudru*: 16c.

Heverlee, *L'Eglise des Annonciades*: 20c Yoors.

Hoogstraten, *St Catherine's*: 16c Claes Mathyssen, Pieter Coecke van Aelst.

Liège, *Cathedral*: 16c. *St Antoine*: 16c, 17c. *St Jacques*: 16c. *St Martin's*: 16c, 17c. *St Paul's*: 16c. *St Servais*: 16c, 17c, 19c. *Hôpital de Bavière*: 16c. *Musée Curtius*: 16c, 17c.

Lierre, *St Gommaire*: 15c, 16c (attributed to Nicolas Rombouts).

Louvain, *Abbaye de Parc*: 17c Jean de Caumont. *Grand-Béguinage Church*: 14c. *Musée Vanderkelen Mertens*: 16c, 17c.

Mons, *St Waudru*: 15c, 16c Nicolas Rombouts, 17c.

Namur, *La Chapelle du Grand Séminaire*: 20c Londot.

Nivelles, *L'Eglise des Récollets*: 20c Blank.

Ostend, *Couvent des Clarisses*: 20c.

St Hubert, Ardennes: *St Hubert's*: 16c.

St Lenaarts, *St Leonard's*: 16c.

Steenhuffel, *St Nicolas and St Geneviève*: 16c.

Tournai, *Cathedral*: 14c, 15c Arnt Nijmegen.

Zichem, *St Eustache*: 14c.

BRITISH ISLES

Aberdeen, *St Machar's Cathedral*: 20c Strachan.

Abinger Common, Surrey, *Parish Church*: 20c Lee.

Addington, Bucks., *St Mary's*: 16c–17c (Flemish).

Adel, Yorks., *St John the Baptist's*: 17c Gyles.

Amberley, Sussex: *St Michael's*: 20c Robert Anning Bell.

Ashdown Park, Sussex, *Notre Dame Convent Chapel*: 20c Harry Clarke.

Audley End, Essex, *Chapel of St Mark's College*: 14c, 15c, 18c Peckitt.

Belfast, *St John's*: 20c Geddes.

Birmingham, *Cathedral*: 19c Burne-Jones and Morris.

Bishopsbourne, Kent, *St Mary's*: 16c–17c (including Flemish).

Bristol, *Cathedral*: 14c, 17c, 19c, 20c New.

Bury St Edmunds, Suffolk, *Cathedral*: 16c (Flemish), 19c Clayton & Bell, John Hardman & Co, Warrington, Kempe, Wailes.

Cambridge, *Christ's College Chapel*: 15c–16c William Neve workshop. *King's College Chapel*: 16c Vellert, Flower, Hone, Bownde, Reve, Nicholson, Williamson, Symondes, 19c Clayton & Bell. *Peterhouse College*: 17c attributed to Baptista Sutton. *Trinity College Library*: 18c Peckitt. *Trinity College Hall*: 20c Doyle.

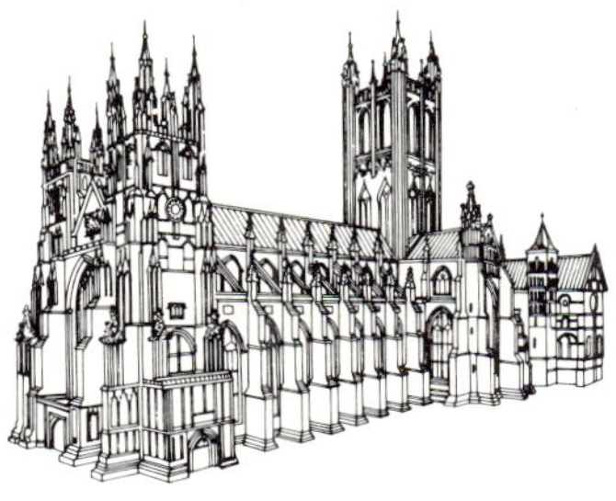

Canterbury, *Cathedral*: 12c, 13c, 16c, 19c, 20c Bossanyi, Comper, Whall. *St Dunstan's*: 20c Lee.

Cheltenham, Glos., *Cheltenham College Chapel*: 20c Davis.

Chester, *Cathedral*: 14c, 15c, 16c, 19c Augustus Welby Pugin, O'Connor brothers, Wailes, 20c Nicholson.

Chetwode, Bucks., *St Mary and St Nicholas's*: 13c, 14c, 19c.

Cork, Co. Cork, *Honan Collegiate Chapel*: 20c Harry Clarke. *University College Chapel*: 20c Harry Clarke.

Coventry, *Cathedral*: 20c Geoffrey Clarke, Forseth, Lee, New, Piper and Reyntiens, Traherne.

Cricklade, Wilts., *St Sampson's*: 20c Travers.

Daresbury, Ches., *All Saints'*: 20c Webb.

Deerhurst, Glos., *St Mary's*: 14c, 15c, 19c Wailes.

Dorchester, Oxon, *Abbey Church of SS Peter and Paul*: 14c, 15c.

Dover, *Maison Dieu (Town Hall)*: 19c.

Dublin, *St Brigid's*, Castleknock: 20c Harry Clarke. *St Joseph's*, Terenure: 20c Harry Clarke.

Durham, *Cathedral*: 14c, 20c Younger.

East Hagbourne, Berks., *St Andrew's*: 14c.

East Harling, Norfolk, *SS Peter and Paul's*: 15c.

Eaton Bishop, Herefords., *St Michael and All Angels*: 14c.

Edinburgh, *Scottish National War Memorial, Edinburgh Castle*: 20c Strachan.

Ely, Cambs., *Cathedral*: 19c Wailes, Warrington, Pugin (also some French glass), 20c Easton.

Eton, Berks., *Eton College Chapel*: 20c Forsyth, Hone, Piper and Reyntiens.

Exeter, *Cathedral*: 14c, 18c Peckitt, 19c, 20c Reginald Bell.

Fairford, Glos., *St Mary's*: 15c, 16c.

Farndon, Ches., *St Chad's*: 17c.

Fladbury, Worcs., *Parish Church*: 14c.

Gilling Castle, near York: 16c Dinickoff.

Glasgow, *Daly's Store*, Sauchiehall St: 20c Mackintosh. *School of Art*: 19c–20c Mackintosh.

Gloucester, *Cathedral*: 14c, 16c, 19c (German), 20c Whall.

Great Malvern, Worcs., *SS Mary and Michael's*: 15c, 16c, 19c.

Great Witley, Worcs., *St Michael's*: 18c Joshua Price.

Hale, Hants, *St Mary's*: 19c (including German).

Halse, Som., *St James's*: 16c (Flemish).

Hampton Court Palace, Middx., *Great Hall*: 19c Willement.

Haselbech, Northants, *Parish Church*: 20c Younger.

Hereford, *Cathedral*: 13c, 14c, 15c, 19c Hardman, Wailes, Warrington, Kempe.

Hillesden, Bucks., *All Saints'*: 16c, 19c.

Hingham, Norfolk, *St Andrew's*: 14c, 16c (German).

Horton, Bucks., *St Michael's*: 19c Kempe.

Ickworth, Suffolk, *St Mary's*: 16c–17c (Flemish).

Leicester, *City Museum*: 15c.

Leighton Buzzard, Beds., *Soulbury Church*: 20c M. C. Farrar Bell.

Lichfield, Staffs., *Cathedral*: 14c, 16c Arnt Nijmegen, 18c Eginton.

Lincoln, *Cathedral*: 13c, 14c, 18c Peckitt, 19c, 20c Geoffrey Clarke, Skeat, Stammers, Webb.

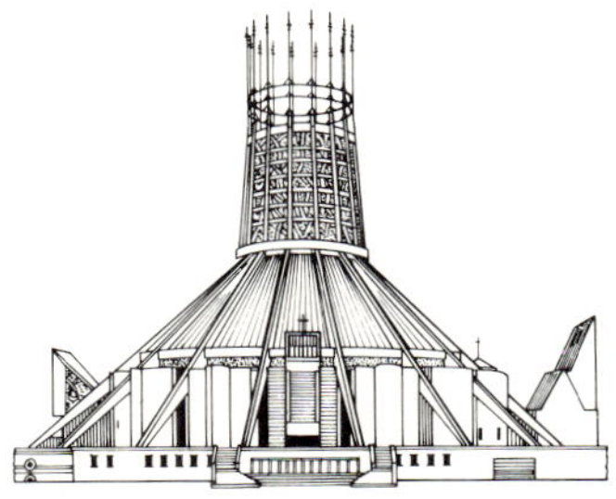

Liverpool, *Anglican Cathedral*: 20c Hogan. *Roman Catholic Cathedral*: 20c Hogan, Piper and Reyntiens, Richards, Traherne.

London, *St Paul's Cathedral, American Chapel*: 20c Thomas. *Westminster Abbey*: 13c, 18c William Price (the younger), Joshua Price, 20c Easton, Thomas. *All Saints'*, Margaret St: 19c Gibbs. *St George's*, Hanover Square: 16c attributed to Arnt Nijmegen. *St Margaret's*, Westminster: 16c, 20c Piper. *Carpenter's Hall*: 20c Lee. *Hatchetts Restaurant*: 20c Bradley. *Lincoln's Inn*: 17c Bernard van Linge, 20c Moore. *National Westminster Bank*, Throgmorton St: 20c Tysoe. *Queen's Hotel*, Crouch End: 20c. *Tate Gallery*: 20c Bossanyi. *Victoria and Albert Museum*: Extensive collection of English and European glass 12c–19c.

Long Melford, Suffolk, *Holy Trinity*: 15c.

Longridge, Lancs., *St Lawrence's*: 20c Brian Clarke.

Lowick, Northants, *St Peter's*: 14c.

Ludlow, Salop, *St Lawrence's*: 14c, 15c, 16c.

Margaretting, Essex, *St Margaret's*: 15c.

Merevale, Worcs., *St Mary the Virgin's*: 14c.

Middleton, Lancs., *St Leonard's*: 16c.

Middleton Cheney, Bucks., *All Saints'*: 19c Ford Madox Brown.

Norwich, *Cathedral*: 14c, 19c Hedgeland, 20c Forsyth, Nicholson. *St Peter Mancroft*: 15c, 16c, 20c Anderson.

Nottingham, *Boots Factory*: 20c Hollaway.

Nowton, Suffolk, *St Peter's*: 16c (Flemish).

Oundle, Ches., *Oundle School Chapel*: 20c Chagall, Piper and Reyntiens.

Oxford, *Christ Church Cathedral*: 14c, 17c Abraham van Linge, William Price, 19c Burne-Jones and Morris. *All Souls College, Antechapel*: 15c John of Oxford. *Balliol College Chapel*: 16c, 17c Abraham van Linge. *Brasenose College*: 18c Pearson. *Lincoln College Chapel*: 17c Bernard van Linge. *Magdalen College, Antechapel and Hall*: 17c Greenbury. *Merton College Chapel*: 13c, 14c. *New College Chapel*: 14c Thomas of Oxford, 15c, 18c Jervais (after Sir Joshua Reynolds), William Price (the younger), Peckitt. *Queen's College Chapel*: 17c Abraham van Linge, 18c Joshua Price. *University College Chapel*: 16c, 17c Abraham van Linge, 18c. *Wadham College Chapel*: 17c Bernard van Linge, 18c. *Worcester College Chapel*: 19c Holiday.

Penshurst, Kent, *St John the Baptist's*: 17c, 20c Lee.

Rendcomb, Glos., *Rendcomb College*: 19c Hardwick.

Rivenhall, Essex, *St Mary and All Saints'*: 12c (French), 13c, 15c, 16c.

Rottingdean, Sussex, *St Margaret's*: 19c Burne-Jones.

St Albans, Herts., *Cathedral*: 16c, 20c Comper, Webb.

St Neot, Cornwall, *St Anietus*: 15c, 16c, 19c.

St Peter Port, Guernsey, Channel Islands, *St Stephen's*: 19c Morris.

Salisbury, *Cathedral*: 13c, 18c Eginton, Pearson, 19c Burne-Jones and Morris, 20c Reginald Bell.

Shrewsbury, Salop, *St Mary's*: 14c, 16c (French, German, Flemish), 19c.

Stamford, Lincs., *Browne's Hospital*: 15c.

Staveley, Derby., *St John the Baptist's*: 17c Gyles.

Stoke d'Abernon, Surrey, *St Mary's*: 15c, 16c, 17c (including French and German).

Stoke Poges, Bucks., *St Giles's*: 19c (German).

Strawberry Hill, Twickenham, Middx., *Walpole's villa*: 17c.

Sturminster Newton, Dorset, *St Mary's*: 20c Harry Clarke.

Swansea, *St Mary's*: 20c Manessier, Piper and Reyntiens.

Temple Guiting, Glos., *Parish Church*: 16c.

Tewkesbury, *Abbey*: 14c, 20c Webb.

Thornton-Cleveleys, Lancs., *Christ Church*: 20c Brian Clarke.

Truro, Cornwall, *Cathedral*: 19c Clayton & Bell, Warrington.

Tudeley, Kent, *All Saints'*: 20c Chagall.

Twycross, Leics., *St James the Great*: 12c–13c (French).

Tyneham, Dorset, *St Mary's*: 20c Travers.

Warwick, *St Mary's*: 15c John Prudde, 17c (Flemish).

Gazetteer

Waterperry, Oxon, *St Mary the Virgin's*: 13c.
Wellingborough, Northants, *All Hallows*: 20c Hone.
Wellington, Berks., *Wellington College Chapel*: 20c Easton.
Wells, *Cathedral*: 14c, 16c, 17c, 18c, 20c Nicholson.
Wickhambreux, Kent, *St Andrew's*: 19c Rosenkrantz.
Willesborough, Kent, *St Mary's*: 14c.
Wimpole, Cambs., *St Andrew's*: 14c, 19c.
Winchelsea, Sussex, *St Thomas's*: 20c Strachan.
Winchester, *Cathedral*: 14c, 15c, 16c, 19c Burne-Jones, Evans, Kempe, Powell, 20c. *College Chapel*: 14c, 17c, 19c, 20c.
Winscombe, Som., *St James's*: 15c, 19c William Morris and Co.
Withcote, Leics., *St Jude's*: 16c.
Wragby, Yorks., *St Michael's*: 16c–18c (Swiss).
Yarnton, Oxon, *St Bartholomew's*: 15c, 16c (including Flemish).
York, *Minster*: 12c, 13c, 14c, 15c John Thornton of Coventry, 18c Peckitt. *All Saints'*, North St: 14c, 15c. *Holy Trinity*, Micklegate: 15c, 19c Kempe. *St Denys's*: 14c, 15c. *St Martin's*, Coney St: 15c. *St Martin-le-Grand*: 15c, 20c Stammers.

CANADA

ALBERTA
Calgary, *Christ Church*: 20c New.
NEW BRUNSWICK
Saint John, *St Mark's United Church*: 20c Blaney.
ONTARIO
Oshawa, *St Andrew's United Church*: 20c Weisman.
Toronto, *St James's Cathedral*: 20c Taylor. *Sunnybrook Hospital*: 20c Weisman.
Waterdown, *Notre Dame Academy*: 20c Weisman.

CZECHOSLOVAKIA

Brno, *Moravian Gallery*: 15c.
Čečovice, *St Nicholas's*: 14c.
Český Krumlov, *Castle, St George's Chapel*: 15c.
Hluboká, *Castle*: 14c, 15c, 16c.
Karlštejn, *Castle, St Catherine's Chapel*: 14c.
Kolín, *St Bartholomew's*: 14c.
Konopiště, *Castle*: 15c.
Kost, *Castle, St Anne's Chapel*: 15c.
Křivoklát, *Castle Museum*: 16c.
Litoměřice, *Regional Gallery of Pictorial Art*: 14c, 15c.
Nadslav, near Jičín, *St Prokopius*: 14c.
Orlík, *Castle Chapel*: 14c.
Plzeň, *West Bohemia Museum*: 14c.

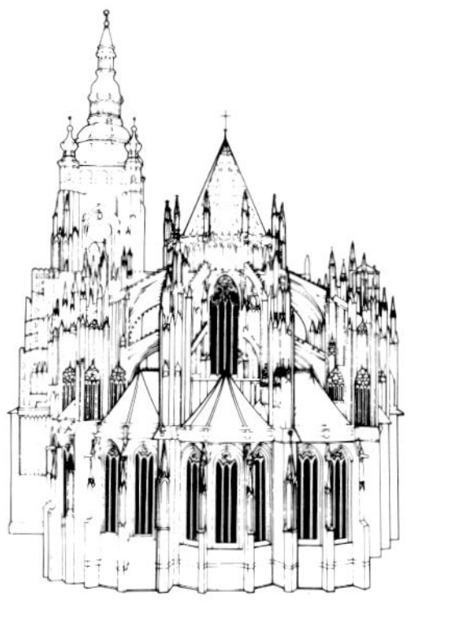

Prague, *Cathedral*: 19c Swerts, Sequens, Lhota, Müller, Maixner, 20c Kysela, Švabinský, Mucha, Bouda, Svolinský, Soukup, Brychtová, Libenský. *National Museum*: 14c, 15c, 16c. *Museum of the City of Prague*: 15c, 16c. *Museum of Applied Art*: 13c, 14c, 15c (including Swiss and German).
Úboč, *St Nicholas's*: 14c.
Žlunice, *SS Peter and Paul*: 14c.

DENMARK

Abildgård, Jutland, *Parish Church*: 20c Agger.
Allerslyst, Jutland, *Parish Church*: 20c Havsteen-Mikkelsen.
Århus, *Cathedral*: 20c Vigeland.
Copenhagen, *Esajas Church*: 20c Skovgaard. *Højdevangs Church*: 20c Nielsen. *Stefans Church*: 20c Kragh. *Messias Church*, Hellerup: 20c Skovgaard. *National Museum*: 13c, 14c, 15c, 16c, 17c.
Esbjerg, *Trinity Church*: 20c Urup-Jensen.
Gershøj, Zealand, *Parish Church*: 20c Skovgaard.
Holbæk, Jutland, *Parish Church*: 20c Iversen.
Humlebæk, Zealand, *Parish Church*: 20c Havsteen-Mikkelsen.
Klarup, Jutland, *Parish Church*: 20c Havsteen-Mikkelsen.
Kregme, Zealand, *Parish Church*: 20c Skovgaard.
Lem, Jutland, *Parish Church*: 20c Jørgensen.
Lumsås, Zealand, *Parish Church*: 20c Kragh.
Lyngby, near Copenhagen, *Christian the Tenth Church*: 20c Jørgensen.
Mårslet, Jutland, *Parish Church*: 20c Jørgensen.
Odense, *Kingo Church*: 20c Skovgaard.
Ordrup, Zealand, *Parish Church*: 20c Havsteen-Mikkelsen.
Risskov, Jutland, *Parish Church*: 20c Iversen.
Roager, Jutland, *Parish Church*: 13c.
Skovshoved, Zealand, *Parish Church*: 20c Lollesgaard.
Svendborg, Fúnen, *St Jørgens Church*: 20c Havsteen-Mikkelsen. *Church of Our Lady*: 20c Havsteen-Mikkelsen. *St Nicolai Church*: 20c Iversen.
Tarm, Jutland, *Parish Church*: 20c Havsteen-Mikkelsen.
Tune, Zealand, *Parish Church*: 20c Sparre.
Vallekilde, Zealand, *Free Church*: 20c Skovgaard.
Vejle, *Saviour's Church*: 20c Nielsen.
Viborg, *Cathedral*: 20c Bindesbøll. *Black Brother's Church*: 20c Bindesbøll. *Vestervang Church*: 20c Jørgensen.
Viby, Jutland, *Church of Peace*: 20c Jørgensen.
Virring, Jutland, *Parish Church*: 14c.
Virum, near Copenhagen, *Parish Church*: 20c Urup-Jensen.
Voel, Jutland, *Parish Church*: 20c Nielsen.

EAST GERMANY

Brandenburg/Havel, *Cathedral*: 13c, 15c. *St Pauli*: 14c.
Erfurt, *Cathedral*: 14c, 15c. *Augustinerkirche*: 14c. *Barfüsserkirche*: 13c, 14c.
Halberstadt, *Cathedral*: 14c, 15c.
Havelberg, *Cathedral*: 15c.
Meissen, *Cathedral*: 13c.
Merseburg, *Cathedral*: 13c.
Mühlhausen, *St Blasius*: 14c.
Naumburg, *Cathedral*: 13c, 14c, 15c.
Stendal, *Cathedral*: 15c. *St James's*: 14c, 15c.
Weimar, *Goethe House*: 12c, 14c.
Wilsnack, *Heiligblutkirche*: 15c.

FINLAND

Espoo, *Church*: 20c Forsström.
Helsinki, *Johannes Church*: 19c. *Kannelmäki Church*: 20c Toivola. *Roihuvuori Church*: 20c Hietanen. *Tammisalo Church*: 20c. *Hietaniemi Chapel*: 20c Forsström. *National Museum*: 13c, 14c, 15c, 16c.
Kokkola, *Church*: 20c Vainio.
Oulu, *Cathedral*: 20c Forsström. *Oulunsuu Church*: 20c Pusa.
Seinajoki, *Lakeuden Risti*: 20c Aalto. *Törnävä Church*: 20c Karjarinta.
Turku, *Cathedral*: 19c Wertschkoff.
Vuoksenniska Imatra, *The Church of the Three Crosses*: 20c Aalto.
Vuolijoki, *Otamäki Church*: 20c Vainio.

FRANCE

Alençon, *Notre Dame*: 15c, 16c.
Amiens, *Cathedral*: 13c, 15c.
Angers, *Cathedral*: 12c, 13c, 14c, 15c André Robin, 16c. *St Serge*: 12c, 15c.
Assy, *Notre Dame de Toute Grace*: 20c Rouault, Chagall.
Auch, *Cathedral*: 16c Arnaud de Moles.
Audincourt, *Church of the Sacred Heart*: 20c Léger.
Autun, *Cathedral*: 15c, 16c.
Auxerre, *Cathedral*: 13c, 14c, 15c, 16c.
Bayonne, *Cathedral*: 16c.
Beauvais, *Cathedral*: 13c, 14c, 15c, 16c. *St Etienne*: 13c, 16c Engrand, Jean, Nicolas and Pierre le Prince, Romain Buron.
Blénod-les-Toul, *St Médard*: 16c.
Bourges, *Cathedral*: 12c, 13c, 15c, 16c Jean Lécuyer, 17c. *St Bonnet*: 16c Jean Lécuyer. *Palais de Jacques Coeur*: 15c.
Brou, *Notre Dame*: 16c.
Carcassonne, *St Nazaire*: 14c.
Caudebec-en-Caux, *Notre Dame*: 15c, 16c.
Châlons-sur-Marne, *Cathedral*: 12c, 13c, 15c, 16c. *Notre-Dame-en-Vaux*: 12c, 16c Mathieu Bléville.
Chantilly, *Château*: 16c.

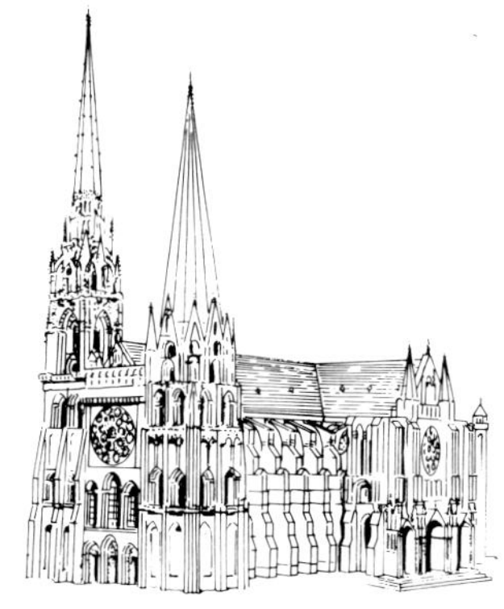

Chartres, *Cathedral*: 12c, 13c, 14c, 15c. *St Pierre*: 13c, 14c, 16c.
Clermont-Ferrand, *Cathedral*: 12c, 13c, 14c, 15c.
Colmar, *Collegiate Church of St Martin*: 13c, 14c.
Conches, *Ste Foy*: 15c, 16c Arnoult de Nimègue, Romain Buron.
Coutances, *Cathedral*: 13c, 15c, 16c.
Dol-de-Bretagne, *Cathedral*: 13c.
Dreux, *Chapelle Royale St Louis*: 19c Ingres, Delacroix. *St Pierre*: 13c, 16c, 17c.
Ecouen, *St Acceul*: 16c.
Evreux, *Cathedral*: 13c, 14c, 15c, 16c, 17c. *St Taurin*: 16c.
Evron, *Notre Dame de l'Epine*: 14c.
Eymoutiers, *St Etienne*: 15c, 16c.
La Ferté-Milon, *Notre Dame*: 14c, 16c Mathieu Bléville. *St Nicolas*: 16c.
Laon, *Cathedral*: 13c.
Le Mans, *Cathedral*: 12c, 13c, 15c, 16c.
Louviers, *Notre Dame*: 15c, 16c.
Lyons, *Cathedral*: 12c, 13c, 15c. *Musée des Beaux Arts*: 12c, 13c, 14c, 15c, 16c.
Metz, *Cathedral*: 14c Hermann von Munster, 15c Theobald von Lixheim, 16c Valentin Busch, 20c Chagall, Villon, Bissière.
Montmorency, *St Martin's*: 15c, 16c.
Moulins, *Cathedral*: 15c, 16c.
Mulhouse, *Temple of St Etienne*: 14c.
Nancy, *Musée Lorrain*: 13c, 14c, 15c, 16c.
Niederhaslach, *St Florentin*: 13c, 14c.
Obazine, *Abbey Church of the Nativity of Notre-Dame*: 12c.
Paris, *Notre Dame Cathedral*: 13c. *St Etienne-du-Mont*: 16c, 17c. *St Eustache*: 17c. *St Germain des Prés*: 13c. *St Germain l'Auxerrois*: 15c, 16c, 19c. *St Gervais*: 16c, 17c. *St Merri*: 16c. *St Séverin*: 14c, 15c, 19c. *Ste Chapelle*: 13c, 15c. *Musée Cluny*: 12c, 13c, 14c, 15c, 16c, 17c. *Musée des Arts Décoratifs*: 14c, 15c, 16c, 19c, 20c. *Musée du Louvre*: 13c, 14c, 15c, 16c, 17c.
Poitiers, *Cathedral*: 12c, 13c. *Ste Radegonde*: 13c.
Pontigny, *Abbey Church*: 12c.
Pontoise, *Cathedral*: 16c.
Quimper, *Cathedral*: 15c.
Reims, *Cathedral*: 13c. *Basilique St Rémi*: 12c, 13c.
Riom, *Ste Chapelle du Palais de Justice*: 15c.
Ronchamp, *Church of Notre Dame du Haut*: 20c Le Corbusier.
Rosenweiler, *Notre Dame de l'Assomption*: 14c.
Rouen, *Cathedral*: 13c, 14c, 15c, 16c. *Abbey Church of St Ouen*: 14c, 15c, 16c. *St Godard*: 16c Arnoult de Nimègue. *St Patrice*: 15c, 16c. *Musée des Antiquités de la Seine Maritime*: 13c, 14c, 15c, 16c, 17c.
St Denis, near Paris, *Abbey Church*: 12c, 13c, 19c.
St Jean-aux-Bois, *Abbey Church of St Jean*: 13c.
St-Nicolas-de-Port, *St Nicolas*: 15c, 16c.
St Omer, *Musée de St Omer*: 15c, 16c.
St Quentin, *Collegiate Church of St Quentin*: 13c, 15c, 16c.
Saverne, *Notre Dame*: 14c, 15c Hemmel von Andlau.
Sées, *Cathedral*: 13c, 14c.
Sélestat, *St George's*: 13c, 14c, 15c.
Semur-en-Auxois, *Collegiate Church of Notre Dame*: 13c, 15c, 16c.
Sens, *Cathedral*: 13c, 15c, 16c.
Soissons, *Cathedral*: 13c.
Strasbourg, *Cathedral*: 12c, 13c, 14c, 15c, 16c. *St Thomas's*: 14c. *St Guillaume*: 14c, 15c. *Musée de l'Oeuvre Notre Dame*: 12c, 13c, 14c, 15c, 16c.
Thann, *Collegiate Church of St Thiebaut*: 15c.
Toul, *Cathedral*: 13c, 14c, 16c. *Collegiate Church of St Gengoult*: 13c, 14c, 16c.
Toulouse, *Cathedral*: 14c, 15c, 16c.
Tours, *Cathedral*: 13c, 14c, 15c.
Troyes, *Cathedral*: 13c, 14c, 15c, 16c, 17c Linard Gontier. *La Madeleine*: 15c, 16c. *St Urbain*: 13c, 14c, 15c. *Library*: 16c–17c Linard Gontier.
Varangeville, *Chapel of St Dominique*: 20c Braque. *St Valéry*: 20c Braque.
Vence, *Chapel of the Rosary*: 20c Matisse.
Vendôme, *Abbey Church of La Trinité*: 12c, 13c, 14c, 15c, 16c.
Verneuil-sur-Avre, *La Madeleine*: 15c, 16c.
Vézélise, *St Come and St Damien*: 16c.
Vieux Thann, *Eglise St Dominique*: 15c.
Walbourg, *Ste Walpurge*: 15c Hemmel von Andlau.
Westhoffen, *St Martin's*: 13c, 14c.
Wissembourg, *St Peter and St Paul's*: 12c, 13c, 15c.
Zetting, *St Marcel*: 15c.

HOLLAND

Amsterdam, *Oudekerk*: 16c, 17c. *Stock Exchange*: 20c A. J. der Kinderen, Joop Nicolas. *Technical College*: 20c Van Doesburg.
Drachten, *Agricultural College*: 20c Van Doesburg.
Eindhoven, *Philips Factory*: 20c Joop Nicolas.
Etten, *Parish Church*: 20c Charles Eyck.
Gouda, *St John's*: 16c Dirck and Wouter Crabeth, 17c, 20c Charles Eyck.
Hilversum, *Town Hall*: 20c Joop Nicolas.
Nijmegen, *St Joseph's*: 20c Jan Toorop. *Philips Factory*: 20c.
The Hague, *St Jakobskerk*: 16c.
Tilburg, *Church of the Sacred Heart*: 20c Joop Nicolas.
Utrecht, *University*: 19c A. J. der Kinderen.

ICELAND

Reykjavik, *National Art Gallery*: 20c Tryggvadottir. *National Theatre*: 20c Breidfjord.

ITALY

Arezzo, *Cathedral*: 16c De Marcillat. *SS Annunziata*: 16c De Marcillat. *San Francesco*: 16c De Marcillat.

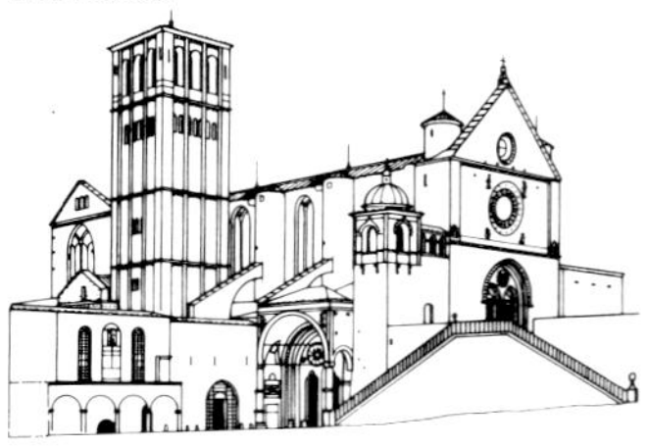

Assisi, *San Francesco, Upper Basilica*: 13c. *Lower Basilica*: 14c Simone Martini, 15c.
Bologna, *San Petronio*: 15c. *San Giovanni in Monte*: 15c.
Cortona, *Calcinaio Church*: 16c De Marcillat.
Florence, *Cathedral*: 15c Ghiberti, Del Castagno, Uccello, Donatello. *Orsanmichele*: 15c. *Santa Croce*: 14c Gaddi, Di Banco, 15c Baldovinetti. *Santa Maria Novella*: 14c Di Cione, Da Firenze, 15c Ghirlandajo, Filippino Lippi. *Santo Spirito*: 16c Perugino. *Laurentian Library*: 16c. *Palazzo Vecchio*: 16c.
Lucca, *Cathedral*: 15c Filippino Lippi, Baldovinetti.
Massa Maritima, *Cathedral*: 14c.
Milan, *Cathedral*: 15c De Mottis, Da Varallo, Foppa, 16c, 19c Bertini family. *San Nazzaro*: 15c. *Cathedral Museum*: 15c.
Orvieto, *Cathedral*: 14c Maitani.
Pavia, *Certosa*: 15c De Mottis.
Perugia, *Cathedral*: 15c Ghiberti, 16c. *San Domenico*: 15c Di Nardo.
Pisa, *Cathedral*: 14c, 15c Baldovinetti. *San Paolo a Ripa*: 14c. *San Francesco*: 14c.
Prato, *Cathedral*: 15c Filippo Lippi, Da Pelago.
Rome, *Santa Maria del Popolo*: 16c De Marcillat.

Siena, *Cathedral*: 13C Duccio, 16C. *Santuario della Madonna della Grotta*: 13C. *Palazzo Pubblico*: 14C Lorenzetti.
Val d'Ema, *Certosa*: 15C, 16C.
Venice, *SS Giovanni and Paolo*: 15C. *Santa Maria dei Miracoli*: 15C. *Accademia*: 14C. *Museo Vetrario*: 14C, 15C.

MEXICO
Mexico City, *Palacio de las Bellas Artes*: 20C Tiffany.

NORWAY
Bærum, *Haslum Crematorium*: 20C Kristiansen.
Bergen, *Church of Landås*: 20C Remfelt.
Bodø, *Cathedral*: 20C.
Drammen, *Bragerns Church*: 20C Wold-Thorne.
Hammerfest, *Church*: 20C.
Hinna, Rojaland, *Parish Church*: 20C Sparre.
Nøtterøy, Vestfold, *Parish Church*: 20C Haarvaads-Holm.
Oslo, *Cathedral*: 20C Vigeland. *Hasle Church*: 20C Moseid. *Vålerengen Church*: 20C Vigeland.
Rjukan, *Parish Church*: 20C Moseid.
Senja, Troms, *Berg Church*: 20C Moseid.
Stavanger, *Cathedral*: 20C Sparre.
Steinkjer, *Parish Church*: 20C Weidemann.
Tromsdalen, Troms, *Parish Church*: 20C Sparre.
Trondheim, *Cathedral*: 20C.

POLAND
Cracow, *Wawel Hill Cathedral*: 20C Mehoffer. *St Mary's*: 14C, 20C Mehoffer, Wyspiański. *Franciscan Church*: 20C Wyspiański. *Jama Michalikowa café, Floriańska St*: 20C Uziebło, Frycz. *American Research Hospital for Children*: 20C Willet Studios. *Medical Association Building*: 20C Wyspiański. *National Museum*: 14C, 15C.
Gdansk, *St Barbara's*: 20C Massalska.
Grodek, near Bialystok, *Orthodox Church of the Nativity of the Holy Virgin Mary*: 20C Stalony-Dobrzański.
Nysa, *Cathedral*: 20C Stalony-Dobrzański.
Poznań, *Church of the Holy Virgin Mary*: 20C Taranczewski.
Rozwadów, *Holy Mother Church*: 20C Stalony-Dobrzański.
Sochaczew, *Church of the Holy Virgin Mary of the Rosary*: 20C Kuligowski.
Toruń, *Pomeranian Museum*: 14C, 16C, 17C.
Warsaw, *Cathedral*: 20C Taranczewski. *Footwear Centre*: 20C Bartłomiejczyk.
Władysławowo, *Church of the Ascension of the Holy Virgin Mary, Patron of Polish Emigrants*: 20C Kulesza.
Wrocław, *Cathedral*: 20C Wojciechowski, Michalak, Pekalski. *Church of the Holy Virgin Mary of the Sand*: 20C Reklewska. *National Museum*: 16C, 17C.

SPAIN
Astorga, León, *Cathedral*: 16C Rodrigo de Herreras.
Avila, *Cathedral*: 15C, 16C Juan de Valdivieso, Arnao de Flandes, Diego de Santillana, Alberto and Nicolás de Holanda. *Museum*: 16C Nicolás de Holanda (or one of his associates).
Barcelona, *Cathedral*: 15C–16C Gil Fontanet. *Chapel of the Colonia Güell*: 19C Gaudí. *Church of Los Santos Justo y Pastor*: 16C Jaime Fontanet. *Pedralbes Monastery*: 14C, 16C Gil Fontanet. *Santa Maria del Mar*: 14C Severin Desmazes, 15C Antonio Llonye, 17C, 18C Saladrigas, 20C. *Santa Maria del Pino*: 18C Ravella. *Museo Gaudí*: 19C.
Burgos, *Cathedral*: 14C, 15C Juan de Arqr, 16C. *La Cartuja*: 15C, 17C.
Cuenca, *Cathedral*: 16C Giraldo de Holanda.
Gerona, *Cathedral*: 14C Ramon Gilabert, 15C, 16C, 20C.
Granada, *Cathedral*: 16C Teodoro of Holland, Jean de Campin.
Huesca, *Cathedral*: 16C Francisco de Valdivieso.
León, *Cathedral*: 13C Adam and Fernán Arnol, Juan Pérez, Pedro Guillermo, 14C, 15C Johan, Lope, Valdovin, Nicolás Francés, Juan de Almunia, Juan de Arqr, 16C Diego de Santillana, Francisco de Somoza, Rodrigo de Herreras, 19C, 20C.
Oviedo, *Cathedral*: 16C Diego de Santillana, Francisco de Somoza.
Palma, Majorca, *Cathedral*: 16C, 19C, 20C.
Pamplona, Navarra, *Cathedral*: 15C.
Salamanca, *Cathedral*: 16C Alberto and Nicolás de Holanda. *Santa Ursula Convent*: 15C.
San Cugat Del Vallés, Barcelona, *Monastery*: 15C, 16C.
Santas Creus, Tarragona, *Monastery*: 13C, 14C.
Segovia, *Cathedral*: 16C Nicolás de Holanda, Arnao de Vergara, Nicolás de Vergara (the elder), Pierre de Holanda, Pierre de Chiverri, Gualter de Ronch.
Seo de Urgel, Lérida, *Cathedral*: 15C.
Seville, *Cathedral*: 15C Enrique Alemán, 16C Cristóbal Alemán, Arnao de Vergara, Arnao de Flandes, Carlos de Brujas, Nicolás de Vergara (the younger), Vicente Menardo, Juan Jacques, Juan Viván, Bernaldino de Gelandia.
Tarragona, *Cathedral*: 14C Guillen Lanturgat.

Toledo, *Cathedral*: 14C, 15C Juan Dolfin, Loys Coutin, Enrique Alemán, Pedro Bonifacio, Cristóbal, Fra Pedro, Pablo, Crisóstomo, Pedro, 16C Nicolás de Vergara (the elder), Nicolás de Vergara (the younger), Vasco de Troya, Alejo Ximénez, Gonzalo de Córdoba, Juan de la Cuesta, 18C Francisco Sánchez Martínez. *Museo de Santa Cruz*: 16C Arnao de Vergara.

SWEDEN
Alskog, Gotland, *Church*: 13C.
Arlöv, Skåne, *Parish Church*: 20C Jørgensen.
Barlingbo, Gotland, *Church*: 13C.
Boda, Småland, *Glassworks*: 20C Hoglund.
Dalhem, Gotland, *Church*: 13C.
Endre, Gotland, *Church*: 13C.
Eskilstuna, *Ansgars Church*: 20C Fisher, Bergholtz.
Etelhem, Gotland, *Church*: c.1300.
Göteborg (Gothenburg), *Bishop's Palace Church*: 20C Fisher, Bergholtz. *Crematorium*: 20C Forseth.
Grötlingbo, Gotland, *Church*: 14C.
Halmstad, *Parish Church*: 20C Forseth.
Hälsingborg, *St Mary's Church*: 20C Bergholtz, Emond, Forseth, Olson.
Hejde, Gotland, *Church*: 14C.
Laholm, Halland, *Parish Church*: 20C Olson.
Lojsta, Gotland, *Church*: 13C.
Lund, *Cathedral*: 20C Vigeland.
Lye, Gotland, *Church*: 14C.
Malmö, *St Peter's Church*: 20C Gehlin.
Mästerby, Gotland, *Church*: 14C.
Mora, Dalarna, *Zorn Museum*: 13C, 14C.
Odensvi, Västmanland, *Parish Church*: 14C.
Rone, Gotland, *Church*: 13C.
Säfle, Skåne, *Parish Church*: 20C Erixson.
Sjonhem, Gotland, *Church*: 13C.

Skara, Västergötland, *Cathedral*: 20C Beskow.
Sköllersta, Närke, *Parish Church*: 13C.
Stockholm, *Carolean Hospital Chapel*: 20C Forseth. *Gustav Vasa Church, Columbarium*: 20C Forseth. *Oscarskyrkan*: 20C Vigeland. *English Church*: 20C Forseth. *Museum of National Antiquities*: 13C, 14C, 15C, 16C. *Svenska Handelsbanken*: 20C Rohde.
Täby, Uttland, *Church*: 20C Jørgensen.
Tångeråsa, Närke, *Parish Church*: 14C.
Trollhättan, *Parish Church*: 20C Bergholtz.
Uppsala, *University Museum*: 13C, 14C.
Växjö, *Cathedral*: 20C Brazda, Beskow, Hoglund.
Vika, Dalarna, *Parish Church*: 15C.
Visby, Gotland, *Museum*: 13C, 14C, 17C.
Voxtorp, Småland, *Parish Church*: 20C Fisher.

SWITZERLAND
Basle, *Historical Museum*: 14C, 15C, 16C, 17C. *Schützenhaus*: 16C. *Town Hall*: 16C. *University, Regency Chamber*: 16C.
Bern, *Cathedral*: 15C Hans Acker. *Historical Museum*: 15C, 16C, 17C.
Biel/Bern, *St Benedikt*: 15C.
Blumenstein/Bern, *St Nicholas's*: 14C.
Fribourg, *St Nicholas's*: 20C Mehoffer. *Fondation Gottfried Keller*: 16C. *Musée d'Art et d'Histoire*: 14C, 15C.
Hauterive/Fribourg, (former) *Monastery Church*: 14C.
Kappel/Zurich, *Cistercian Church*: 14C.
Königsfelden, near Brugg/Aargau, (former) *Abbey Church*: 14C.
Köniz/Bern, *Church of the Teutonic Order*: 14C.
Lausanne, *Cathedral*: 13C.
Lucerne, *Historical Museum, Town Hall*: 16C, 17C, 18C.
Münchenbuchsee/Bern, *Johanniterkirche*: 13C, 14C.
Muri/Bern, *Convent Church*: 16C.
Romont/Fribourg, *Notre Dame de l'Assomption*: 14C, 15C.
Staufberg/Aargau, *St Nicholas's*: 15C.
Wettingen/Zurich, *Abbey Church of Maria Maris Stella*: 13C, 16C.
Zurich, *Swiss National Museum*: 12C, 13C, 14C, 16C, 17C, 18C, including extensive collection of domestic panels.

UNITED STATES

ALABAMA
Tuskegee, *Tuskegee Institute Chapel*: 20C J. and R. Lamb.

ALASKA
Anchorage, *First United Presbyterian Church*: 20C Willet Studios.

CALIFORNIA
Belvedere, *Christian Science Church*: 20C Cummings.
Davis, *St James's*: 20C Pinart.
Fort Ord, *First Brigade Chapel*: 20C Sachs.
Fresno, *First Armenian Presbyterian Church*: 20C Sachs.
Los Angeles/Glendale, *Forest Lawn Memorial Park*: 20C.
Los Gatos, *First Methodist Church*: 20C Pinart.
Menlo Park, *Christian Science Church*: 20C Sachs.
Palo Alto, *All Saints' Episcopal Church*: 20C Sowers.
Roseburg, *St Joseph's*: 20C Kepes.

San Francisco, *Grace Cathedral*: 20C Connick, Henry Lee Willet, Loire. *Masonic Memorial Temple, Nob Hill*: 20C Norman. *St Dominic's*: 20C Connick. *St Ignatius*: 20C Cummings Studio.
San Rafael, *St Paul's Episcopal Church*: 20C Burnham.

COLORADO
Colorado Springs, *Air Force Academy Chapel*: 20C Judson Studios.
Denver, *Temple Emanuel*: 20C Pinart, Labouret Studios, Paris, Wagner Studios.

CONNECTICUT
Greenwich, *Temple Shalom*: 20C Sowers.
Hamden, *Temple Mishkan Israel*: 20C Pinart, Duval.
Stamford, *First Presbyterian Church*: 20C Loire.
Woodbridge, *Congregation B'nai Jacob*: 20C Duval.

DELAWARE
Wilmington, *Cathedral Church of St John*: 20C William Willet, Henry Lee Willet, D'Ascenzo.

DISTRICT OF COLUMBIA
Washington, *Cathedral of St Peter and St Paul*: 20C Saint, Henry Lee Willet, Burnham, Reynolds, Francis & Rohnstock, Bossanyi, Le Compte, Tower (of Kempe Co.), Hone, Birkle, Sanborn, Setti, Reyntiens, Winfield. *Folger Shakespeare Library*: 20C D'Ascenzo.

FLORIDA
Jacksonville, *St John's Cathedral*: 20C Wilson.
Winter Park, *Morse Gallery of Art*: 19C–20C Tiffany.

GEORGIA
Athens, *First Methodist Church*: 20C Willet Studios.
Columbus, *Temple Israel*: 20C Miller.
Savannah, *Mickve Israel*: 19C Butler & Sons.

HAWAII
Honolulu, *St Andrew's Episcopal Cathedral*: 20C Lamb Studios. *State Building*: 20C Karawina.

ILLINOIS
Chicago, *Bethlehem Lutheran Church*: 20C Nicolas. *Loop Synagogue*: 20C Rattner. *St Andrew's Church*: 19C Burne-Jones, Holiday, Harry Goodhue. *St Chrysostom's*: 20C Connick.
Mooseheart, *House of God*: 20C Nicolas.
Peoria, *St Paul's Episcopal Church*: 20C Frei.

INDIANA
Fort Wayne, *Trinity English Evangelical Lutheran Church*: 20C Wright Goodhue, R. Toland Wright.

LOUISIANA
Shreveport, *Holy Trinity Church*: 20C Pinart.

MARYLAND
Baltimore, *Mary Our Queen Cathedral*: 20C Connick, Henry Lee Willet, Schmitt, Durhan, Loire, Burnham, Rambusch.

MASSACHUSETTS
Beverly Farms, *St John the Evangelist*: 20C Connick.
Boston, *Arlington Street Church*: 20C Tiffany. *Church of the Advent*: 19C Whall, Kempe. *Emmanuel Church*: 20C Connick, Comper, Kempe, Young, Crowninshield. *Robinson Memorial Chapel*: 20C Connick. *St Anthony's Shrine*: 20C Pinart. *Trinity Church*: 19C La Farge, Burne-Jones, 20C. *Museum of Fine Arts*: 19C Tiffany, 20C La Farge.
Brookline, *All Saints'*: 20C Goodhue, Connick.
Cambridge, *Memorial Hall, Harvard College*: 19C La Farge, Whitman.
Methuen, *First Congregational Church*: 19C La Farge.
Newton, *Temple Mishkan Tefila*: 20C Sowers.
North Easton, *Unity Church*: 20C La Farge, Connick.
Worcester, *Art Museum*: 19C, 20C La Farge.

MICHIGAN
Cranbrook, *Christ Church*: 13C (French), 20C D'Ascenzo, Guthrie, Wright Goodhue, Lloyd Wright, Powell.
Detroit, *Blessed Sacrament Cathedral*: 20C William Willet. *St Paul's Cathedral*: 20C Henry Lee Willet,

Gazetteer

Heaton, Butler & Bayne, Connick, Powell. *St Mary of Redford*: 19C–20C Burnham, Connick, Wright Goodhue.
Flint, *De Waters Art Center*: 20C Rattner.

MINNESOTA
Minneapolis, *St Mark's*: 20C Connick, Heaton, Butler & Bayne.
St Paul, *Cathedral of St Paul*: 20C Connick, Bancel La Farge. *St John the Evangelist*: 19C–20C Connick, Heaton, Butler & Bayne. *Temple B'Nai Aaron*: 20C Saltzman.

MISSOURI
Columbia, *Stephen's College*: 20C Marioni, Sowers.
St Louis, *Faith Evangelical and Reformed Church*: 20C Frei Studios. *City Art Museum*: 13C (French), 15C (French, English, German), 20C La Farge.

NEW HAMPSHIRE
Peterborough, *All Saints'*: 20C Connick.
West Lebanon, *Holy Redeemer*: 20C Sowers.

NEW JERSEY
Bayonne, *St Vincent de Paul*: 20C Clarke.
Princeton, *University Chapel*: 19C–20C Connick, D'Ascenzo, Reynolds, Francis & Rohnstock, Burnham, Wright Goodhue, Weeder, Butler & Recke, Henry Lee Willet.

NEW YORK
Albany, *Temple Beth Emeth*: 20C Sowers.
Buffalo, *St Paul's Cathedral*: 20C Young, Guthrie & Lakeman. *Temple Beth Zion*: 20C Shahn.
Islip, *St Mark's Episcopal Church*: 19C–20C Connick, Tiffany, Heaton, Butler & Bayne.
New York City, *St John the Divine*: 20C Powell, D'Ascenzo, Connick, Lakeman, Henry Lee Willet, Burnham, Heinigke, Reynolds, Francis & Rohnstock, Young, Metcalf & Norris, Hardman, Kempe, Clayton & Bell. *St Patrick's Cathedral*: 20C Woodroffe, Connick. *Church of the Ascension*: 19C La Farge, Tiffany. *Church of the Incarnation, Madison Avenue*: 19C La Farge, Young, Heaton, Butler & Bayne, Clayton & Bell, Cottier, Burne-Jones. *Bellerose Jewish Centre*: 20C Weitzman. *Congregation Habonim*: 20C Sowers. *Temple Emanu-El*: 19C–20C Tiffany. *Holy Trinity Church*, Brooklyn: 19C W. and J. Bolton. *Plymouth Church*, Brooklyn: 20C J. and R. Lamb. *Rhinelander Memorial Church of the Holy Trinity*: 19C Holiday. *Riverside Church*: 20C Wright Goodhue, Reynolds, Francis & Rohnstock, D'Ascenzo, Burnham. *St James's*: 20C Connick, Young, D'Ascenzo. *St George's*: 20C J. and R. Lamb. *St Vincent Ferrer*: 19C–20C Connick, Guthrie, Locke, Harry Goodhue. *American Airlines Terminal, Kennedy International Airport*: 20C Sowers. *The Cloisters*: 13C–14C (French), 15C–16C (Flemish, German). *KLM Royal Dutch Airlines office*: 20C Kepes. *Maxwell's Plum Restaurant*: 20C Le Roy. *Metropolitan Museum of Art*: 12C–13C (French, German), 15C (English, French), 16C (English, French, German, Swiss), 19C La Farge, 20C Tiffany, Heinigke, Lloyd Wright. *Milton Steinberg House*: 20C Gottlieb. *United Nations Secretariat*: 20C Chagall.
Pelham, *Christ Church*: 19C W. and J. Bolton.
Port Chester, *Congregation Kneses Tefereth Israel*: 20C.

Rochester, *Temple Beth El*: 20C Wiener, Weitzman.
Tarrytown, *Union Church of Pocantico Hills*: 20C Chagall, Matisse.
West Point, *United States Military Academy*: 20C William Willet.

NORTH CAROLINA
Winston Salem, *St Paul's*: 20C Wright Goodhue, Reynolds, Francis & Rohnstock.

OHIO
Cincinnati, *Christ Church*: 19C–20C Connick, Heaton, Butler & Bayne, R. and G. Metcalf.
Cleveland, *Trinity Cathedral*: 20C William Willet, Young, Connick. *Church of Our Saviour*: 20C Wright Goodhue. *Temple Emanuel*: 20C James. *Blue Grass Restaurant*, Maple Heights: 20C Winterich Studios.
Gambier, *Kenyon College*: 20C D'Ascenzo, Connick.
Toledo, *Museum of Art*: 13C–16C (European).

PENNSYLVANIA
Harrisburg, *Pine Street Presbyterian Church*: 19C–20C Connick, Wright Goodhue, Burnham.
Mercersburg, *Mercersburg Academy Chapel*: 19C–20C D'Ascenzo, Reynolds, Francis & Rohnstock, Wright Goodhue, Connick, Butler, Guthrie, Tower of Glass Studio, Dublin.
Philadelphia, *Church of the Holy Child*: 20C D'Ascenzo. *Washington Memorial Chapel*: 20C D'Ascenzo. *Reform Congregation Keneseth Israel, Elkins Park*: 20C Emerson, Tiffany, D'Ascenzo, Rambusch.
Pittsburgh, *Calvary Protestant Episcopal Church*: 20C William Willet, Connick, Heaton, Butler & Bayne, Reynolds, Francis & Rohnstock, Harry Goodhue. *East Liberty Presbyterian Church*: 19C–20C Connick, Wilbert, Burnham, Reynolds, Francis & Rohnstock, D'Ascenzo, Willet Studios. *Heinz Memorial Chapel*: 20C Connick. *Shaare Torah Temple*: 20C Parrendo. *Tree of Life Synagogue*: 20C Hickman. *University of Pittsburgh*: 20C.
Wilkinsburg, *St James's*: 20C Wright Goodhue.

RHODE ISLAND
Newport, *Emmanuel Church*: 20C Harry Goodhue, Young, Clement Heaton.
Providence, *Church of the Redeemer*: 19C–20C Connick, Guthrie.
Woonsocket, *B'nai Israel*: 20C Arikha.

VERMONT
Rutland, *Christ the King*: 20C Wright Goodhue.

WASHINGTON
Olympia, *Gloria Dei Lutheran Church*: 20C Pinart.

WISCONSIN
La Crosse, *Christ Church*: 19C–20C Tiffany, Connick.

WEST GERMANY

Aachen, *Cathedral*: 20C Schaffrath, Wendling, Benner. *St Joseph's, Adalbertastrasse*: 20C Schaffrath. *St Foillan*: 20C Buschulte. *Lourdheim*: 20C Katzgrau. *Art Museum, Wilhelmstrasse*: 20C.
Altenberg, near Cologne: *Abbey Church*: 13C, 14C.
Augsburg, *Cathedral*: 11C, 14C, 15C. *SS Ulrich and Afra*: 15C Holbein the Elder.
Bad Honnef, *St Martin's*: 20C Poensgen.
Bad Kissingen, *Catholic Parish Church*: 20C Meistermann.
Bad Zwischenahn, *St Maria*: 20C Schaffrath.

Berlin, West, *Kaiser Wilhelm Memorial Church*: 20C Loire.
Birkesdorf, *St Peter's*: 20C Schaffrath.
Blutenburg, near Munich, *Convent Chapel*: 15C.
Bottrop, *Heilig-Kreuz-Kirche*: 20C Meistermann. *St Konrad*: 20C Klos.
Bremen-Neue Vahr, *Heilig-Geist-Kirche*: 20C Schreiter.
Bremerhaven, *St Michael's*: 20C Schreiter.
Bremerhaven-Lehe, *St John's*: 20C Schreiter.
Bücken, *Collegiate Church*: 13C.
Bürgstadt, *St Margaret's*: 20C Schreiter.
Cologne, *Cathedral*: 13C, 14C, 15C, 16C. *St Georg*: 20C Thorn Prikker. *St Gereon*: 14C. *St. Kunibert*: 13C. *St Maria in den Trümmern*: 20C Gies. *Schnütgen Museum*: 14C, 15C, 16C. *West German Radio Station*: 20C Meistermann.
Cologne-Kalk, *St Marien*: 20C Meistermann, Gies.
Cologne-Marienburg, *St Maria Königin*: 20C Böhm.
Cologne-Niehl, *St Christoph*: 20C Meistermann. *St Clemens*: 20C Buschulte.
Dinslaken, *Christus-Kirche*: 20C Poensgen.
Drolshagen, *St Clemens*: 20C Buschulte.
Duisburg, *St Anna*: 20C Katzgrau.
Düren, *Eucharistiner Kloster*: 20C Buschulte. *Karmelkloster*: 20C Schaffrath.
Eichstätt, *Cathedral*: 16C Holbein the Elder.
Emden, *Town Hall*: 16C.
Eschweiler, *Liebfrau Kloster*: 20C Katzgrau.
Essen, *Minster*: 20C Buschulte, Gies, Schaffrath, Campendonk, Schreiter, Manessier.
Essen-Borbeck, *St Dionysus*: 20C Buschulte.
Esslingen, *Barfüsserkirche*: 14C. *Frauenkirche*: 14C. *St Dionys*: 14C. *Merckel'schen Schwimmbad (former swimming pool)*: 19C Graf.
Frankfurt, *Historisches Museum*: 13C, 14C, 15C, 16C, 17C.
Freiburg, *Cathedral*: 13C, 14C, 15C Hans Acker, 16C. *Augustiner-Museum*: 13C, 14C, 15C, 16C.
Freising, *St Martin's*: 15C.
Friedberg, *Marienkirche*: 15C.
Gelsenkirchen, *Reform Synagogue*: 20C.
Goslar, *Cathedral*: 16C. *Marktkirche*: 13C. *Museum*: 13C.
Haan, near Düsseldorf, *St Mary's*: 20C Poensgen.
Hagen, *St Meinholf*: 20C Buschulte. *Karl Ernst Osthausen Museum*: 20C Thorn Prikker. *Railway Station*: 20C Thorn Prikker.
Haina, *St Mary's*: 14C.
Hamburg, *St Marienkirche*: 20C Schreiter.
Hanover, *Marktkirche*: 15C.
Heilbronn, *St Kilian's*: 15C.
Heiligkreuztal, *St Anna's*: 14C.
Helmstedt, *Abbey Church Marienberg*: 13C.
Herford, *St John's*: 14C, 15C, 16C.
Hohenzollern, near Hechingen, *Castle Chapel*: 13C.
Julich, *Prosterkirche*: 20C Wendling, Schaffrath. *St Rochus*: 20C Speiling.
Karlsruhe, *Landesmuseum*: 13C, 14C, 15C, 16C.
Kassel, *Museum*: 14C.
Kitzingen, *St John's*: 20C Schreiter.
Kyllburg, *Parish Church*: 16C.
Landsberg am Lech, *Parish Church*: 16C.
Leutesdorf/Rhein, *Kapelle des Exerzitienhauses Johannesbund*: 20C Schreiter.
Leverkusen-Fettehenne, *Mathiaskirche*: 20C Schaffrath.

Lüneburg, *Town Hall*: 15C.
Marburg, *St Elisabeth's*: 13C, 14C.
Mönchen-Gladbach, *St Vitus's*: 13C.
Munich, *Frauenkirche*: 15C Hemmel von Andlau, 16C. *Maria-Hilfe-Kirche*: 19C. *Michaelskirche*: 16C Hans and Georg Hebenstreit. *Bavarian National Museum*: 14C, 15C, 16C.
Münnerstadt, *St Maria Magdalena*: 15C.
Münster, *Cathedral*: 16C. *Landesmuseum*: 12C, 13C, 14C.
Neukloster, *Cistercian Church*: 13C.
Neuss, *Christus-Kirche*: 20C Thorn Prikker.
Nuremberg, *St Lorenz*: 14C, 15C Hemmel von Andlau, 16C. *St Sebald's*: 14C, 16C. *Germanisches National-Museum*: 12C, 13C, 14C, 15C, 16C, 17C, 18C. *Tucher House*: 16C.
Nuremberg-Wöhrd, *St Bartholomew's*: 16C.
Pilgerzell, near Fulda, *Catholic Church*: 20C Poensgen.
Ratzeburg, *Cathedral*: 20C Buschulte.
Regensburg, *Cathedral*: 14C. *Dominican Abbey of the Holy Cross*: 14C.
Rothenburg ob der Tauber, *St James's*: 14C, 15C.
Saarbrücken, *Liebfrauenkirche*: 20C Buschulte.
Schweinfurt, *St Kilian's*: 20C Meistermann. *St Michael's*: 20C Schaffrath.
Sennestadt, *Jesus-Christus-Kirche*: 20C Lander.
Sobernheim, *St Matthew's*: 20C Meistermann.
Soest, *St Patroklus*: 12C, 13C, 15C. *St Pauli*: 13C, 14C. *Wiesenkirche*: 14C, 15C.
Straubing, *St James's*: 15C.
Stuttgart, *Landesmuseum*: 13C, 14C, 15C.
Trier, *St Matthew's*: 15C, 16C.
Tübingen, *St George's*: 15C Hemmel von Andlau.

Ulm, *Cathedral*: 14C Jacob Acker, 15C Hans and Jacob Acker, Hemmel von Andlau workshop, 20C Kohler, Von Stockhausen.
Ulm-Bofingen, *Guter-Hirte-Kirche*: 20C Schaffrath.
Urach, *St Amandus*: 15C Hemmel von Andlau.
Walbeck, *St Nicholas's*: 20C Klos.
Wienhausen, *Abbey Church*: 13C, 14C, 15C.
Wimpfen am Berg, *Parish Church*: 13C, 15C.
Würzburg, *Cathedral*: 20C Meistermann.
Xanten, *St Victor*: 14C, 15C, 20C Gottfried.

Glossary

Abrading, abrasion Removal of coloured areas of flashed glass by scraping or grinding away with a flint.
Acid-etching Process of removing coloured flashing. The area of flashing to be removed is first outlined. The rest is masked with bituminous paint, while hydrofluoric acid eats through the exposed portion to the paler-coloured layer below.
Aisle Side division of a church, parallel to the nave.
Ambulatory Semicircular or polygonal aisle running around the eastern end of a church, behind the altar.
Annealing Final, cooling process in glass manufacture.
Antique glass Hand-made, blown glass, which has the irregular, crumbly texture of medieval glass.
Antitype New Testament scene which, in medieval doctrine, is prefigured by a type, an Old Testament scene.
Apse Semicircular or polygonal eastern end of a church.
Atrium In Roman architecture an inner courtyard; also the forecourt, sometimes cloistered, of Early Christian and Byzantine churches.

Badger Wide, soft brush, with hairs three to four inches long, used to produce smooth or stippled effects on a wash of paint.
Baptistery Part of a church, or adjacent building, used for baptisms.
Baroque Architectural style of the seventeenth and early eighteenth centuries, characterized by curves and extravagant ornamentation.
Basilica Originally a large, oblong Roman assembly hall, often with a semicircular apse; in Early Christian and later architecture a church built on this plan with the nave higher than the aisles.
Bas-relief Sculpture which projects slightly from its background.
Bema In Early Christian churches a raised platform for the clergy. In later church architecture it was developed to form embryonic transepts.
Bestiary Allegorical, medieval moralizing book describing real and mythological beasts.
Biblia Pauperum see **Poor Man's Bible**
Blockbook Late medieval book printed from wooden blocks upon which the text and illustrations were carved in relief.
Boss Raised carved ornament, usually at the intersection of the ribs in a vaulted ceiling.
Bottle glass see **Norman slab**
Buttress Projecting support built on to the exterior of a wall to counteract the outward thrust of an interior arch or vault.
Byzantine Early Christian architecture, typified by the church plan on a Greek cross, by domes, and by internal mosaic decoration.

Calm (plural calmes) Strip of lead used in stained-glass windows.
Cameo glass Two-layered glass; when carved the upper white layer stands in relief against the darker background.
Canopy Glass framework within a window imitating an architectural niche and surrounding figures or a scene.
Capital Crowning feature of a column.
Cartoon Full-size design for a stained-glass window.
Cathedral glass Commercial, machine-rolled stained glass widely used in the United States.
Champlevé Enamelling in which metal areas are gouged out and the hollows filled with enamel, leaving a raised metal outline.
Chancel Eastern part of a church, reserved for clergy and containing the altar and choir.
Chevet French term for the eastern end of a church comprising the apse, its surrounding ambulatory and radiating chapels.
Choir Eastern part of a church in which the choristers sit, usually separated from the nave by a screen or rail; sometimes applied to the whole chancel.
Cinquefoil see **Foil**
Clerestory Upper tier of a church, pierced with windows.
Cloisonné Enamelling in which different colours of enamel are separated by narrow cloisons, or strips, of metal, usually gold, which are soldered on to a metal base.

Cloisters Covered arcade around an open space, connecting the domestic part of a monastery to the church.
Corbel Bracket or block projecting from a wall to support a roof beam or other horizontal feature.
Crocket Carved decorative projection on Gothic pinnacles or gables.
Crossing Intersection of transepts and nave in a church.
Crown, or spun, glass Blown glass, rare today, spun into a flat disc with a thick central knob.
Cullet Scrap or waste glass remaining after cutting the pieces for a window.
Cusp Projecting stonework point at the intersection of two arcs in Gothic tracery.
Cutline Tracing of the lead-line pattern from the cartoon.
Cylinder glass see **Muff glass**

Dalle de verre Pieces of glass, usually about one inch thick and often chipped or faceted on the surface, which are set into concrete or epoxy resin.
Decorated Late thirteenth-century to mid-fourteenth-century phase of English Gothic architecture, characterized by geometric and later by flowing tracery.
Diapered Covered with a geometric pattern of small squares or lozenges.
Dividing iron Medieval tool; the tip was heated to crack glass.

Enamelling Application of enamel paint to glass.
Endomosaic Combination of stained glass and mosaic.
Epoxy resin Synthetic, colourless adhesive, used instead of leading to hold together pieces of stained glass, particularly dalle de verre.
Eye window Circular window with no stone tracery.

Faceted glass see **Dalle de verre**
Favrile glass Iridescent glass, patented by Tiffany in the 1880s, produced by the exposure of hot glass to metallic fumes and oxides.
Fillet Thin strip of glass.
Firing Process of heating painted glass so that the paint and glass fuse smoothly and securely.
Flashed glass Two-layered glass, the bottom layer of white or light-coloured glass, the thinner top layer of a darker colour.
Flux Solvent, usually soda ash, used to assist the melting of silica in glass manufacture. Also, as borax, used to assist the fusion of paint to glass.
Flying buttress Arch or half-arch abutting against an outside wall and carrying the thrust of a vault to an outer support.
Foil Small arc opening in Gothic tracery; the number of foils is indicated by a prefix—trefoil (three), quatrefoil (four), cinquefoil (five).
Fused glass Pieces of coloured glass bonded to a sheet of glass by heat.

Glass appliqué Collage of pieces of coloured glass glued with epoxy resin to clear plate glass.
Glazing bar Iron window bar.
Golden Legend (Legenda Aurea) Book describing the lives of the saints, written by Jacobus de Voragine c. 1275.
Gothic Style of architecture, dating from the mid-twelfth century, generally associated with the pointed arch, the flying buttress and the rib vault.
Greek cross Cross with four arms of equal length.
Grisaille (from the French "grisailler", to paint grey) Clear glass, ornamented in muted colours with delicate, often foliar patterns and leaded into decorative designs.
Grozing Biting away the edge of a piece of glass with pliers.
Grozing iron Medieval notched tool used to nibble glass into shape.

Halation Phenomenon whereby light-coloured glass surrounded by darkness or solid masonry produces a blurred effect, the light seeming to spread beyond the actual boundaries.
Heel-ball Black wax composition used in the process of stained-glass restoration to make rubbings of glass panels on thin paper.

Isothermal glazing System of protective outer glazing.

Jesse Tree Genealogical tree, showing Christ's descent from Jesse, popular in many forms of medieval art including stained glass.

Labours of the months Activities ascribed to each month of the year; recurrent theme in medieval manuscripts as well as in stained glass.
Lancet Tall, slim, pointed window.
Lathekin Small, sharpened piece of wood or bone used for opening and straightening leads.
Latin cross Cross with one long arm and three short arms.
Lead Strip of lead, grooved on both sides, to hold pieces of stained glass in place.
Leading-up Assembly of glass with leads.
Legenda Aurea see **Golden Legend**
Light Opening between the mullions of a window.
Linenfold Woodcarving on medieval wall panelling and seating which resembles the folds of linen.

Matt Muted, uniform finish.
Medallion windows Windows composed of variously shaped small panels, often arranged in a narrative sequence.
Millefiori Roman ornamental patterned glass resembling mosaic.
Misericord Carved underside of hinged seat in choirstalls.
Mould-blown glass Glass blown into an open-topped mould.
Muff, or cylinder, glass Most commonly used form of stained glass; produced by cutting off the end of an elongated balloon of glass which is then split along its length to form a flattened sheet.
Muller Pestle, usually of granite or glass, with which pigment is ground.
Mullion Vertical stone shaft which divides window lights.

Narthex Western arcaded porch, or vestibule, of Early Christian and some later basilican churches.
Nave Main part or central aisle of a church, extending from the entrance to the transepts or choir.
Norman slab, or bottle, glass Glass blown into a square mould, each side of which is cut into a sheet of glass. It is rarely used today.

Occhio (plural occhi) Italian eye window.
Ogee S-shaped curve.
Ojo de buey Spanish bull's-eye window, round and devoid of stone tracery.
Opalescent glass Glass developed in the late nineteenth century by La Farge and Tiffany, in which streaks of colour, when fused, give a milky, iridescent appearance.

Perpendicular English Gothic architectural style of the late fourteenth and fifteenth centuries, characterized by strongly defined vertical lines; see also **Tracery**, Perpendicular.
Pier Solid masonry support, usually thicker than a column but fulfilling the same function.
Pinnacle Slender, pyramidical or conical architectural ornament, used to terminate buttresses and gables.
Plan Architectural design of a church.
Plating Backing of thin plain or coloured glass used to reinforce fragments of ancient glass.
Poor Man's Bible (Biblia Pauperum) Medieval devotional book, in manuscript and blockbook form, summarizing the prophetic parallels between events in the Old and New Testaments.
Pot glass, pot metal Antique glass coloured throughout with one colour.

Quarry Square or diamond-shaped pane of glass used particularly in grisaille windows.
Quatrefoil see **Foil**

Reamy glass Irregular streaky glass, made from a mixture of glass of different hardnesses.
Reredos Decorated wooden or stone screen behind the altar.
Rib Projecting band, either structural or decorative, separating the divisions of a groined vault.
Rococo Eighteenth-century development of Baroque architecture, characterized by a proliferation of ornamental details.
Romanesque Architectural style based on the techniques of Roman architecture and characterized by round arches and thick columns and walls.

Rose window Circular window with tracery radiating in petal-like shapes.
Roundel Circular panel of glass.

Sacristy Repository for sacred vessels in a church.
Seedy glass Bubbly antique glass.
Silver stain Silver compound, usually silver nitrate, which when fused to glass produces a yellow colour.
Slab glass see **Dalle de verre**
Smear shading Method of shading details such as drapery and features by applying pigment sparingly with parallel brush strokes; prevalent until the fourteenth century.
Speculum Humanae Salvationis (Mirror of Human Salvation) Illustrated medieval devotional book relating the Bible story from the fall of Lucifer to the Redemption of man.
Springing line Point at which an arch rises from its supports, or, in a window, at which a mullion curves.
Spun glass see **Crown glass**
Stippling Method of painting which creates the effect of minute points of light all over the glass.
Strap-work Interlacing bands forming geometric patterns on glass.
Streaky glass Glass in which the colour appears as streaks, rather than being uniformly dispersed.

Template Full-size paper or card pattern of a window; also piece of tracing paper or card used, particularly in France and Germany, as a pattern around which glass is cut out.
Tracery Ornamental stonework in the upper part of a Gothic window. PLATE tracery: the earliest, most elementary form, in which simple shapes are cut out of the stonework; BAR tracery: thirteenth-century development in which patterns are formed by thin stone ribs; GEOMETRIC tracery: earliest form of bar tracery distinguished by symmetrical shapes; FLOWING tracery: more curvaceous, fourteenth-century style of bar tracery; FLAMBOYANT tracery: fifteenth-century French form characterized by flame-like curves; PERPENDICULAR tracery: comparatively sober style characterized by vertical lines which succeeded flowing in late fourteenth-century England. RECTILINEAR tracery: fifteenth-century development of Perpendicular characterized by a system of rectangular panels.
Transepts Two projecting arms, usually between the nave and chancel, of a cruciform church.
Transom Horizontal iron bar which divides a window.
Trefoil see **Foil**
Triforium Arcaded gallery below the clerestory, sometimes glazed, facing on to the nave.
Type Old Testament scene, which, in medieval doctrine, was believed to prefigure a scene from the New Testament, the antitype.
Typological window Window depicting Old and New Testament scenes, symbolically juxtaposed.
Typology Medieval doctrine that events in the New Testament are foreshadowed symbolically by events in the Old Testament.

Vault Arched ceiling or roof. BARREL OR TUNNEL vault: the simplest form which, unbroken in its length, resembles a tunnel. CROSS OR GROIN vault: formed by the intersection at right angles of two tunnel vaults; RIB vault: development of cross vaulting in which the arched diagonals known as groins are replaced by arched ribs built across the sides and diagonals of a vaulted bay as support; FAN vault: form of rib vault in which ribs radiate in a fan-like pattern from the springing point of an arch.
Verre doublé see **Flashed glass**

Wash Thin coat of paint.
Wheel window Round window in which the stone tracery radiates from the centre like the spokes of a wheel.

Yellow stain see **Silver stain**

Index

The gazetteer and glossary have not been indexed. The various forms of "Saint", with reference to churches, are written as S.

A

Aachen Cathedral, 77, 160, 161
Aaron, rod of, 37
Abraham, 76, 153
Abrasion, 48–9, 104, 182
Aciding, acid-etching, 49, 182–3
Acker, Hans, and family, 39, 115
Adam, 71, 114
 and Eve, 108, 133, 139, 145
Adam the Forester, 82
Adoration of the Magi, 80–1, 100–1, 137; see also Magi
Adornes family, 131
Adventures in Light and Colour, Connick, 162
Aelst, Pieter Coecke van, 126
Aesop's fables, 29
Agnes of Habsburg, 96
Agony in the Garden, El Greco, 39
Air Force (US) Academy Chapel, 164
Aisle, 14–15, 16, 17, 72
Aix-la-Chapelle *see* Aachen
Alban, St, 112
Albert I, of Austria, 96
Albert Memorial, London, 151
Albertus Magnus, 80
Alcazar, Toledo, 109
Aldegrever, 61
Aldrin, Edwin, 163
Alexander the Great, 10
Alexandria, 10, 11
Alfred jewel, 12
Alfred the Great, 12
Alice in Wonderland, Carroll, 29
Aligret, Simon, 104
Alkalinity, damage to glass from, 190
All Hallows, Wellingborough, 33
All Saints', Middleton Cheney, 153
All Saints', North Street, York, 28, 33, 86, 112
Alma-Taddema, Sir Laurence, 154
Alpha and Omega, 32, 87
Alsace, stained glass in, 92–3
Altars
 depiction in glass of, 98
 siting of, 14, 17
Altenberg, Abbey Church, 14, 18, 81, 84
Aluminium silicates, 8
Ambulatory, 14–15
Amenhotep IV, 10
American Airlines Terminal, New York, 164
Amersham Church, 150
Amiens Cathedral, 17, 22, 72
Amsterdam, modern glass in, 174
Ancient world, glass in, 10–11
Andlau, Peter Hemmel von, 37, 114–15, 117, 137, 140
Andrea da Firenze, 61, 95
Angels, 20–1, 30–1, 76, 77, 108, 111, 113, 120
Angers Cathedral, 22, 37, 42, 69, 78, 105
Animals, 25–6, 32–3, 44–5, 86, 87, 89, 113, 115, 135, 136, 139
Anne, St, 34, 56, 74, 75, 96, 115
Annealing processes, 8, 185
Annunciation, The, 14, 25, 41, 45, 76, 96, 103, 104, 117, 121, 122, 123, 133, 137, 146–7, 155
Anselm, Bishop of Tournai, 102
Anselm, St, 70
Anthony of Padua, St, 94–5
Antioch, cult of relics in, 80
Antique glass, 8–9, 180–1
Antwerp, artists from, 133, 134; see also S. Lierre
Antwerp Cathedral, 130
Apocalypse, 30, 32, 78, 79, 86–7, 105, 123
Apocryphal works, 25–6
Apostles, The, 12, 28, 32, 34, 35, 68, 69, 76, 92, 96, 107, 118, 130
Apothecaries, Milan Corporation of, 123
Apparition at Arles, 95

Appliqué *see* Glass appliqué
Apse, 16
Aquitania, Duke of, 74
Arab peoples *see* Islam
Aragon, 106; see also Spain
Arcade, 16
Arch, 16–17, 64
Archangels, 34–5
Architecture
 parallels in costume, 54
 relationship with glass, 16–17, 50–1, 64, 68, 72, 84, 86, 97, 142, 158, 160, 164, 168, 171
 representation in glass, 50–1, 84, 90, 96, 115, 123, 124, 138, 140; see also Canopies and Secular buildings, glass in;
 steel framing, 16, 17; see also Twentieth century
Arezzo *see* S. Annunziata, S. Francesco
Arezzo Cathedral, 141
Arian Baptistery, Ravenna, 12
Aristotle, 44, 97
Arms *see* Heraldry
Armstrong, Neil, 163
Arnao de Flandes, Vergara
Arnold, St, 148
Arnouldt de la Pointe *see* Nijmegen
Arqr, Juan de, 106
Arrow-heads, obsidian, 8
Art
 constraints on medieval, 24–7
 conventions in medieval, 32–3, 98
 in history of stained glass, 60–3
 see also Painting *and under individual styles*
Art Nouveau, 63, 146, 154–7, 172
Arthurian legends, 29
Artists, status of, 60–1
Arts, The, depiction of, 109, 111
Arundel Castle, 145
Ascension, Church of the, Birmingham, 188
Ascension, The, 68, 69, 118, 121, 132
Ass, symbolism of, 25–6
Assheton, Sir Richard, 40
Assisi *see* Francis, St, S. Francesco
Assumption of the Virgin Mary, 25, 75, 118, 120
Assy *see* Notre Dame de Toute Grace
Atmospheric pollution, 190–1
Auch Cathedral, 50
Audincourt *see* Sacred Heart
Augsburg, 124
Augsburg Cathedral, 13, 42, 60, 64, 66–7, 69, 114, 190, 191
Augustine of Canterbury, St, 24, 70
Augustine of Hippo, St, 140
Aureoles *see* Haloes
Austen, Jane, 124
Australia, modern glass in, 173
Austria, Baroque style in, 142
Autun Cathedral, 20, 31
 Museum, 31
Auxerre, 78
Avila *see* S. Pedro
Avila Cathedral, 106, 132, 133

B

Backing plates, 192–3
Bacon, Francis, 56
Bacon, Sir Francis, 31
Badger brush *see* Brushes
Balaam and the Ass window, Gouda, 129
Baldwin II, Emperor of Constantinople, 78
Balliol College Chapel, Oxford, 144
Banding, 188
Baptism, symbols of, 32
Baptism of Christ, 12
Baptism of Christ window, Gouda, 128, 129
Baptistery, 12, 17, 119, 121, 168
Barcelona, 106
Barcelona, Art Nouveau in, 154, 155
Barcelona Cathedral, 106–7
Bardi Chapel *see* S. Croce
Bargello Museum, Florence, 118
Barnabas, St, 134
Baroncelli Chapel *see* S. Croce
Baroque architecture, 142, 145

Barry, Charles, 150–1
Basilica, Roman, 15, 16; see also Byzantine architecture
Bas-reliefs, 31
Bathsheba, 141
Battle of Britain window, Westminster Abbey, 55, 58–9
Bavarian National Museum, Munich, 99
Bayeux Tapestry, 46
Beauchamp Chapel *see* S. Mary, Warwick
Beauvais *see* S. Etienne *and* Le Prince family
Beauvais Cathedral, 16, 37, 72
Becket, Thomas, St, 58, 70, 82, 112, 142
Beckingham family, 135
Bede, the Venerable, 76
Bedford Book of Hours, 105
Behaim, Martin, 117
Belgium, modern glass in, 174–5; see also Flanders
Bell, Alfred, 60, 151
Bell-Founders' window, York, 41, 86, 88
Benedict Biscop, 12–13
Benedictine Order, 67, 106
Benefactions *see* Donations
Béranger, 148
Berlin *see* Kaiser Wilhelm Memorial Church
Bernard of Clairvaux, St, 68, 72, 74, 102
Bernhardt, Sarah, 63
Berry, Jean, Duke of, 104
Bertini, Giovanni, and sons, 149
Beskow, Bo Viktor, 174
Besserer Chapel *see* Ulm Cathedral
Bestiaries, 44, 45, 86
Beverley Minster, 15
Bible, The
 as source of inspiration, 24–7, 44–5, 80, 86–7, 89, 98, 108, 110, 112, 113, 115, 133, 149; see also New Testament, Old Testament.
 illumination of, 36
Biblia Pauperum see Poor Man's Bible
Bing, Samuel, 155, 157
Birds, 44–5, 89, 97–8, 135, 154
Birmingham *see* Ascension, Church of the
Bishop's Eye, Lincoln, 22
Bishopsbourne *see* S. Mary
Black Death, 84, 86, 90
Blanche of Castile, 75, 77, 79
Bléville, Mathieu, 139
Blinding of Elymas, The, Raphael, 127
Blowing iron, 10–11
Blue Grass Restaurant, Cleveland, 164
Boaz, 57, 67
Bobby of Rochester, 82
Böblinger, Matthäus, 115
Boda glassworks, Sweden, 175
Böhm, Dominikus, 160
Bologna, glass workshops, 123
Bolton, John, and William, 149
Bonaiuto, Andrea di, 120
Bonifacio, Pedro, 104
Books of Hours, 52, 104, 105
Borders, 20, 42–3, 45, 64, 86, 120, 121
Boss, roof, 15
Bossanyi, Ervin, 43, 63
Boston, Museum of Fine Arts, 154
Botticelli, Sandro, 119, 122
Bottle glass *see* Norman slab glass
Bourges, Hôtel de Ville, 104
Bourges Cathedral, 12, 33, 37, 39, 72, 78, 79, 100, 104
Bownde, Richard, 134
Bradley, Ray, 158
Brandiston Hall, Norfolk, 52–3
Brangwyn, Frank, 155
Braque, Georges, 62, 158, 170
Breidfjord, Leifur, 174
Britain
 modern glass techniques in, 179, 188, 189
 restoring stained glass in, 190–4
 twentieth-century glass in, 158, 168–9
 see also England
British Museum, 10, 11, 24, 26

Brown, Jimmy, 164
Bruges *see* Adornes family, Holy Blood
Brujas, Carlos de, 132
Brunelleschi, Filippo, 61, 118, 119, 121
Brushes, for painting, 183, 184–5
Brussels, Art Nouveau in, 155
Brussels Cathedral, 126, 127, 130
Bullion glass, 9
Bull's-eye windows, 22, 133
Bunnell, Kathie, 165
Burg Kreuzenstein collection, 37
Burgos Cathedral, 72, 106
Burgundy, House of, 102
Burne-Jones, Edward, 21, 29, 30, 62, 146, 152–3
Buron, Romain, 61, 139
Burrell Collection, Glasgow, 52, 135
Bury St Edmunds Cathedral, 151
Busch, Valentin, 61, 140
Buschulte, Wilhelm, 160, 161
Buttressing, 16–17, 98
Byram Hall, Yorks, 194
Byzantine architecture, 15, 16, 64
 use of glass in, 12, 158
Byzantine art, 12, 13
 depiction of Christ in, 12, 38, 39
 influence of, 12, 42, 67, 69, 92
 move away from, 94–5

C

Cadmium selenium, 9
Cage-cups, Roman, 11
Calcium silicates, 8
Calcium sulphate, damage to glass from, 191
Calvinism *see* Protestantism
Cambridge University, glass for colleges of, 144–5; see also individual colleges
Camden Society, 151
Campin, Jean de, 133
Cana, Marriage Feast at, 53, 77
Canaan, grapes of, 25, 141
Candlestick, seven-branch, 33, 167
Canopies, 50–1, 62, 84, 90–1, 92, 94, 104, 105, 111, 113, 115, 120, 134, 138
Canterbury Cathedral
 glass, 22, 32, 33, 43, 53, 56, 63, 64, 70–1, 82
 history, 35, 64, 70–1, 142
 restoration of glass, 191, 192–3, 194
 see also Becket
Canterbury Tales, Chaucer, 82
Caravaggio, 38
Cariti, Bernard, 84
Carroll, Lewis, 29
Cartoons, for stained glass, 26, 128, 153, 168, 178, 179
Castagno, Andrea del, 61, 118, 120–1
Castile, castles of, 43, 79; see also Spain
Catacombs, 39
Cathedral schools, 64
Catherine de Medici, 138, 140
Catherine of Alexandria, St, 35, 69, 96, 104, 114
Cecilia, St, 80
Celtic art, influence of, 173
Cementing, 187; see also Fixing
Central Synagogue, London, 166–7
Ceres, 29
Cervantes, Miguel de, 132
Chagall, Marc, 58, 62, 166, 167, 170, 177, 182
Chair of Mercy window, Cologne, 117
Châlons-sur-Marne, glass workshops, 139; see also Notre-Dame-en-Vaux
Chamberlain, Sir William, 40
Chance, William Edward, 146
Chancel, 14, 15
Chantilly, Château, 139, 140
Chapelle Royale, Dreux, 148
Chapels, side, 14
Charlemagne, 77, 92

Charlemagne window, Chartres, 75, 77
Charles V, Holy Roman Emperor, 126, 127, 130, 131, 132, 133
 window, Brussels, 126, 127
Charles I, King of England, 55, 56
Charles VI, King of France, 105
Charles VII, King of France, 78
Charles VIII, King of France, 138
Charles IX, King of France, 138
Charles the Bald, 64
Chartres
 medieval prosperity of, 74, 116
Chartres Cathedral
 architecture, 16, 17, 72, 74
 cult of Virgin, 64–5, 74–5
 donations, donors, 40, 75, 76, 77
 glass, 13, 22, 23, 30, 32, 36, 37, 40, 50, 64, 71, 72, 74–5, 76–7, 120
 history, 64, 74
 influence of glass, 71, 78
 quality of light in, 18, 72, 74, 75, 76
 school, 64
Chaucer, Geoffrey, 82
Chester Cathedral, 50, 142
Chester Miracle Plays, 26
Chetwode Church, 43
Chevet, 14, 98
Chiaroscuro, 38–9
Chicago World Fair, 157
Chilperic I of Neustria, 102, 103
Chivalry, Age of, in Germany, 80–1
Choice of glass, 180–1
Choir, screened, 16
Christ
 depiction of, 22, 24, 25, 27, 32, 33, 36–7, 52, 69, 75, 76, 79, 90, 93, 96, 97, 98, 100–1, 103, 105, 107, 108, 113, 114, 115, 117, 118, 121, 128, 129, 132, 141
 face of, 13, 38–9
 genealogy of, 36–7, 71; *see also* Jesse Tree;
 symbols associated with, 32–3
 see also individual themes
Christ and the Virgin, glorification of, 22
Christ Church, Dinslaken, 160
Christ Church Cathedral, Oxford, 21, 42, 51, 144, 153
Christ in the Garden of Olives, Gauguin, 39
Christianity, Christian Church
 and paganism, 30–1
 characteristics of architecture and plan of, 14–15, 16–17
 characteristics of early art, 12–14, 30–3
 modern attitudes to glass, 158
Christopher, St, 35
Churchill, Winston, memorial window, 172
Cimabue, Giovanni, 95
Cione, Nardo di, 120
Cipriani, Giovanni Battista, 56
Circles, significance of designs based on, 20–1, 22–3, 32
Circular windows *see* Rose windows
Circumcision window, Florence, 119
Cisneros, Jiménez de, 108, 111
Cistercian Order, 72, 106
Clare, St, 96
Clarke, Harry, 158, 182
Classical architecture, 16; see also Renaissance architecture
Classical literature, as source of inspiration, 28–9
Classicism *see* Neo-classical style *and* Renaissance
Clayton, John Richard, 151
Clayton & Bell, 60
Clément of Chartres, 60, 61
Cleopatra, 151
Clerestory, 14, 16, 64
Climate
 effect on glass, 190, 191, 194
 effect on use of glass, 72
 see also Italy, Spain
Cloisonné enamel, 12
Cloisters, 15
Clopton family, 112, 113
Clothes *see* Costume
Clovis I, King of the Franks, 78
Cluny *see* Benedictine Order

200

Coats of arms, 46–9; see also Heraldry
Coeur, Jacques, 100, 104
Coignières Church, 177, 178, 189
Collage techniques, 177, 189
Collectors, 144, 145
Colmar, Bible windows, 37
Cologne
  glass in early synagogue, 166
  glass workshops, 137
  Radio Station, 158, 160
  see also Dominican Church, S. Ursula
Cologne Cathedral
  architecture, 72, 80–1
  glass, 42, 45, 48, 49, 80–1, 84–5, 117, 137
  history, 80–1, 142
  relics in, 80–1
Colombes Church, 171
Colour, colours
  and light, 18–19, 106
  in heraldry, 47, 48–9
  modern use of, 62–3; see also Twentieth century;
  national preferences for, 67, 80, 84, 92, 93, 97–9, 160
  production methods in glass, 8–9, 11, 84, 145, 146
  quality of, 36, 37, 63, 64, 69, 72–8, 107, 110–11, 118–19, 120–1
  symbolic use of, 17, 32, 33, 58, 168
  theories, 18, 146
  vulnerability to decay, 191
  see also Enamelling
Columbus, Christopher, 100, 106
Comper, Sir Ninian, 56, 57, 60
Composition (Mondrian), Kehlmann, 165
Conches see S. Foy
Concrete, glass set in, see Dalle de verre
Connick, Charles J., 162
Connick Studios, 29, 162
Conrad II, Emperor, 92
Conrad of Hirsau, 67
Conrad Schmitt Studios, 164
Constantine, Emperor, 15
Constantinople, cult of relics in, 80; see also Hagia Sophia and Baldwin II
Contrasts, Pugin, 150
Conversion of St Paul, 162–3
Copper, 8
Copper wire, 188
Cornelisz, Jacob, 126
Corporal Acts of Mercy, 112
Corpus Christi, festival of, 26
Corpus Vitrearum Medii Aevi, 191
Cosin, Bishop, 144
Costume
  depiction of, 48, 54–5, 56, 112, 113, 114, 116, 119, 138, 139, 140, 141
  parallels in architecture, 54
Counter-Reformation, 38, 142
Cousin, Jean, 128
Coutin, Loys, 109
Couturier, Le Père, 170
Coventry Cathedral, 18, 31, 51, 58, 158, 168–9, 174
Coventry Miracle Plays, 26
Cowick Priory, Devon, 49
Coxcie, Michiel, 126
Crabeth, Dirck, 126, 128–9, 131
Crabeth, Wouter, 126, 128–9, 131
Craft guilds
  disputes with foreign artists, 134
  heraldic arms of, 46, 48
  power of, 103, 118, 119
  windows given by, 40–1, 75, 76, 77, 98, 102, 103, 105, 123
Creation, The, 20, 76, 166–7
Cristóbal, 110
Cross, significance, symbolism of, 14–15, 22, 32–3, 39, 45, 67; see also Crucifixion
Crown (spun) glass, 9, 180, 181
Crucifix see Cross, Crucifixion
Crucifixion, The, 20, 25, 37, 41, 69, 95, 98, 108, 111, 113, 123, 131, 144, 162
Cruciform planning see Cross
Crusades, 46, 54
Crux dissimulata, 32
Cruyt, Marcus, 131

Crystal Palace, 151
Cubism, 62, 160, 171
Cullet, 8, 180
Culmer, Richard (Blue Dick), 142
Cult of the Carts, Chartres, 74
Cummings, Harold, 164
Cupid and Psyche, 139, 140
Cusp, 20
Cuthbert, St, 89
Cutline, 178–9, 181–2, 186
Cutting techniques, 178–9, 181–2
Cylinder (muff) glass, 8–9, 180, 181

D

D'Ascenzo, Nicola, 162
Dalle de verre, 9, 51, 158, 160, 164, 171, 172, 177, 179, 181, 182, 187, 188
Damage to glass, causes of, 190–1
Daniel, 24–5, 66–7, 71, 77, 88, 190
Danse Macabre, 27
Dante, Divine Comedy, 12
Daphni, 39
Daresbury Church, 29
Darkness, associations of, 14
Darmstadt Museum, 33, 45
Darricarrere, Roger, 164
David, King, 24, 34, 37, 66–7, 75, 114, 153
Day, Lewis, 22–3
Day of Atonement, 167
Day of Judgement, Jewish, 167; see also Last Judgement
Day of Resurrection see Resurrection
De Clare family, 56, 91
De Diversis Artibus, (Upon Various Arts), Theophilus, 10, 177
De Mochis see Much
De Nimègue, Arnoult, see Nijmegen
De Voragine, Jacobus, 28, 35
Dean's Eye, Lincoln, 72
Decay of glass, causes, symptoms of, 190, 191
Decimil, St, 35
Decorated Gothic style, 50, 84, 86, 88, 89, 90; see also Gothic style, Tracery
Delacroix, Eugène, 62, 148, 149
Delaunay, Robert, 173
Demons, 32–3
Denis, St, 105, 131
Deocarus, relics of, 117
Deposition of Christ, 118, 121, 131, 144
Design
  characteristics of modern, 158, 160, 164–5, 170–1, 174–5
  importance of paper, printing on, 26–7
  influence of Art Nouveau on, 146, 154–5, 156–7
  influence of painting on, 61, 62–3, 67, 95, 96, 103, 104, 117, 124, 126, 137
  influence of Pre-Raphaelites on, 146, 152–3
  medieval conventions of, 24, 26–7
  preparation stage of, 26, 177
  reconstruction of, during restoration, 193
  sources of, 24–9
  see also individual aspects
Devéria, Eugène, 149
Devil, The, 30–1, 132, 139, 144
Diamond cutters, 181
Diane de Poitiers, 138, 140
Diatreta, 11
Dickens, Charles, 29, 82
Didron, Adolphe Napoléon, 149
Diepenbale, Valerius, 141
Dijon, illuminated Bible, 36
Dinslaken see Christ Church
Dionysius, 6, 69
Dionysus, 11
Dismantling a window, 192
Division ties, 188
Doesburg, Theo van, 174
Dolfin, Juan, 108, 109, 111
Dome, 16, 118, 121
Dominican Church, Cologne, 80, 81
Dominican Church, Strasbourg, 93
Dominican Order, 14
Dominique, St, 170

Donatello, 61, 100, 118, 119, 120–1
Donations, donors, 40–1, 75, 84, 116, 117, 129, 177
  by craft guilds, 40–1, 75, 76, 77, 98, 102, 103, 105, 123
  by labour unions, 163
  depiction of, 40–1, 56, 68, 69, 75, 76, 77, 84, 86, 91, 96, 104–5, 112, 113, 124, 126, 128, 130–1
Doom themes see Last Judgement
Dorchester Abbey, 37
Double glazing, 194
Dove, 33, 36, 37, 41, 71, 115, 137
Dowsing, William, 142, 190
Doyle, Harcourt, 158
Drake, Thomas Tyrwhitt, 150
Dreux see Chapelle Royale
Duccio, 61, 95
Ducereau, J. A., 137
Durandus, 15
Dürer, Albrecht, 45, 48, 56, 61, 117, 128, 129, 136–7, 138, 139
Durham Cathedral, 17
Duycking, Everett, 148

E

Eagle, symbolism of, 32, 35
East Hagbourne Church, 52
East Harling Church, 40
Eastern Orthodox Church, 24, 30
Easton, Hugh, 55, 58–9
Eaton Bishop Church, 91
Ecce Homo, Guido Reni, 39
Ecouen, chapel at Château of, 139, 140; see also S. Acceul
Edward I, King of England, 72
Edward II, King of England, 90
Edward IV, King of England, 89
Edwin, King of Northumbria, 71
Eginton, Francis, 145, 151
Eginton, William Raphael, 151
Egypt, ancient, glass from, 10–11
Eighteenth century
  costume in, 55
  decline of glass during, 142–5
El Greco, 39
Eleanor de Clare, 91; see also De Clare family
Eleanor of Aquitaine, 68
Eleanor of Portugal, 117
Eleventh century
  characteristics of glass in, 64–5
  in Alsace, 13, 38
  in Germany, 13, 64, 66–7
Eligius, St, 123
Elijah, 167
Elisabeth of Hungary, St, 81, 138
Elizabeth I, 57
Elizabeth of Habsburg, 96
Elizabeth of York, 88, 134
Ely Cathedral, 151
Emanu-El, Congregation, New York, 166
Emblems of saints, 34–5; see also Symbolism
Enamelling, enamel paints
  application of, 183, 184
  significance of introduction, 49, 52, 53, 56, 124, 135, 142, 146, 148, 149
  value in heraldry, 49, 145
Endomosaic, 164
Engelbert II, 130
England
  basis of church planning in, 14–15
  depiction of donors in glass of, 40–1, 91
  destruction of medieval glass in, 142, 190
  Gothic style in, 20, 21, 70, 72, 84, 86, 90, 91, 100, 134
  imported glass in, 126, 135, 136, 144, 149
  synagogue glass in, 166–7
  use of grisaille in, 72, 82–3
  eleventh century, 64
  twelfth century, 64, 70–1
  thirteenth century, 72, 82–3
  fourteenth century, 84, 86–91
  fifteenth century, 100–1, 112–13
  sixteenth century, 124, 134–5
  seventeenth century, 142
  eighteenth century, 142, 144–5
  nineteenth century, 146–7, 150–3, 155

twentieth century, 158, 168–9, 188, 189
English Civil War, 55, 142
English Stained Glass, Read, 146
Engrand le Prince, see Le Prince, Engrand
Engraved glass, 139, 168
Enrique Alemán, 106, 109, 110, 132
Ensingen, Ulrich von, 115, 122
Epernay, Moët et Chandon factory, 148
Ephesus, Basilican church at, 22
Epiphany, 110
Epoxy resin, 158, 164, 177, 179, 181, 187, 189, 192, 193; see also Dalle de verre
Equipment
  for restoration, 192–3
  for window-making, 177–87
Erfurt Cathedral, 45, 98, 99
Escutcheon see Shields
Essen Minster, 161, 171
Esslingen see S. Mary
Etching, 49, 182–3
Eton College Chapel, 39, 158
Eugene III, Pope, 102
Evangelists, The, 32, 33, 34, 35, 44, 77, 106
  symbols of, 32, 34, 35, 44, 76, 77
Eve, creation of, 27; see also Adam and Eve
Evelyn, John, 55
Everyday life, impressions recorded in glass, 52–3; see also Costume, Labours of the months
Evil see Good and evil
Evreux Cathedral, 21, 31, 40, 42, 43, 50, 84, 100, 105
Exeter Cathedral, 145
Exodus from Egypt, 116, 117, 167
Eyck, Charles, 175
Eye window see Occhio
Ezekiel, 71, 75, 77

F

Faces
  depiction of, 12–13, 56–7, 78, 84, 114, 132, 141, 151, 184
  of Christ, 38–9
Faceting, 63, 172, 182
Fairfax, Thomas, 142
Fairford see S. Mary
Faith, representation of, 139
Fall, The, 76
Farndon see S. Chad
Fashions see Costume
Faulkner, C. J., 152
Favrile glass, 157
Ferdinand and Isabella, 106, 109, 130
Ferrières, Raoul de, 40, 84
Festival of Lights, 167
Fête des Fous, 37
Fifteenth century
  characteristics of glass in, 37, 52, 100–1
  costume in, 54–5
  in England, 100–1, 112–13
  in Flanders, 102–3
  in France, 100, 104–5
  in Germany, 100, 114–17
  in Italy, 100, 118–23
  in Spain, 106–11
  in Switzerland, 49
Figures, styles of portrayal, 22, 37, 55, 56–7, 64, 69, 91, 105, 113, 120, 126, 134, 140, 141
Fillets, 20, 42
Fire
  destruction of cathedrals by, 64, 67, 70, 99
  symbolism of, 32, 41
Firing process, 185
First Presbyterian Church, Stamford see "Fish" Church
Fish, symbolism of, 15, 33, 34
"Fish" Church, Stamford, 15, 17, 21, 162, 164, 172
Fisher, Alfred, 189
Fisher, Geoffrey, Archbishop, 56
Five Prophets windows, Augsburg, 13, 42, 64, 66–7
Five Sisters window, York, 29, 71, 82, 83, 88, 194

Fixing process, 188–9
Flanders
  artistic influence of, 106, 132–9
  depiction of donors in glass of, 41, 128–9, 130–1
  Gothic style in, 102–3
  tapestries in, 102, 103, 126, 127
  fifteenth century, 100, 102–3
  sixteenth century, 124, 126–7, 130–1
  see also Flemish school
Flandes, Arnao de, 132–3
Flashed glass, 8, 48, 84, 145, 182, 183
Flashing, abraded, 48, 49, 104
Flaubert, Gustave, 29
Flemish school, influence of, 50–1, 61, 100, 104, 106
Fleur-de-lys, 42, 43, 47, 49, 77, 79, 104
Flight into Egypt, The, Giotto, 95
Flint, 8, 10
Florence
  Laurentian Library, 141
  medieval prosperity of, 116, 118, 119
  fifteenth century in, 118–21
  see also Orsanmichele, S. Croce, S. Maria Novella, S. Spirito
Florence Cathedral, 22, 61, 118–21
Floris, Frans, 129
Flower, Barnard, 134
Flowers, 22, 44–5, 114, 115, 135, 137, 139, 150, 154
Fly, visual conceit, 28
Foliage, 22, 42–3, 45, 114
Fonseca, Cardinal, 49
Fonthill Abbey, 145
Foppa, Vicenzo, 122, 123
Forseth, Einar, 174
Forsyth, Moira, 158
Four Seasons window, 157
Fourteenth century
  characteristics of glass in, 84–5
  costume in, 54
  technical progress in, 84
  in Alsace, 92–3
  in England, 84, 86–91
  in France, 84
  in Germany, 84–5, 97–9
  in Italy, 94–5
  in Spain, 106, 108, 111
  in Switzerland, 96
Fra Angelico, 38, 39
France
  Art Nouveau in, 155
  artistic influence of, 71, 106, 172
  Baroque style in, 142
  basis of church planning in, 14
  costume in, 54–5
  depiction of donors in glass of, 40–1, 69, 104, 139, 140
  destruction of glass workshops in, 142
  Gothic style in, 20–1, 68–9, 72, 100, 140
  impact of Renaissance on, 138–40
  Romanesque style in, 68–9
  synagogue glass in, 166
  use of grisaille in, 72, 84
  eleventh century, 64
  twelfth century, 64–5, 68–9, 70, 71
  thirteenth century, 72–9
  fourteenth century, 84, 92–3
  fifteenth century, 100, 104–5
  sixteenth century, 124, 138–40
  seventeenth century, 142
  eighteenth century, 142
  nineteenth century, 146, 148, 149
  twentieth century, 158, 170–1, 188, 189
Francés, Nicolás, 107
Francesca, Piero della, 141
Francis I, King of France, 140
Francis of Assisi, St, 32, 41, 44, 94–5
Franciscan Order, 14, 94, 95
Frankfurt, 114
Frankfurter, Felix, 167
Frederick II, Emperor, 116
Frederick III, Emperor, 117
Freedom of Conscience window, Gouda, 129
Frei Studios, 164
Freiburg, 98
Freiburg Minster, 33, 35, 41, 43, 50, 72, 81, 97, 98, 114, 136–7
  Museum, 33, 137

201

Index

French, Leonard, 173
French, Old, heraldic language, 46–7
French Revolution, 142
Frescoes, 14, 50, 94–5, 100, 119, 120
Fretwork, Islamic, 12–13
Frideswide, St, 153
Fuggers, 100
Fulgurite, 8
Fundamentalism, 142
Fused glass, 158, 177, 189

G

Gabriel, Archangel, 34, 117
Gaillon, palace at, 138
Gallatin, James, 146
Ganymede, 28, 29
Gaudí, Antoni, 154, 155
Gauguin, Paul, 39
Gautier, Théophile, 110
Geometric designs
　in borders, 43, 106
　in church plan, 14–15
　in tracery, 20–1, 106
George III, King of England, 56
George IV, King of England, 151
George VI, King of England, 57
George, St, 35, 55, 56
Gerard, John, 45
Gérente, Henri, 149
Gerlachus, 33, 60, 67
Germany
　artistic influence of, 91, 92–3, 94, 106, 134
　Baroque style in, 142
　basis of church planning in, 14
　costume in, 54–5
　depiction of donors in glass of, 41, 116–17
　destruction of glass workshops in, 142
　Gothic style in, 72, 80–1, 97–9, 100, 136
　use of colour in, 84; *see also* Colour, national preferences;
　use of grisaille in, 81, 84, 97
　eleventh century, 13, 40, 64, 66–7
　twelfth century, 64, 66–7
　thirteenth century, 72, 80–1
　fourteenth century, 84–5, 97–9
　fifteenth century, 100, 114–17
　sixteenth century, 124, 136–7
　seventeenth century, 142
　eighteenth century, 142
　nineteenth century, 146, 149
　twentieth century, 158–9, 160–1
Gethsemane *see* Prayer in the Garden
Ghibellines, 118
Ghiberti, Lorenzo, 61, 100, 118–21
Ghirlandajo, Domenico, 119
Gibberd, Frank, 17
Giotto, 38, 95
Gislebertus, 31
Gitschmann von Ropstein, Hans, 136–7
Glaber, Ralph, 64
Glasgow, Art Nouveau in, 155
Glasgow Cathedral, 149
Glass
　chemistry of, 8–9
　choice of, 180–1
　in ancient world, 10–11
　invention, history of, 10–11
　natural occurrence of, 8
　see also different types
Glass appliqué, 177, 189
Glaziers
　families of, 56, 106, 115, 128–9, 132, 133, 139
　identity and status of, 60–3, 84, 86, 177
　modern, 158; *see also* Twentieth century;
　Worshipful Company of, 46
Gloucester Cathedral, 50, 90
God
　depiction of, 32–3, 67, 87, 99, 128, 133
　Protestant objection to images of, 128, 129, 142
Goddard and Gibbs, 60, 188, 189
Godfrey, Thomas, 148
Goethe, 124
Gold, use of, 8, 12

Golden Legend, De Voragine, 28, 35
Goldsmiths, 12, 123
Golfer, The, Gloucester, 90
Good and evil, 14, 30–1
Good Samaritan, 76
Good Shepherd, 153
Gorleston Psalter, 86
Gospels, scenes from, *see* New Testament
Gothic Revival, 9, 16, 17, 21, 39, 43, 51, 62, 146, 148, 150–1
Gothic style
　adoption of term, 17, 72
　evolution, characteristics of, 15, 16–17, 20–1, 42–3, 45, 50–1, 64, 68, 69, 72
　rejection of, 16, 17, 138, 140
　principles of, 46–7
　in England, 20, 21, 50, 70, 72, 84, 86–7, 88–9, 90–1, 134
　in Flanders, 102–3
　in France, 20–1, 50, 68–9, 72–3, 92–3, 100, 104–5, 140; *see also* Chartres;
　in Germany, 72, 80–1, 97–9, 100
　in Italy, 61, 72, 94–5, 122–3
　in Spain, 72, 106–7, 133
　see also Gothic Revival, Tracery
Gouda *see* S. John
Granada Cathedral, 132, 133
Grasset, Eugène, 154
Graz, Landesmuseum, 25
Great Exhibition, 151
Great Malvern Priory, 26, 27, 33, 45, 58, 113
Great Schism, 100
Great Witley Church, 142–3
Greece, ancient
　glass workshops in, 10
　legacy of geometric forms from, 14
　legends of, as design source, 28, 29
　medieval interest in, 97
Greenbury, Richard, 56
Gregorian mass, 108
Gregory I, Pope (St), 12, 70
Gregory of Tours, 102
Grien, Hans Baldung, 61, 136, 137
Grimms' fairy tales, 29
Grisaille glass, 18, 40, 72, 81, 82, 83, 84, 88, 89, 92, 94, 97, 126
Ground glass, 49
Grozing, 181, 182, 187
Gruenke, Bernard, 164
Güell, Eusebio, 154, 155
Guelphs, 118
Guilds *see* Craft guilds
Guillaume de Marcillat *see* Marcillat
Guthlac Roll, 26
Guy de Laval, 41
Gyles, Henry, 144–5

H

Habakkuk, 88
Habsburg, House of, 54, 96, 126, 130–1
Hadassah-Hebrew University Medical Center, 166, 167
Hagia Sophia, 16
Hakone
　glass in Fujiya Hotel, 172
　glass in Museum of Modern Art, 172
Halation, 18, 23
Hale Church, 57
Hallenkirche, 57
Haloes, 33, 34, 67, 137
Hammarskjöld, Dag, 58
Hampton Court, 151
Hans von Ulm, 115
Har Zion Temple, Philadelphia, 167
Harling family, 40
Havsteen-Mikkelsen, Sven, 175
Healy, Michael, 158
Heaven and hell, 31
Heinigke, Otto, 162
Henlein, Peter, 117
Henry II, King of England, 82
Henry III, King of England, 79
Henry VI, King of England, 89
Henry VII, King of England, 21, 88, 134
Henry VIII, King of England, 124, 134, 135, 142
Henry II, King of France, 138, 140

Henry III, King of France, 138
Henry de Mamesfeld, 91
Henry of Navarre, 58
Henry the Black, 92
Heraldry, heraldic emblems
　canting, punning arms, 48
　Church's attitude to, 28, 124, 129
　depiction of, in glass, 21, 48–9, 76, 77, 79, 86, 88, 89, 96, 104, 111, 112, 114, 126, 130, 131, 135, 144, 151, 158
　history, language of, 46–7
　principles of, 46–7
　production techniques of, 48–9
Herbals, 45
Herod, 26
Hickman, Helen Carew, 167
Hillesden *see* S. Nicholas
Hirsau, Abbey of, 67
Hirsvogel, Veit, 56, 137
Historical themes, 51, 58–9, 124, 129
Hogan, James, 177
Hoglund, Eric, 175
Holanda, Alberto and Nicolas de, 133
Holbein, Hans, the Younger, 48, 56, 124
Holiday, Henry, 151
Holland, liberation of, 129
Hollaway, Antony, 158
Holy Blood, Chapel of the, Bruges, 130
Holy Family, Church of the, Barcelona, 155
Holy Ghost, Holy Spirit, 32, 33, 36, 37, 44, 67, 96, 168
Holy Land, 35
Holy Trinity *see* Trinity
Holy Trinity Church, Micklegate, York, 86, 112
Holy Trinity Church, New York, 151
Hone, Evie, 33, 39, 158
Hone, Galyon, 61, 134
Hoogstraten *see* S. Catherine
Horta, Victor, 155
Horton Church, 151
Hosea, 66–7
Hôtel Solvay, Brussels, 155
Houses of Parliament, 150–1
Howard-Vyse memorial window, 149
Hugh le Despenser *see* Le Despenser family
Huizinga, Johan, 100
Humanism (and realism), 56, 100
Hundred Years' War, 79, 84, 90, 100, 104, 112
Hunt, W. Holman, 39, 152
Hutton, John, 168
Huysmans, J. K., 23
Hydrofluoric acid, 182

I

Iceland, glass in, 174
Iconoclasm *see* Protestantism
Iconography, Christian, 24–7, 28, 32–3, 34–5, 36–7, 38–9; *see also* Design, Symbolism
Icons, 30
Ildefonso, St, 108
Illuminated manuscripts, 24, 26, 67, 104
Imagery
　Cistercian objections to, 72
　effects of Reformation on, 48, 56, 58, 124, 128, 135, 144
　Jewish objections to, 166–7
　see also Design, Iconography, Protestantism, Symbolism
Immaculate Conception, 32
Indulgences, sale of, 136
Indus Valley, 10
Ingres, Jean, 62, 148, 149
Innsbruck, Landesmuseum, 28
International Committee of History of Art, 191
Ireland, modern glass in, 158
Irish School, 158
Iron oxide, 9, 184
Ironwork, 22, 64
Irradiation, 18

Isaac, 24
Isaiah, 25, 37, 71, 77
Islam, influence of, 12–13, 106, 108
Islip, John, 135
Islip, Long Island, Episcopal Church at, 157
Isothermal glazing, 194
Italy
　artistic influence of, 95, 96, 100, 132, 136, 138–40
　Gothic style in, 61, 72, 94–5, 122–3
　origins of Baroque in, 142
　origins of Renaissance in, 95, 118–21
　significance of climate in, 72, 94
　thirteenth century, 61, 95
　fourteenth century, 84, 94–5
　fifteenth century, 100, 118–23
　sixteenth century, 124, 141
　nineteenth century, 149

J

Jacob's dream, 27, 37, 144
Jakobskirche, Straubing, 60
James Powell and Sons, Whitefriars, 60, 146, 152–3
James the Greater (the Pilgrim), St, 34, 35, 104, 106, 108, 139
James the Less, St, 34
Jameson, Anna B., 35
Japan
　artistic influence of, 155, 172
　glass in, 158, 172
Jared, Patriarch, 71
Jereboam, 25, 74
Jeremiah, 37, 77, 167
Jerome, St, 41, 44, 131
Jervais, Thomas, 62, 145
Jesse Tree, 20, 36–7, 45, 48, 49, 57, 67, 69, 71, 76, 90, 91, 114, 117, 138, 139
Jewellery, influence of, on glass, 12
Jews, Judaism
　festivals, 167
　representation of, 25, 76, 116, 135
　symbols of, 25, 33, 166–7
　synagogue glass, 166–7
Joan of Arc, 78, 100, 113
Joanna of Castile, 130, 137
Jogues, Isaac, 58
Johann I von Nassau, 48
Johannesbund Convent, Leutesdorf, 160
John, St (Apostle and Evangelist), 32, 35, 69, 77, 79, 92, 106, 108, 110, 123, 153
John of Damascus, St, 123
John of Gaunt, 48
John the Baptist, 79, 92, 128, 129, 144
Johnson, James Rosser, 18
Jonah, 24, 25, 51, 80, 129, 144
Jonas, 66–7
Jonas, H., 175
Joseph (New Testament), 100–1, 112, 113, 149
Joseph (Old Testament), 82
Joseph of Arimathea, Van Orley, 127
Joshua, 57
Judas, 33
Judgement of Solomon, 92
Judith, 129
Judson Studios, Los Angeles, 164
Juliana of Nicomedia, St, 132
Julius II, Pope, 141
Jung, Carl Gustav, 22
Justinian, Emperor, 15, 22

K

Kaiser Wilhelm Memorial Church, Berlin, 51, 172
Kehlmann, Robert, 165
Kempe, Charles Eamer, 60, 151
Keneseth Israel, Elkins Park, 167
Kepes, Gyorgy, 163, 164
Ketal, Cornelis, 128, 129
Kilchsperger, Hans Jacob, 124
Kiln, 185
Kinderen, A. J. Der, 175
King's College Chapel, Cambridge, 21, 126, 134, 151

Kirchheim, Johannes von, 92
Klarup Church, Jutland, 175
Klimt, Gustav, 155
KLM Royal Dutch Airlines, New York, 163, 164
Kloster Lorsch *see* Lorsch
Koberg Bible, 25
Königsfelden, Switzerland, 39, 43, 54, 84, 96
Krafft, Adam, 117
Kulmbach, Hans von, 61, 137
Kunhofer, Konrad, 117
Kunibert, St, 80
Kyburg, arms of, 49

L

La Farge, John, 146, 149, 154, 155
Labours of the months, 22, 52–3, 77, 100, 105
Lakeman, Ernest, 162
Lalaing family, 130
Lamb, symbolism of, 32, 33, 44
Landscape in glass, 51, 61, 117, 118, 121, 123, 126, 134
Lanfranc, 70
Laon Cathedral, 72, 78
Larivière, Charles, 148
Lassus, Baptiste Antoine, 149
Last Judgement, 14, 15, 25, 30, 31, 72, 76, 93, 105, 166–7
Last Supper, 33, 114, 123, 129, 130, 153
Lathekin, 186, 187
Latin cross, 14–15
Lattice-work, stone, 16
Laud, William, Archbishop, 144
Laurelton Hall, Long Island, 157
Law and the Prophets, 70, 71
Lawrence, St, 118, 120
Lawson, John, 179, 188
Le Corbusier, 170, 171
Le Despenser family, 56, 91
Le Mans Cathedral, 37, 68, 69, 78, 100, 104–5
Le Prince, Engrand, 60–1, 138, 139
Le Prince family, 139
Leading, lead-lines, 12, 49, 61–2, 146, 153, 160, 178, 183, 186, 187, 193
Leading-up, 186–7
Lead-lining, 183
Lee, Lawrence, 168
Lee, Robert E., 58
Legend of St Julian Hospitator, Flaubert, 29
Legenda Aurea, De Voragine, 28, 35
Léger, Fernand, 32, 62, 158, 170–1, 173
Leo X, Pope, 136
Leocadia, St, 108
Leodegar, St, 35
León, Luiz de, 132
León Cathedral, 23, 72, 106, 107, 132
Leonardo *see* Vinci
Levant, inspiration from, 13
Leyden *see* Relief of Leyden
Liberty's, London, 155
Lichfield Cathedral, 126, 142
Lierre *see* S. Gommaire
Light
　and architecture, 16, 17, 142
　and colour, 18–19, 74–5, 76–7, 94, 106, 110–11, 168
　effect of, on glass, 8, 9
　glare, 18, 23, 183
　spiritual qualities of, 68, 144, 166–7
Light of the World, Holman Hunt, 39
Lilford Lodge, Oxford, 150
Lily, symbolism of, 32, 34–5, 41, 45, 113, 118, 137, 138
Limbourg brothers, 104
Limestone, 8–9
Lincoln Cathedral, 14, 22, 43, 50, 72, 83, 142, 145, 151
Linge, Abraham van, 51, 144
Linge, Bernard van, 144
Lion, symbolism of, 32, 34, 35, 37, 44, 46, 47, 118, 136
Little Red Riding Hood, 29
Liverpool Cathedral, 17, 51, 158, 168
Loire, châteaux of, 138
Loire, Gabriel, 51, 162, 164, 172, 177, 178, 179, 180, 184, 188, 189
Londot, Louis Marie, 175

Long Melford Church, Suffolk, 40, 45, 112, 113
Longley, Thomas, Bishop, 89
Loop Synagogue, Chicago, 167
Lorraine, destruction of glass workshops in, 142
Lorsch Abbey, 13
Lot's wife, 25
Louis IV, King of France, 138
Louis VI ("the Fat"), King of France, 68
Louis VII, King of France, 68, 82
Louis IX (St Louis), King of France, 44, 72, 75, 77, 78, 79, 148
Louis XIII, King of France, 57, 142
Louis II, of Anjou, 105
Louis of Bourbon, 76
Louviers *see* Notre Dame
Low Countries *see* Belgium, Flanders, Netherlands
Loyola, Ignatius, 132
Lübeck, medieval prosperity of, 116
Lucifer *see* Devil
Ludwig I of Bavaria, 62, 149
Ludwig the Bavarian, 117
Luke, St, 32, 35, 60
Lüneburg Town Hall, 114
Lusson, Antoine, 149
Luther, Martin, 136
Lutheranism *see* Protestantism
Lyceum Theatre, New York, 157
Lycurgus cup, 11
Lyons Cathedral, 37, 72, 78

M

Machiavelli, 119
Mackintosh, Charles Rennie, 155
Mackmurdo, Arthur, 155
Madonna *see* Virgin Mary
Madox Brown, Ford, 29, 152, 153
Magdalen College, Oxford, 56
Magi
 depiction of, 24, 25, 32, 61, 80, 81, 82, 137
 relics of, 80–1
Maidstone, United Reform Church, 152–3
Maison Dieu, Dover, 55
Maison Tassel, Brussels, 155
Malines Cathedral, 130
Mandala see Circles
Mandeville, Sir John, *Travels*, 10
Manessier, Alfred, 171, 173
Marburg *see* S. Elisabeth
Marcillat, Guillaume de, 141
Margaret of Parma, 131
Marioni, Paul, 53, 164, 165
Mark, St, 32, 35, 99, 131
Marshall, P. P., 152
Martens, Michel, 175
Martha and Mary windows, Oxford, 51
Martin, St, 128, 144
Martini, Simone, 95
Martyrs, 28, 34, 35, 52, 70, 80, 82, 97, 105, 132
Mary Magdalene, St, 35, 107
Mary of Burgundy, 137
Mary Tudor, 129, 131
Masonic Memorial Temple, San Francisco, 164
Massacre of St Bartholomew, 138
Massacre of the Innocents, 26, 144
Mater Dolorosa, 34; *see also* Virgin Mary
Matilda, Queen of England, 58
Matisse, Henri, 62, 158, 170, 173
Matthew, St, 32, 34, 35
Maximilian I, Emperor, 56, 130, 131, 136, 137
Maxwell's Plum, Manhattan, 164
Medallion windows, 64, 74, 75, 76, 77, 78, 79
Medici family, 63, 100, 119, 122, 138, 140
Megillah, 167
Meistermann, Georg, 158, 160
Melchizedek, 153
Memorial windows, 58–9; *see also* Donations, War Memorial windows *and individual examples*
Menardo, Vicente, 132
Menorah, 167

Merchant bankers, 100
Mérimée, Prosper, 149
Merton College Chapel, Oxford, 43, 84, 91, 152
Mesnil-Aubry, Church of, 140
Methuselah, 71
Metz, history, 139–40
Metz, Maréchal de, 149
Metz Cathedral, 62, 76, 114, 140
Mexico City, National Theatre, 157
Michael, Archangel, 30, 33, 34, 144
Michelangelo, 24, 119
Middle Ages
 anonymity of glaziers in, 60, 84
 constraints on design in, 24, 26, 27
 depiction of donors in, 40–1
 glass technology in, 9, 10
 impetus to church building in, 64
 window-making processes in, 26, 177, 178, 181, 182, 184, 185, 186
 see also individual centuries, countries, styles
Middleton Cheney *see* All Saints'
Mignot, Jean, 122
Milan Cathedral, 114, 122–3, 141, 149
 Museum, 122
Millais, John Everett, 152
Millefiori glass, 11
Milton, John, 151
Milton Steinberg House, New York, 167
Miniatures, 67, 105
Minne, Minnesänger, 80
Miracle plays, 26, 30, 86
Miracles, 35, 64, 76, 82, 86, 88, 89, 108, 134, 135
Miró, Joan, 158
Mirror of Human Salvation, 27
Misericord window, Strasbourg, 93
Misericords, 44
Moët et Chandon factory, 148
Monash University, Melbourne, 173
Monasteries
 dissolution in England, 124, 134–5
 illuminated manuscripts from, 24, 26, 67
 see also individual orders
Mönchen-Gladbach, 37
Monetary Gain, 165
Moneylenders, Christ's expulsion of the, 141
Monkey's funeral, 86
Monkwearmouth, monastery at, 12–13
Monreale Cathedral, 14
Mons *see* S. Waudru
Monsters, symbolism of, 44–5
Montmorency, House of, 139, 140
Moon
 glass on, 8
 rock, 163–4
 symbolic representation of, 69
Moore, Rupert, 158
"Mooress, The", Strasbourg, 49
Moors, in Spain, 106, 108
 depictions of, 139
 see also Islam
Morris, Jane, 152
Morris, May, 57
Morris, William, 31, 55, 57, 62, 146, 151, 152–3, 155, 191
Morse Gallery of Art, Florida, 157
Mosaic Law, 39, 70, 71, 166, 167
Mosaic technique, 11
Mosaic windows, at Florence, 120
Mosaics, Byzantine, 16, 32, 39, 42
Moses, 24, 25, 27, 67, 75, 91, 166
Mottis, Cristoforo de, 123
Mouchettes, 20
Mount Sinai, 167
Mouths 25, Röling, 174
Much, Konrad, 141
Mucha, Alphonse, 63
Muff (cylinder) glass, 8–9, 180, 181
Munich, 114
Munich, glass workshops, 62, 149
Münster Landesmuseum, 33, 49, 67
Murad, Mosque of, Turkey, 43
Murillo, 132
Musical instruments, 20–1, 30, 86, 113
Mystery plays *see* Miracle plays
Mythology, scenes from, 28–9, 139, 140, 141

N

Nash, John, 150
National Gallery of Victoria, Melbourne, 173
National Portrait Gallery, London, 134, 135
Nativity, The, 22, 25–6, 44–5, 52, 61, 96, 98, 99, 110, 112, 113, 118, 121, 139, 145, 149
Natron, 10
Naturalism, 37, 44–5, 94–5, 114, 124, 136, 146
Nave, 14, 16, 17, 72
Nebuchadnezzar, 74
Neo-classical style
 effect on glass, 62
 emergence of, 142
Netherlands, The
 depiction of donors in glass of, 129
 destruction of glass in, 124
 painted panels in, 124
 Renaissance style in, 126–7
 roundels in, 126, 144, 145
 War of Independence in, 130, 131
 fifteenth century, 100
 sixteenth century, 126–131
 seventeenth century, 145
 twentieth century, 174–5
 see also Flanders, Flemish school
Neuweiler, Timotheus window, 67
New College, Oxford, 62, 91, 145, 191
New Testament, as source of inspiration, 14–15, 24–7, 44, 64, 80, 82, 87, 122, 123
New York, glass in, 58, 62, 162, 163, 164, 166, 167
Newton, Isaac, 56
Nicaea, Second Council of, 24
Nicholas, St, 35, 76, 88, 126
Nicholas Nickleby, Dickens, 29, 82
Nicholson, James, 134
Nightingale, Florence, 58
Nijmegen, Arnt, 102–3, 126, 138–9
Nine Worthy Conquerors, 100
Nineteenth century
 religious art in, 30, 31, 39, 45
 revival of glass in, 146
 in England, 146, 150–3
 in France, 146, 148, 149
 in Germany, 146, 149
 in Italy, 149
 in United States, 146, 148, 149
 see also Art Nouveau, Gothic Revival, Pre-Raphaelites
Nineveh, 10, 51, 144
Noah, 75, 115, 184, 186, 188
Noah's Ark, 11·5
Noli me Tangere, Fra Angelico, 39
Noli me Tangere window, Barcelona, 107
Norfolk, Duke of, 56
Norman, Emil, 164
Norman architecture, 70; *see also* Romanesque
Norman slab glass, 9, 180, 181
Normandy, glass-painters in, 138–9
Norway, modern glass in, 174, 175
Norwich, parish churches, 112; *see also* S. Peter Mancroft
Norwich Cathedral, 15
Nostell Priory, 144
Notaries, Milan College of, 123
Notre Dame, Paris, 15, 23, 72–3, 79
Notre Dame, Semur-en-Auxois, 41, 105
Notre Dame de la Belle Verrière, Chartres, 13, 64–5, 76, 77
Notre Dame de Toute Grace, Assy, 170
Notre Dame du Haut, Ronchamp, 17, 170, 171
Notre-Dame-en-Vaux, Châlons-sur-Marne, 33, 53, 139
Notre Dame of Louviers, 139
Notre Dame *see* Antwerp Cathedral
Nuremberg
 Germanisches National-Museum, 54, 117
 glass in, 116–17, 124
 history, 116
 medieval craftsmanship in, 116, 117
 medieval prosperity of, 116
 see also Dürer, S. Lorenz, S. Martha, S. Sebald, Tucher

O

Obazine Abbey, 72
Obsidian, 8
Occhio, 22, 95, 118, 120, 121
Ogee, 20
Ohyama, Yoshiro, 172
Ojo de buey, 22, 133
Old Dispensation, 71
Old Glory, 165
Old Testament, as source of inspiration, 14, 24–7, 33, 36–7, 44, 64, 66–7, 79, 80, 82, 86–7, 108, 110, 117, 123, 142, 153, 177, 189
Opalescent glass, 146, 149, 156–7, 160, 164
Orchard, The, Rohde, 175
Orientation of church, 14–15
Orley, Bernard van, 126, 127
Orsanmichele, Florence, 119
Orthodox Church *see* Eastern Orthodox
Oscarskyrkan, Stockholm, 174
Ox, symbolism of the, 25–6, 32, 35
Oxford University, glass for colleges of, 144–5; *see also individual colleges*
Oxides, 8, 9
Oyster Bay window, Tiffany, 156, 157

P

Paganism, and Christianity, 14, 30–1
Paine, Thomas, 163
Paint
 chemical composition of, 184
 decay of, 191
 protection of, during window restoration, 192, 193
Painting, influence on stained glass, 50, 61, 62–3, 67, 95, 96, 103, 104, 117, 118, 124, 126, 137, 170–1, 172, 173
Painting on glass, 37, 49, 53, 56, 57, 61, 62, 100, 124, 137, 141, 142–5, 148–9, 158, 183, 184; *see also* Enamelling
Palazzo Cornaro, Venice, 50
Palladium, 64, 74, 77
Palma Cathedral, 18–19, 22
Paper, invention of, 26
Paris
 Cluny Museum, 67
 destruction of glass in, 142
 Musée des Arts Décoratifs, 154
 sixteenth-century glass in, 140
 see also Notre Dame, S. Chapelle, S. Denis, S. Germain
Parkinson's *Herbal*, 45
Parler family, 98, 115, 117, 122
Paschal lamb, 33, 44
Passion of Christ, 25, 76, 93, 96
 emblems of, 20, 32, 33, 97
Passion plays, 26
Paterson, Samuel, 111
Patrixbourne *see* S. Mary
Patrons, 100, 102, 104, 119, 138, 139, 177; *see also* Donations
Paul, St, 89, 134, 162–3
Pavia *see* S. Michele
Paxton, Joseph, 151
Peace, theme of, 58
Peace window, Canterbury, 43, 63
Pearson, Eglington Margaret, 145
Pearson, James, 145
Peckitt, William, 145, 194
Pelican, symbolism of, 37, 98
Penancers, 88
Peninsular War, 106
Penshurst Church, 58
Pentecost, 110, 119
Peregrinus, 67
Pérignon, Dom, 148
Perpendicular style, 20, 50, 84, 86, 88–9, 134; *see also* Gothic style, Tracery
Persian, heraldic language, 46, 47
Perspective, 50, 84, 92–3, 94, 95, 96, 117, 121, 123, 124, 129, 134, 137; *see also* Realism
Perugino, Pietro, 119
Peter, Friar, 110
Peter, St, 34, 99
Peterborough Cathedral, 142

Peterhouse College, Cambridge, 144
Philadelphia, Independence Hall, 148
Philip I, King of Castile, 130, 131, 137
Philip II, King of Spain, 109, 126, 129, 131
Philip the Good of Burgundy, 102, 131
Pieter the Cripple, 129
Pilgrimages, 35, 70, 74, 80, 82, 86, 90, 106, 135
Piper, John, 17, 158, 168, 172
Pitti Palace, Florence, 118
Pitting, of glass, 190, 191, 192
Pittsburgh, University of, 29
Plants, 44–5; *see also* Flowers, Foliage *and individual items*
Plateria, 133
Plating, 177, 192–3
Plato, 97
Pliny the Elder, *Historia Naturalis*, 10, 44
Pliny the Younger, 11
Poensgen, Jochem, 160
Poitiers Cathedral, 69, 78
Poor Man's Bible, 25, 26–7
Poor Man's Bible windows, 27, 82, 97, 98
Portland vase, 11
Portraiture, 40–1, 56–7; *see also* Donors, Faces, Figures
Post-Impressionism, 172
Pot metal glass, 9, 111, 146
Potash, 9, 10
Powell *see* James Powell and Sons
Prague Cathedral, 63, 98
Prayer in the Garden window, Florence, 118, 119, 121
Pre-Raphaelites, 30, 31, 45, 51, 55, 57, 62, 146, 152–3, 155
Presentation in the Temple window, Florence, 118, 119, 121
Price family, 145
Pricke of Conscience, Rolle, 28, 112
Prikker, Jan Thorn, 43, 160, 174
Princeton University Chapel, 162
Printing, development of, 26–7
Prodigal Son, Vigeland, 174, 175
Prophetic Quest windows, Elkins Park, 167
Prophets, 13, 36, 37, 42, 64, 66–7, 69, 70, 71, 108, 111, 118, 119, 120, 138, 190, 191
Protection of windows, 194
Protestantism, 39, 48, 56, 58, 115, 124–5, 132, 134–5, 136–7, 140, 142, 144, 174; *see also* Reformation
Proust, Marcel, 29
Prudde, John, 113
Public houses, glass in, 155
Pugin, A. C., 150
Pugin, A. W. N., 150–1
Pulcheria, St, 60
Purification of the Temple, 129, 141
Purser, Sarah, 158
Pyramus and Thisbe, 28

Q

Quaratesi Palace, Florence, 118
Quarry panes, 45, 84, 89, 100, 135
Quartz, 8, 10
Quatrefoil, 20
Queen of Sheba, 24, 80, 82, 129, 145
Queen's College Chapel, Oxford, 144
Queen's Hotel, Crouch End, 155

R

Rainbow Tower, Hakone, 172
Raphael, 126, 127, 129, 132, 139, 140
Raphael, Archangel, 35
Rattner, Abraham, 167
Ravenna, mosaics at, 12; *see also* S. Vitale
Read, Herbert, 146
Realism, 22–3, 40, 44, 45, 50, 51, 52–3, 55, 56, 61, 84, 92, 94–5, 98, 100, 103, 104, 105, 117, 118, 124, 132, 134
Reamy glass, 9, 165
Rebecca, Biagio, 145
Reconstruction of window, during restoration, 193

Index

Records, in restoration of window, 192
Red and White Peonies, La Farge, 154
Red Sea, 74, 116
Reeded glass, 8
Reformation, 38, 39, 48, 56, 58, 115, 124–5, 134–5, 136–7, 140, 142, 190
Regensburg Cathedral, 42, 60, 72, 98–9
Reichenau, Benedictine Abbey at, 12
Reims, 11
Reims Cathedral, 20, 22, 23, 72, 78, 79
Releading, 193
Relics, sacred, 34, 35, 64, 68, 70, 74, 75, 77, 78, 80, 81, 82, 94–5, 106, 108, 117
Relief of Leyden window, Gouda, 51, 58, 129, 131
Relief of Samaria window, Gouda, 129
Reliquaries, 35
Rembrandt, 39, 56
Renaissance, 16, 40, 50, 60–1, 84, 118–19, 124, 132, 134
  architecture, 17, 118, 132, 133, 139, 141
  style in glass, 40, 43, 45, 50, 61, 118–19, 124, 126, 127, 132, 133, 134, 138, 139, 140
Rendcomb College, 29
René of Anjou, 29
Reni, Guido, 39
Restoration of windows, 82, 142, 146, 149, 151
  modern techniques of, 190–5
Resurrection, The, 24, 25, 33, 44, 96, 99, 118, 121, 162
Resurrection of the dead, 37, 76, 105, 115
Reve, Thomas, 134
Revelation, Book of, 31, 77, 79, 86–7; see also Apocalypse
Reykjavik
  National Art Gallery, 174
  National Theatre, 174
Reynolds, Sir Joshua, 62, 145, 151, 191
Reyntiens, Patrick, 17, 158, 168, 172
Rhesa panel, Canterbury, 191, 194
Ribera, 132
Richelieu, Cardinal, 142
Rieter window, Nuremberg, 43, 116, 117
Rievaulx Abbey, 82
Robin, André, 105
Rococo style, 142, 145
Roger of Pont l'Evêque, Archbishop, 71
Röling, Marte, 174, 175
Rolle, Richard, 28, 112
Rolled glass, 160
Romanesque style
  adoption of term, 16, 72
  evolution, characteristics, 14, 16–17, 22, 24, 31, 32, 39, 64, 67, 80–1, 92
  in Alsace, 92
  in England, 70, 71
  in Flanders, 102
  in France, 68–9
  in Germany, 16, 67, 80, 81
  in Italy, 95
  in Spain, 106
Romantic movement, 16, 17; see also Gothic Revival
Rombouts, Nicolas, 130
Rome, ancient
  architecture in, 118
  catacombs, 29
  glass in, 8, 9, 10–11
  legends, as source of inspiration, 29
Rome, medieval, 35, 80; see also S. Maria del Popolo
Ronchamp see Notre Dame
Roosevelt, Theodore, 156
Rosary, Chapel of the, Vence, 62, 170, 173
Rose windows, 16, 22–3, 72–3, 74, 75, 76, 77, 78, 105, 108–9, 110, 111, 162
Rosenkrantz, Arild, 146–7
Rossetti, Dante Gabriel, 29, 152
Rottingdean Parish Church, 30
Rouault, Georges, 62–3, 158, 170

Rouen, Musée Départemental, 52, 53; see also S. Godard, S. Nicolas, S. Ouen, S. Vincent
Rouen Cathedral, 29, 60, 61, 72, 103
Roundels, 49, 52, 90, 100, 113, 126, 144, 145
Rublev, Andrei, 30
Rudolf I, of Habsburg, 96
Ruskin, John, 79, 152, 153, 191
Ruth, 57
Rütter, Hans, 49

S

S. Acceul, Ecouen, 140
S. Albans Cathedral, 48
S. Andrew, Cuffley, 189
S. Annunziata, Arezzo, 141
S. Bartholomew, Yarnton, 45, 100
S. Catherine, Deerhurst, 42
S. Catherine, Hoogstraten, 126, 130
S. Chad, Farndon, 55
S. Chapelle, Paris, 37, 72, 78, 79, 149
S. Croce, Florence, 95
S. Denis, Paris, 17, 24, 33, 36, 37, 68–9, 71, 72, 166
S. Denys, York, 86, 112
S. Dionysius, Esslingen, 97, 98
S. Dominique, Varangeville, 62, 170
S. Elisabeth, Marburg, 72, 81
S. Etienne, Beauvais, 138, 139
S. Etienne, Metz see Metz Cathedral
S. Foy, Conches, 61, 139, 140
S. Francesco, Arezzo, 139
S. Francesco, Assisi, 38, 94–5
S. Georg, Cologne, 43
S. George, London, 126
S. Germain des Prés, Paris, 78
S. Giles, Stoke Poges, 149
S. Godard, Rouen, 138
S. Gommaire, Lierre, 103, 130, 131
S. Gudule, Brussels, 40–1; see also Brussels Cathedral
S. Guillaume, Strasbourg, 114
S. John, Ephesus, 22
S. John, Gouda, 39, 45, 49, 51, 58, 124, 126, 128–9, 131
S. John the Divine, New York, 162
S. Kilian, Schweinfurt, 160
S. Kunibert, Cologne, 80–1
S. Lambrecht, Convent of, 25
S. Leonard, Middleton, 40
S. Lierre, Antwerp, 130
S. Lorenz, Nuremberg, 22, 25, 34, 37, 43, 116–17, 136
S. Lorenzo, Florence, 118
S. Marco, Florence, 38
S. Margaret, Westminster, 54
S. Maria del Popolo, Rome, 141
S. Maria Königin, Cologne, 32, 160
S. Maria Novella, Florence, 95, 119, 120
S. Martha, Nuremberg, 117
S. Martin, Halle, 102, 103
S. Martin, Montmorency, 40, 41, 139, 140
S. Martin, Tours, 12, 13
S. Martin-le-Grand, York, 86, 112
S. Mary, Bishopsbourne, 135
S. Mary, Cologne-Kalk, 160
S. Mary, Esslingen, 97, 98
S. Mary, Fairford, 14, 27, 30, 31, 33, 134
S. Mary, Hälsingborg, 174
S. Mary, Patrixbourne, 136
S. Mary, Shrewsbury, 33
S. Mary, Warwick, 100, 112, 113
S. Michael, Schweinfurt, 161
S. Michele, Pavia, 16
S. Neot Church, Cornwall, 20, 26, 34, 35
S. Nicholas, Hillesden, 35, 134, 135
S. Nicolas, Rouen, 142
S. Ouen, Rouen, 84, 138
S. Patrick, New York, 58
S. Pedro, Avila, 22
S. Peter, Rome, 15, 136
S. Peter and S. Paul, Hirsau, 67
S. Peter and S. Paul, Washington, 58, 162–4, 172
S. Peter Mancroft, Norwich, 26, 100–1, 112, 113
S. Sebald, Nuremberg, 56, 117, 137
S. Spirito, Florence, 118, 119

S. Stephen, Westminster, 72, 90
S. Ursula, Cologne, 160
S. Vincent, Rouen, 139
S. Vitale, Ravenna, 15
S. Waudru, Mons, 130
S. Zeno Maggiore, Verona, 22, 36
Sabbath, Jewish, 167
Sacred and Legendary Art, A. B. Jameson, 35
Sacred Heart, Church of the, Audincourt, 32, 62, 171
Saints, 28, 34–5, 58, 87, 94–5, 96, 99, 111, 119, 120, 132, 140, 145; see also individual saints
Salamanca Cathedral, 132, 133
Salisbury Cathedral, 14, 72, 83, 142, 191
Saltzman, William, 167
Salzburg, 114
Samson, 136
Samuel, 153
Sand, 8, 10
Santiago de Compostela, 35, 106
Santillana, Diego de, 132
Saul, 57
Scales, 34, 71
Scandinavia, modern glass in, 174–5
Scarabs, 10
Schaffrath, Ludwig, 160–1
Schreiter, Johannes, 160
Schweinfurt see S. Kilian, S. Michael
Sciences, The, depiction of, 109, 111
Scotland, Art Nouveau in, 155
Scott, Sir George Gilbert, 151
Scrolls of the Law, 167
Sebaldus, St, 116–17
Sebastian, St, 35, 48, 132, 133
Secular buildings, glass in, 28–9, 48–9, 52–3, 56–7, 58, 100, 104, 106, 114, 124, 126, 135, 144–5, 146, 148, 150, 154–60, 163–5, 172–3, 174–5
Secular literature, as source of inspiration, 28–9
Secular subjects, in glass, 22, 28–9, 48–9, 52–3, 56–7, 58, 86, 100, 104–5, 106, 114, 124, 126, 135, 144–5, 146, 148, 150, 154–60, 163–5, 172–3, 174–5; see also Heraldry, Twentieth century
Segovia Cathedral, 132, 133
Selenium, 18
Seligenthal Abbey, 54
Self-portraits, 60, 67, 136, 138, 139
Sens Cathedral, 22, 37, 78
Serpents, 26, 33, 37, 44, 67, 87, 90
Seven, significance of, 32, 79
Seven Deadly Sins, 25, 139
Seventeenth century
  costume in, 54–5
  decline of glass during, 142
  in England, 142, 144–5
  in France, 142
  in Germany, 142
Sevestre, Geoffroi de, 76
Seville Cathedral, 106, 109, 132, 133
Sèvres porcelain factory, stained-glass studios at, 62, 148, 149
Sforza family, 122–3
Shahn, Ben, 167
Shakespeare
  Love's Labours Lost, 100
  Measure for Measure, 152
  Richard II, 48
Shardeloes Manor, 150
Sheet glass, 8
Shelley family, 48
Shem, 71
Sherfield, Henry, 142
Shields, heraldic, 46–9
Shofar, 167
Siena Cathedral, 72
Sigebert of Neustria, 102
Silica, 8, 9, 10
Siloe, Diego de, 133
Silver nitrate, 184
Silver stain, 37, 50, 84, 86, 93, 111, 114, 124, 126, 138, 139, 184–5

in Germany, 124, 136–7
in Italy, 124, 141
in Netherlands, 124, 126–31
in Spain, 124, 132–3
in Switzerland, 124–5
Sixtus, St, 117
Skara Cathedral, 174
Sketch, for stained glass, 177
Skeat, Francis, 158
Skinner, Mrs Orin E., 29
Skirlaw, Bishop, 86
Slab glass, 158, 161, 173; see also *Dalle de verre*, Norman slab glass
Soda ash, 8
Soda lime, 9
Soest, Wiesenkirche, 114
Soissons Cathedral, 37, 78
Solomon, King, 33, 92, 138, 139, 145
Solomon and Sheba windows, 24, 80, 82, 129, 145
Solvay, Armand, 155
Song of Roland, 75
Sorel, Agnes, 104
Soul, depiction of, 21, 30, 32, 33, 34, 75, 76
Southwark, glass workshops at, 134
Southwell Minster, 45
Sowers, Robert, 164, 165
Space window, Washington, 163–4
Spain
  Art Nouveau in, 154, 155
  Baroque style in, 142
  Gothic style in, 106–7, 108, 132–3
  influences on art of, 106
  Renaissance style in, 132–3
  Romanesque style in, 106
  significance of climate in, 72
  thirteenth century, 106, 107
  fourteenth century, 106, 107, 108, 111
  fifteenth century, 100, 106–11
  sixteenth century, 124, 132–3
Speculum Humanae Salvationis, 27
Speculum Virginum, 67
Spence, Sir Basil, 168
Speyer Cathedral, 16, 67
Spring, Eugène Grasset, 154
Spring Buds, Breidfjord, 174
Spun (crown) glass, 9, 180, 181
Squaring-up, 178
Stain see Silver stain
Stained glass
  and architecture, 16–17, 20–1 22–3, 50–1; see also Architecture; decline of, 16, 100, 134, 142–5
  emergence as art form, 12–13, 60–3
  manufacture of, 8–9, 146, 180–1
  window-making processes, 177–89
  see also Design, Light, *and related aspects*
Stamford see "Fish" Church
Star of David, 18–19, 22, 33, 166
Steigel, Heinrich Wilhelm, 148
Steinbach, Erwin von, 92
Stendhal Cathedral, 117
Stephen, St, 77, 118, 120
Stephen's College, Columbia, 165
Stigmata, 32, 95
Stippling, 84, 183, 184
Stoss, Veit, 117
Strasbourg
  Guild Chamber, 49
  history, 92
  Musée de l'Oeuvre Notre-Dame, 38
  see also Dominican Church
Strasbourg Cathedral, 20, 31, 37, 42, 64, 72, 81, 86, 92–3, 114, 139, 142
"Strasbourg Style", 114–15
Straubing see Jakobskirche
Strawberry Hill, 145, 150
Streyters, Arnold, 131
Strozzi, Palazzo, 21
Suger, Abbé, 17, 24, 37, 68–9, 72, 166
Sumeria, glass in, 10
Sundials, 144–5
Swann's Way, Proust, 29
Sweden, modern glass in, 174–5
Swiss National Museum, Zurich, 58, 67, 124
Switzerland
  craftsmen in, 48, 49
  heraldic roundels in, 49, 144, 145

painted panels in, 124–5
fourteenth century, 96
fifteenth century, 49
sixteenth century, 49, 124–5
eighteenth century, 144, 145
see also Königsfelden and Tell, William
Symbolism, symbols, 20, 22, 30–1, 32–7, 44–5, 53, 67, 79, 113, 167, 171, 173; see also Colour, Passion, emblems of, Evangelists, symbols of
Symbolist school, 157
Symondes, Symond, 134
Symphony Tower of Joy, Hakone, 172
Synagogue, medieval representation of the, 70, 71, 92
Synagogues, glass in, 166–7
Syria, ancient, glass in, 10–11

T

Tapestries, 102–3, 126, 127, 152
Tegernsee, Abbey of, 67
Tektites, 8
Tel-el-Amarna, glass in, 10
Tell, William, 58
Templates, for window-making, 178, 179, 181, 182, 186, 193
Temple B'nai Aaron, Minnesota, 167
Temple Beth Tikvah, New Jersey, 167
Temple Beth Zion, New York, 167
Temptation of Christ, 27
Ten Commandments, 167
Tenniel, Sir John, 29
Tennyson, Alfred, 152
Teodoro of Holland, 133
Tewkesbury Abbey, 50, 56, 91
Theodora, 67
Theodoric, Emperor, 12
Theophilus, 10, 177, 178, 181, 182, 186
Thirteenth century
  characteristics of glass in, 72–3
  costume in, 54
  in Alsace, 92
  in England, 72–3, 82–3
  in France, 72–9
  in Germany, 72–3, 80–1
  in Italy, 95
  in Spain, 106, 107
Thirty Years' War, 142
Thomas, Brian, 158
Thomas of Bayeux, 71
Thomas of Oxford, 60, 91
Thornton, John, 60, 86, 87
Three Marys window, Louviers, 138, 139
Tiffany, Louis Comfort, 146, 149, 154, 155, 156–7, 162, 164
Tiffany Studios, 166
Timotheus window, Neuweiler, 67
Timothy, 153
Tobias, 35, 144
Toledo Cathedral, 49, 72, 106, 108–11, 132–3
Topkapi Palace, Istanbul, 12
Tosinghi-Spinelli see S. Croce
Tothill family, 150
Tournai Cathedral, 102–3, 126, 130, 138
Tower of Babel, 122
Tracery, 20–1, 22–3, 78, 86, 90
Transept, 14–15, 16
Transubstantiation, 34
Tree
  of Knowledge, 26, 37
  of Life, 32, 37
  symbolism of, 37
  see also Jesse Tree
Tree of Life Synagogue, Pittsburgh, 167
Trefoil, 20
Très Riches Heures, 104
Tribes of Israel windows, Jerusalem, 166
Triforium, 16, 17
Trinity, The, 17, 32–3, 113, 129, 142, 158
Trinity Church, Brooklyn, New York, 149
Trinity College, Cambridge, 56
Trinity Lutheran Church, Decatour, 164

Trousseau, Pierre, 104
Troyes Cathedral, 32, 78, 139
Tryggvadottir, Nina, 174
Tübingen, 114
Tucher family, 28, 29, 137
Tudeley Church, Kent, 58, 62
Tudor arms, 48–9
Tudor rose, 135
Tunnoc, Richard, 41, 86, 88
Twelfth century
  characteristics of glass in, 64–5
  in Alsace, 92, 93
  in England, 64, 70–1
  in France, 64–5, 68–9, 70, 71
  in Germany, 64, 66–7
Twentieth century
  characteristics of architecture in, 14–15, 16–17, 21, 51, 158
  characteristics of glass in, 31, 39, 43, 51, 53, 62–3, 158–9
  in Australia, 173
  in Belgium, Holland, 174–5
  in England, 158, 168–9
  in France, 158, 170–1
  in Germany, 158, 160–1
  in Ireland, 158
  in Japan, 172
  in Scandinavia, 174–5
  in United States, 158, 162–5
  window-making processes in, 177–89
Typological windows, 24, 25, 26–7, 80, 82, 129
Tysoe, Peter, 158

U

Uccello, Paolo, 61, 118, 120, 121
Ulm, medieval prosperity of, 116
Ulm Cathedral, 33, 39, 60, 100, 114–15
Ultrasonic cleaning, 192
United Nations Building, New York, 58
United States of America
  modern glass techniques in, 179
  synagogue glass in, 166–7
  eighteenth century, 148
  nineteenth century, 146–9
  twentieth century, 158, 162–5
University College Chapel, Oxford, 51, 144
Uriel, Archangel, 35
Ursula, St, 81

V

Valencia Cathedral, 22
Vålerengen Church, Oslo, 174, 175
Van de Velde, Henri, 155
Van Egmond, Bishop of Utrecht, 128
Van Eyck, Jan, 61, 100, 102–3
Van Ort, Artus *see* Nijmegen
Varallo, Nicolò da, 123
Varangeville *see* S. Dominique
Vasari, Giorgio, 141
Vaulting, 16–17, 72, 134
Vega, Lope de, 132
Velasquez, Diego, 132
Vellert, Dirck, 61, 126, 134
Vence *see* Rosary, Chapel of the
Vergara, Arnao de, 132–3
Vergara, Nicolas de, 111, 133
Verre doublé (flashed glass), 8, 84, 145
Vices, 25, 93, 139
Victoria, Queen, 58
Victoria and Albert Museum, London, 29, 30, 35, 41, 43, 49, 52, 53, 55, 126, 130, 152
Vigeland, Emanuel, 174, 175
Vincennes, Chapel of castle of, 140
Vincent, St, 69, 129
Vinci, Leonardo da, 119, 123
Vine, symbolism of the, 37, 44, 45, 140
Viollet-le-Duc, Eugène, 18, 68, 146, 149
Virgin Mary
  birth of the, 25, 53
  coronation of the, 95, 99, 103, 118, 120, 121
  cult of the, 64, 65, 67, 74, 75
  death of the, 69, 75
  depiction of the, 20, 32, 33, 34, 35, 36–7, 41, 64–5, 68, 69, 72–3, 74–5, 76, 77, 79, 84, 90, 91, 93, 96, 97, 99, 100–1, 103, 104, 105, 107, 108, 111, 112, 113, 114, 115, 117, 120, 121, 137, 138, 139, 144
  legends of the, 28
  miracles of the, 119
  Protestant objection to images of the, 142
  symbols associated with the, 32–3, 45
  visitation of, 97, 115, 142
Virgin of the Catholic Kings, The, 106
Virgins, 81, 97
Virtues, 12, 25, 32, 34, 45, 62, 67, 70, 71, 93, 111, 113, 139, 145
Vischer, Peter, 117
Visconti family, 122
"Vitrail", Viollet-le-Duc, 18
Von Daun, Philipp, 48
Von Salm family, 48
Voyage in Spain, Gautier, 110
Vyner Memorial window, Oxford, 153

W

Wadham College Chapel, Oxford, 144
Walpole, Horace, 145, 150, 158
Walter de Merton, 91
Walton, Isaak, 28
Waning of the Middle Ages, The, Huizinga, 100
War Memorial windows, 55, 56, 57, 58–9, 129
Wars of the Roses, 100
Warwick, Earl of, 112, 113
Warwick *see* S. Mary
Washington, George, 58
Washington Cathedral *see* S. Peter and S. Paul, Washington
Wastell, John, 134
Water
  depiction of, 32, 33, 115
  significance of, 14
Webb, Christopher, 60
Webb, Geoffrey, 29
Webb, Philip, 57, 152
Wellingborough *see* All Hallows
Wells Cathedral, 20, 70, 72, 90
Wellwood family, 48
Wendling, Anton, 160
Westerburg, Siegfried von, 80
Westlake, N. H. J., 134
Westminster Abbey, 55, 58–9, 145
Weyden, Rogier van der, 61, 100, 103
Wheel windows *see* Rose windows
Whistler, James McNeill, 155
White House, The, 156
Whitefriars *see* James Powell and Sons
Whittington, Sir Richard, 100
Wickhambreux Church, Kent, 146–7, 155
Wiesenkirche, Soest, 114
Wild, Hans, 114
Wilde, Oscar, 156
Wilfrid, St, 71, 86
Willement, Thomas, 151
Willet, Henry Lee, 162
Willet, William, 162
Willet Studios, 162, 164
William, Abbot of Hirsau, 67
William Fitzherbert, St, 86, 89
William of Churton, 55
William of Orange, 58, 129, 131
William of Sens, 14, 70
William of Wykeham, 91
William Skinner House, New York, 156
William the Englishman, 70
Williamson, Francis, 134
Willow Tearooms, Glasgow, 155
Winchester Cathedral, 28, 142
Winchester College, 60, 91
Wine press, symbolism of, 140
Wingfield, Sir Robert, 40
Winn, Mr, 144
Winscombe Church, Somerset, 40
Winston, Charles, 146
Winterich Studios, 53, 164

Wissembourg, 13, 37, 38
Wistar, Caspar, 148
Wolgemut, Michael, 117, 136
Wolsey, Cardinal, 134
Wolveden window, York, 88
Woman taken in adultery window, Arezzo, 141
Woodroffe, Paul, 58
"Wool" churches, 112–13
Worcester College, Oxford, 151
Wordsworth, William, 134
Wragby Church, 144
Wright, David, 173
Wyatt, James, 191
Wynkyn de Worde, 28

Y

Yarnton Church, 45, 100
Yellow stain *see* Silver stain
Yom Kippur, 167
York
  medieval wealth of, 86, 116
  parish churches in, 86, 112
  see also All Saints', Holy Trinity, S. Denys, S. Martin-le-Grand
York Minster
  architecture, 72, 86, 88–9
  cartoons used for windows, 178
  effects of Civil War on glass, 142
  glass, 29, 32, 41, 43, 71, 72, 76, 82, 83, 86–9, 142, 145, 194
  history, 71, 191
  light in, 18
  see also Five Sisters window
York Mystery Plays, 26, 86
Young, Henry Wynd, 162
Young Buckeye Tree, Bunnell, 165
Younger, Alan, 158

Z

Zacharias, 35
Zeiner, Lukas, 49
Zeus, 28, 29
Zeverdonck, Denis van, 131
Zodiac, signs of, 22, 77, 105, 167
Zouche, Archbishop, 89
Zurich
  arms of, 49
  glass by Chagall in, 62

Acknowledgements

The publishers have received invaluable help and advice in the preparation of *Stained Glass* from a great many individuals and institutions. They would like to extend their thanks to them all, and in particular to the following people:
Alan Alder, Hartley Wood & Co, Monkwearmouth; J.A. van Alphen, Eerste Ambassadesecretaris (Culturele Zaken), Royal Netherlands Embassy, London; F.S. Andrus, Lancaster Herald of Arms; Dr Pawel Banas; Rabbi M. Berman; A.E. Bicknell; Muriel Blackett; Arthur Butterfield; Kathy Chapman; R.J. Charleston, Keeper of the Department of Ceramics, Victoria and Albert Museum, London; Brian Clarke; Frederick W. Cole; Dr William Cole; Robert Cumming, Tate Gallery, London; H.W. Cummings, Cummings Studio, San Rafael, California; Alistair Duncan; Sue Farr; Pauline Faulks; Dr Gottfried Frenzel, Institut für Glasgemäldeforschung und Restaurierung, Nuremberg; Mogens Frese; Dr Eva Frodl-Kraft, Institut für Österreichische Kunstforschung des Bundesdenkmalamtes, Vienna; Dr J. Golding, Courtauld Institute, London; Rev. Odd Øverland Hansen; Dr D.B. Harden; Sven Havsteen-Mikkelsen; Ann Hume, Assistant Editor, *Washington Cathedral*; Rev. B. Kenney, Apostolic Delegation, London; Jill Kerr, Librarian, Courtauld Institute, London; Dennis King; Carlos Knapp; Paul Kunkel; John Lawson, Goddard and Gibbs, London; Lucinda Liddell; Professor Giuseppe Marchini; David O'Connor, Radcliffe Fellow, University of York; Señor Luis Villalba Olaizola, Minister for Cultural Affairs, Spanish Embassy, London; Sir Cecil Parrot, Professor of Central and South European Studies, University of Lancaster; Caroline Swash, British Society of Master Glass Painters; Eva Ulrich, Institut für Glasgemäldeforschung und Restaurierung, Nuremberg; Helen Varley; Konrad Vetter; Helen Weis, Willet Studios, Philadelphia; York Glaziers Trust; Eric Young.

Photographs

Sonia Halliday and Laura Lushington would personally like to thank the following, without whose help their photography of the stained glass in this book would not have been possible: Martine Klotz; Dr Brigitte Lohmeyer, German Embassy, London; The Dean of Gloucester, the Very Rev. Gilbert Thurlow; Gabriel Loire, Lèves; Miss F. van Haelewyck, Belgian Embassy, London; Dr Dietmar Lüdke; Nico Metselaar; Professor G. Marchini; Dr Arnold Wolff; John Piercy of London for the very high standard maintained in processing all their original transparencies taken on Kodak Ektachrome-X; Linhof Professional Sales Division, Connaught Cameras Ltd, London, for supplying and servicing the Super Technika V $2\frac{1}{4} \times 3\frac{1}{4}$; and Kafetz Cameras Ltd, London, for supplying the Bilora Tripods.

Most of their photographs were taken on the Asahi Pentax 6×7 and they are very grateful for all the help and co-operation of Peter Railton and John Raddon of Rank Photographic, Distributors of Asahi Pentax Equipment in Great Britain.

The publishers and the photographers would also like to acknowledge the kind co-operation of the following in connection with the photography for this volume:

Belgium: Brussels Cathedral; Tournai Cathedral; Basilica of St Martin, Halle; Church of St Catherine, Hoogstraten; Collegiate Church of St Gommaire, Lierre.

England: The Deans and Chapters of Canterbury, Gloucester, Lincoln, Norwich, Oxford, St Albans, Wells, Westminster, Winchester and York; the Provost and Council of Coventry Cathedral; Dorchester Abbey; Great Malvern Priory; Tewkesbury Abbey; St Mary's Church, Addington; Church of St Mary, Amersham; Church of St Mary, Bishopsbourne; Church of St Mary and St Nicholas, Chetwode; St Neot Church, Cornwall; All Saints' Church, Daresbury; Church of St Michael and All Angels, Eaton Bishop; St Mary's Church, Fairford; St Michael's Church, Great Witley; All Saints' Church, Hillesden; Holy Trinity Church, Long Melford; All Saints' Church, Middleton Cheney; Church of St Peter Mancroft, Norwich; St Mary's Church, Patrixbourne; Church of St Margaret, Rottingdean; St Stephen's Church, St Peter Port, Guernsey, St Mary's Church, Shrewsbury; Church of St Giles, Stoke Poges; All Hallows Church, Wellingborough; St Andrew's Church, Wickhambreux; Church of St Michael and Our Lady, Wragby; St Bartholomew's Church, Yarnton; All Saints' Church, North Street, York; Central Synagogue, London; the Provost and Scholars of King's College, Cambridge; the Warden and Fellows of Merton College, Oxford; the Warden and Fellows of New College, Oxford; the Warden and Fellows of University College, Oxford; Eton College; Chapel Studio; Mr J. Bossanyi; Mrs A.C. Huggins, Brandiston Hall, Norfolk; Miss Joan Nind, Oxford; John Piper; the Reyntiens Trust; Victoria and Albert Museum, London.

France: Secrétariat d'Etat à la Culture (and particularly the representatives of the Conservations Régionales des Bâtiments de France); Angers Cathedral; Autun Cathedral; Bourges Cathedral; Chartres Cathedral; Evreux Cathedral; Cathedral of Notre Dame, Paris; Poitiers Cathedral; Reims Cathedral; Rouen Cathedral; Sens Cathedral; Strasbourg Cathedral; Troyes Cathedral; Church of St Serge, Angers; Church of the Sacred Heart, Audincourt; Church of Notre-Dame-en-Vaux, Châlons-sur-Marne; Church of Sainte Foy, Conches; Church of St Martin, Montmorency; La Sainte Chapelle, Paris; Basilica of St Denis, near Paris; Notre Dame du Haut, Ronchamp; La Chapelle royale St-Louis, sépulture de la famille d'Orléans, à Dreux; Municipal Library, Troyes; Moët et Chandon, Epernay; Chantilly Château.

Germany: Aachen Cathedral; Cologne Cathedral; Essen Minster; Freiburg Cathedral; Regensburg Cathedral; Ulm Cathedral; Altenberg Abbey Church; St Georg, Cologne; St Kunibert, Cologne; Marienkirche, Cologne-Kalk; Frauenkirche, Esslingen; Johannesbund Convent, Leutesdorf; St Lorenz, Nuremberg; St Sebaldus, Nuremberg; Wiesenkirche, Soest; Jakobskirche, Straubing; Hessisches Landesmuseum, Darmstadt; Augustiner-Museum, Freiburg; Münster Landesmuseum.

Holland: St John's Church, Gouda.

Italy: Arezzo Cathedral; Florence Cathedral; Basilica of St Francis, Assisi; Basilica of Santa Croce, Florence; Arian Baptistery, Ravenna.

Spain: Barcelona Cathedral; León Cathedral; Toledo Cathedral; Chapel of the Güell Colony, Barcelona.

Switzerland: Königsfelden Church.

United States: Congregation Emanu-El, New York; KLM Royal Dutch Airlines, New York.

Most of the photographs were specially taken by Sonia Halliday and Laura Lushington, who are credited as SH/LL. Other abbreviations: V&A Victoria and Albert Museum, Crown Copyright; BM Reproduced by permission of the British Museum Board; AFK A.F. Kersting; CP Cooper Bridgeman; MC Milan Cathedral; CH Claus and Liselotte Hansmann.

Pictures read top line first, left to right
1 SH/LL **2** SH/LL **4** The Morse Gallery of Art, Winter Park, Florida **6** SH/LL **8** All pictures reproduced by permission of the Director of the Institute of Geological Sciences, London **10** BM; BM **11** BM; BM **12** Kunsthistorisches Museum, Vienna; Ashmolean Museum, Oxford; SH/LL; SH/LL **13** SH/LL **14** SH/LL/Photo, A.C.F. Birch; Angelo Hornak **15** SH/LL **16** Bavaria Verlag **17** SH/LL/Photo, Martine Klotz; F.L. Harris; SH/LL **18** SH/LL; SH/LL **19** Wim Swaan **20** SH/LL **21** SH/LL **22** SH/LL; Scala; SH/LL; SH/LL; SH/LL; SH/LL **23** SH/LL; SH/LL **24** BM (Cotton Vespasian A.I. f30v) **25** SH/LL; Bildarchiv Preussischer Kulturbesitz; SH/LL; CH **26** BM (Harley Roll Y6 PV111.BM facs. 282); SH/LL; SH/LL; Mansell Collection **27** Mansell Collection; Bodleian Library, Oxford; BM (Ms Kings 5 f18) **28** CH; SH/LL; SH/LL **29** CP; BM; Angelo Hornak; Courtesy of E. Maxine Bruhns, Nationality Classrooms, University of Pittsburgh **30** SH/LL; Michael Holford **31** SH/LL; F.L. Harris; SH/LL; SH/LL **32** SH/LL **33** SH/LL **34** SH/LL **35** SH/LL; SH/LL; Susan Griggs/Photo, Adam Woolfit; Bulloz; V&A; SH/LL; Bodleian Library; SH/LL **36** Musée des Beaux Arts, Dijon; SH/LL; SH/LL; SH/LL **37** SH/LL **38** SH/LL **39** BM/Photo, Michael Holford; SH/LL; SH/LL; SH/LL; CP; SH/LL; SH/LL; SH/LL; CP; CP; SH/LL **40** SH/LL **41** SH/LL **42** SH/LL **43** SH/LL **44** SH/LL **45** SH/LL; SH/LL; SH/LL; Bodleian Library, Oxford; Bodleian Library, Oxford; AFK; CP; SH/LL; SH/LL **46** BM (Harley Ms 4205 f30) **48** SH/LL **49** SH/LL; SH/LL; SH/LL; SH/LL; SH/LL; V&A/Photo, Angelo Hornak; V&A/Photo, Angelo Hornak **50** SH/LL; SH/LL; SH/LL **51** SH/LL **52** Giraudon; Burrell Collection, Glasgow Art Gallery and Museum; SH/LL; SH/LL; Giraudon; SH/LL **53** Giraudon; Giraudon; SH/LL; SH/LL; SH/LL; SH/LL; SH/LL; V&A/Photo, Angelo Hornak **54** CH; SH/LL; CH; CH **55** SH/LL; C.M. Dixon; SH/LL **56** SH/LL; SH/LL; CP **57** SH/LL; Lawrence Lee; Photo, Grut's; SH/LL; Mansell Collection **58** CH; SH/LL; SH/LL; Leland A. Cook; Three Lions **59** AFK **60** SH/LL **61** Scala; Scala; SH/LL; SH/LL **62** SH/LL; CP **63** Giraudon; Dilia/with kind permission of Karel Neubert, Prague; Muriel Blackett; Zefa/Photo, Ronald Sheridan **65** SH/LL **66** Gottfried Frenzel **67** BM (Arundel 44 f2v); SH/LL **68** Robert Harding **69** SH/LL; SH/LL **70** SH/LL **71** SH/LL; Nicholas Servian F.I.I.P., Woodmansterne Ltd **73** SH/LL **74** SH/LL **75** SH/LL **78** SH/LL **79** SH/LL; SH/LL **80** SH/LL **81** Archiv für Kunst und Geschichte; Praun Photo/Courtesy of Erzbischöfliches Diözesan-Museum, Cologne; SH/LL; SH/LL **82** SH/LL; SH/LL; Michael Holford; SH/LL **83** SH/LL; SH/LL **85** SH/LL **86** Bodleian Library, Oxford; SH/LL **87** SH/LL **90** SH/LL; SH/LL **91** SH/LL; Mary Evans; Mansell Collection; Mary Evans; SH/LL; SH/LL **92** SH/LL; Elek Books Ltd/Photo, Wim Swaan; SH/LL; Elek Books Ltd/Photo, Wim Swaan **93** SH/LL; SH/LL **94** Scala; SH/LL; SH/LL **95** SH/LL; SH/LL; SH/LL **96** Bernisches Historisches Museum; SH/LL; SH/LL **97** SH/LL; SH/LL **98** SH/LL; from *Schätze Deutscher Kunst* by Gerhard Ulrich **99** SH/LL; CH **101** SH/LL **102** SH/LL; Giraudon; SH/LL; Cloisters Collection, Metropolitan Museum of Art, New York **103** SH/LL; SH/LL; Giraudon **104** SH/LL; Mansell Collection; SH/LL **105** SH/LL; SH/LL; BM (Add. Ms 18850 f 9); SH/LL **106** SH/LL; Salmer **107** SH/LL; Wim Swaan; SH/LL **108** Foto Mas; SH/LL; SH/LL **109** Bill Stirling; SH/LL **112** SH/LL; Mansell Collection; SH/LL **113** SH/LL **114** Josef Makovec; SH/LL; CH; SH/LL **115** SH/LL; Archiv Münsterbauamt; BM (Add. Ms 11639 f 521v) **116** SH/LL; SH/LL **117** Archiv für Kunst und Geschichte; Stadt Nürnberg; Stadt Nürnberg; Lala Aufsberg; Stadt Nürnberg **118** SH/LL; SH/LL; Scala **119** SH/LL; P. Marzari; Scala; Scala; C.M. Dixon **122** MC; MC; Mauro Pucciarelli **123** MC; MC; Scala **125** CH **126** SH/LL **127** Musées Royaux des Beaux Arts, Brussels; V&A; SH/LL **128** SH/LL **129** SH/LL **130** SH/LL **131** SH/LL **132** SH/LL; Wim Swaan; SH/LL **133** Spectrum Colour Library; Didier le Blanc **134** National Portrait Gallery, London; SH/LL; AFK **135** Burrell Collection, Glasgow Art Gallery and Museum; SH/LL; SH/LL; SH/LL **136** BM; CP; SH/LL **137** Giraudon; CH; SH/LL; SH/LL **138** Jean Roubier **139** Giraudon; all others SH/LL **140** SH/LL **141** SH/LL; SH/LL **143** SH/LL **144** SH/LL; Mary Evans; SH/LL; SH/LL **145** SH/LL; National Portrait Gallery, London; SH/LL **147** SH/LL **148** SH/LL **149** Leland A. Cook; Mansell Collection; SH/LL **150** SH/LL; SH/LL; Mansell Collection **151** SH/LL; SH/LL; AFK **152** National Portrait Gallery, London; Mansell Collection; Fitzwilliam Museum, Cambridge; Fitzwilliam Museum, Cambridge; CP; Michael Holford **153** SH/LL; Chicago Institute of Art; SH/LL **154** Giraudon; Museum of Fine Arts, Boston; SH/LL; SH/LL **155** Phillips/Wood Associates; Angelo Hornak; Snark International; CP **156** The Morse Gallery of Art, Winter Park, Florida **157** Lamps/Photo, Sotheby's of Belgravia; all other pictures The Morse Gallery of Art, Winter Park, Florida **159** SH/LL **160** SH/LL **161** SH/LL; Brian Clarke; SH/LL **162** SH/LL/Courtesy of Gabriel Loire Studios **163** Scott d'Arazien Inc; "Cathedral Age 1974" (Washington Cathedral) **164** Warner le Roy; Winterich Studios, Cleveland, Ohio; Emil Frei Studios, St Louis, Missouri **165** Alistair Duncan; Office of Public Information, Stephen's College, Columbia, Missouri; Paul Kunkel; Robert Kehlmann **166** C. Harrison Conroy Co, Newton, New Jersey; AFK **167** SH/LL; Temple Keneseth Israel, Elkins Park, Pennsylvania; Lamb Studios, New Jersey; Willet Studios, Pennsylvania **168** Camera Press; Nicholas Servian F.I.I.P., Woodmansterne Ltd; Angelo Hornak; AFK; SH/LL **159** SH/LL **170** SH/LL; Giraudon; Giraudon **171** SH/LL; Private Collection, Montreal; SH/LL **172** Orion Press; Yoshiro Ohyama; Carl Purcell/Colorific **173** Leonard French; Leonard French; David Wright **174** Marte Röling/Photo, Henk Juriaans; Van Tetterode Glasobjekten, Amsterdam; Leifur Breidfjord **175** Shostal Associates; Shostal Associates; Søren C. Olesen; the Rev. Odd Øverland Hansen/Photo, Frank-Tore Melby **176** SH/LL **178** SH/LL **179** Angelo Hornak; SH/LL **180** SH/LL **184** SH/LL **185** SH/LL **186** SH/LL **187** SH/LL **188** SH/LL; SH/LL; James Clark & Eaton Ltd/Courtesy of John Lawson, Goddard & Gibbs **189** SH/LL; Angelo Hornak; Angelo Hornak; SH/LL; SH/LL **190** Gottfried Frenzel **191** The Stained Glass Works, Canterbury Cathedral **194** The Stained Glass Works, Canterbury Cathedral.

Photographs on introductory pages:
Thirteenth century, Bourges Cathedral, France
Fifteenth century, Great Malvern Priory, England
Nineteenth century, Heckscher House window, by Louis Comfort Tiffany, now in the Morse Gallery of Art, Florida
Twentieth century, Essen Minster, by Johannes Schreiter

Additional picture research: Jackie Webber

Artists

9 Alan Suttie **10/11** Shireen Fairclough **14** Kevin Maddison **14/15** Peter Morter **15** Alan Suttie **16, 17** Peter Morter **18, 20, 21** Alan Suttie **22** Peter Morter **34** Trianon (Colour) **46/47** Dan Escott **50** Kevin Maddison **54/55** Arthur Barbosa **60** Alan Suttie **64** Anne Winterbotham **69** Alan Suttie **72** Anne Winterbotham **75** Venner Artists **76/77** Gary Hincks **77** Venner Artists **82** Alan Suttie **84** Anne Winterbotham **87** Alan Suttie **88/89** Andrew Farmer **89, 93, 95, 97, 98** Alan Suttie **98** Mike Saunders **100** Anne Winterbotham **102, 106, 109** Alan Suttie **110/111** Gary Hincks **111** Alan Suttie **115** Venner Artists **117** Kevin Maddison **119** Alan Suttie **120/121** Gary Hincks **121** Alan Suttie **123** Mike Saunders **124** Anne Winterbotham **128, 129, 141** Alan Suttie **142, 146, 158** Anne Winterbotham **167** Alan Suttie **168** Venner Artists **178–188** Coral Mula **192/193** Christopher Nichols **194** Alan Suttie **Gazetteer artwork** Kevin Maddison, Alan Suttie, Venner Artists.

Bibliography

The following list of titles is a select bibliography of the books and journals that have been consulted during the preparation of *Stained Glass*.

GENERAL
Anderson, M. D., *History and Imagery in British Churches* 1971. Armitage, E. L., *Stained Glass* 1959. Bushnell, A. J., *Storied Windows* 1914. Ferguson, G., *Signs and Symbols in Christian Art* 1954. Fletcher, Sir Bannister, *A History of Architecture on the Comparative Method* 17th Ed., 1961. Fossing, P., *Glass Vessels Before Glass Blowing* 1940. Hall, J., *Hall's Dictionary of Subjects and Symbols in Art* 1974. Harden, D. B., *Archaeological Journal: Ancient Glass* 1969-72. Jameson, A. B., *Sacred and Legendary Art* 1890. Mâle, E., *The Gothic Image* 1961. Panofsky, E., *Meaning in the Visual Arts* 1955. Piper, J., *Stained Glass: Art or Anti-Art* 1968. Rackham, B., *Victoria and Albert Museum: A Guide to the Collections of Stained Glass* 1936. Rosser Johnson, J., *The Radiance of Chartres* 1964. Rushforth, G. McN., *Medieval Christian Imagery* 1936. Schiller, G., *Iconography of Christian Art I* 1969. Sowers, R., *Stained Glass: An Architectural Art* 1965, *The Lost Art* 1954.

AUSTRIA
Frodl, W., *Glasmalerei in Kärnten 1150-1500* 1950. Frodl-Kraft, E., *Corpus Vitrearum Medii Aevi Österreich—Wien* 1962. Kieslinger, F., *Die Glasmalerei in Österreich* 1947.

CZECHOSLOVAKIA
Matouš, F., *Corpus Vitrearum Medii Aevi/Tschechoslowakei* 1975.

ENGLAND
Baker, J., *English Stained Glass* 1960. Clifton-Taylor, A., *The Cathedrals of England* 1972. Day, L. F., *Windows* 1909. Eden, F. S., *Ancient Stained and Painted Glass* 1933. Knowles, J. A., *The York School of Glass Painting* 1936. Le Couteur, J. D., *English Mediæval Painted Glass* 1926. Nelson, P., *Ancient Painted Glass in England 1170-1500* 1913. Read, Sir H., *English Stained Glass* 1926. Sherrill, C. H., *Stained Glass Tours in England* 1909. Woodforde, C., *English Stained and Painted Glass* 1954, *The Medieval Glass of St Peter Mancroft, Norwich* 1934, *The Norwich School of Glass Painting in the Fifteenth Century* 1950. British Society of Master Glass Painters Journal.

FRANCE
Aubert, M., *Le Vitrail Français* 1958. Aubert, M. and Goubet, S., *Gothic Cathedrals of France and Their Treasures* 1959. Beyer, V., *Das Strassburger Münster* 1969. Beyer, V., Choux, J. and Ledeur, L., *Vitraux de France* 1970. Delaporte, Y., *L'Art du Vitrail aux XII et XIII Siècles* 1963. Gaudin, F., *Le Vitrail* 1928. Henderson, G., *Chartres* 1968. Miller, M. B., *The Cathedral—Chartres* 1968. Oldenbourg, Z., *L'Epopée des Cathédrales* 1972. Perrot, F., *Le Vitrail à Rouen* 1972. Sherrill, C. H., *Stained Glass Tours in France* 1908. Witzleben, Elisabeth von, *French Stained Glass* 1968.

GERMANY
Fischer, J. L., *Handbuch der Glasmalerei* 1914. Gall, E., *Cathedrals and Abbey Churches of the Rhine* 1963. Hatje, U., *Knaurs Stilkunde* 1963. Krummer-Schroth, I., *Glasmalereien aus dem Freiburger Münster* 1967. Paffrath, A., *Altenberg—Der Dom des Bergischen Landes* 1974. Pinder, W., *Deutsche Dome des Mittelalters* 1910. Rode, H., *Die mittelalterlichen Glasmalereien des Kölner Doms, CVMA Deutschland IV, 1* 1974. Sherrill, C. H., *Stained Glass Tours in Germany, Austria, and the Rhine Lands* 1927. Wentzel, H., *Meisterwerke der Glasmalerei* 1954. Wentzel, H. (ed.), *Corpus Vitrearum Medii Aevi Deutschland I* 1958.

ITALY
Berenson, B., *The Italian Painters of the Renaissance* 1959. Brivio, E., *Le Vetrate del Duomo di Milano* 1973. Marchini, G., *Italian Stained Glass Windows* 1957. Sherrill, C. H., *A Stained Glass Tour In Italy* 1913.

LOW COUNTRIES
Helbig, J., *Corpus Vitrearum Medii Aevi: Belgique I* 1961, *Corpus Vitrearum Medii Aevi: Belgique II* 1968. Sherrill, C. H., *Stained Glass Tours in Spain and Flanders* 1924. Troche, E. G., *Painting in the Netherlands—15th and 16th Centuries* 1936. Van de Walle, A. J. L., *Gothic Art in Belgium* 1971. Wilenski, R. H., *Flemish Painters—Vols I and II* 1960.

SCANDINAVIA
Anderson, A., *Corpus Vitrearum Medii Aevi: Skandinavien* 1964.

SPAIN
Alcaide, V. N., *La Vidriera del Renacimiento en España* 1970, *Corpus Vitrearum Medii Aevi: España I* 1969. Berrueta, M. D., *La Catedral de León* 1951. Bevan, B., *History of Spanish Architecture* 1938. Booton, H. W., *Architecture of Spain* 1966. Gade, J. A., *Cathedrals of Spain* 1911. Gomez-Moreno, M., *Catalogo Monumental de España* 1925, *Provincia de León* 1926. Gomez-Moreno, M. E., *La Catedral de León* 1974. Harvey, J. H., *The Cathedrals of Spain* 1957. Jedlicka, G., *Spanish Painting* 1963. Rudy, C., *Cathedrals of Northern Spain* 1946. Sherrill, C. H., *Stained Glass Tours in Spain and Flanders* 1924. Street, G. E., *Some Account of Gothic Architecture in Spain* 1865. Tatlock, R. R., *Spanish Art* 1927.

SWITZERLAND
Beer, E. J., *Corpus Vitrearum Medii Aevi Schweiz I* 1956, *Corpus Vitrearum Medii Aevi Schweiz II* 1965. Dürst, H., *Vitraux anciens en Suisse* 1971. Sherrill, C. H., *Stained Glass Tours in Germany, Austria and the Rhine Lands* 1927. Stettler, M., *Swiss Stained Glass of the Fourteenth Century* 1949.

UNITED STATES
Broderick, R. C., *Historic Churches of the United States* 1958. Connick, C. J., *Adventures in Light and Color* 1937. Lloyd, J. G., *Stained Glass in America* 1963.

NINETEENTH CENTURY AND ART NOUVEAU
Battersby, M., *The World of Art Nouveau* 1968. Harrison, M., *Pre-Raphaelite Paintings and Graphics* 1971. Henderson, P., *William Morris—His Life, Work and Friends* 1967. Holiday, H., *Stained Glass as an Art* 1896. Koch, R., *Louis C. Tiffany—Rebel in Glass* 1964. Sewter, A. C., *The Stained Glass of William Morris and his Circle Vol. I* 1974. Sweeney, J. J. and Sert, J. L., *Antoni Gaudi* 1960. Waters, W., *Burne-Jones: an illustrated life of Sir Edward Burne-Jones 1833-98* 1973. Winston, C., *Inquiry Into Ancient Glass Painting Vols. 1 & 2* 1867.

TWENTIETH CENTURY
Chagall, M., *The Jerusalem Windows* 1968. Gieselmann, R. and Aebli, W., *Kirchenbau* 1960. Kampf, A., *Contemporary Synagogue Art* 1966. Kaploun, U., *The Synagogue* 1973. Marteau, R., *The Stained-Glass Windows of Chagall 1957-1970* 1973. Smith, G. E. K., *The New Churches of Europe* 1964.

HOW A STAINED-GLASS WINDOW IS MADE AND RESTORED
Douglas, R. W. and Frank, S., *A History of Glassmaking* 1972. Metcalf, R. and G., *Making Stained Glass* 1972. Newton, R., *The Deterioration and Conservation of Painted Glass* 1974. Reyntiens, P., *The Technique of Stained Glass* 1967. Schuler, F., *Flameworking: Glassmaking for the Craftsman* 1970. Theophilus (trans. R. Hendrie), *De Diversis Artibus (A Treatise Upon Various Arts)* 1847. Whall, C., *Stained Glass Work* 1905.